ARCHITECTS OF ART THERAPY

ARCHITECTS OF ART THERAPY

MEMOIRS AND LIFE STORIES

Edited By

MAXINE BOROWSKY JUNGE

and

HARRIET WADESON

CHARLES C THOMAS • PUBLISHER, LTD.
Springfield • Illinois • U.S.A.

Published and Distributed Throughout the World by

CHARLES C THOMAS • PUBLISHER, LTD.
2600 South First Street
Springfield, Illinois 62704

©2006 by CHARLES C THOMAS • PUBLISHER, LTD.

ISBN 0-398-07685-5 (hard)
ISBN 0-398-07686-3 (paper)

Library of Congress Catalog Card Number: 2006048173

With THOMAS BOOKS *careful attention is given to all details of manufacturing and design. It is the Publisher's desire to present books that are satisfactory as to their physical qualities and artistic possibilities and appropriate for their particular use.* THOMAS BOOKS *will be true to those laws of quality that assure a good name and good will.*

Printed in the United States of America
CR-R-3

Library of Congress Cataloging-in-Publication Data

Architects of art therapy : memoirs and life stories / edited by Maxine Borowsky
  Junge and Harriet Wadeson.
    p. cm.
  ISBN 0-398-07685-5 (hard) -- ISBN 0-398-07686-3 (paper)
  1. Art therapists--United States--Biography. 2. Art therapy--United States. I.
Junge, Maxine Borowsky. II. Wadeson, Harriet, 1931-

RC489.A7A72 2006
616.89'165600922--dc22   2006048173

To our students, with love.

CONTRIBUTORS

Gladys Agell, PhD, ATR-BC, HLM, was the Director of the art therapy program at Vermont College of Norwich University. She was Editor and Associate Editor of the *American Journal of Art Therapy.* She was President of the *American Art Therapy Association* (AATA), 1983-1985, and is a licensed psychologist. Currently she is in private practice and lives in Vermont.

Frances Anderson, EdD., ATR-BC, HLM, is Professor Emerita from Illinois State University where she established the art therapy Masters program and was Distinguished Professor of Art. She also taught at the School of the Arts and the School of Education, College of Charleston. She was Editor of *Art Therapy, Journal of the American Art Therapy Association.* She has worked with special needs children. Frances Anderson has published many research-based articles and seven books including *The Art of Healing Children, Children Draw from Within,* and *Art for All the Children: A Creative Sourcebook for the Impaired Child.*

Robert Ault, MFA, ATR-BC, HLM, initiated the art therapy Masters program at Emporia State University, Kansas. For many years, he was an art therapist at the Menninger Clinic in Topeka, Kansas. He has taught and presented workshops nationally and internationally. He was the second President of AATA, 1971–1973. His book is titled *Drawing on the Contours of the Mind.* Currently he is a painter and works in private practice. He lives in Kansas.

Mildred Lachman Chapin, M.Ed,, ATR-BC, HLM, at present, is advisor and faculty member for Prescott College's Master of Arts Program in Counseling, with a specialty in Expressive Arts. She has been *Newsletter* Editor for AATA as well as holding many other posts in the association. For many years, her focus has been the art therapist as artist. She is the author of *Reverberations: Mothers and Daughters,* and is an exhibiting painter. She lives in Arizona.

Cay Drachnik, MA, ATR-BC, HLM, is a former professor at California State University at Sacramento and was President of AATA, 1987–1989. Her book is *Interrupting Metaphors in Children's Art.* She is a prize-winning painter who lives in northern California.

Linda Gantt, Ph.D, ATR-BC, HLM, is the owner and Executive Director of Trauma Recovery Institute in Morgan-Town, West Virginia. She has taught at George Washington University and is on the faculty of the medical school at West Virginia University. Her books are: *The Formal Elements Art Therapy Scale: The Rating Manual and The Trauma Recovery Institute Treatment Manual.* She is known as an advocate for research and has worked on establishing an art therapy drawing scale commensurate with the DSM. She lives in West Virginia.

Gwen Locke Gibson, MA, ATR-BC, HLM, was born in a small town in Pennsylvania. She was an art therapist at the Baltimore City Psychiatric Day Treatment Center and Johns Hopkins University Hospital. She received her Masters from Johns Hopkins University. Before that, she was a laboratory technician at the University of Pennsylvania Graduate Hospital and Wills Eye Hospital. She was President of AATA, 1979–1981. In retirement, each week she takes a piano player and ten singers into a retirement home to lead sing-alongs. She is a painter and a potter who lives in Maryland.

Don Jones, ATR-BC, HLM, registered as a Conscientious Objector during World War II. He was assigned to Marlboro State Hospital in New Jersey where he wanted to find a way to combine his two main interests, art and theology. From 1942–1945, he collected patient drawings and paintings and, with his own paintings, made them into a book: *PRN in a Mental Hospital Community.* In 1951, he went to the Menninger Clinic in Kansas where he developed an extensive expressive arts therapies program. In 1966, he became the Director of Adjunctive Therapy at Harding Hospital in Ohio, one of the first hospital-based art therapy training programs in the United States. He was AATA's first Publications Chair and fourth President, 1975–1977. He lives in Ohio.

Maxine Borowsky Junge, PhD, ATR-BC, HLM (Editor), is Professor Emerita at Loyola Marymount University, Los Angeles, where she was Chair of the Marital/Family, Clinical Art Therapy Department. She has also taught at Immaculate Heart College in Los Angeles, Goddard College, Vermont, and Antioch University, Seattle. She has been in clinical practice since 1973, with family art therapy as her primary focus. She has published broadly and is the author of *A History of Art Therapy in the United States and Creative Realities: The Search for Meanings.* She is a painter, draughtswoman, and photographer, who currently lives on Whidbey Island, Washington. She is one of the Editors of this book.

Edith Kramer, ATR-BC, HLM, is known as one of the first two major theoreticians of the art therapy profession. Her theory involves the process of sublimation through art and the creative process, itself, as healing. She was the second person to receive the HLM award. She has taught in most of the east coast art therapy programs, and was involved in starting quite a few. Her books are: *Art Therapy in a Children's Community, Art as Therapy with Children, Childhood and Art Therapy* and *Art as Therapy: Collected Papers.* Throughout her long career, she has painted and advocated that art therapists make their own art. She continues to paint in New York and Austria. David Henley helped Edith Kramer with her chapter.

Helen Landgarten, MA, ATR-BC, HLM, is Professor Emerita at Loyola Marymount University, Los Angeles. She initiated the art therapy program at Immaculate Heart College in Hollywood in 1974 and moved it to Loyola Marymount in 1980. She was Chair of the LMU art therapy department until 1988. She originated the term "clinical art therapist." By this she meant the art therapist as a primary clinician. For many years, she was an art psychotherapy clinician at the Thalians Community Mental Health Center-Cedars-Sinai Hospital, Los Angeles. Her art therapy books are, *Clinical Art Therapy, Family Art Psychotherapy, Adult Art Psychotherapy,* and *Magazine Photo Collage: A Multicultural Assessment and Treatment Technique.* She is a painter who lives in Southern California.

Myra Levick, PhD, ATR-BC, HLM, established the creative arts therapy program at Hahnemann Hospital and Medical College, Philadelphia, the first graduate art therapy program in the country. She was the Director of Adjunctive Therapies and the Coordinator of the art therapy program there for many years. She was the first President of AATA, 1969–1971. She was Editor of *The Arts in Psychotherapy: An International Journal* and has published over 50 articles in national and international journals. Her books are: *They Could Not Talk and So They Drew: Children's Styles of Coping and Thinking, Mommy, Daddy, Look What I'm Saying: What Children are Telling You Through Their Art,* and See *What I'm Saying: What Children Tell Us Through Their Drawings.* She wrote the chapter on Felice Cohen for this book, in addition to her own memoir. She lives in Florida.

Vija Lusebrink, PhD, ATR-BC, HLM, trained to be a medical technician in Latvia where she was born. She came to the United States in 1950. She is Professor Emerita at the University of Louisville Graduate Program in Art

Therapy and the Institute of Expressive Therapies. She has been a guest faculty member at California State University at Sacramento, Notre Dame College, University of New Mexico, University of Florida, and Marylhurst College. She discovered nonverbal modes of communication in California at the time of the Human Potential Movement. She became interested in Jung and studied Gestalt Therapy at the Esalen Institute. She worked as an art therapist and researcher at Agnews State Hospital and later obtained a grant based on the application of sand-tray therapy with cancer patients. Her book is *Imagery and Visual Expression in Therapy*. She is a painter and, in addition to her own memoir, wrote the chapter on Janie Rhyne for this book. She currently lives in northern California.

Shaun McNiff, PhD, ATR, HLM, is currently University Professor at Lesley University in Cambridge, Massachusetts, where he started the expressive arts graduate program. He was President of AATA, 2001–2003, and is a prolific writer. He has published 11 books including *Art-Based Research, Depth Psychology of Art, Educating the Creative Arts Therapist: A Profile of the Profession* and *The Arts and Psychotherapy*. He lives in Massachusetts.

Virginia Minar, MS-AEd, ATR-BC, HLM, holds a Wisconsin Life Certificate in Art & Special Education K-12. She received her art therapy training at the University of Wisconsin. She has taught at Alverno College and Mount Mary College. She was President of AATA, 1995–1997. The focus of her clinical work has been special education, children and cancer patients. She has written *Expressive Therapies, the Arts and the Exceptional Child: An Annotated Bibliography*. She is a poet and currently lives in Las Vegas.

Arthur Robbins, EdD, ATR, HLM, is a Professor of Creative Art Therapy at Pratt Institute, Brooklyn, and was a founder of that program. He is also the founding director for the Institute for Expressive Analysis, NYC. He is a Licensed Psychologist and a psychoanalyst, as well as a sculptor. His books include: *Creative Art Therapy, Between Therapists: The Processing of Transference and Counter-Transference, The Psychoaesthetic Experience,* and *The Artist as Therapist.* He has made a video, "Dancing on Blood." He lives in New York City.

Judith Rubin, PhD, ATR-BC, HLM, is Professor Emerita at the Pittsburgh Psychoanalytic Institute and a faculty member at the University of Pittsburgh. She was the fifth President of AATA, 1977–1979, and the "Art Lady" for "Mr. Rogers Neighborhood" TV program. She has served on the editorial boards of many journals and published five books including *Child Art Therapy, The Art of Art Therapy, Approaches to Art Therapy,* and *Art Therapy:*

An Introduction. She has produced five audio-visual productions including the DVD "Art Therapy Has Many Faces." In this book, she is the author of the chapters on Margaret Naumburg and Elsie Muller, as well as her own memoir. Currently, she lives in Pittsburgh and Florida.

Rawley Silver, EdD, ATR-BC, HLM, has published many research-based articles and books, including *Developing Cognitive and Creative Skills through Art, Art As Language, Three Art Assessments,* and *Aggression and Depression Assessed through Art.* She was a faculty member at the College of New Rochelle. Her particular interest is art with the deaf. Currently, she lives in Florida.

Bobbi Stoll, MA, ATR-BC, HLM, is a certified trauma specialist and has served as a clinician with many organizations and populations, including the American Red Cross where she worked in Disaster Services. In 1989, she founded the International Networking Group of Art Therapists. She was President of AATA, 1993–1995. Currently, she is a painter and works in private practice. She wrote the chapter for this book on Shirley Riley in addition to her own memoir and lives in southern California.

Harriet Wadeson, PhD, ATR-BC, HLM (Editor), began her art therapy career at the National Institutes of Health, directed the Art Therapy Graduate Program at the University of Houston/Clear Lake and the University of Illinois at Chicago, where she is Professor Emerita. She currently heads a post-graduate art therapy program for Northwestern University. She has published 68 professional articles, numerous chapters for psychology and art therapy texts, and five books, including *Art Psychotherapy, The Dynamics of Art Psychotherapy,* and *Art Therapy Practice: Innovative Approaches with Diverse Populations.* She has presented her work in 15 countries, led professional delegations to four countries, and received awards for her art and professional accomplishments. She has held many positions in AATA, most recently Associate Editor of its journal. In addition to her own memoir in this book, she wrote chapters on Hanna Kwiatkowska and Bernard Levy. She lives in Evanston, Illinois, and is one of the Editors of this book.

Katherine J. Williams, PhD, ATR-BC, wrote the chapter on Elinor Ulman for this book. She is Professor Emerita at George Washington University, Washington, D.C., where she was Director of the graduate art therapy program. She is also an adjunct professor at Naropa University, Colorado. She has written articles for many journals and is a published poet.

INTRODUCTION

The richness in the art therapy profession stems from those who pioneered its development. They are a creative, spirited collection of people bound by their mission to develop this unique, hybrid discipline. Otherwise, they differ vastly from one another in backgrounds, temperaments, talents, approaches to the work, and visions of art therapy.

The American Art Therapy Association (AATA) was formed in 1969. Although a few pioneers were practicing several decades earlier, art therapy as a formal profession is still quite young. We are fortunate, therefore, that many of the profession's early "architects" are still living, although some of our earliest pioneers are already deceased.

As we, the editors of this book, moved into retirement ourselves, we felt it a necessity to gather personal histories of those who have been prominent in shaping art therapy while they are still among us. The urgency of our enterprise came home to us in the initial stage of our work when one of our authors who had agreed to write a chapter, died suddenly.

So many art therapists have added significant ramifications to our diverse field that we recognized that selection of those to be included would involve difficult decisions. We were able to solve that problem quite simply, however, by letting the American Art Therapy Association make the selections for us: The highest honor awarded in art therapy is the American Art Therapy Association Honorary Life Membership (HLM). It was first awarded to Margaret Naumburg, whom many consider to be "The Mother of Art Therapy," at the inaugural meeting of the American Art Therapy Association in 1969 at Airlie House outside Washington, D.C. Since then, an AATA Honors Committee has nominated art therapists for the HLM award. This nomination is then ratified by a vote of the entire membership. Although the Honors Committee deliberates each year, in some years no art therapist is put forward for the HLM award. As editors, we recognized the thorough process of review leading to nomination and ratification of AATA's Honorary Life Members. Those who have been so honored became those we invited to write a personal memoir for this book. We asked them to include what brought them to art therapy, how they entered the field, their major accomplishments and struggles in the field, what art therapy has meant to them in their lives, and their predictions, recommendations, and admonitions for the future of the profession. We also encouraged them to include personal aspects of their lives. For the eight HLMs who are deceased, we contacted art therapists who knew them well with a request for a brief biography.

Who are these pioneering art therapists of this book? The most stunning characteristic of this sample of art therapy leaders is that most are women: Of the 28 HLMs in this book, 23 are women. At a time when middle-class women stayed in their homes as wife and mother, before the Women's Movement of the late twentieth century, these women ventured out to start the art therapy profession. During that period, women of this kind often felt isolated and different in their yearnings, but through art therapy and the American Art Therapy Association (established in 1969), they discovered a group of professional colleagues and friends who shared their unique aspirations. The evolution of art therapy as a profession was primarily driven by women of courage who were unusual in that they left home and hearth to found a profession of importance and creativity, to educate future generations of art therapists, and to propel their innovative profession toward broad acceptance in the mental health hierarchy. Still today, most art therapy training programs are directed by women. Beginning on the East Coast and in the Midwest, art therapy soon developed on the West Coast as well, to become a national profession.

Another interesting aspect of this group's experience is that many benefited from mentors who helped them along the way, before that word was common. These mentors, who were both male and female, served as important role models. Some were art therapy pioneers; others were psychiatrists and psychologists interested in stimulating the development of this new profession.

Although histories of art therapy are available elsewhere, this collection is unique in that it provides personal reflections from many different vantage points, often inside scoops on behind-the-scenes machinations of art therapy's development not found in other sources. It is a very personal history of art therapy's beginnings and thoughts by its creators about its current and future state, as well as its history. Art therapy's colorful creators come to life in their own words. Their voices differ vastly from one another, some theoretical, some extremely personal, some practical, some whimsical, all embodying significant wisdom, from the place of art therapy among the helping professions to the business end of practice, to spiritual growth through art, and beyond. We believe that this diversity among those who have helped to build art therapy's structure has served as a template for the development of the profession into a "coat of many colors."

Many of our authors have been trail-blazers. Charting new territory can be perilous, and some of these memoirs describe roadblocks, challenges, and failures, as well as the successes these pioneers experienced. Between the lines, the reader can see the creative drive that propelled those who have developed the art therapy profession. Art therapy bridges the worlds of art and human services, so both advocates and adversaries were encountered in each, as we presented new visions of how art could be used for healing and growth.

The book is organized more or less chronologically. Part I "Beginnings" is composed of chapters about art therapy's pioneers who were practicing before 1960. In many respects, these individuals were the progenitors of art therapy. Part II "Growth" covers the second wave of art therapy leaders who entered the field in the 1960s. Although art therapy was still little known at the time, this decade covers the establishment of the profession's first journal and the beginnings of art therapy training programs and ends with the organization of a professional association. Some who entered the field at this time were students of those in Part I. Part III "Expansion" is composed of AATA Honorary Life Members who began their art therapy careers in the 1970s. During this period, art therapy training programs proliferated, so that some benefited from newly-established formal art therapy education. Others had been working in related areas such as art and psychology, and moved into art therapy in the early 1970s.

In their various venues of influence, the authors presented here are highly accomplished visionaries whose dedication to the development of art therapy has been remarkable. The influence of these few has expanded in ever-widening circles to change the lives of countless others. Through their chapters, we chart the development of an important mental health profession. We hope that the ways paved by these "architects of art therapy" will serve as an inspiration, not only for those involved in art therapy today, but for the generations of art therapists to come.

Maxine Borowsky Junge
Whidbey Island, Washington

Harriet Wadeson
Evanston, Illinois

ACKNOWLEDGMENTS

We thank Benjamin Junge and Keith Sinrod for their generous technical assistance. Harriet Wadeson composed the cover for the book and Maxine Borowsky Junge came up with the idea for this collection. We thank our memoir contributors for their interesting lives and for their hard work creating the profession of art therapy.

CONTENTS

III. EXPANSION: ART THERAPISTS WHO BEGAN IN THE 1970S

*Deceased

ARCHITECTS OF ART THERAPY

What we, or at any rate, what I refer to confidently as memory—meaning a moment, a scene, a fact that has been subjected to a fixative and thereby rescued from oblivion—is really a form of storytelling that goes on continually in the mind and often changes with the telling. Too many conflicting emotional interests are involved for life ever to be wholly acceptable, and possibly it is the work of the storyteller to rearrange things so that they conform to this end.

—William Maxwell
So Long, See You Tomorrow

Part I

BEGINNINGS: ART THERAPISTS WHO
BEGAN PRIOR TO 1960

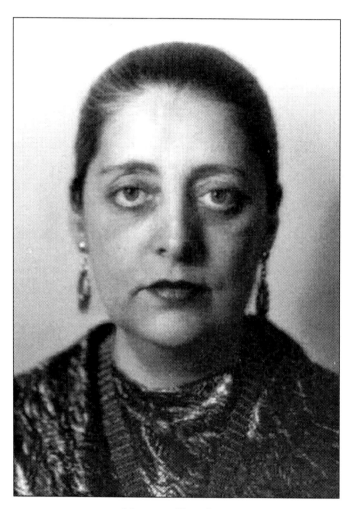

Margaret Naumburg

Chapter 1

MARGARET NAUMBURG (1890–1983)

The Mother of Us All

Judith A. Rubin

When the American Art Therapy Association held its first conference in September of 1970, there were disputes about many issues, but no one questioned the choice of Margaret Naumburg as the first Honorary Life Member. At the age of 80 the founding mother of art therapy looked elegant, spoke fluently, and delivered a stimulating address on the importance of training in the psychiatric interview. As always, she modeled for her audience the high standards that had given the discipline its earliest credibility among those in other professions.

The daughter of Max and Theresa Naumburg, Margaret grew up in a well-to-do New York German-Jewish family. Her older sister, Florence, became an artist and a teacher, and is now acknowledged as a pioneer in the therapeutic use of *art as therapy.* (Florence Cane wrote *The Artist in Each of Us* published in 1951.) In contrast, Margaret's pioneering work developed over time in the direction of what is now known as *art psychotherapy.*

According to her son, psychiatrist/psychoanalyst Thomas Frank, Margaret was "constrained and miserable . . . as a child;" fueling her desire to liberate other children to express themselves freely. A Renaissance woman, she pursued learning in a wide range of disciplines, always from the experts. After attending Vassar, then Barnard (B.A., 1912), Margaret studied with such innovators in education and psychotherapy as John Dewey, Maria Montessori, and Jacob Moreno. Analyzed by both a Jungian and a Freudian, she was comfortably eclectic and open-minded in her approach to both education and therapy. She was a truly amazing woman.

Note: Further details about Margaret Naumburg's life and work can be found in the tributes and obituaries in *Art Therapy* (1983, *1*: 4–7); the *American Journal of Art Therapy* (1982, *22*: 10–11; 28–29); and *Art Psychotherapy* (1984, *11*: 3–5).

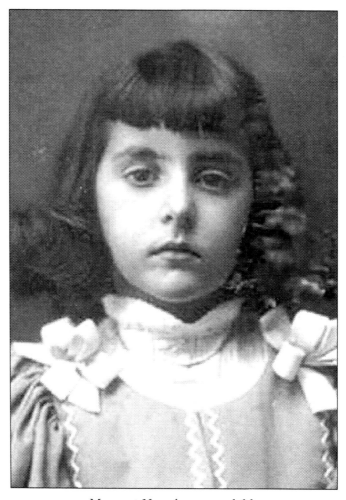

Margaret Naumburg as a child.

In 1914, Naumburg founded the Children's School (later Walden), a widely admired embodiment of progressive education. The arts and psychoanalysis were central, as was her conviction that children would thrive if they
could follow their own interests. In 1916, she married poet Waldo Frank; they
moved in *avant garde* artistic circles with people like Georgia O'Keefe and
Charlie Chaplin. Their son Tom attended the school, as did Florence's twin
daughters. In 1920, Florence Cane, Margaret's sister, became the art teacher
at Walden, where she developed methods to release creativity, including the
scribble drawing, which Margaret later adapted to release unconscious
imagery in art therapy.

After leaving the school, Margaret wrote a book about education, *The
Child and the World*, in 1928. Margaret insisted I read this book in 1975 before

interviewing her for a film. Although I had read and reread all of her art therapy publications, she was adamant that I read her first book, because "the seeds of art therapy were all there." Despite her advancing age and declining capacities, she was right. For she had not only directed Walden, she had also "directed the spontaneous, free art expression of groups of children," which sowed vital seeds in her.

In 1941, Margaret met Dr. Nolan D.C. Lewis, Director of the New York State Psychiatric Institute, who gave her the opportunity to study the use of art with disturbed inpatients. This resulted in her first book of child case studies in 1947, which was soon followed by two more books on her work with a schizophrenic adolescent (1950) and with a neurotic adult (1953). She also initiated the very first courses in art therapy (at the New School for Social Research and New York University), offered private seminars in her home, and gave generous guidance to many who later contributed significantly to the field. Elinor Ulman wrote: "In those early days, Margaret Naumburg virtually was art therapy."

In 1966, she published *Dynamically Oriented Art Therapy*, where she defined her approach as it had finally evolved. Her case studies rival Freud's, with the added bonus of vivid illustrations; and her scholarly literature reviews were extremely thorough. The quality of her work as a writer and lecturer

Margaret Naumburg (3rd from left) with her students, including
Hanna Yaxa Kwiatkowska (2nd from left).

undoubtedly facilitated the eventual acceptance of art therapy by the mental health establishment.

A fellow analyst once referred to a Director of our Institute as an *"analytic nun,"* since she had devoted her life to psychoanalysis to the exclusion of all else. That could also be said of Margaret Naumburg, for whom art therapy became the central passion of her life, her *raison d'etre*. In addition to her extensive publications, she was always eager to give lectures and to train others, so that art therapy would live on.

Like all innovators, Margaret Naumburg was able to draw ideas and practices from a wide variety of sources and to synthesize them in such a way that something new was created. Like all pioneers, she had to fight hard for her creation; she was a tenacious advocate for art therapy during its most critical formative stage.

I think that she was a genius; and that we are incredibly fortunate to have had her as our primary progenitor. Although others also thought and wrote about "art therapy" in the mid-twentieth century, I doubt that the profession itself would exist today as a separate discipline without Margaret Naumburg's courageous and energetic efforts.

Edith Kramer at an American Art Therapy Association book
signing standing beneath the poster of her painting
"Three Art Therapists," 2001.

Chapter 2

EDITH KRAMER

ART AS THERAPY

EARLY YEARS IN EUROPE

I was born in Vienna, Austria, in 1916, in the midst of the First World War, in a country that would soon be among the defeated: a hungry and depleted nation. My family was Bohemian in the truest sense, with artists, actors, Communist sympathizers, many of whom moved in Viennese psychoanalytic circles. Ever since I can remember, the center of my life was the making of art: drawing, painting and sculpting. My mother, who herself was artistically talented, nurtured my passion. My earliest drawings did not survive, for they were made on the black slate tablets that all young school children then used for writing and drawing. Paper was in short supply during those postwar years and was too expensive to give to children. These slates however, could be wiped clean and used indefinitely, providing me with an endless supply of drawing material.

When I was ten years old, the noted artist and art teacher, Friedl Dicker, saw my drawings and declared that she would take me on as a student when I became a little older. At the age of 13, I was permitted to participate in drawing classes that Friedl then held for teachers.

Friedl was associated with the famous "Bauhaus" in Weimar, Germany. This was a school conducted by a number of artists including Paul Klee, Walter Gropius and Joseph Itten. Itten developed a specific method for teaching art: He asked his students to separately depict certain formal elements in their art, such as rhythm, texture, linear composition, tonal value and cold and warm color. Later, he would have the students deliberately combine these elements in their work.

Friedl enthusiastically embraced Itten's teaching methods. In her exercises, she would beat out various rhythms, calling them out in increasing and decreasing volume. She would have her students draw as quickly as she

11

called out–rhythmic images, such as how bamboo grows in bursts–quickly, up, up, until the new leaves unfold. She asked us to imagine and then draw various textures, such as knitted material, sand, or gravel. Dicker had us draw figures in different situations, such as people carrying weight on their backs or in their arms, posed going up or down hill. She dictated all sorts of pictorial elements to her students, making us draw as quickly as she gave her commands. As a young artist I learned an enormous amount from those exercises.

Dicker was an ardent Communist during a time when Austria was dominated by a reactionary regime that would soon become part of Hitler's *Reich*. Friedl was arrested for harboring false passports that were used by many political refugees. After serving time in an Austrian prison, she immigrated to Prague, where she married her cousin Pavel Brandeis and became a Czech citizen.

When I graduated from the *Realgymnasium* in 1934 at age 18, I followed Friedl to Prague to become her disciple in the classical sense. I was to obediently help in the household and manage the children in the kindergarten classes she taught at the time. I followed her advice in my own work and submitted to her often scathing criticisms. She taught me to be severely self-critical, which is a capacity that has sustained me throughout my life as an artist.

During this time I also assisted Friedl in her in work with children of political refugees who lived in camps provided by the Czech government. It was during this work with uprooted children that I first experienced how art could help them regain their emotional equilibrium. In the art of these children, many of whom were traumatized, were signs of emotional disturbances that would later become familiar to me as an art therapist. Many of their pictures were chaotic, with distorted body images, sterile, repetitious, showing the ominous defense of "identification with the aggressor." Many drew pictures of Hitler, who had become the incarnation of evil for these children and yet had become a symbol of power with whom they identified.

By 1938 it was becoming increasingly dangerous for Jews to remain in Europe. Despite many opportunities to flee, Friedl and Pavel made the fateful decision to remain in Prague. Perhaps they, like many others, refused to believe the horrific fate that lay in store for European Jewry. They were also torn between the urgent need to flee and the determination to continue their fight against Fascism. In any event, in December of 1942 they were deported to Camp Terezin, otherwise known in German as "Theresienstadt." This camp was a propaganda tool of Hitler, which housed many world-famous Jews in a kind of "Potemkin Village." It was maintained solely to impress the

---

Note: According to the *American Heritage Dictionary of the English Language*, Fourth Edition, 2000, a "Potemkin Village . . . is something that appears elaborate and impressive but in actual fact lacks substance . . . after G.A. Potemkin who had elaborate fake villages constructed for Catherine the Great's tours of the Ukraine and the Crimea."

world, particularly the Red Cross, with the Third Reich's supposed benign and even charitable treatment of the Jews, though most would later be deported to death camps. Despite their eventual fate, inmates of Terezin created an intense cultural and intellectual life, with thousands of classes and lectures given by hundreds of scientists and other professionals. Friedl promptly established art sessions for children in the camp that would prove to be her greatest legacy. Surviving inmates from Terezin who attended Friedl's art sessions remember them with joy. They report how she encouraged the children to evoke in their art, all that was good in both their present and past lives. This sustained them and helped them endure the deprivations and dangers of life in a concentration camp. In a sense Friedl did for those doomed children what we do in our therapeutic work with older adults for whom the future holds little promise: We encourage them to evoke good experiences in their past life that can sustain them as their health declines.

Some of the children whom Friedl worked with were especially traumatized, such as the group that arrived from Germany whose fathers had been shot before their very eyes. Friedl had created a therapeutic art community. Those adults or children who had little interest in making art were helpful in other important ways, such as the scavenging of precious art materials. They collected scraps of colored paper useful for collages, pencil stubs for drawing or mud that could be modeled as clay. In this way, these individuals could engage in respected and productive functions. Friedl also made costumes for dramatic productions, gave lectures on art and in 1943, arranged for exhibitions of the children's work. Although many of these children perished in the death camps, a great deal of their art survives. Much of the child art of Terezin, as well as Friedl's own art, were discovered by Elena Makarova, who organized traveling exhibitions throughout Europe and at the Jewish Museum in New York. Viewers attending these exhibits were struck by the strength and vitality of the children's work. It is a testament to the adults and parents as well, whose Jewish tradition especially cherished and protected their children, and who also deeply valued their art.

Friedl sustained the quality of life and emotional health of innumerable children at Terezin. During her two years in the camp, she fulfilled her destiny as an artist, teacher and humanitarian. In October of 1944, Friedl was one of 1500 women and children who boarded a train to Auschwitz. The following day she entered the gas chamber at Birkenau. To this day I honor Friedl's memory. Her work has had a profound effect on my life as an artist, a teacher of children and eventually as an art therapist. Indeed, all art therapists should know of Friedl's story and respect her as one of the earliest art therapists and the "grandmother" of art therapy.

[handwritten margin note: Terezin? shown in Jewish museum in Prague?]

IMMIGRATION TO NEW YORK CITY

In 1938, I fled Hitler's Europe, arriving finally in New York City where my Aunt Elizabeth awaited me. Elizabeth worked at the time in a beauty parlor, but would soon resume her career as a character actress both in New York and Hollywood. I found work at the famed "Little Red School House," which is one of New York's original progressive schools and is still flourishing today in Greenwich Village. Like many other institutions in New York, the Little Red School House made use of the influx of talented refugees from Europe. The school was searching in particular for a sculptor who could teach children in the wood shop, as the carpenters they had previously employed were too demanding and severe with the children. I had worked with Friedl's children, had sculpted in wood and stone, and had experience as a carpenter. I was happy to work with the 7-13-year-old children in the carpentry shop in exchange for room and board. My quarters were in an ancient attic space that was unheated on weekends. The classroom teachers took it upon themselves to collect a few dollars each week for my pocket money. During my three years at this prestigious school I gained experience working with New York's brightest and most imaginative children. We created an array of sculptures from wood as well as innumerable toys, small stools and other items.

With the advent of World War II, most of the men were in the service, and women were increasingly employed to fill in the work force. I found work in one of the small tool and die shops that lined Grand Street in New York's SoHo district. As a machinist, I was the only woman in the shop. For two years I learned to operate all of the machines, read blueprints and prepared various metal components for the professional tool and die makers. Also I obtained permission to remain in the shop after completing my shift, in order to draw the workers at their machines. Recently these war-time drawings and prints of men plying what would become a dying craft were mounted in a exhibition by The Barbara Levy Gallery.

In 1947, I traveled to Europe, touring war-torn France on a motorbike. For an artist, France had something new to see almost every mile—particularly the famed caves at Lascaux. The Cro-Magnon cave-paintings at Lascaux were then still open to the public. I marveled at these great murals which were anything but primitive—they were fantastic art works indicative of a creative and sophisticated culture.

It was a wonderful voyage, but finally I had to decide where to reside. France was full of artists and its landscape and architecture had been depicted in art for centuries. New York City, on the other hand, was new territory. I returned to New York ready to make a modest living as a painter and sculptor, celebrating the industrial scenes that I had first depicted in the machine shops of lower Manhattan. It became clear, however, that I could not support myself solely as an artist. I was then 33 years old and needed to find a livelihood. I also needed to continue the psychoanalytic treatment I had begun in Prague with Dr. Anni Reich, which also required money. Another psychoanalyst, Dr. Viola Bernard, was on the board of the Wiltwyck School for Boys and arranged that I be hired at Wiltwyck's therapeutic treatment home for disadvantaged and delinquent boys, ages 8–13, from New York City. It was also Dr. Bernard who pronounced me an "art therapist" rather than teacher, as few art teachers at the time would work with such disturbed children. For the next seven years I commuted three days a week from Manhattan to upstate New York to work with these delinquent and aggressive children. It was at Wiltwyck that I began to develop my ideas that would later become Art as Therapy.

ART AS THERAPY

While at Wiltwyck I heeded the words of Dr. Bernard to "Write things down. . . . You think you'll never forget, but you will!" And so for seven years I wrote a diary every night of my art therapy work with the boys of

Edith Kramer at Wiltwyck School for Boys, 1950s.

Wiltwyck, noting misgivings, victories, mistakes and surprises. Those illegible scribbles, comprehensible only to myself, were indeed invaluable when I decided that there might be a book in my work. I applied to the professional advisory board at Wiltwyck for leave of absence and a small stipend for financial assistance during my sabbatical. By 1958 the book was published and titled *Art Therapy in a Children's Community.* It provided the reader with an overview of my psychodynamic approach based upon the Freudian model, as well as case accounts which demonstrated practical applications of art therapy. I described many anecdotes of the art therapy process and the many interesting children with whom I worked. Some of these boys remain in touch with me to this day. In the book's introduction I attempted to define art therapy and the art therapist's tasks:

> The basic aim of the art therapist is to make available to the disturbed persons the pleasures and satisfaction which creative work can give and by his insight and therapeutic skill to make such experiences meaningful and valuable to the total personality.

In *Art Therapy in a Children's Community,* with this definition in hand, I then set about framing my approach, in which child psychology was firmly placed within the Freudian psychoanalytic model. I wrote:

> In his function as therapist he has to accept the unbeautiful manifestations of sexual and aggressive impulses in the raw, along with the results of confusions and incomplete sublimation.

Cultivating a nonjudgmental stance of therapeutic acceptance, I also emphasized the element of artistic integrity as part of our overall Art as Therapy approach:

> But this attitude of acceptance, which is essential in all therapy, must not dull the artist's capacity for discrimination. The teacher (therapist) has to preserve his integrity as an artist in order to be able to distinguish between the fake and the genuine, between blocks and limitations, regression and progress, superficial pretense and true sublimation, so that he can help each individual to reach whatever degree of artistic sublimation the individual is capable of in each instance.

Next, I articulated the relationship between artistic endeavor and the complex act of "sublimation." Sublimation in art therapy became the centerpiece of both my theory and practice. Briefly defined (according to Freud), subli-

---

Note: The sexist language of the day has been retained in the original quotations.

mation is any process in which primitive asocial impulses are transformed into a socially productive act, so that the pleasure in the achievement of the social act replaces the pleasure which the original urge would have afforded. About sublimation, I wrote:

> Artistic sublimation begins as the artist replaces the impulse to act out his fantasies with the act of creating equivalents for his fantasies through visual images. Those creations become true works of art only as the artist succeeds in making them meaningful to others. The complete act of sublimation, then, consists in the creation of visual images for the purpose of communicating to a group very complex material which would not be available in any other form. Form and content become an inseparable whole.

I sought to link sublimation and other psychodynamic processes of individual development within the context of the individual's relationships and to his or her place in society:

> The instinctual energy which is not discharged becomes, at least in part, available to the ego, is used in the development of skills and accomplishments which give the individual greater mastery over his environment and improve his capacity for positive object relationships so that he becomes a more valuable member of society. The gratification which this accomplishment affords replaces instinctual gratification.

Finally, I attempted to frame the process of sublimation with a degree of flexibility and variation, both between the artist/patient and artists at-large: That in sublimation, drive energy is rarely fully neutralized and one must acknowledge the frailties of the idiosyncratic nature of the artist's persona:

> This explains why we often find in artists the highest level of sublimation coexisting with instinctual and impulsive behavior. The balance between sublimation, repression, and instinctual gratification varies with individual artists. The artist may be impulse-ridden or ascetic; he may be a slow, steady worker or alternate between periods of heightened productivity and blocking. But a certain tolerance towards direct instinctual gratification in some form or other seems inevitable.

The text was well received by reviewers. The journal *Contemporary Psychology* cited the book's "individualized guidance of children based upon an understanding of psychodynamics." *Psychoanalytic Quarterly* wrote that the book provided: "New insight into the process of art therapy by linking psychoanalytic knowledge with her [the author's] ability as an artist." It was significant that *Art therapy in a Children's Community* was the only existing systematic account of utilizing art as therapy with disturbed children, besides Margeret Naumburg's seminal *Studies of the "Free" Expression of Behavior Problem Children as a Means of Diagnosis and Therapy*, published first in 1947. Thus, it appeared that there was an audience hungry for information and the shared experiences of someone working in this fledgling field.

In 1961, I mounted an exhibition of the art of the Wiltwyck boys entitled "Art and the Troubled Child," which was opened with fanfare by former First Lady Eleanor Roosevelt. The exhibition, which later toured the United States, showcased the unique artistic talents of some of the Wiltwyck children, rather than focusing solely on their pathology.

Edith Kramer (r) opening her "Art for the Troubled Child" exhibit, attended by
Eleanor Roosevelt (l), 1961. (Photo by H. Stroyman)

Soon after my book was published, I received a "fan" letter from Elinor Ulman, an artist and art therapist who was conducting therapeutic art sessions with children at the Washington, D.C. General Hospital. In her letter, dated October 5, 1958, Elinor wrote: "You so beautifully clarify the peculiar value of the artistic process itself—neither as a mere lubricant for an essentially verbal process of communication, nor primarily a supplement to other ways of getting at unconscious revelation of personality."

Soon after, Elinor visited me at my fifth floor walk-up on the "Bowery" on the lower east side of Manhattan, and we quickly became friends. We found that we were the only people we knew who seemed to be knowledgeable about Art as Therapy within the therapeutic teams that at the time supervised and conducted the patient's treatment. We both rather enjoyed our isolation as art therapists, however, and were skeptical of forming any organization which promoted our field. However, Elinor accurately foresaw that as art therapy gained ground, it was inevitable that most of our colleagues would want to join forces as a profession. Elinor wisely decided to act in a leadership role and we both became active in forming our association, according to the precepts that the both of us embraced. She acted decisively and in 1961, began publishing the field's first refereed journal the *Bulletin of Art Therapy*. The *Bulletin* was unique by today's standards as its articles encouraged responses from readers. Authors often responded back to their critics in the following issue, which had the effect of promoting discourse and debate those in our burgeoning field. Besides journal articles, it also had a reader's forum for letters, many of which were sent by faculty and Master's students from Pennsylvania State University's art education program. These were students of Viktor Lowenfeld, the great art educator, who early on helped promote the "therapeutic aspects of art education." The *Bulletin* also allowed individuals working within art therapy to find each other and exchange experiences, conferences, exhibits, new publications, and programs that were developing in universities and hospitals. In 1963, Elinor sent out questionnaires in search of persons who considered themselves "art therapists." She obtained 35 responses. However, the number of people subscribing to the *Bulletin* was considerably larger, comprised of art teachers, occupational therapists, child care workers, nurses, and psychotherapists. Clearly the art therapy field was up and running.

THE HISTORIC RIFT

As soon as the field began to organize, a division appeared which was to perturb art therapy throughout its existence and which seems to survive to this day: There were those who considered art as the essential element of our emerging profession, as opposed to those who aspired to make a special place for art therapy within the realms of psychotherapy. Adherents to the latter group coined the term "Art Psychotherapy." Elinor and I considered the term ponderous. It seemed to appeal to those individuals who were eager to employ specific strategies that centered around the need for the client to talk about the work. They seemed to feel that a session where interesting art was produced, without any following discussion, was insufficiently "therapeutic." Yet, as the cave paintings of Lascaux bear out, art has been a form of eloquent communication since the beginnings of human existence. In the spoken or written word, cultural differences can impede understanding. However, the language of art is universal.

In my twenty-some years of work as an art therapist, most of the children and adolescents could not use words to explain their feelings. More often, words were used as weapons: to insult others, to threaten, or to self-protect, and although important as defense mechanisms, I thought their language was terribly limited as a form of communication. In the Art as Therapy approach, the children were able to speak a more differentiated language, one that elaborated their ideas as they discovered how many blues, greens and browns they could create, and they loved it!

The difference between Art as Therapy and Art Psychotherapy perhaps has more to do with the age group and social environment of the individuals under our care. It is significant that early in her career, Naumburg worked with disturbed children from the greater New York area, and our approaches were very similar. It is unfortunate that few art therapists seem to read Naumburg's early material with children and are aware of this fact. It was only after she began her work with middle-class adults, many of whom found art making daunting, did Naumburg evolve and change her methods. Her technique of Dynamically-Oriented Art Therapy then became more aligned with the talking-based free associative techniques of classical psychoanalysis. According to my understanding, it is only in population and setting that our approaches begin to differ, but the supposed rift in our field persists.

Naumburg's adult patients had learned to discuss ideas, to argue with each other and their children, to give reasons for the demands and expectations they made. In contrast, the children I worked with had been neglected, screamed at, bribed into compliance or beaten. For these minority boys from the slums of New York, art was often a new experience, which did not burden them with the vicious arguments, accusations, threats and violence they knew. To maintain the art studio as a kind of sanctuary, I avoided discussions that were apt to deteriorate into vituperation. Instead, I let the art speak for itself.

During sessions when I attempted to discuss their problems or their pictures, they would cry out: "Stop preaching, Mrs. Kramer!" They were very fragile children, who were engrossed in their work and did not want to be interrupted. Comments on individuals' art work usually occurred after the children completed their work and had overcome the struggles that such work entailed. We would talk together over crackers and juice, or while washing brushes or while sorting out their art for storage in their portfolios. This was often a time of quiescence for these otherwise active boys. With their defenses relaxed, I was able to broach topics that would be impossible during their intense art-making sessions. Of course, some art "psychotherapy" inevitably occurred, during instances when the children spontaneously discussed their pictures. In other situations, patients had developed specific confidence in me as art therapist, and with this alliance, I was able to deal with specific issues related to their therapeutic care. However, this limited psychotherapeutic work was not considered more important or demanding than art therapy.

ACUTE CARE AND ART AS THERAPY WITH CHILDREN

After leaving Wiltwyck, I began to work with more acutely disturbed children on the child psychiatric unit at Albert Einstein Medical College at Jacobi Hospital in New York City. This was a psychiatric ward for children between three and nine years of age who had been diagnosed with borderline disorders. It was here for the next 13 years that I became part of an expressive therapy team, with individual therapy, dance therapy, occupational therapy and a therapeutic educational program. In those days children could stay as long as three years on the ward, so extensive long-term work was possible. Being younger and more severely disturbed than the boys of Wiltwyck, most of the children at Jacobi were incapable of achieving sublimation. My work in this more acute setting taught me how to help these children express themselves and thus relieve the psychic pressures through their art. Art is compatible with a great deal of mental disturbance. As long as there is movement (for better or for worse), art can contain and express much that is terrible and terrifying. I described these children in my second book, *Art as Therapy with Children*, which was published in 1971 and has since been translated into a dozen languages.

In *Art as Therapy with Children*, I described children such as six-year-old Henry, who had survived an attempt on his life by his psychotic mother when he was four and a half. Hospitalized for two years, he continuously reenacted destruction and rescue by incessant destruction of toys, which alternated with restoring them with skillful repair jobs. This behavior was again reenacted in art therapy as he spilled and cleaned up paint, as well as destroying his own art work. Incapable of making figurative art beyond some primitive stick-figures, Henry was able to self-represent by creating innumerable stereotypes that symbolized his Jewish culture, such as the Star of David. Such compulsive activity enabled Henry to bind his aggression and helped him behave in a less chaotic fashion. He often made gifts of these symbols for his nurses, which cemented relationships while also establishing his own tenuous feeling of identity.

Much of *Art as Therapy with Children* was also based upon my work at the Jewish Guild for the Blind, where, as part of their therapeutic programs, I worked with children who were partially or completely blind. Here, I found that blind children's capacity to gain control over their own person and of their environment was greatly restricted. For security, information and understanding, children must rely heavily on the spoken word. However, since they learn the language of those who see, much information remains distorted and unintelligible. Because of this dependence upon the sighted, the blind child is apt to become overly compliant or passive. To strengthen identity and to develop initiative and independence, it is important to give blind children every opportunity to express their own ideas, no matter how limited or bizarre. When we accept their ideas unconditionally, it is possible for blind children to grow beyond their limited perceptions or fantasies.

For instance, I worked in art therapy with a blind twelve-year-old boy named "Christopher" who would often perseverate upon animal themes that centered on the concept of speed and power. Much of his discussion was obsessive and joyless in the autistic manner, until I assisted him in making a large-scale sculpture of a rhinoceros. Although Christopher's obsessions with animal traits remained, he had now created an image that expressed anger and the desire to be protected and strong. He dealt with his difficulties in a constructive rather than neurotic way, though obsessions with questioning his teachers and therapists over the traits of different animals continued unabated. After further sculpture sessions, one of which involved creating a tree with six birds and bird nests, Christopher began to relinquish some of his symptomatic behavior and renounced some of his fantasies. Now thirteen, he began to show an interest in real animals, not just in their grandiose qualities. Two therapeutic outcomes occurred in the case that are symbolic of this population: The first entails my assisting this blind child to compensate for his sensory deficits. The second focused on helping him build ego-function by encouraging interests that were not based solely in fantasy, but firmly in reality.

In *Art as Therapy with Children*, I continued my ideas explored in my first book, on the problem of "quality in art" within the art therapy setting. In art therapy, unconditional acceptance of patients and their art is of paramount importance. However, this tenet does not mean that we are blind to the enormous qualitative differences between those products which, for want of a better word, we call "art." The art therapist encounters a great variety of products that have a range of characteristics: from those works that are formless and chaotic, to those that are conventional and stereotyped, and those pictographic expressions whose meanings are known only to the artist. Each of these outcomes, which seem to fall short of being art in the truest sense of the word, may possess intrinsic therapeutic value, such as when a person with schizophrenia eventually shares with the therapist the secret meaning of his stick figures: this in itself would constitute a therapeutic victory. However, in the Art as Therapy paradigm, it seems a worthy debate to help sort out the hallmarks of what I have termed true art or "formed expression." Three elements seem essential. Art, it can be argued, is always emotionally charged: it arises from and evokes feeling. Second, art possesses inner consistency. This means that the art requires a degree of courage and truthfulness, rather than defense or deception. Last, quality art always possesses an economy of means so that the work would be diminished if any elements were added or taken away.

In each of these elements, art therapists or critics can begin to measure the quality of formed expression: whether it be in the named scribbles of a three-year-old, the tactile sculptures of the blind, or the sophisticated conceptually-based paintings of a professional Master of Arts Degree painter. With this conceptual framework in hand, art therapists and art critics alike can assess both the quality of artistic expression as well as the work's relationship to the artist. When artistic efforts become fully formed, there is a greater likelihood that sublimation too will be achieved. These concepts are a major conceptual thread running throughout *Art as Therapy with Children* and, I believe, remain one of my foremost theoretical contributions to the field.

UNIVERSITY TEACHING

Shortly after my first book was published, I began to teach courses on art therapy. Since there was a void in art therapy training, both Margaret Naumburg and I began teaching: she at New York University and Columbia University, and I at The New School for Social Research and Turtle Bay Music School. While still practicing at Jacobi Hospital and later, at the Guild for the Blind, I began to teach courses based upon my clinical experiences. The art of juggling art therapy practice along with long stretches of time in the studio, now also included the demand of teaching students on the university level–thus began a regimen that lasted some twenty years. In the early 1970s, I followed Naumburg at New York University (NYU), which then expressed an interest in forming a graduate degree in art therapy. Being a person who is at home most in the studio, and entirely impatient and intolerant of the politics of full-time academia, I deferred, only to teach adjunctively in the program. I agreed, however, to search for the right person to administer such a program. I called upon a then-young art historian and art therapist, Dr. Laurie Wilson, who in 1976, agreed to take on the position of navigating our fledgling program through the university system. For days,

Laurie and I holed up in my lower east-side apartment, and over Lithuanian bread and spinach soup, embarked on the endless process of forming a state-approved program. Working out courses, faculty, clinical internships, admission requirements, etc., it eventually all came together. Under the leadership of Laurie, NYU would become one of the elite training programs in the nation and the world. Students from the New York area, from across the United States and Europe began to flood our enrollments and still do to this day.

One of the hallmarks of what would become the NYU "method" was the idea that a productive art experience was itself inherently therapeutic—so long as the art therapist has long practiced as an artist, intensively and with joy. Art therapy candidates had to have attained sufficient fundamental artistic skill and sensibility to empathically facilitate such a process. The art therapy exercises utilized in our training emphasized nonverbal interventions, which I termed in 1986, "The Art Therapist's Third Hand." "The Third Hand," as my late friend and colleague Vera Zilzer has said, "Requires the ability to make art in many different handwritings." In order to enable the client's very intimate material to become therapeutically fruitful, the art therapist must adapt many different abilities, developmental levels and personalities. Interventions focus on helping the art along, often through the making of suggestions regarding art media, technique, or content. These suggestions are made without being intrusive, without distorting meaning or imposing pictorial ideas or preferences which might be developmentally or culturally alien to the client. Students within the New York University program learn to cultivate Third Hand interventions through specific exercises.

In the first part of this exercise, students are given images created by clients in art therapy that have obvious issues, and are required to copy them exactly, in every detail. Only through drawing can we begin to *know* the client's image. Secondly, the students are asked to fantasize meaning: How would the patient's art look if he or she were miraculously cured of pathology? Here we attempt to enter the student's countertransference and cultivate what Ernst Kris called "the conflict-free-sphere." We ask this in order to prevent fantasies from entering the student's perception of the artwork. After creating the "fantasy" picture, students are then asked to refer back to their copy of the patient's original. They are then asked to consider a *realistic* change that one might expect with an effective Third Hand intervention: Perhaps a finer brush to create a less distorted facial feature; or a lightly drawn line around the nose of the client's portrait that relieves the stress of multiple erasures; or perhaps the art therapist mixes the right skin tone for a child from India or an African American. Each of these interventions is applied in the smallest of increments. This is especially critical for those who are fragile and apt to easily give up when setbacks inevitably occur. Unlike "directives," Third Hand interventions are gifts to the client, with no strings attached. For instance, one fifteen-year-old African American boy, reported by my friend and colleague Dr. David Henley, had asked him to mix an accurate skin color for a self-portrait he was painting. The boy had become frustrated after several failed attempts to attain the right tone. After Henley helped mix an accurate skin color, this teen chose, inexplicably, to ignore the pot of paint. Henley accepted this child's rejection of his intervention without question. Left untouched, the boy eventually created the skin color that was aligned with his ego-ideal, in this case the lighter skin color of a basketball star. Faced with the realistic facial tone of his dark complexion, this child's tenuous and frail sense of self prevailed and a projection ensued. The art therapist supported the child, by remaining "the benign mother" attuned to the client's capacities, but without interference.

In this way, students within the NYU program become immersed in the subtle nuances of the client's art process. These interventions are based upon the client's artistic and emotional needs, unfettered by the art therapist's own tastes or preferences. Rather than asking the client canned or formulaic questions of "how they feel," that are so often the bane of much art therapy, intervention occurs on more profound levels. It occurs through the language of art itself: in the musty smell of clay, the power of deep reds, the control of a finely pointed brush or as our last case attests, by permitting a client to ignore the art therapist's intervention altogether.

Edith Kramer (r) receiving an honorary doctorate at Vermont College of Norwich University, with Gladys Agell (l).

These interventions may eventually lead to a body of knowledge that is useful for writing up case material. Reflection and data gathering occur as the student learns to write systematic process notes using an outline that Laurie Wilson and I developed for the NYU program. In this way, detailed observations could be recorded, that once accumulated, could be transferred and translated into research papers or theses.

In today's art therapy, much emphasis is placed upon a scientific approach to research. Recently as I perused an issue of *Art Therapy, The Journal of the American Art Therapy Association*, I searched in vain for interesting art. Instead I was distressed to find an unending array of graphs, pie charts and numerical figures that were utterly boring and mostly incomprehensible. At New York University, I always taught my thesis students that art therapy is best situated in the humanities, in which the naturalistic method of research can be most effectively used in our field. The noted primatologist, Jane Goodall, pioneered this method, which, simply stated, requires extensive observations of the client's behavior in their environment. The art therapist has to simply ply her craft and become attuned to her client's behaviors. Sit with your patients, study how they relate, how they approach their art process, and the resulting art and then record these dynamics in your diary. Once there are sufficient observations (which in Goodall's case entailed some 20 years of observation!), the observer might have sufficient data to analyze and perhaps even to claim some understanding of the phenomena. It is this method that has served me well over some forty years, and I believe, will never go out of style, despite the current leanings of our field to become more scientific.

The New York University approach has also served its graduates well. During the last twenty years, the program has graduated many distinguished alumni who have gone on to advance our methods and influence countless students as professors of other university art therapy programs: Karen Dannecker at Berlin University, the late Rene Bouchard at Albertus Magnus, Ellen Horovitz at Nazareth College, Michael Franklin at Naropa University, Lani Gerity, Catherine Paras and Ikuku Acosta all of New York University. David Henley of Long Island University, an authority on child art therapy in his own right, has long been a standard bearer for my ideas. Putting Art as Therapy into practice, he has generated numerous publications and research of his own. He was also of great assistance to me in researching and preparing this manuscript for publication.

IN CONCLUSION

On December 8, 2005, the current chair of the NYU art therapy program, Ikuku Acosta, organized a celebration of my retirement from university teaching by gathering together many individuals who were instrumental in my career in this field. Laurie Wilson, the keynote speaker, recounted the early days of the NYU art therapy program's founding, while the renowned child psychoanalyst and dear friend Anni Bergmann reflected over our collaborations that spanned some forty years! Gladys Agell, Judy Rubin, David Henley all presented, while my friends and colleagues Lani Garity, Irene Rosner, and Martha Haeseler read brief salutations. Asked to address the audience of art therapists and students, I exhorted them all to continue to make their own art: To curb the burnout that comes with exhausting clinical work, by restoring our zest and identity through the joys of creative work.

Edith Kramer in her studio holding her painting of the
New York Transit Authority's machine shop, 1997.
(Photo by H. Stroyman)

At the time of this writing, I am almost 90 years of age. Yet my journey now continues vigorously onward in my work as an artist and lecturer. In painting studios in New York City and the Alps of Austria, where since 1958, I have spent every summer in our family home in the mountains, I continue my work as an artist. My task remains to paint and sculpt the world around me with humility, vigor and truthfulness: To depict both the horrors and the beauty of our world in a way that does poetic justice to the reality that surrounds me. If you live long enough, good things will come. As Goethe said: "What is desired in youth one has in old age in abundance."

Don Jones' self-portrait "Portrait of an Artist Posing as an Artist."

Chapter 3

DON JONES

STILL WATERS RUN

Inner images are the creative tools of artists, the metaphors of poets, the visions of mystics, the "eurekas" of scientists and the wordless, natural play of children.

–Don Jones

In *Wisdom of the Heart*, Henry Miller says "somewhere along the way one discovers that whatever one has to tell, is not nearly so important as the telling itself." In my telling, too, I wish to create for you, from a collection of random anecdotes, more of an aesthetic experience than a story. It is a revealing of my lifelong dance among three equal ways of knowing, which have shaped my being–science, art, and contemplation.

Words do well to document some occasions but may not speak to the depth on a subjective level. So, I write to the meaning of feelings, poetry, metaphors, and imagery. The meaning of feelings may express the sense of reverence implicit in what one reads between the lines as well.

As a child, I learned early, out of necessity, the capacity to be by myself and to turn that state of aloneness into creative solitude. I am a young boy in my hometown, Towanda, Pennsylvania, with Table Rock Mountain on my left, the river next to it, and a flat main street one block wide. The rest of the town is built on a 45-degree slope up the mountain. I live in that house up at the top of the town. In the early evening I often climb up the slope to rest on a huge boulder. It is bigger than an elephant! I lay on my back in the growing darkness to watch the Milky Way emerge. Soon in the now blue-black heavens, a shining path extends across the entire sky, brilliant and clear. "Awesome!" I drop childish wishes into the deep well, waiting for them as shooting stars to splash on the surface of the sky. (At least, looking up at the sky when lying on my back gives me that "creature feeling.") It is scary enough every time that it precipitates a sense that it is time to go home to my safe house in this "nothin' never happens in this quiet little town!"

Scientist-astronomer? Poet-artist? Philosopher-mystic? No, simply a child opening to life in "wordless wonder," a capacity that has served me as insights into life's two primary issues of Eros and Thanatos, the fear and fascination with life and with death.

So, don't try to remember the words I write. After all, our working memories for either spoken or written words last about ten seconds, not that one necessarily will forget the meanings, content or feelings.

I invite you not to expect a narrative list about *who*, but about *what* I am, while participating in the process of my becoming. Join me in a mutually subjective mood and mode around my reflecting pool, and meditate with me. See into my "wondrous wordless world" of "unrational" knowing, where science, art, and contemplation have become one, mixed in the swirl-pool of my living-learning experiences. I say about "Portrait of an Artist Posing as an Artist," the subject is continuously changing.

Life has taught me this special openness and freedom of viewpoint about therapy and living that I offer to you as a life model. My telling, in the first person, might well be illustrated with the many self-portraits, saved by my mother, painted since childhood into the present depicting the gradual changes in my "becomings."

The three spheres, science, art and contemplation, are equally valid and valued, though, for me, none has exclusive knowledge of the actual "reality" of the world. Science though seems to claim more space currently. Each is merely an interpretation of a world view categorized in its own language-words and symbols! Judged by my "wordless wonder," however, each arrives at the same "WOW!" when expressed as basic human, "neuroaesthetic" responses and assumptions about life and the cosmos.

I believe, too, that my personal art experiences record and suggest ways of expanding the frontiers of sensitivity training, study and growth, for students and teachers alike in our art therapy profession. Never has the role of the arts and artists been more vital in this tilted, lost world! However, this is a time when there is some insistence among some senior art therapy educators who believe, succumbing to the categorical error of judging one field's values by another, that for academic respectability in the eyes of our peers, artist-clinicians must become scientists. Meanwhile, scientific researchers are being challenged by their own experimental data. Their equations indicate paradoxical connections that have defied both their own common sense and human intelligence. They have instead sought out metaphors of the arts, and have begun to resort to poetry, images, and parables to add meanings to their scientific observations.

The famed scientist Neils Bohr declared, "When it comes to atoms and quantum theory . . . the hallmark of modern science is that it has run out of common sense, and run headlong into our metaphorical, poetic self, and some part of our self that (must) mythologize." When scientists speak, using images such as "black holes," "big bangs," "warps and strings," the artist in me loves it!

My tale has two plots—one funny and one more serious. You can laugh with me at this part from childhood to the present, milestones marking my unique journey of discovery, as long as you look and listen for my serious thoughts as well. It might well begin like this:

> Born, March 15, 1923, 9 River Street, Towanda, Pennsylvania.
> Died, March 15, 1927, a near-death, a Shaman's first lesson.
> Resuscitated, March 15, 1927, a curious beginning!

I was born, literally, on the bank of a great stream, just a few miles south of the confluence where the Allegheny and the Chemung rivers flow into the Susquehanna on its thousand-mile way to the Chesapeake Bay and the Atlantic Ocean. About thirty feet above the level of the river, across a single railroad spur and a narrow gravel road, perched my maternal grandparents' house. The front parlor, the room where I was born, has a window that looks out across the mile-wide river valley,

My grandparents were practical people. Grandfather lived and died tragically working on the railroad. "Great Nanny," subsequently, expected bad news from every letter or phone call she received. She seemed troubled by most things, except when she baked. Then, it was a creative, free-hand, non-recipe, pinch of this, a dash, a blub of molasses from the jug, a spit-moistened finger-touch to the hot coal-fired oven floor, a hiss to gauge the right temperature, and she and I were ready for wondrous bread, biscuits, and pies.

Two blocks away, my paternal grandparents lived. William Jones was a Steuben glass cutter-artisan and his wife in her early years was a teacher in a small women's college. Grandma Jones filled my mind with the history of ancestors who came from Wales to America in the 1600s, who were craftsmen, scholars, and singers. There were stories of families who fought in the American Revolution. Grandma listed relatives' names from the Civil War too, the Morgans, the Whitneys, the Beechers. When I was a child, she gave me an elegant, leather bound book, *The Beautiful, the Wonderful and the Wise.* The book was filled with line engravings of the arts of the ages, a reference for me for fifty or more years until it was retired to decorate our library top shelf.

My father was a "poet-without-paper," saddened by the Great Depression of the thirties, but who made trips to the library, major wondrous events for my two older brothers and me. Best of all was meeting his retired vaudeville friends who came to our home and introduced us to the arts of "song, dance and fancy patter," and humorous recitations. We became performers.

My mother was the original Winnecott's "good-enough, environmental mother," who only had an eighth- grade education but later taught in the Social Work School at Cornell University in Ithaca, New York. We did not think of ourselves as poor, but as "challenged" to make our own toys, music, games and poetry which shaped us into artists. My brother Lyman was a gifted political writer and poet, Earl a singer, opera coach and poet, and I, an artist-clinician, theologian and as youngest brother, a "closet poet." As it turned out, we felt "We were rich, indeed!" Thus continued the family myth of the evidence of creative Welsh blood in our veins!

My mother hung framed prints like "Boy with Rabbit" and Gainsborough's "Blue Boy" in our living room, "to brighten up the house!" As a boy I replaced them with my own drawings, to my mother's delight, when she came home from work. But once, when I was twelve, my mother was furious about the Mexican siesta mural I had painted on the slanted ceiling of her bedroom in our little rented, one-and-a-half storied house. But I found she was not angry with me! She was furious about the landlord who complained! There is so much to tell of such important lessons from my "becomings."

But first an anecdote about a sad clown whose humorous-serious performance illustrates my method and style of "openness-compassion" in relationships. Emmett Kelly is a master mime (wordless like me) and an icon for the saddest of clowns. He seemed able to captivate his viewers and enmesh them in the whole story of his human pathetic-funny existence. Imagine!

Notice him, wandering aimlessly about in the midst of the chaotic Barnum and Bailey, Ringling Brothers, three-ring circus under the big tent. Childlike, he holds a balloon, which delights him so completely that he stumbles directly into the path of a charging horse and rider. Now, fear for his safety with that trembling feeling in your groin, because he has dropped the balloon and is unaware of his danger. This looks like an accident that wasn't supposed to happen! As he bends over to pick it up, the galloping horse and rider leap over him! Sigh, he doesn't even notice! The horse circles the ring but the rider has dropped her bouquet. The clown picks it up and races to give it to the beautiful lady but in haste blindly collides with the flank of an elephant and tumbles, rolling backwards.

We laugh at his clumsiness and sigh for his safety. He is shy and embarrassed, noticing that other clowns tease and echo our responses. We are hooked now as he picks up the flowers and presses them to his heart. He is in love! Some of us are mirroring his gesture. He rushes to return the flowers as the lady offers a kiss. But the circus's strongman seizes the bouquet and steals the kiss, while the poor-soul clown stands poised with closed eyes waiting. At this point, the uniformed ringmaster arrives in his top hat, a Dali mustache, with a whip, broom and dustpan in his hands. Gesturing towards the elephants, he is angrily instructing the clown to sweep up the elephants' droppings.

Sad, put down, with a grown-up, menial job, he turns to leave, but pauses long enough to raise his floppy shoe and slyly, in frustration, stamp his foot. The music stops abruptly! In wonder, he dares to lift and stamp the other foot. All the lights go out!

One spotlight now shines down directly on him. Alone, he begins to sweep the circle of light which grows smaller and smaller. Finally, there is only one tiny spot left. He sweeps it into the dustpan. It is completely dark now! Then, lights are back on an instant later but he is gone, has disappeared! We are caught between laughing and weeping.

What has happened? What is the nature of the communication that took place? By what means does the human content of such moments become known implicitly to us, instantaneously shared? How is it transmitted across space and time without cognitive thought, conscious participation or ego memory? Is it something we can achieve in other human relationships?

I resonate with the sad clown who has opened and laid bare his being for all to see. My life has revealed an access to his secret, and I must share it. One phrase, "Openness creates openness!" To the degree that I remain open, my clients and others will be safe to be open with me. Can you begin to see how such openness achieved, might apply to our work and personal relationships? But what is this skill of openness in psychological and emotional terms? Does it have evolutionary human survival value? In a 1977 lecture on therapeutic relationships, I said: Openness involves risk, seeking anxiety, not developing calluses, feeling the "pain," avoiding process words, like "chronic," "collateral damage," and other abstractions that are monstrous, like easy labels, predetermined beliefs and short-circuiting theories, resorting to neutral words, "countertransference," " projective identity"? Fancy inventions for feelings in most common circumstances "love and unloved."

The clown opened to us, shared with us his naiveté, his innocence, awkwardness, embarrassment, danger, love lost, menial job, frustration and depression, a lifetime all at a glance, reinforced by the gestalt of his "bedraggled," physical image. Is this unique process a model for a realistic way of an instant sophisticated assessment? In turn, without thinking or planning, we have opened ourselves to understanding his life and participated in an intimate way.

Learning this openness is the simple, profound secret of my "becoming" able to be inside and outside simultaneously. Science has demonstrated that an electron can be in two places simultaneously. Can this kind of cooperative communication be taught and learned in our art therapy programs to balance the statistical sciences demanded? I hope to demonstrate this for you with another example, a keynote address of mine which I call, *One Plus One Equals Three.* Bruce Moon in his book, *Working with Images*, reports:

September 1974: I was 23 years old. It was my first day in the Clinical Internship in Art Therapy at Harding Hospital. Don Jones asks if I had a sketchbook? I assumed he wanted me to have something in which to document clinical observations. I brandished a notebook and asked, "Do you want me to write progress notes?" "No, Bruce, I want you to come and work with me to draw and write poetry!" "Why?" I asked. Don did not explain. He said, "You figure it out."

 In that instant, I loved what I had seen in the student! In the deepest spiritual sense, I loved him and his anticipated future. Yes, the word is "love"–a neglected word in our sensitive human services field.

How did I know him so profoundly in an instant? How to see in that moment into his head and future? It was of course, one of those unspoken "intersubjective" occasions so familiar to me, a skill having evolved from my unique life experiences. I MUST TELL YOU MORE!

FIRST EVENT -The Family Myth -I was born Welsh

> *"Blessed is the man born Welsh, not with a silver spoon his mouth, but music*
> *in his heart and poetry in his Soul."*–Anon.

SECOND EVENT-I was born left-handed. *Sinestral,* from the Latin, sine', sinister, left-bank, "widdershin" the witches' counter-clockwise dance, as opposed to *Dexter* meaning right.

The teachers in my early education thought writing with one's left hand was bad, and one needed to be punished, exorcised, and made ambidextrous, with two right hands. My retraining was severe, so, I learned to write, right! However, neurological detours occurred. I stuttered and stammered in school, K through 12, and was mostly painfully, awkwardly mute, speaking seldom. But, my brain had a mind of its own.

I pleaded, "But I was born left-sided."
Those wise teachers thought they knew
When they decided to make me "write"
What surprising wrong, that it might do,
To part my mind and split my tongue in two.
Not ambidextrous, but *sinestros* now.
Still silent, mute, I slide serpent-like
into Eden where the Muses dwell
To hide and draw outside the lines.
Use <u>two</u> left hands, a pair of eyes in single sight,
And make a "work" of art to scumble over Heaven

With many shades of Hell. Then, I might design
And fake my own Paradise as well.

Jones writes: "While using my childhood technique of learning to master drawing with both hands, my reflection appears as if looking up from beneath an 'icy surface.'" I began to draw and develop my creative defensive skills of "watch-and-see-and-feel-everything-in-sight quiet awareness!" It was that sense of "quiet awareness" that became the basis of a guided imagery technique to elicit an "embodied-felt-sense-response," as opposed to encouraging third-person detailed case material.

Don Jones' painting "Fingers Hold Glass."

THIRD EVENT- On my fourth birthday, I drowned, falling through thin pond ice in March, but was resuscitated. (A death and reborn Shaman's first lesson.) The narrative of that event became well-known to me from childhood, stories recorded in the national newspapers, scrapbook clippings, and the lifesaving medal my six-year-old brother received for dragging me out. However, I was simply in the third person, an actor in a story. The actual experience was repressed to be gradually elicited unconsciously by my arting-out processes many years later.

My grandmother, the worrier, often said to me in my childhood, "It was a terrible thing! You should be dead, yet, already by now!" enforcing as well my conscious suppression of the incident. I thought I understood what she meant and was trying to express, but the details frightened me.

I began drawing at age four. To draw on, I used to save the white cards that divided the shredded wheat biscuits (my favorite breakfast food to this day). It took sixteen years of drawing boats, learning to render hands, by holding a piece of glass, and early adolescent painting attempts to master water surfaces. "How original and creative!" I assumed I was. I finally actually lived out the repressed traumas related to being abused for being left-handed, and reenacted the drowning death (a real "embodied-felt-sense" experience). I saw the thin ice on the water surface from underneath as I lost consciousness. It had been familiar for years, described in the third person as if it were a narrative told while sorting and reviewing old snapshots.

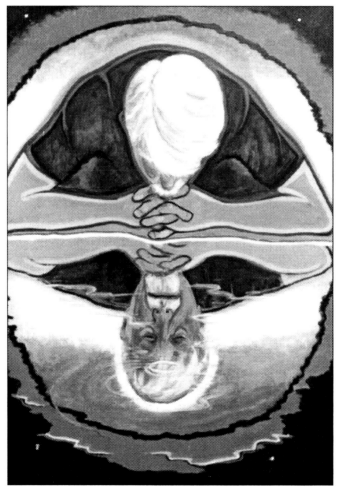

Don Jones' painting "I Reflect on Water."

Important experiences of both joy and sadness, and especially of trauma, become part of a silent past affecting our present lives. These original experiences are inscribed in memory in a form that retains the real-time flow of their original unfolding. It is an amputated psychic past, like a phantom-limb pain hidden in live-action video clips that are stored in the closet of the present. Such feelings distort present behaviors and responses. The clips when discovered in random "spring-cleaning" occasions, are most effectively played back through expressive arts techniques in the form of real-time episodes with live imagery, sound track, color, not like silent films with narrative subtitles. Of course, now, having the conscious insights of the drowning incident, and the years of practice in mastering, I am still intoxicated by water and have painted numberless water scenes. But self-portraiture is my way to meditate in that silent place, my Eden, constantly, re-creatively searching for my present identity. My first and only show of these self-portrait slides was at the Wisconsin Art Therapy Symposium at Mt. Mary College, Wisconsin, April 2005.

ANOTHER EVENT important in my becoming occurred at age 13. I was already a practiced, quiet observer in all my relationships and increasingly more and more psychologically free, "open" to subjectively evaluate and critique circumstances. It was particularly telling in observing my own family's internal dynamics, which were troubled by my father's unpredictability and the economic times of the Great Depression. We lived frugally and creatively in a difficult, mixed neighborhood where I secretly wished to study ballet, but took up boxing and tumbling instead. Though the youngest, I became the peacemaker in the family and my retreat was painting outdoors. This is my TREE, when I first became truly conscious that my brain had changed my mind about the different meaning of doing art which helped me to comprehend and survive. It was a moment of transcendence, understood later, like the eighth step of Hatha Yoga,"Samadhi," the self-collectedness when a meditator and an object are one. Vincent Van Gogh in Letter 543 wrote: "I have a terrible lucidity at moments, these days when nature is so beautiful, I am not conscious of myself anymore, and the picture comes to me as in a dream."

More recently, neurologists have identified and been able to witness this state of Absolute Unitary Being, with brain imaging. I actually became the tree in the process of painting. The tree said to me, "I will survive."

I recalled at this same age an incident from my earlier childhood, when I was about six years old. My two brothers were in school and my mother took me to an afternoon movie, *All Quiet on the Western Front.* It is the tragic story of a young German student coerced into the army with tales of ideal heroism. Through gradual disastrous experiences, he finds himself finally alone overnight in a bomb crater with a mortally wounded, young enemy soldier.

In an "all quiet," dawn moment, a butterfly lands on the twig of a shattered limb near him. He reaches out to touch this thing of beauty, and is shot, killed by the last bullet fired in World War One.

Don Jones' painting "The Tree and I Are One."

Before recalling this years later, I had painted several interesting paintings of hands, skulls and butterflies. Our brain does have a mind and appropriate timing of its own that serves us.

Peacemaker became a way of life, not only as negotiator, but as therapist for my extended family. I developed in resonance and "com-passion"(shared passion), gradually expanding into my "world view" which became both political and moral.

My guide was Gandhi. It seemed I actually felt the wound when I heard he was shot! My philosophy became, "I am not my brothers' keeper, I am my brothers!" I grew in an increasing expanded world identification and feeling for life similar to the awesome childlike experience of lying on my back at night seeing the Milky Way upside-down.

I supported the peace movement before World War Two. In spite of my church's objection and the F.B.I. questions, I registered as a Conscientious Objector, dropping out of college, where I was majoring in pre-med and pre-theology. I might have claimed exemption because of these studies, but I volunteered for alternative Civilian Public Service. After six months in the labor camp, I was a human guinea pig for the Army Medical Corp's Commission on Acute Respiratory Diseases researching "Atypical Pneumonia." I became the conscientious objector (C.O.) Assistant Administrator of the project, recruiting, and arranging travel plans for young men in other camps across the country, providing orientation, morale support, and editing a newsletter for intercommunication during medical isolation periods.

At times when we were not in individual clinical isolation, we C.O.s would socialize and greet each other, "Peace Brother!" By the end of this six-month program, the technical military medical staff from Fort Bragg was saluting each other, officers and enlisted men with, "Peace Brother!" too.

I volunteered and next worked three-plus years in the Marlboro State Mental Hospital in New Jersey. This experience became my "university of psychiatry." That hospital of 2800 beds during the war was almost entirely staffed by C.O.'s. We worked alone in cottages housing 150 patients, twelve-hour shifts six days a week. I write in more detail about this experience because of its significance in my finding clues to the power of the arts in healing, the roots of my art therapy beginnings, and my psychological insights.

Upon arriving at the hospital, after a long bus ride from the labor camp in the hills of Virginia, I was met and given a uniform consisting of white pants and shirt and a black bow tie, handed a set of burdensome keys, and directed across the grounds to a cottage. Opening the heavy oak door loaded with hardware, I was greeted by another young man about my same age, 19 or 20, "Oh! You are my relief replacement."

I found myself backed up against the door inside alone, facing a dayroom full of sound and sights and odors, and humanity in conditions that were beyond my description. These indelible images are still flashbacks imprinted on my psyche and experienced in real time still. In his work *The Mentally Ill in America*, Deutsch described "sick people shackled, strapped, straitjacketed and bound to their beds, curable cases sinking into chronicity . . . ward upon wards of patients sitting in idleness and stripped of human dignity." In some of the wards there were scenes that rivaled the horrors of the Nazi concentration camps.

As the door closed, noisily locked from the outside, I became aware of a man, agitated and pacing back and forth at the far end of the dayroom. Spying me with a wild glance, he came rushing towards me with hands reaching out. (Time out, to review my short life in those slow motion moments that followed.) Closer, and then directly in front of me, he thrust his hands out from buttonless hospital-issue clothes and ragged torn sleeves into the space above my head. He grasped some unseen "things," threw them to the floor and stomped furiously. I thought in that enlightening moment, "By God! If this 'crazy' man can sense my terror and vulnerability, in whatever form it appeared to him, and then rush to defend me, I have nothing to fear from people here in this alien place!" That was my only orientation. I wondered then about this mysterious form of "co-subjective" communication that I came to trust. Did the patient know it too?"

Multiply that incident by three years, twelve hours a day, six days a week, with no tranquilizing drugs yet created and one can gain a sense of my education in this universe of primitive psychiatry. These abandoned, hopeless men and women were and are never still anonymous abstractions to me. I painted and drew them and their plight. My earlier life experiences in openness, resonance, com-passion and co-subjective exchanges had somewhat prepared and aided me in surviving on these back wards. I could see that this wordless exchange was a human given, a useful survival skill. There were insightful creative moments too.

"Sophie" was threatening and destructive most of the time, but she did elaborate expressive graphics on the walls of her seclusion room and sometimes when "let-out," she would continue her work on the walls of the hall. Her graphics were curiosities for special visitors, but no one ever paid attention to Sophie! Once when I had a brief day off and the Jersey Central Railroad could offer a one-and-half hour trip to New York City, I went to the Museum of Modern Art to see the temporary showing of Picasso's "Guernica." I couldn't help comparing the similarities of these two artists, a presage of the art therapy movement.

In Cottage 13, the segregated men's cottage, where "mother" was a prefix for every word, I worked the 7:00 P.M. to 7:00 A.M. shift. There I found "B.B. Blues," regressed, burned out by cocaine, he had played piano for Cab Calloway on Broadway. Helplessly dysfunctional most of the time, and yet if paid one or two cigarettes, he could play jazz and the blues all evening. Music and dancing until bedtime became our only therapy and sedation. For me it was a "mother"of an experience, and again another early hint of the healing power of the uses of the arts.

There were many frequent difficult encounters also, most requiring instantaneous responses in which fortunately I had developed some practice and skill. Again, earlier life experiences in openness and resonance kept me focused "on the other person" and aided me in my survival alone in the back wards at night.

Don Jones' painting "Confined in the 'Disturbed' Building."

One night in the darkened hall, lit only by dim blue night-lights in the ceiling, I felt two heavy hands pressing on my shoulders and a dark, angry voice behind me threatened, "Say your prayers, white boy! You're the one who gave me that black pill!" Alone, my instant action was to turn around, holding his hands on my shoulders and facing "Joe" while speaking gently, "Joe, I know it's hard to sleep with all those terrible voices in your head, but go and try to rest. It is almost morning" . . . "Yes, 'Boss!'"

It was such occasions that later were to become the sources of my frequent famous clichés to students and interns, "Seek anxiety, stay open." "Never react, but always respond!" "Therapy is about them not about you!"

I began to see that intuitive wordless exchanges must be a part of any treatment interaction and could also be useful in tight moments. It was such unique experiences that made me valuable subsequently to the Menninger Clinic. My painting out my own "film-clips" of the terrible plight of the patients and my felt responses later earned me an invitation to join the Menninger Clinic full-time, a position that lasted 16 years. At the same time I served as part-time pastor of a small country Methodist church, spending summer vacations completing theology studies in seminary. In each field, I maintained my artistic independence and creative views about both analysis and theology. I raised "innocent" "what if" and "yes, but" questions about the work.

My original one easel in the clinic's Occupational Therapy shop was replaced by degrees with a creative arts building including studio spaces for all the arts and stipends for art interns. A work and education unit was added. Through the arts, I introduced a concept of "process versus content-analysis." I taught and promoted the idea that even the most psychotic artworks created in art therapy were "affect-images" and important attempts at self-healing. Fortunately, as an artist-clinician, I was among the very few who could comfortably participate in this process and share these expressive images with the difficult, disturbed patients, who otherwise would have been rejected as untreatable, to be sent "someplace else!" (One analyst suggested that "someplace else" was just jargon for "I wish they were dead.")

My Marlboro hospital experiences alerted me to the importance of the influence of an "automatic environment" that might be either therapeutic or toxic when unexamined in detail. I soon saw the possibilities of fusing the Menninger psychoanalytic theory, based on an individual 50-minute hour, with a psychodynamic milieu therapy treatment. Using all of the aspects of the "automatic environment" to observe and treat clients more intensively, one could extend the influence of a team prescription into the 24- hour life spaces of the patients. I worked to develop a "sociotherapeutic" model. First as Director of the Creative Arts Division and later as Co-Director of the Adjunctive Therapy Department, I wrote and presented many position papers to the staff. Michael Maloney in his Master's thesis wrote:

> With the support of Dr.s Karl and Will Menninger, Don Jones became a significant leader in retooling the treatment methods used in VA, state, and private psychiatric hospitals. Don lectured and presented this new philosophy of the sociotherapeutic milieu system throughout the United States.

Similarly, I viewed Jungian theory as translating patients' interesting narratives into elegant literature and mythology while intellectually short-circuiting com-passion and the immediacy of possible direct expression. I continue to question the narrative-interpretation abstract approaches, told in the third person, twice removed from immediacy and possible resolution. Is the information too quickly being "shoe-horned" into a diagnostic category or an uncompromising belief system? (Ah Ha! Freud lives!) "What if?" I questioned, "the theories are flawed?" Do the statistics of the scientific psychological tests, originally designed as personal interviews to seek clues, really describe human beings?"

Words, your box is too simply built, and thin
To ease the weight of grief, I would put in.
Numbers, you are too finite, in spare specifics
No beings survive, within such stark statistics.
(If only words could weep, and phrases sigh!)

With the background of the state hospital experiences and the Menninger intensive training, I was ready in 1967 to respond to the invitation from Dr. George Harding in Ohio to join the Harding Hospital staff and institute a milieu program similar to that I had designed in Topeka.

The next twenty-two years were opportune for the rapid advancement of the field of art therapy. It gradually developed as a profession. Harding was open to original ideas. We built studio spaces for the arts, introduced the use of isomorphic metaphors and guided imagery as techniques to be used in art psychotherapy groups. The years 1967 to 1988 saw the establishment of a clinical internship in art therapy at Harding, the introduction of art therapy courses at Columbus College of Art and Design, and an undergraduate degree program at Capital University. I became a founder of both the Ohio Buckeye Art Therapy Association and the American Art Therapy Association.

Art therapy became recognized as one of the most precise psychotherapeutic approaches. In my numerous papers, I have variously described art as a time machine providing immediate real-time access to the sources of trauma, the hidden "film clips," as a darkened theater, where past pain can be felt and relieved in the present, as a unique ultra-sound probe. I am always searching for the right metaphor, as is our profession. We are reminded though that we are still in our first generation! Vincent Van Gogh wrote to his brother Theo: "I have a terrible need . . . shall I say the word?. . . of religion. Then I go out at night and paint the stars."

While studying at theological seminary, I read Rudolph Otto's book, *The Idea of the Holy.* It is a seminal study of the "un-rational" aspects of the religious experience. Otto stated that "fascinans" might be ascribed to the arts as well as to religion. He used terms like "mysterium," "tremendum," and "numinous" in describing both art and religion, (and I contend he might have included science).

Finally, a view of my personal journey in search of the sacred. The Gospel of John begins with, "In the beginning was the Word. . . ." But, there was no need for words in the Beginning, words being a human invention. There were then, only "thought-words" that is, ideas which are perceptual-images becoming ART in the hands of the first humans who were all born artists. Therefore, in the beginning Art was made to overcome Chaos. What fun for me, to think upside down! I always wonder what would happen if?

> Hell is sky high and Heaven earth-bound.
> While gravity is there to guarantee,
> If I am tossed up, I must fall down.
> And there I'd be, back on the ground.
> My world, my home, my hospital, my Heaven!

The sacred is no more obvious in ritual than in science or the arts. This was my view as artist-pastor of the country church in the little village of Rossville where I served for fifteen years while working at Menninger's. I wrote over a thousand sermons. Today, I would translate what Moses thought he heard on the mountain, from: "I AM THAT I AM!" into "I AM THAT I AM BECOMING!"

In Rossville, we made art every Friday night in my garage studio behind the parsonage, ultimately painting murals in two of the churches, the community center and the high school auditorium. The artists were local town's people, among them the butcher, the weekly newspaper editor, farmers, neighbors with their children and mine, and some staff members from Menninger's. The community eventually got used to the unusual happenings on Friday nights. It was no surprise then for them to see on one Christmas morning, two twelve-foot Baroque-style gilded angels flying from the bell-tower of our church. On some wonderful, intuitive level they began to know, feel and welcome the creative power of ART that I felt as part of their lives. I left an acre of art there! It takes ART to make a Village-Soul!

It was in Topeka that I made the "Equality Kids," a poster illustration used extensively during my participation in the NAACP movement, 1954, the year of *Brown versus the Topeka Board of Education.* I have in intervening years created many paintings on other social issues.

Currently, 2005, I share art Studio 3J with Karen Rush Jones, M.A., ATR-BC, who is an art therapist with a Hospice Bereavement Program. I am in the studio daily painting and exhibiting, writing, and seeing clients in my private practice, often as a "therapist's therapist," and I mentor art therapy students. Since 1988, when "becoming" retired, I have done expressive arts in hospice, neuro-rehabilitation, adult care, and a two-year program with mentally ill inmates in an Ohio prison. I have also traveled frequently, presenting seminars, papers and workshops at art therapy education programs and at American Art Therapy Association conferences, as well as giving sermons and helping in the founding of two new Unitarian Universalist churches.

Having reached this age but yet being neither saint nor sage, I am hoping in my spiritual sojourn to finally make THE PAINTING, the one that will explain my lifelong fascination and awe with art, science and contemplation, and the processes of my human "becoming and being."

EPILOGUE

When I received the Honorary Life Member award from AATA in 1988, these were some of my remarks. I called my remarks "Graces, Epiphanies and Exclamations":

My theme is, "Life is full of graces, epiphanies and exclamations. I am here by the *grace of* the influence of those who have stood here, those bypassed who might have stood here, and those yet to be on this spot (in a spotlight), symbolically speaking. (Am I the sad clown, finally open?)

If it were not for those who will yet stand here, I would not feel comfortable or complete. Anything worth doing takes more than one lifetime but each of us is allotted only one span. So, I am your root! You are my continuity! . . .

Epiphanies . . . Doing creative activities is such an experience for me but, there have been even higher sacred moments of human exchange with patients doing the work of art in therapy. Such high occasions for me occurred as I was involved with the "pioneer-founders." Bob Ault and I, in Topeka, had a dream . . . Myra Levick graced and managed many of those early occasions . . . Felice Cohen's applied humor, salvaged tough moments and tight situations . . . Elinor Ulman added a clarity and intensity of purpose.

There were *exclamations* . . . as we hammered out practical details. We went round and round . . . discovering that we moved not in divergent but in concentric circles. The centrifugal force of our vision centered our efforts . . . soon others were caught up in the swirl of energy and exuberance . . . even so, we were reminded that art therapy's development is not so much determined by individuals as by the force and logic of the creative process. In the minutes before being installed as the fourth President of AATA, I spontaneously recalled and shared with Bob Ault my childhood memory of a small, wide-eyed, anxious boy going to the circus. The ringmaster announced that the first twelve kids to race to the center could ride on an elephant. A dozen of us climbed on. The beast rose up from a kneeling position. Suddenly came the awareness that it was alive and moving and that riding on the back of an elephant was by its grace and with

its indulgence. . . . (A reminder to me that all who serve this organization do so with the assent of the collective, creative brawn of the membership body.) Doing art is a phenomenal expediter of expression of insight, of comprehension and more . . . The aesthetic spirit is life saving and life-giving. My hope is that it will be beauty and poetry that may help to save the world. The experiences of conception, birth, nurturing and growth of the American Art Therapy Association have been full of graces, epiphanies and exclamations for me. I cannot resist one final exclamation to all of you, THANK YOU!
–Don L. Jones ATR-BC, HLM

Note: I must give special thanks to Micheal Maloney, who, for two years, pressed me to open my hundreds of papers and memories for his thesis, *A Pioneer: The Theoretical Contributions by Don Jones to the Field of Art Therapy.* It began a search, after retirement in 1988, that has revived my interest and participation in art therapy up to the present moment. Thanks, Michael!!

Elinor Ulman

Chapter 4

ELINOR ULMAN, 1910–1991

SHORT REFLECTIONS ON A LONG
AND PRODUCTIVE LIFE

Katherine Williams

I agonized over my first paper for Elinor Ulman, the legendary wielder of a relentless blue pencil. Returning to school after a hiatus in my education, I assumed I would be in the market for another career upon the return of my assignment. Heightened alertness inspired by fear has allowed me, all these years later, to still see Elinor's clear, unassuming script at the bottom of the last page, complimenting me on my writing, asking a thoughtful question that propelled me to think further on my topic, and noting that I had used a word which, upon consultation with the dictionary, she could assure me did not exist in the English language. So much of my experience of Elinor is captured in that comment—her generosity, her thirst for discourse and engagement in the study of art therapy, and her fearless commitment to uphold the standards of excellence in writing.

Elinor's reputation for fierceness was not unfounded. She did not suffer fools and could ignite instantly when one of her passions was challenged. Judy Finer and I were asked to take notes at an early meeting of art therapy educators. Imagining ourselves basking in the glow of combined collegial wisdom, we were astounded to witness a spectacle more like an ideological catfight among our elders. Amazed as I was by this experience, I can't even remember what the fight was about. But I do remember that when she pounced on her prey, Elinor's claws were as sharp and skillful as any of her beloved Vermont barn cats. Elinor's keen interest in ethics and her belief in the importance of rigorous training in the field of art therapy led her at times to engage in vehement debate. But it was real debate—she was capable of changing her perspective through thoughtful discourse. So even though her forcefulness and passion did create enemies, they also fueled the pursuit of excellence that marked everything she did.

She graduated Phi Beta Kappa from Wellesley (1930), studied oil painting in France (1932–1934), brush painting in China (1934–1936), and landscape architecture in the United States (1943). From 1934–1940, she painted and taught private pupils. Her paintings were exhibited at the Corcoran Biennial, the Phillips Gallery in Washington, the Baltimore Museum of Art, and at the 1939 New York's World's Fair.

Elinor never stopped learning, and it was this freshness of mind that kept her engaged with students and writers throughout her life. From 1942–1953, she worked as a draftsman, cartographer, and technical illustrator, while beginning to explore the process of teaching art to handicapped children and offering art materials to participants at an alcoholic rehabilitation program. Emboldened by these experiences, Elinor focused her ferocious energy on establishing art therapy at D.C. General Hospital, where she developed the Ulman Assessment Procedure (1955–1965). She committed her financial and intellectual resources to initiating and editing the *Bulletin of Art Therapy*, which became the *American Journal of Art Therapy* (1961–1984); and, with Bernard Levy, started the art therapy program at George Washington University, one of the first Master's Degree programs in the country (1971). She also taught for many summers at the Vermont College art therapy program, which awarded her an honorary degree in 1985. The articles she wrote based on these experiences, the authors whose work she invariably improved through her careful editing, the anthologies of art therapy literature of which she was editor, and the students she taught made her a primary influence on the thinking and writing of a generation of art therapists.

Elinor's discriminating eye could pick up a comma splice, select outstanding artwork from amidst the world's cluttered offerings, choose and order simple, beautiful spaces in which to live, and pick the perfect kitten for my daughter, selected after days of close observation of the whole litter tumbling across the straw in her barn. She was not an adventurous cook, but my mouth waters as I remember the chopped liver sandwiches and fragrant Earl Grey tea she brought to her evening supervision sessions. And I still have the turquoise and pink metal cookie tin with folding handles that she filled with dark chocolate brownies, her customary donation at potluck dinners. In her later years, Elinor was uncomplaining about her failing health, rejoicing when the temperature in her pond was warm enough to permit a dip, delighting in the pleasure of looking off into the green hills visible from her Vermont porch, and continuing to savor language deeply, as editor and reader.

I concluded my words at her memorial service by quoting one of Elinor's and my favorite authors. Because of Elinor's appreciation of the natural world and the particular sort of humility that she possessed, I believe she would relish being compared to Charlotte, the literary spider. So I end here, as I did then, using E.B. White's words: "It is not often that someone one comes along who is a true friend and a good writer. [Elinor] was both."

Elinor Ulman receiving an honorary doctorate at Vermont College of Norwich, 1985.

Hanna Yaxa Kwiatkowska

Chapter 5

HANNA YAXA KWIATKOWSKA (Deceased, 1980)

FAMILY ART THERAPY PIONEER

Harriet Wadeson

Hanna (pronounced "Hanya") Kwiatkowska never wanted to reveal her age or the year in which she was born, so they are not included here. I was Hanna's first student, having met her at the National Institutes of Health, where in 1961 I attended an art presentation she had arranged. Afterwards we went to her office and she told me about art therapy. I had never heard of it before, even though I had done it without knowing in volunteer work with mental patients. I asked Hanna how I could get an education in this field, and she said, "I'll train you." Thus began our 13-year working relationship.

Hanna was born into an aristocratic family in Poland. (My ancestors might have been serfs of hers.) She went to school in Switzerland and spoke fluent French as Polish aristocrats did in the early part of the twentieth century. Hanna was to become fluent in Russian, Portuguese, and of course English, in addition to her native Polish and French. When she was a child, the maids in her household would become ecstatic over the art she made and the poems she wrote, the latter bringing one of them to tears.

As an adult, Hanna became a sculptor. She married a Polish diplomat, Alexander Kwiatkowska, and the couple moved to China, where he was assigned for several years. "Kwiat," as he was known, joined the Polish Free Forces and fought for England throughout World War II, during which Hanna lived in Brazil. After their many years of wartime separation, they were reunited, and the couple moved to New York.

It was there that Hanna met Margaret Naumburg and became her first art therapy student. Later, when Hanna introduced me to Margaret, it was evident that each was very proud of the other. An award-winning semi-abstract clay piece titled "The Family" that Hanna had sculpted was predictive of the art therapy work for which Hanna was to become renowned.

Hanna Kwiatkowska (l) with Margaret Naumburg, 1970)

In 1955, Kwiat joined the State Department in Washington, D.C., and Hanna began work as an art therapist at St. Elizabeth's Hospital, a large mental institution in Washington. Subsequently, she was hired at the National Institute of Mental Health (NIMH) in 1958, where I began work with her three years later. Murray Bowen, one of the founders of family therapy, had set up family studies there, which were continued by Lyman Wynne, under whom Hanna worked. Although family art therapy began accidentally when family members visited patients and attended their art therapy sessions, Hanna soon found both their individual and conjoint art pieces revealing of family dynamics. As a result, art therapy became a regular part of family evaluations. The major focus of these studies was families of schizophrenics. The research was directed by Lyman Wynne. Hanna also participated in work with Loren Mosur, who headed some interesting monozygotic twin investigations. Hanna developed a protocol in which family members made free pictures, scribble drawings, family portraits, abstract family portraits, and a conjoint picture. With William Dent, she worked on creating a manual for rating the artwork in family art therapy. Hanna published her book, *Family Therapy and Evaluation through Art* in 1978. Throughout these years, she was also a frequently invited guest lecturer, spreading the word about art therapy.

When Elinor Ulman established the George Washington University (GW) Art Therapy Graduate Program in the early 1970s, she called upon her good friend and colleague Hanna Kwiatkowska to serve on the faculty. Hanna became a beloved mentor to many students throughout the 1970s. She often spoke of how GW misprinted the title of her course, Art Therapy Technique, by labeling it "Art Therapy Techniques." She was adamant that art therapy is not simply a series of techniques.

Hanna was active in the formation of the American Art Therapy Association (AATA), serving on its first Executive Board as Research Chair. She secured Arlie House outside Washington for the site of the first AATA conference in 1970. When she was awarded AATA's fourth Honorary Life Membership (HLM) in 1973, the vote was unanimous. She became choked up as she accepted the honor, saying that she hadn't expected to be so moved.

During the many years I knew Hanna, from 1961 until her death in 1980, she suffered from the results of a botched surgery to her leg when she was a child. She had frequent hospitalizations and occasional additional surgeries. She used a cane and sometimes needed crutches. Because her balance was compromised, from time to time she fell, adding to her disability. Frequently, she appeared to me to be smiling through her pain.

In 1978, I moved from Washington, so the last time I saw Hanna was at the 1979 AATA conference, for which I returned to D.C. She was already ill from cancer, from which she died several months later, but she claimed that the reason she attended only one day of the conference was because she was moving to a new apartment. Several years later, the memory of being with her on that day inspired me to write a poem:

THE LAST LESSON

I sat at your feet
as I had done at the beginning.
You were almost transparent
in your flowered chiffon with the brooch at your neck.
Shadows flickered beneath your tissue paper skin,
and you seemed a pale leaf
soon to be caught up by the wind.

In the long ago maze of being teacher and student,
we used to speak of luscious delicacies,
profiteroles, paté, amaretto soufflé.
But you were silent about your indigestion,
and I left the room when the doctor returned your calls.

This last time,
even in the midst of being feted
by colleagues and students,
you apologized (as you had so often done),
this time for missing most of the Annual Meeting.
You were moving, you said,
and spoke of apartments and vans.
Yes, you were moving,
fluttering so delicately
in your dappled chiffon.
The wind was stirring
and soon you would be gone.

But wind carries with it
more than thin, veined leaves.
Seeds too are spread,
floating from parachutes of milkweed silk,
dandelion balloons,
and the wings of opened maple pods.
Your students have become teachers
tilling the soil you have cultivated.

That last time I looked into the dark seas of your eyes,
where the wind was beginning to ripple the surface,
I told you what I wanted you to hear.
I didn't speak of coffee mouse or sabayon sauce.
People pressed around us
and presented you with a cake.
I don't know if you heard me,
but still, it was important for me to speak.
I said that you visited my dreams,
and in spite of time and distance,
you were with me often.

I still see your fragile face fluttering in the wind,
the deep sigh in your dark eyes,
and the canes and crutches of all those years.
And only now,
years since that last goodbye,
as I plow fields where your students and mine
have become planters,
do I reap the full harvest of your teachings.

The wind roars the name of that last lesson:
Courage.

Harriet Wadeson, 1983

Elsie Ferrar Muller's drawing of her work for AATA.

Chapter 6

ELSIE FERRAR MULLER (1913-1996)

A CALMING PRESENCE

JUDITH A. RUBIN

Elsie Muller was born in Worcester, Massachusetts, the daughter of Frederic and Anne Bonnet. She earned a Bachelor's degree in 1934 from Alfred University (New York), became a licensed social worker, and taught at Alfred until 1936, when she married Frederick Muller (d. 1961). Elsie began graduate work at the University of Missouri in 1962, earning a degree in social work in 1968. She was a member of NASW and ACSW, and the National Register of Clinical Social Workers, but I believe that her heart was in art therapy.

She was a close friend of Margaret Howard of Tulsa, Oklahoma, whom I first met at a meeting chaired by Irene Jakab, a psychiatrist then at Topeka State Hospital. Elsie and Marge, like many in that era, had gone to New York for classes with Margaret Naumburg. Sandy Kagin (now Graves-Alcorn), who studied with Marge and spent time with the two friends, remembers: "Elsie was a very spiritual woman. She truly believed that you could take any experience and make it a positive one. I loved being around her because she had a depth of character missing in many people. She was a dear, sweet woman."

Elsie worked as an art therapist at the Gillis Home for Children and later the Ozanam Home for Disturbed Adolescent Boys in Kansas City, Missouri, from 1958 to 1970. In 1968, she published *Family Group Art Therapy: Treatment of Choice for a Specific Case*, which she had presented at a conference of the American Society of Psychopathology of Expression. I remember reading

---

Note: In writing this, I have drawn extensibely on the obituary published by Elinor Ulmanan in *The American Journal of Art Therapy* (1996), and on the recollections of Robert Ault, Sandra Kagin [Graves-Alcorn], and Irene Jakab, in addition to my own memories of Elise Muller.

61

that article at the recommendation of Hanna Kwiatkowska, whose work had inspired and informed Elsie's.

From 1970 to 1978, Elsie worked as a social worker in Kansas City, but she used art whenever possible. One of the first things I remember Elsie telling me was that, even though she had been well trained as a social worker in verbal therapy, she had found that adding art opened many new avenues for those she served. She was a true believer in the healing potential of art, for she had experienced it herself and knew its power.

Elsie was a founding member of the American Art Therapy Association (AATA) and served on the Executive Board from 1969–1973 as Chair of the Constitution Committee. During one particularly heated meeting, she decided to draw to discharge some of the tension she was feeling. She was also AATA's Parliamentarian from 1970–1974. She was universally liked and admired. Because she was so well regarded by everyone as a stabilizing force in the association's early, tumultuous years, Elsie received the HLM Award in 1976.

I remember her saying that she didn't think she deserved the honor and didn't feel she belonged in the company of those who had preceded her. Yet she was the voice of calm in the chaos of AATA's beginnings. Bob Ault said: "As parliamentarian, she kept us to the rules, and she was highly respected. She helped us with her calm presence."

I remember Elsie's kindness, teaching me all she had learned as Constitution Chair when I took that position on the Board in 1973. She remained on the Committee and was always available for help when I called her. She died in 1996 in the Palouse Hills Nursing Home in Pullman, Washington, where she had retired in 1986. She was 83.

Part II

GROWTH: ART THERAPISTS WHO BEGAN IN THE 1960s

Robert Ault

Chapter 7

ROBERT AULT

THE ART THERAPY LIFELINE
OR
HOW WAS YOUR PRACTICE? "IT HAD ITS UPS AND DOWNS," SAID THE ELEVATOR MAN

I would like to have lived my life so that when I die even the undertaker would be sad.
—Mark Twain

THE BEGINNING

I was born and raised in Corpus Christi, Texas, blessed with loving parents, four brothers, a secure home, with lots of relatives around. I was the middle child, the one who was best at making peace when the five of us squabbled. When I was in the fifth grade I had a teacher named Miss Love, who called my mother one day and reported that she thought little "Bobbie Ed" had some art talent and would benefit from art lessons. Thus began a lifetime of involvement in art making, and later in the use of art in the service of helping people to heal. Another important factor was my involvement in the Boy Scouts. Skills that I learned as a boy still serve me today. For many, it was a good time to grow up, but very tough if you were a young man in Texas in the '40s and '50s more interested in art than football. The girls preferred jocks, not artists. I was admitted to the South Texas Art League at the age of 14 and already had my mind made up to follow a career in the arts. My goal was to get a bachelors degree in art at Texas University, go to graduate school, teach at a university, and be an artist. It almost happened that way.

I did get my Bachelor of Fine Arts (BFA) at Texas in painting and applied for graduate fellowships at the University of Tennessee and at Wichita State in Kansas. The letter from Wichita came first with an offer of a fellowship that would make a graduate degree possible. So after a visit, I accepted. My teaching duties would not be at the University, but would be at the Institute of Logopedics, a speech correction institute there in Wichita. They wanted to set up an art program and thought a cheap way of doing it was to offer a fellowship to a graduate student. I decided I could put up with anything for two years while I continued painting and completed my Masters of Fine Arts (MFA).

Robert Ault as a child.

The Institute was a different world for me. Many of the kids wore helmets and stumbled around; their arms and hands seemed to have a life of their own, and they talked with great difficulty. I learned they suffered from cerebral palsy and aphasia or other forms of brain damage. I was sent to a room where a woman was helping students make art or do other creative work. I helped her and it was a kick. I loved it and soon loved my students. I found in the art room a place that challenged my creativity and ability to interact in meaningful ways. It was a place for all that family and scouting stuff that I mentioned earlier.

There was a boy named Lynn who came to the art room. He was 14 and had suffered whooping cough with high fever for several days. He'd survived, but with severe expressive-receptive aphasia; he could not understand or speak language. His housemother noticed that he liked to draw so she sent him to me. I didn't know what to do other than to play with him by drawing each other, which he really enjoyed. One day I got the idea of drawing a cartoon sequence of Lynn sitting at the table, getting up and going out the door, going outside the building, and coming in the back door and sitting down. He looked it over, got up and ran out and around the building and back to his seat. Both our lives changed at that moment. I became an art therapist, and Lynn started a journey of communicating visually. Together, we developed a set of symbols for Lynn and sent these to all the offices at the Institute, and people used Lynn to go get mail, coffee, etc., by using the symbols. I graduated and left the Institute. Years later my wife met Lynn's speech teacher and asked about him. She said that after I left, his parents took him home to a small town in Nebraska. She added, "You know those symbol things Bob was doing? Everyone in his town has a set." This is what this art therapy profession and the people in it have always been about for me and why I would give my professional life to it. It doesn't get any better than that.

One other important thing happened while I was in Wichita: Besides two years of experience at the Institute and finishing my MFA, I met a wonderful young woman from southern Kansas, and fell in love. I returned briefly to Texas, but was miserable and quickly followed her to Topeka, proposed, and married her. That was 45 years ago and I still think it was one of my better decisions. We have raised two wonderful children and now have four grandchildren.

In 1961, if you did not join the army reserve, you were drafted for two years, so like many other young men, I joined the reserve and served six months active duty and five and a half years of reserve duty in Topeka. What a shock to the whole system that was. Like the South Texas of my youth, the army liked football players more then artists. I had been married two weeks when I shipped out to Fort Leonard Wood in Missouri. It was a few miserable weeks, but my wife, Marilynn, brought me oil crayons and paper that I would fold in my clothing hidden in the footlocker. At night I would go to the latrine and draw. Art helped with the assault to my individuality, my creativity, my loneliness, my values, my very being, as I learned the art of killing.

On Christmas leave, I came home to Topeka, went out to the Menninger Foundation and applied for a job in the activity therapy department. There was an opening in the recreation section and to my surprise I was hired. So, in February 1961, when I left Fort Leonard Wood, I began working at Menningers. Menningers was a different environment for me. I had never been in a psychiatric hospital, other than a visit to the Texas State Hospital with a psychology class (that scared the hell out of me). After checking in the first day, I was told another staff member was sick and I needed to take a group out to the garden to work. So I took several patients and a variety of garden tools out to a garden to chop weeds. An elderly woman sat on the ground and proceeded to chop with the hoe. I asked her to stand up like the rest of the group and she replied, "Sonny, let your brains save your butt!" That was some of the best advice I ever got and my career quickly took a different turn. I started going over to the Creative Arts Shop and having lunch with Don Jones and the other staff there.

There are at times very special loving relationships outside one's family. Among these I believe one of the strongest to be that of the mentor. I have been blessed with several, including my long-time friend Don Jones and Dr. Karl Menninger. Don and I worked together for a number of years at Menningers' and I learned so much from him. I still call him Pop and he calls me Son. We shared an office that had once been that of Dr. C.F. Menninger, the father of Dr. Karl and William Menninger. He was a collector of rocks, and the walls of our office had display cases filled with rock samples. It was a small but comfortable space, and Don and I would often sit in the office after hours and talk and dream of the idea of using art to work with patients. We didn't call ourselves art therapists. Those were a handful of people on the East Coast who did art analysis, yet we saw our patients change and get better, and we believed that the art process itself was curative. We also talked about someday trying to organize a national organization where people like ourselves could get together and talk about these things.

It was wonderful having a father figure in my life who talked art. I loved my own father but he was a business man, as were my brothers and when we talked, both my parents had difficulty understanding what I did or why accumulation of wealth wasn't important to me. One day I called home and told my folks that I had accepted an appointment to a university. My dad replied, "Does that mean you are a professor?" I answered, "Yes." From that day on he referred to me or introduced me as his professor son, never his artist or art therapist son. So Don took on a multilayered meaningful role with me, and I will always be grateful to him for it.

Note: Menninger Clinic and Foundation in Topeka, Kansas, were founded in the 1920s as one of the first milieu therapy programs in the United States. Psychodynamically oriented, Menningers' always had "activities therapies," including art and music. In the 1930s Mary Huntoon was an artist working at the Clinic, whose title changed from "art instructor" to "art therapist."

For several years we would have a creative arts open house at Menningers' and convert the creative arts clinic and the adjoining hallways and rooms into a large gallery to display the art works of both patients and staff. Open to the public, the exhibit was very well attended. The patients acted as docents and took groups around explaining what was done there and answered questions. One of the patients later reported he had someone in his group who kept asking to see the "psychotic art." When the group came into the main room the fellow looked around and pointed to a painting across the room and declared, "This is what I mean!" He pointed to an oil painting of an eagle flying over a pond, seeing a dove reflected in the water. It was the only painting in the room painted by a staff member–Mr. Don Jones. We all got a real laugh hearing how the patient explained to the guest that was the boss's painting.

Robert Ault with a client.

In the '60s I was psychoanalyzed at Menningers'. Being a staff member, I qualified as a training case at a below cost rate. It was quite an experience and I feel I learned a great deal from it and benefited greatly from it. The week before I was assigned a psychoanalyst, I drove to my office late one evening. As I entered the parking lot, there was Dr. Hartacollis, with his Mercedes up on a jack trying to change his back tire. I turned my lights around, got out and asked if he needed any help. He said he couldn't figure out how to keep the tires from rotating so he could get the lugs off. I pushed down on the emergency brake and it fixed the problem. He dismissed me when I offered further help. I went on to my office. A few days later I was told he would be my analyst. Over the next year as I lay on the analytic couch looking at the ceiling, we spent hours talking about that incident. How could a guy with doctorates in both psychology and medicine who was a psychoanalyst not have the common sense to put on the brake to change a tire?

My supervisor and friend Don Jones left Menningers' and moved to Ohio to work at Harding Hospital. It was shortly after the move that the letter came from Myra Levick to attend a meeting in Philadelphia to discuss the formation of a national art therapy organization. I attended from Menningers' and Don was there from Harding Hospital. We were both elected to a committee to put together a constitution and bylaws along with Myra Levick, Felice Cohen, and Elinor Ulman. The irony was that if Don and I had both still been at Menningers', one of us would have attended the meeting and the other would have stayed and kept the clinic open. As it turned out, we were able to work together on our life's project.

At the meeting I met for the first time a very bright, attractive, dynamic woman from Hahnemann Hospital in Philadelphia. Myra Levick had organized the meeting and was determined that we get on with the business of organizing in spite of some real opposition. There was another person there, an elderly woman who walked with a cane, was hard of hearing and was very disruptive to the meeting at times. When things were said that she disagreed with, she would bang her cane on the floor and speak out. I finally turned to Don and asked who she was. It was Margaret Naumburg.

Another woman also spoke a lot. She was very gracious and funny and had a Texas drawl that I loved. She was Felice Cohen from Houston. Felice was very supportive of the idea of organizing, as were Don and I, and we seemed to counter the objections of Margaret and Elinor Ulman. Finally, the time came to nominate the people for the Ad Hoc committee, and Elinor nominated Margaret along with several others. When the vote was taken, the winners were Myra, Felice, Elinor, Don, and myself. Margaret was furious, got up, shook her finger at us and announced, "I'm not through with you!" and stormed out of the room. I sat there in shock. The grandmother of our profession had just shaken her finger at me. That was the only time I saw

Margaret Naumburg in person, but the story doesn't end there. In the following years we exchanged a number of very warm and caring letters. Shortly before her death, she asked me to review her book, and she seemed receptive to my comments about the importance of using what she had created for patients all over the country. I am glad that our paths crossed in this way and there was a different kind of closure.

After being elected to the committee to write a constitution and bylaws for the formation of the American Art Therapy Association (AATA), I met with Bill Sears several times, one of the founders of the Music Therapy Association, to discuss the structure of their organization. I also went through several constitutions of other professional organizations, including that of the American Speech and Hearing Association. Before the meeting in Louisville, where AATA was to adopt a constitution and bylaws, I was convinced that we needed a strong national structure that would eventually allow state organizations to join in. I felt this was the need, rather then trying to start with state structures and a weak federal organization. The day before I came to Louisville, my secretary typed up a copy of this constitution and bylaw model, and it was reproduced on the old purple ink mimeograph machine we had in the office. This was before the availability of Xerox and computers.

At the committee meeting we debated from early afternoon till late at night to decide on the proper structure for the organization. Elinor Ulman had brought another model, one of a weak federal organization with the emphasis on state structures. The rest of us felt it was a ploy to delay as long as possible the American Art Therapy Association from happening. Finally, she agreed on the strong federal structure if we would agree not to elect officers for a year. We agreed in the middle of the night and went to bed, but telephoned people who were at the meeting and asked them to vote yes on accepting the constitution and bylaws and vote no on the delay. Elinor called her colleague Bernie Levy, who flew out to Louisville that night, and the next day he made a passionate speech to delay. He was voted down and the group voted in the constitution and proceeded to elect officers. The American Art Therapy Association was born.

Over the years I have met and greatly admired so many people in our profession that it would be impossible to name them all or even begin to tell the stories. One of the people though that I struggled with was Elinor Ulman. I'm not sure why. I know that she and Margaret Naumburg and others had spent their life energy fighting, as pioneers just to do the work. They were as committed as Southern Baptist ministers to the idea of art therapy. They were also committed to the ideas of Freud and analysis, and art therapy was like their child. They weren't interested in some young guys from Kansas, or Ohio, coming in and taking this from them, and they fought all of us. Elinor fought most fiercely with Myra Levick, and, in my opinion, much energy and time were wasted. Elinor once told me she believed that you had to forge things out of the fire of conflict and debate. She found it hard to believe you could also forge from cooperation and compromise.

When I was serving as AATA's 2nd president, I had a particularly potent exchange with Elinor via correspondence. I don't remember the issue now, but Elinor had written a rather bitter letter to me wanting me to take an action that I did not believe was in the best interest of the American Art Therapy Association. I wrote her a letter back, and instead of being angry, I tried to be as respectful as possible and appreciative of all she had contributed. I remember saying to her that we needed each other, as what we were doing with AATA was much bigger than anything we could do alone, and I asked for her help. She wrote me a very nice letter back and thanked me and said she agreed. From then on, I felt that we worked together in a much more agreeable manner.

I also met Elinor's good friend and colleague, Bernie Levy. I loved Bernie, and his death in 1984 was a big loss to all of us. We had a party at his home one evening and I got to see firsthand his lovely watercolors. We worked on AATA boards and argued at times but always with respect and care. There was never any hostility. He was funny, he was bright, he was one of the few other men in the AATA, and he was a good guy. My students at Emporia State spent some time at one of the conferences visiting with his wife and they all fell in love with her.

THE MIDDLE YEARS

At one American Art Therapy Association conference, the men of AATA met. A group of about 20 men met to discuss the issue of being the sexual minority of our profession. I don't think any of us had ever felt discriminated against or anything like that, in fact just the opposite. At that time art therapy primarily attracted women and the American Art Therapy Association was composed primarily of women. About a dozen women showed up for the meeting. We asked them why they were there, and they said they just wanted to know what we were up to.

One of the men in the AATA that I became friends with was Robert Wolf from New York. We would often meet at conferences and spend time together talking. He taught at Pratt Institute and was a fine sculptor as well as a very nice colleague, one I highly respected. One day, I received a lovely letter from Bob with photographs of two sculptures that he had created. He asked me to pick out one to be sent to Menningers' in commemoration of my work there as an art therapist. I was dumbfounded by the honor. I did pick out a lovely marble piece and it arrived and was displayed in the dining room. When Menningers' moved to Houston in 2004, much of the art collection was sold, but Bob's piece was given to the Topeka and Shawnee County Public Library's Art Collection. I still feel very honored and touched by his kindness.

I took over as President of AATA in Milwaukee in 1971, following a fiery business meeting with much division and anger. Myra Levick closed the meeting and handed me the gavel. I felt that I had inherited a hive of bees with no gloves or smoker. A group of friends asked me to go with them to a late lunch, and I turned them down and told them I just wanted to be alone for a while. So, I walked around the streets of Milwaukee until time to go to the airport. I caught a plane to Chicago, and a later flight to Kansas City. The seating was open and I went to the back corner seat, feeling the weight of the world on my shoulders. The plane filled and a young woman sat next to me. She asked me what kind of work I did. I told her I was an art therapist. She then proceeded to tell me of a full-blown paranoid delusional system that began with her husband spraying poison on the trees in her yard. When we landed she asked if she should see a psychiatrist and I answered yes. She shook my hand, thanked me, and deplaned.

I got my bag and found my car and drove to Topeka. It was sixty miles away and it was pouring down rain with a heavy wind, a typical Kansas storm. I was exhausted and remember watching the wipers work back and forth on the windshield as if saying, "Dumb guy, dumb guy." When I finally got home, my wife Marilynn had already gone to bed. I went upstairs and crawled in bed next to her, wet clothes, shoes and all. I just needed to snuggle in a warm safe place. The next day, I went to work, sorted through my notes, and began my two years as president of my beloved AATA.

In 1970, I attempted to start a Masters in Art Therapy program at Kansas University (KU). KU is not only the home of the famous Kansas Jayhawks basketball team, but it is where Music Therapy was started. Several times I met with Bill Sears, one of the founders of music therapy. In one of the conversations I asked Bill when music therapy had come into it's own as a profession and he spontaneously answered, "The day Thayer died." Thayer Gaston was the other founder of music therapy, and I thought it very significant that Bill believed it to be so important for the elders to let go of the organization.

Kansas University in Lawrence, Kansas, is only 20 miles from Topeka and as music therapy had started in the music education department, I thought art therapy would be a good fit in the art education department in the same building. I was hired by KU in 1970, but I was never allowed to teach a class in Lawrence, until I resigned in 1973. I was told that it would upset the psychology department too much, whom the art people believed were running rats crazy. The psychology folks talked of the arts people as a bunch of hippies who shouldn't be on campus. I taught classes in Topeka at Menningers', and students either had to be recruited from the Topeka area or drive over from Lawrence. I was told each semester that we would be able to start a program shortly. What I finally figured out was that KU wasn't interested in an art therapy program; they were interested in my not starting one at another university. Finally I resigned. That same week a group from Emporia State University, 60 miles away, asked that I talk to them about art therapy at Menningers'. I told them I had just resigned from Kansas University and was looking for another University to start a program. The next day I got a call from Emporia and a month later we had a Master of Science in Psychology with a specialty in Art Therapy in place and operating. It was the fifth masters in the country and the only Master of Science in art therapy for many years. The program, now in it's 33rd year, is alive and well and is a great source of pride and inspiration for me. Emporia State will also be the site for the permanent location of the AATA archives.

A very special thing happened to me along the course of these middle years. I was selected to receive the Honorary Life Membership award. Marilynn came with me to the meeting in Los Angeles. I knew of course that the award would be given, but what I didn't expect was that when I was asked to come forward, people stood up and clapped. It freaked me out. My colleagues and friends actually stood and clapped as I walked to the podium. That was a very special moment, one I will not forget.

Working at Menningers' 32 years was a mixed bag. I loved being a part of an excellent hospital and learning environment. I loved the people that I met and my colleagues. I loved the support they gave me as we put together the AATA and when I served on the board, but I hated the institutional prejudice. If you were not a doctor or a psychiatrist, you were a second-class citizen. I had the opportunity to go through analysis, and with some pressure was allowed to go through psychotherapy training, but was given only the worst cases and was not paid as other psychotherapists. I was doing some outside work with business organizations then and had gathered a lot of experience with using art therapy in the business world. I had tried for a number of months to get into the Menninger Management Institute, but was repeatedly turned down. The Management Institute was a part of the organization that conducted weeklong seminars for business executives, doctors, military leaders, and other groups. It was started after World War II, by Dr. Will Menninger, and had been attended over the years by 40,000 people. It was thought to be one of the finest such institutes in the world.

I persisted and finally, one day over lunch, the Director of the Institute asked me if I had ever been in the scouts. I said yes. He asked what rank and

I said I was an Eagle Scout. He perked up and said, "Then you know how to cook breakfast over a campfire. We could use someone to help with our executive seminars on the river trips." I picked up my tray, said some very nasty things to him and left. A few months later he resigned as Director of the Institute and Dr. Conroy took over. I had worked with him in the hospital and spoke to him about my working at the Management Institute. He signed me on and I spent the last twelve years of my years at Menningers' teaching, introducing art therapy, counseling, and loving working with the teams in what I called the varsity of Menningers. Bob Conroy was a prince of a fellow and the best person I ever worked with. The teams were allowed to be creative, always with respect and support, and it was fun to introduce visual ideas into the seminars.

One summer, a colleague asked if I would cover two weeks for him at an Ozark Hospital while he and his wife were on a trip. Each day I was introduced to the patients who had checked into the emergency room the previous night. The catchment area was in the southern hills of Missouri. One day I was assigned to a very depressed man of about 40, bearded, wearing overalls, who lived up in one of the "hollers," and had never been out of the county. Although we talked that afternoon, it was unclear just what was going on that would cause him to be depressed. His everyday life would make me depressed, but he was a survivor. That evening he again talked of suicide and I placed him on precautions. The next morning when I arrived at the clinic he was waiting for me and was furious. He had not been able to go out and smoke the night before. We went to a room and he ranted at me for a couple of minutes. He began to cry, reached in his shirt pocket and showed me a picture of himself standing beside a casket with his dead father in it. He cried bitterly telling me that his father had recently died, something he had not mentioned before. I listened and tried to support him. He immediately began to feel better and was ready to go home. He asked if he could have a picture of the two of us before leaving and I agreed. So a nurse got the Polaroid and before she took the picture, he took a piece of paper and wrote a message on it and held it up in front of him. We each got a picture and he left. My picture is still on my dresser. It is of me with a smaller, bearded man in overalls holding a piece of paper that reads, "This man helped me. He can help you too." This is why I chose to do this work for 50 years and never felt bored or wished I had chosen a different profession.

I had the pleasure of working with a nun who had come to Topeka to be in treatment at Menningers'. She wanted art therapy and looked me up and we began meeting. She did mostly contour drawings and her treatment went well until one day she came in and announced that Catholic services had shredded all 30 years of her educational work. She drew herself being put through a shredder. I had a shredder at home and brought it over to the studio and had the idea of shredding images and weaving them back together with paper and making art out of them, infusing them with new energy and life. We both worked on these projects. The metaphor worked very well with her as she put her own life back together. For me it opened a new way of painting that lasted nearly seven years.

The years as an art therapist passed by quickly with many terrific people in my life. During those years, my wife and I raised a wonderful son and daughter, one a scientist and the other a social worker, whom we couldn't be more proud of. Both seemed to have inherited a good social concern and have devoted their lives to making the world a better place. As with an earlier story, it just doesn't get much better than that.

I tried to get our daughter Keri interested in art therapy, but she wouldn't have anything to do with it, as it was my thing and she wanted her independence. Instead, she got a degree at KU in psychology and a second one in art history. She spent her junior year in Scotland and traveled around Europe and saw much great art. After returning to Kansas University she stayed on to earn a second degree in art history. I offered to pay her way to the Kansas Art Therapy conferences, but she would not go, or would only go incognito, hoping no one would know she was my daughter. After graduation, she moved to Portland, Oregon, and got a job in a psychiatric hospital. After several weeks, the staff realized she also had a degree in art history and asked her to start an art group. I got a very pathetic call one night from her saying, "Papa, can you tell me something about art therapy." There are some sweet moments in life.

Edith Kramer is someone I only knew from a distance, yet she was significant in my life. I met her and we had exchanged a few comments over the years, but had never really had a long conversation. One day I was sitting in one of her presentations at an AATA conference in New York and she remarked, "I have always struggled with learning by the written word." A light went off in my head and I thought, "Edith Kramer! The writer of the books! I know exactly how she feels. I also struggle with the written word, but I am a whiz at seeing and doing processes!" I remembered elementary school and the shame of the worst spelling test papers being placed on the bulletin board each Friday. Mine often were pinned up next to my drawings and I thought I wasn't very bright. I struggled with this until Edith's golden words freed me.

Through all 32 years on the professional staff at Menningers', I was never allowed to have a business card. The hierarchy ruled that those of us who were art therapists, music therapists, etc., just weren't professional enough, even though I carried a full load of psychotherapy cases, charged full fees for my services, and served on the faculty of the Menninger Management Institute. At the end of the Management seminars, the executives would often ask for my card and I would give them my studio card and write the Menninger address and phone number on the back.

Finally, I went to a friend who was the secretary for the Psychotherapy Department and told her of my situation. She was shocked and proceeded to forge the name of the director of the department on a purchase order. I received a box of a thousand crisp new cards a week later. I sent two to my parents, gave one to my wife, sent one to each of my kids, and put one in my billfold. A couple of days later, a letter came from Menningers' offering an early buy out which I took. Anyone wanting 994 obsolete business cards should contact me.

For two years I had the pleasure of serving on the Kansas Arts Commission. One day after evaluating a stack of grant applications, I was driving to Kansas City for a meeting when I passed Lawrence, Kansas. We had been struggling to figure how to place money in various art projects or with groups. This was on my mind as I looked to my left and saw the grain elevators where the movie *The Day After*, about an atomic war, had been shot. The image of rockets being fired off from the scene was vivid as the movie had just been shown on television. The radio was on in the car and the news was announcing that the new budget for the defense department was something like fifty billion dollars. We spend more money each year on one B1 bomber then we spend for all the arts. Anyway, I began to think, what if we made the National Endowment for the Arts part of the Defense budget. Even one percent would give us a great deal of money to make peace with the nations we were at war with. We could have art exchanges, or other cultural exchanges. I knew that each year Russian athletes visited Kansas and were welcomed at the statehouse and by the local population. We could gradually increase the percentage each year. What a better way to spend our money. I wrote Bob Dole, our Senator from Kansas, about the idea, but he never replied.

THE LATER YEARS

I left Menningers' in 1993, and Emporia State in 1995. I opened Ault's Academy of Art in 1978. It is where I still spend most of my time these days. I have six art classes and it has always run full. There are about 50 students a week, plus I have a half-time private practice of art therapy and psychotherapy. Now, I have cleared two days a week to paint. I don't travel very much anymore or go teach as I did all those years. I have always felt that when the time came my role would change from being an active player with the AATA to being more selfish with my time, to have time to be an active artist, to exhibit, to sell my work, and to enjoy a less stressful existence. That along with the normal aging process has forced a slower pace. I don't miss the activity of the AATA, I had my day. I do miss my extended family but I still keep close ties with many of them. I miss my students and cherish the times when I hear from them or get to see them, and I have a boatload of memories of good clinical work, past patients, colleagues, and good friends.

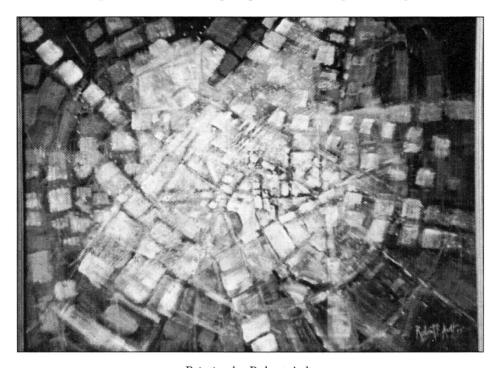

Painting by Robert Ault.

I couldn't possibly begin to name all my students or colleagues past or present who have added such richness to my career for fear that I would leave someone out. You all know who you are and how I feel about each of you. One student and colleague that I do want to say something about though is Janet Smith. Janet is a Cherokee Indian from Oklahoma who came to Emporia State in mid-life and completed her Master of Science Degree in Art Therapy. She is a tall, attractive, and bright woman who is also an artist. She was an excellent student and after she graduated from Emporia State we hired her for a year to help teach. She then returned to Oklahoma, where she worked for many years for the Cherokee Nation and introduced art therapy to Native American populations all over the country. She became a highly distinguished art therapist and one I am so proud of. I am honored to have been a part of her training.

Every year the University asks each College to elect an outstanding recent graduate and we elected Janet from the College of Education and Psychology. Usually it is a school superintendent. They had a big dinner at the Student Union Ballroom, and the outstanding graduates from the college of Business and the Liberal Arts College gave their proper speeches. Janet then went to the podium dressed in her native dress. She was lovely, and began by saying, "I am the only one in my family to ever complete high school." She then went on to tell the story of her quest to become an art therapist. The audience was mesmerized. At the end of her speech they stood and cheered. The Dean came to me and shook my hand firmly and said he now understood what this art therapy thing was about and asked what we needed for the program. That night Janet was our star that nailed our often-leaking program boat together and insured its longevity.

There are a couple of other friends I want to comment on before finishing with a couple of final stories. One is my buddy Maxine Junge. We have known each other for many years and shared so much. She is a respected colleague and part of my family as I feel a part of hers. We've stayed in each other's homes, painted together, told our secrets to each other, and shared much joy and some heartache over the years. There are those special people that cross your path whom you come to love and feel very special with. It is so nice to be so honored.

The other is my dear friend Julia Byers. I believe she is one of the most outstanding art therapists in the country, and I honor our friendship and closeness. She has stayed in our home a couple of times while in Kansas and has always been a source of inspiration to me with her international work in the Middle East as well as her brilliant directing of the program at Lesley University. I asked my wife last weekend after we had both talked to Julia on the phone, what do you call such a relationship like this and she answered, "How about Friend." That was good. The special love, kindness and respect are understood.

During my career I met and loved Elizabeth (Grandma) Layton, an elderly woman from Wellsville, Kansas, who had suffered a 40-year-old bout with a bipolar illness. She was isolated and alone for many years but managed to raise five children by herself. At the age of 68 she took a course in contour drawing at a local university and through her art, cured herself. Her artwork and her story became nationally known and she became part of the American cultural treasury. She was a great source of friendship and inspiration and we enjoyed 15 years of closeness. She was the one I called on Mother's Day, after traveling and teaching contour drawing as a psychotherapeutic technique all over the country. She always wanted to hear the stories.

Her art adorns my home and her goodness and genius touched everyone who contacted her. Following her death, this woman who lived in isolation and depression for so many years and found salvation and health through art had 1,500 names of people she was corresponding with. After presentations, people remind me I often speak of her as if she were still alive. Maybe she is, at least I know one heart that thinks so.

My final story is about one of the people in my life that I will always feel a real connection with, Dr. Karl Menninger. I knew and worked with him for 32 years and often interviewed him or had long conversations with him regarding art and art therapy. He didn't always get along with everyone and could be very gruff, but he never was that way with me. For some reason he liked me, and I liked him. He once asked me how many art therapists there were, and I reported we had about 3,000 in the association at that time. He shook his head and said we should have had 30,000 by now. He said one of his great disappointments in his career was that art therapy, music therapy, or other activity therapies had never taken off, as they were so valuable.

We often talked of painting together and finally did, each Friday afternoon, the last three years of his life. He died at the age of 96. I would go to his office and he would take my arm and we'd walk back to a kitchen area where there were a couple of easels set up. He'd often say to me, "Tell me something good that has happened this week. I've been feeling pretty depressed and I always feel better when I'm with you." We proceeded to paint next to each other and talk about music, or art, or life for an hour or so, before he tired and we closed out the week. It was a time I loved and I grew very close to him. He told me one day he knew he was a relic that they kept near the front gate so people could come to see, and this they did, wanting his autograph, his books, his picture, etc. As Emily Dickinson writes, he lived in the "bog of admiration."

One day a memo came saying he was very ill with cancer and staff couldn't visit him in the hospital, so I wrote him a letter and told him how much our time together had meant to me. The next day his daughter called and said they were setting up a watch and asked if I would like to participate. I agreed and sat with him twice. The last time I sat with him he seemed to be asleep, with tubes in his nose, breathing heavily. The next person came to relieve me and before I left I went over to Dr. Karl, touched his forehead and said goodbye. As I was leaving, Dr. Bradshaw, said, "I think he is trying to say something to you." I went back and leaned over him and he whispered to me, "Thanks for helping me Bob." He died that night. All these years later I still drive by his grave and think of him and how much I treasure the gift of him and what he gave me with that comment. He understood perfectly how I felt and why I was there.

I have had a charmed life as an art therapist and I still feel the passion in my gut for what we are about. These days I am concerned with how we can apply what we have learned to the greater population, those that are not ill, but can have a shot at growing up happier and more productive. The experience in the art studio has more than proved to me that the world is full of people who can use the experience of art for a better life. Up to now, psychological treatment has focused on getting people from a -5 (very ill) to 0 (normal). Most of our work has also focused on this portion of the population, those who come to us for therapy. What about the needs of the other 85%, those that range from -1 to +2, but who could grow to +5? It is my belief that in the next few years the arts, led by people from our profession or those with understandings we have generated, will play a significant role in public health and education. We have known for years that people do not need to be sick to respond to art therapy, to grow and change toward a richer and happier life. Hopefully, creative arts centers populated by art therapists will spring up all over the country, and the arts can again be an integral part of everyday life for everyone. Art is something to enjoy and to help define our lives, finding one's own inner voice and creativity. Just maybe, if we as art therapists can hang in there together, we could help visualize and discover the path to a more peaceful world.

Painting by Robert Ault.

Harriet Wadeson

Chapter 8

HARRIET WADESON

A MULTI-COLORED LIFE

My Mother used to say, "In my day. . . ." And I would protest, "TODAY is your day." Now I am older than she was then. When I gaze back on all my many days, I see bright flashes of color, but also long dark streaks of struggle as well.

My childhood in Washington, D.C., looks gray, bleak, arid. I see Sonny, my blue-eyed, tow-headed younger brother, the favorite of both my parents, being taken into bed with my Mother and to the golf course with my Father. My Mother was anxious, but involved. My Father was anxious, but remote. My Mother threatened me when I misbehaved, "Daddy will get the strap." He'd get angry, sometimes out of frustration with my Mother (but a nice Jewish man did not beat a woman), take off his belt, and beat me and my brother.

The sirloin steak my Mother served mapped the family power dynamics. She placed it before my Father, who cut it up and took the heart of the steak for himself. Sonny and I were passed the platter of outside pieces. The outer edge and fat were left for my Mother, who was still in the kitchen.

Only in my Grandmother's eyes did I shine. We'd all go to her apartment for the traditional family dinners—Hanukah, Passover, Rosh Hashanah—they all blend in my memory. My Grandfather read in Yiddish or Hebrew—I don't know which—I never understood what he was reading, and my brother and I sat at the children's table, a card table set up for us and our two male cousins. I was the oldest. The best part was that instead of gefilte fish, the children were given special eggs. They were small yolks with thin brown veins and a gamey taste. They came from inside the kosher chicken, eggs not yet laid. I've never had them since. I think that if I were to be served such eggs now, I would dissolve into tears.

But I was saying (before matzos and unlaid eggs captured my memory) that I was the shining star in my Grandmother's life. When we'd arrive at her apartment for the holiday dinner, she'd open the door and her face would light up at the sight of me. "Hello, Sveetness," she'd say in her Eastern European accent.

Later, when I worked on an adolescent unit at the National Institutes of Health (NIH) and observed family sessions through the observation mirror, I compared my dysfunctional family with theirs and concluded that only my Grandmother's love saved me from an emotional meltdown like theirs.

ART AND PSYCHOLOGY

My Mother also used to say, "Harriet made art before it was fashionable." I drew stories before I could write. I was the cartoonist for my high school paper. (The major challenge was thinking up something funny for each issue.) In college I took more classes in art than in my major, psychology. But I never wanted to become an artist. I didn't think I was good enough. And I didn't want to get caught up in the art world (I don't know how I could have been so wise as a teenager). I had no interest in teaching art either.

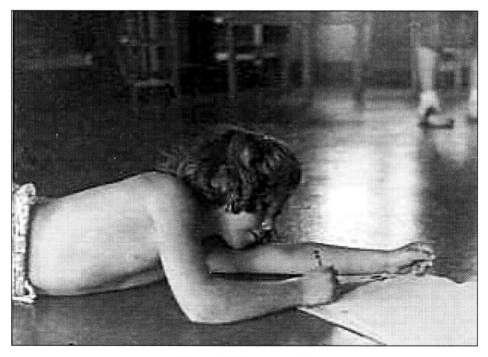

Harriet Wadeson, age 7.

My interest in psychology began when I was about 14, babysitting for my cousin. After I put her to bed, I would peruse the study bookcase of my psychiatrist uncle. I was fascinated by Freud's interpretations of dreams. But of more consequence to my ambitions, I was a typically depressed adolescent, so naturally I wanted to become a therapist. I found it difficult to get close to people, so naturally I wanted to become a therapist. I wanted to understand my own unhappiness, so naturally I wanted to become a therapist. I wanted to be important to others, so naturally. . . . I could go on and on.

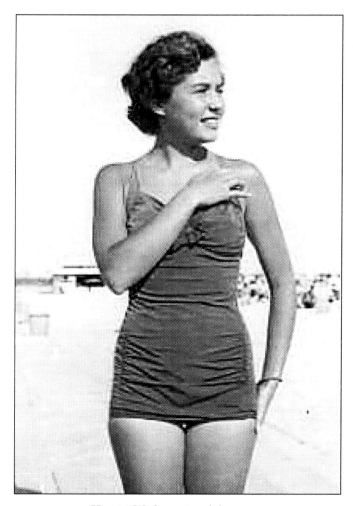

Harriet Wadeson in adolescence.

I attended Cornell University and became a psychology major, working with the famous psychologist Urie Bronfenbrenner on his research project, never dreaming that psychological research would later play such an important role in my life. When I returned to D.C. after graduation, a woodcut print I had made at Cornell won a first prize at the Smithsonian Institution. It was full of angst, and my art teacher titled it "Pieta." I didn't even know what a Pieta was.

But I have neglected to say anything about what was most important in my life in those years: BOYS! I came of age in the 1950s. I was raised to become a wife and mother. "Career women" were those who couldn't catch a man. My parents did not wish for "my daughter, the doctor." My Mother told me to make myself "worthy" to marry "my son-in-law, the doctor." My Father said, "You have a woman's greatest asset—looks." I embraced my culture and all its romantic illusions. I got married. I had children. We lived in Munich for two years while my husband was in the army, and I was thrilled to travel to many countries where I visited the art and architecture I had studied in Art History.

The only thing that was "different" about me was that I wanted something more. When we returned from Europe, I began taking courses at the Washington School of Psychiatry, American University, and Catholic University. I wanted to get a Ph.D. in psychology. There was little money for baby-sitters so I took one course at a time. It would take me 10 years at that rate. Then I met Hanna Kwiatkowska.

Wife – wanted something more

NATIONAL INSTITUTES OF HEALTH (NIH)

A.T.

I was painting and entering art shows with my friend Adele Wynne. Her husband, Lyman, headed up a unit at the Clinical Center of NIH in the National Institute of Mental Health (NIMH). Adele invited me to attend a program there for which Hanna, the unit's art therapist, had brought in a speaker on art of the insane. Afterwards we went to her office and I asked her about art therapy. It sounded like the marriage of my two major interests. "How can I become an art therapist?" I asked Hanna. "I'll train you," she said. And thus began my 13-year career at NIH. That was in 1961 and there were no art therapy masters degree programs then. Because my children were young, I worked half-time.

NIH was eye-opening. It was exhilarating. I felt perched on the leading edge of psychiatric research. Each week I attended a research conference in which luminaries from all over the world presented their research followed by a lively discussion. The eager young residents were often the first to comment, and usually at the end, Lyman Wynne reflected on the discussion with cogent remarks. I never said a word. One night I had a dream that I looked into the closet in my childhood room where there were only green clothes. A voice proclaimed, "Don't dress up for the jealousy conference." And so it was, each young resident trying to outdo the next.

Competition

Harriet Wadeson, traditional bride.

At first I worked with Hanna on an adolescent unit. We ran two art therapy groups together. They had only just begun when she was called away suddenly for several months to Brazil, where her mother had become ill. So without any training, I ran the groups myself. I wasn't much older than some of the patients, who were in their teens and twenties, but exciting things happened. I was overjoyed. NIH was a publish-or-perish institution. That's what everyone there did. So I wrote a paper about the groups, which was published by Elinor Ulman in the second issue of her new *Bulletin of Art Therapy*.

Group

Hanna's office was small, and initially we had to share it. Sometimes I literally sat at her feet on the stool beside her chair as we discussed the patients. In time, she arranged for me to move into an unused hydrotherapy room across the hall. It was small and windowless with built-in cabinets, a sink, and a large hydrotherapy tub that took up most of the floor space. Hanna had a Formica top made for it so I could use it as a table. It was a weird room, but it was mine and I loved it. When the American Art Therapy Association conference was in Washington, D.C., in 2002, I visited NIH for the first time in over 25 years. Nothing was the same—it looked like a Holiday Inn with all the brown and dull green tile replaced by carpeting and painted walls. When I walked down the transformed corridor of 3 West, I spied a door labeled Utility Room. It was my old hydrotherapy room, exactly the same except that the tub had been removed. There was the ugly tile, the old built-ins. I was so happy to see it.

After I had worked with Hanna on the adolescent unit for a couple years, William ("Biff") Bunney, who headed an affective disorders project, was interested in having an art therapist, so I moved to 3 East and a real office with windows. Space was a status thing there. My office was larger and nicer than the cubicles given to the psychiatric residents. I was moving up in the NIH world. Also, I was no longer under the supervision of Hanna. I read. I took courses. I was becoming a confident clinician. I was working with people who were manic, psychotically depressed, and suicidal. I was first author on a paper with Biff on a 24-hour cycling manic depressed patient that was published in 1970 in *The Journal of Nervous and Mental Disease*, one of the most prestigious journals in psychiatry. I also produced an exhibit, "Portraits of Suicide," that won the Benjamin Rush Award for Scientific Exhibits at the American Psychiatric Association conference and was part of the National Institutes of Health 25th Anniversary celebration.

Nevertheless, I was the only female and only non-MD member of the research team. I often felt inaudible. I used to think that if I only said it right, I would be heard. This was before the Women's Movement. I can't describe the relief I felt when a social worker whom I respected highly told me that she experienced the same thing.

After I had worked in mania and depression for eight years and published many papers on the subject (mostly in *The Journal of Nervous and Mental Disease*), Will Carpenter set up a schizophrenia unit at NIMH and invited me to join it. I was delighted. Several months later, Will told me that Hanna had wanted the position, but he thought I "would be more fun to work with." I

was devastated. Had I known Hanna wanted it, I never would have accepted the position. She was my senior. She was my mentor. But Will was my
age. We were young. I could see the dismissal of those who are older. I did
not want this opportunity at Hanna's expense. But I knew I could never discuss it with her because it would embarrass her, and I worried that she
resented me. It all seemed so horribly Oedipal!

stole positio from mentor

Harriet Wadeson with her Portraits of Suicide exhibit.

What can I say about Hanna, art therapy pioneer, originator of family art
therapy, beloved by many students and colleagues? I was her first student,
but I think not quite the compliant daughter she longed for. Nevertheless, she
was very generous towards me, sharing with me all she had learned about art
therapy. After we had been working together for many years, I was the mod-
erator of an opening plenary panel at an American Art Therapy Association
(AATA) conference. I invited Hanna to present on the panel and introduced
her as "my Art Therapy Mother, whom it gives me great pleasure to thank
publicly for the gift of this marvelous profession." When Hanna got up to
speak, she tried to refer to me, but could not remember my name! We were
both terribly embarrassed.

AATA

couldn't remember Harriet's name

Despite my concerns about Hanna, I came to love my work in schizophrenia. The patients were nonmedicated, providing a rare research oppor-

tunity, and opened whole new worlds to me in their drawings of their hallucinations and delusions. Weekly staff meetings were structured around presenting a newly-admitted patient with the first half-hour devoted to a presentation from the psychiatrist, the social worker, a member of the nursing staff, the occupational therapist, and last of all, me. I was given five minutes. I would show the art from an initial evaluation session. I talked fast. The next hour was to be devoted to treatment planning, but the pictures were often so evocative that my five minutes extended over the next hour as the staff wanted to hear more and more about the art therapy.

As my professional confidence continued to grow, I took my first steps onto the international circuit, presenting at a conference on Social Psychiatry in Yugoslavia and an American Psychiatric Association conference in Honolulu. At this time also (the early 1970s) the Human Potential Movement was growing. I brought to our unit such luminaries as Carl Whitaker. I worked with him and Lyman and we all presented together at a Psychiatric Association meeting.

In the mid 1970s, however, NIMH went biochemical and psychodynamic research was ended. All my colleagues left. Will and I stayed on an extra year to finish papers we were writing. In that one year alone, I completed 14 papers and left NIH having published 29, mostly in psychiatric journals.

NIH was a formidable and formative experience for me. Some nights I still have dreams of being there. Although I was later to complete two masters' degrees and a Ph.D., it was at NIH that I gained my major learning. For 13 years I lived in a rarefied atmosphere with the crème de la crème in psychiatric research, abundant funding, and opportunities to initiate my own research. I learned research methodology from leaders in psychiatric research. I was encouraged to publish and did so. Although my highest degree was a BA, I was publishing in journals whose articles were all by MDs, with an occasional Ph.D. I think that the patient art was a strong selling point. I learned clinical practice mostly on my own and from my patients, as I constantly questioned their treatment. One of the residents labeled me "the gadfly for patient rights."

The heady NIH atmosphere had its downside too. Once when I had a dinner party for some of the residents, they spoke of never having been able to talk so freely, as they complained about researchers stealing each others' data and the ruthless competition for research recognition. I experienced some of that myself. One of the MDs who headed up a project wrote a paper on my work without including me as an author or even citing me. After the unit was shut down, the director was interviewed by *Psychiatric News.* The entire article was about my work, but my name was never mentioned. All in all though, I feel extremely fortunate to have had the experience I gained at NIH. I doubt that an untrained individual would be able to get the advantages there today that I had then.

FAMILY

During the 13 years I spent at NIH, my family life underwent more flux than in any period of my life before or since. Shortly after I started work there, I became pregnant for the third time. My child was born two months premature, and I had to deliver him myself (in an ambulance) because my doctor did not believe I was in labor. I was told he was brain damaged and blind and that he would never reach beyond an eight-year-old level. He also had a facial deformity. My husband wanted to institutionalize him. I knew that if this child were to have a life, I would have to give it to him–again. My two other children were bright and beautiful. I thought we were abundantly blessed and could afford to give to this child who came into the world less endowed than the rest of us. But my husband could not tolerate the narcissistic injury of this less than perfect child. He rejected him. I got a divorce. He never forgave me and continued to make life difficult for all of us.

I was 30 years old when my third child was born. With his birth, it was clear to me that my youth had ended. I also felt I had no future. I couldn't imagine what my life would be like when he started to crawl. How would I protect a blind baby from bumping into everything? I thought I would have to watch him constantly, and that would be my life. His development was very slow. It seemed that everyone I knew had a baby at that time. When I was with my friends and their babies, I came away depressed. I had been heartened by the slow steps of my son's development until I saw how far he lagged behind the children of my friends.

Nevertheless, his growth was full of surprises. They began one day when I was feeding him in his highchair. As I brought the spoon to his face, he opened his mouth, and I realized that he could see it. Another surprise was his artistic ability. At a young age he drew in great detail and had an amazing sense of spatial relationships. When he was four he made a choo-choo train that ran around all the walls of his room. The kids were given plenty of paper and told not to draw on the walls, but I did not wash off his train because I found it so delightful.

Although he could see, he remained visually impaired and was diagnosed legally blind. He didn't really fit into the many special schools he attended. When he was 10 I sent him away to camp with his older brother. Since the schedule there was of the kids' own choosing, I figured he would enjoy swimming and crafts even if he couldn't participate in such sports as baseball. So what did he do each day? He came home with a packet of perforated paper targets. His favorite activity was riflery!

Nowhere have I seen the drive for mastery in such raw intensity as in this child. Today the baby who was not supposed to reach beyond an eight-year-old level and who is still legally blind has graduated from college, is happily married, and works as a photographer. Go figure. . . .

Shortly after my divorce, I remarried, this time to a psychoanalyst. It was great to be able to discuss my work with him. But there were many strains--his kids, my kids. And I think we both had unrealistic expectations. He had just suffered a bout with cancer and was unhappy in his previous marriage. I had just given birth to a damaged child. My in-laws blamed me. I think we each hoped that our marriage would rescue us from our unhappiness. Maybe we each married our creation of the other. That was certainly true for me. The mirror of reality was not the pretty picture I had painted. One day I came home from a conference to find a note telling me how to contact his attorney. I was devastated. I had three children, one of whom had special needs, a half-time government job, and no money.

SINGLE MOM

I upped my NIH hours, though I was still employed as a part-time "temporary" (for 13 years) employee without benefits. I found private practice work, at first leading groups with a psychiatrist who split the fees with me and made me vice-president when he incorporated. My next opportunity was not so generous. A psychologist saw groups with a social worker in her home and hired me to replace her. She paid me $40/hour, which was more than I was making at NIH. The social worker got only $10/hour. But the groups brought in $250/hour. Something was wrong with that picture! Ever since, I have been angered to see professionals who can command high fees pay art therapists just a small percentage of what they bring in. The psychologist had agreed to allow me to screen any new client she wanted to admit to a group. I was away for a week and returned to find a new member who was manic and totally unfit for group work. The psychologist insisted that the client stay, so I resigned. A couple weeks later, the social worker told me that the client had driven her car through the large bay window of the psychologist's home. At that point, she was dismissed from the group. Oh sweet "I told you so." I increased my private practice on my own and started doing some art therapy teaching.

I was forty and beginning the single life again. It was hard on my kids. I was dating more than my teen-age daughter (not good), and my older son felt in competition with the men in my life. To my surprise he resented one who came over to rake the leaves. He claimed that was his job. I thought he would be happy to be relieved of it. But my younger, handicapped son enjoyed the attention of the various men who were a part of my life during his growing up. All were better fathers to him than his own father.

[handwritten margin notes: "unfair pay for art therapist", "mischievous attitude! ☺", "older son resented male friend younger son liked attention from them"]

GRADUATE SCHOOL

As my NIH position was ending, I realized I would need more than a BA degree to do what I had already been doing—clinical work and writing for professional publication. So in addition to working 35 hours/week at NIH, bringing up three kids, and working several hours of private practice, I got an MA in psychology and art therapy from Goddard College and then enrolled in a full-time Masters of Social Work program at Catholic University. I persuaded the department chair to allow me to graduate in one year instead of the usual two by plunking down on his desk all the papers I had published, which were more than any of his faculty had written. After leaving NIH, I expanded my private practice and enrolled in a Ph.D. program at Union Institute. For my dissertation, I wrote the book that was often requested of me. During the 1970s there were few books on art therapy available, and those in print were mostly about work with children. *Art Psychotherapy* described my work at NIH with patients diagnosed with affective disorders and schizophrenia as well as group and family art therapy in my private practice.

I had been teaching a course in art therapy at Montgomery Community College and began to teach at NIH's Foundation for Advanced Education in the Sciences. Working with highly motivated students was a pleasant change from working with schizophrenic patients. I set my sights on a career in university teaching. An opportunity was presented to me when I met the director of a new art therapy training program at the University of Houston. She was looking for a replacement while she took a year's leave.

HOUSTON

To move or not to move to Houston? My kids were in college, law school, and one was about to graduate from high school. But I was concerned about leaving my aging parents. When I told them of the Houston offer and my concern about leaving them, my Father said, "Everyone has to grow up and leave home sometime." I was 47!

I drew a picture to help me decide. The left side in cool greens represented the comforts of staying in Washington. A red diagonal jagged lightening-like slash separated the Houston side colored in hot yellows and oranges. A giant me stood on top of a stack of books surrounded by a group of smaller students. My career would take off. I moved.

I found that I loved full-time teaching and the relationships with students. But Houston itself was culture shock. After a year, I was recruited by the

University of Illinois at Chicago (UIC) to start up a new art therapy Masters Degree program. When I met with the Dean in Chicago, he asked what salary I would want. I stated a figure that was much more than I was earning in Houston. He said, "Oh, I think we can do better than that." I asked about tenure, hoping I would be given credit for my time at the University of Houston. He said, "You will come in with tenure." Then I asked about moving expenses, and he granted a very generous amount. It was an offer I could hardly refuse. But I did, because it came late in the spring and I had made commitments for the summer, and there would be no time to move and be ready to teach in the fall. Nevertheless, I allowed that I might be interested the following year.

In the meantime, the University of Houston rescued Judy Chicago's "Dinner Party" art installation, which she was threatening to destroy because she couldn't afford storage space and museums had cancelled exhibits due to its controversial nature. I was eager to teach a "Feminism in the Arts" course that I had developed in conjunction with the exhibit. It turned out to be a wonderful course in which the students, including one man, made a feminist statement in the art form of their choice, and we created our own personal dinner party place settings, wrote a group poem, painted a group mural, ate food at our dinner party, and dressed up for the occasion.

As an academic however, I was naïve. I spoke my mind, and as a result I was eventually done in by university politics at Houston. They became ugly and the University of Illinois at Chicago (UIC) upped their offer, so I moved again. Just prior to leaving Houston, I developed severe disk trouble and was crippled for four months, thus delaying my arrival in Chicago. I was 49 and hadn't expected this sort of debilitation until later in life (such as my more advanced age now with its attendant physical challenges–but I am getting ahead of myself).

CHICAGO

Thus began my 23-year tenure at UIC. When I arrived, the Dean who hired me had already left. He had been a highly successful business man who couldn't stand the sludgy pace of academia. My immediate boss was the Director of the School of Art & Design (A & D). In one of our early meetings he said, "Harriet, after you have been here five years . . ." I thought, "Fat chance, Buddy, no way will I stay in the North Pole." But I didn't say a thing. He remained very supportive of me and art therapy. Unfortunately, he stepped down as Director after two years because he couldn't stand the pressures from the faculty. Successive directors of the School were less supportive of art therapy, and when budget crunches came, art therapy was the first to suffer. Initially, I was allowed to hire an additional full-time faculty member. Six years later when she left after not receiving tenure, her line was removed from art therapy, so for most of the life of the program, I had to run it alone. Fortunately, for the last ten years I had very loyal adjunct faculty who contributed far more than the courses they were paid to teach: Deb Paskind, Deb Behnke, Anne Canright, Gail Roy, and Gail Wirtz.

At the University of Houston, the Behavioral Science faculty was very enmeshed, with two faculty meetings weekly. At UIC, I experienced just the opposite. Art therapy was physically isolated from the rest of Art & Design. At first, I welcomed the change and the autonomy. (At the U of H, it seemed I had to get permission from all the faculty if I needed to burp!) At UIC, despite the strong support and involvement of our own faculty/student art therapy community, the separation from other A & D faculty and students led to alienation and little support. The Director of the School changed many times, and despite my attempts to interest each new Director in our program, it became clear that art therapy was not the jewel in the crown of the University of Illinois at Chicago. Feeling overworked and underpaid, in the mid 1990s I conducted a survey of art therapy educators to investigate the support given to other AATA approved MA programs. I was surprised to discover that I was better off than almost all in salary, tenure, rank, and course load, which is a sad commentary on the place of art therapy in higher education.

Nevertheless, despite the continuous struggle for financial support, our program was highly successful. Each year we had more than twice the number of applicants than we could admit. We were able to select outstanding students and as a faculty group develop an excellent art therapy training program.

When I began teaching in Chicago in 1981, there were very few art therapists in the area. I visited many facilities to tell them about the profession and our program in order to set up internships. Before long, this was no longer necessary, as word had spread about art therapy and the quality of our students, their training, and their contribution to treatment services. Soon facilities were calling us requesting interns and expressing dismay when we did not have a student for them.

I have always felt that the proof of the art therapy training pudding was in the internship eating, so students spent 24 hours/week for three semesters at their internship sites and had a three-hour supervision seminar at the university, many more hours than required by AATA for program approval at that time. Before selecting sites, students had to visit at least six and write a detailed report on each. (One ambitious student visited 21!) We developed many kinds of internship opportunities with various populations in different kinds of settings. My intention was in this way to expand the profession by increasing the variety of venues that would hire art therapists.

Teaching was a fascinating challenge. I loved the creativity in program development, which was ongoing as I continually made changes to improve the quality of our students' education. I loved the interaction with students as well. I selected the experiential courses to teach because I knew I would soon tire of hearing myself speak. Each class, each student, brought a new set of experiences to our work together. At first I was a little fearful of conducting supervision, but I found that I loved the way that the material that needed to be covered arose organically from the issues that students faced in their work with clients.

Just as in my practice of conducting therapy I like using art, I found that the same was true in teaching. So I developed many ways to incorporate art making in learning. Students expressed concepts, processed work with clients, reflected on readings and their experience in art projects. They also role-played different psychiatric and sociological conditions by making art as clients with various diagnoses and practiced being art therapists for them. They terminated from the program with an art piece. We graduated 240 students, of whom I am extremely proud. Many have become art therapy educators themselves. Others have developed ongoing treatment services in the Chicago area, elsewhere in the United States, and in other countries as well.

One of the program's most creative enterprises was our Annual Summer Institute, which ran for 20 years. Held on the wooded shores of Lake Geneva, Wisconsin, 90 minutes from Chicago, the Summer Institute brought in guest faculty from other areas–Bob Ault, Judy Rubin, Sandra Graves, Nancy Knapp, Maxine Junge, Shirley Riley, Doris Arrington, Cathy Malchiodi, Leigh Files, Suzanne Lovell, Jillian Froebe, Jerry Fryrear, Irene Corbit, and others. Students came from all over the United States and from other countries as well. For a number of years, Clay Bodine taught a joyful course in "Creating Rituals," in which we had torch-lit, costumed, drum-beating processions throughout the campus. Teaching there expanded way beyond the classroom to a wonderful freedom of expression. In a beautiful natural setting, our summer art therapy community bonded in the time and space to explore ourselves through our art without the distractions of home, family, and work. Some students said that the Summer Institute changed their lives. It was as close as I have come to my ideal of what education should be.

My life in Chicago encompassed some other colorful activities in addition to my teaching. One of them was street theatre in Clay Bodine's Big Fish Theatre group. I was on his advisory board, and we had great fun performing outlandish seasonal presentations on the streets, in the parks, and even in a restaurant. One time a "Hero's Quest" in Montrose Park caught the attention of a roving Chicago Tribune photographer, and we made the front page of the Sunday Metro section. Another avocation was karate, in which I trained from ages 56 to 65. I was the oldest member of my dojo. It was a strengthening and humbling experience.

Harriet Wadeson at the Art Therapy Summer Institute she directed for 20 years.

AMERICAN ART THERAPY ASSOCIATION (AATA)

When AATA was in its infancy in 1970, Hanna was part of a planning committee to select officers. She called me from their meeting in Louisville to ask me to be Financial Chair. I told her I couldn't even balance my checkbook. She insisted. At the moment of her call, I was embroiled in a tearful break-up with a boyfriend. I told her I couldn't possibly agree then, that I would have to think about it. She insisted on an answer then, so I told her no. It was not easy to say no to Hanna. Some years later, Bob Ault, who was Chair of the Nominating Committee, asked if I would run for President (there was not a competitive nominee in those days). I told him that I might be masochistic, but I wasn't totally crazy, so the answer was no. After I got settled in Chicago, however, I felt that my life had finally become sufficiently stable for me to run for AATA office. At that time, Committee Chairs were members of the Executive Board. The only position that interested me was Publications Chair. I was pleased to win the election and held that position for two terms, six years. In that capacity, I was Newsletter Editor also, which I felt was a very significant position, kind of like the conductor of AATA's communication train. Then I became Research Chair and mainly gave out research awards. I have chaired many other committees in AATA as well, including: the Funding Committee, the Status of Women Committee, the Ethics and Professional Practice Committee, and the Honors Committee. I was a member of the original Research Committee and of the first Journal Editor Search Committee. Currently I am Associate Editor of *Art Therapy, Journal of the American Art Therapy Association.*

In addition to official duties, I had many light-hearted moments in AATA too. One was at the second Art Therapy Educators' Convocation that I hosted in Houston, when I pushed a fully-clothed Shaun McNiff into the swimming pool of my condo. Shaun and I had some other hilarious moments too, such as changing clothes for the Baltimore AATA conference costume dance. He looked far more beautiful in my purple chiffon balloon sleeve blouse and floppy hat than I did. When the conference was at Grossingers in New York, Helen Landgarten decided to become Shaun and put on his clothes that I had been wearing, so I raided Helen's room for some clothes of hers and came away with a white fur wrap. Helen outdid me by far, however, when she squirted her face with Redi-Whip for a beard.

Certainly, one of the highlights of AATA conferences for me was the 25th anniversary celebration in Chicago, for which Sandra Graves (now Alcorn) and I put together a multi-media opening called "The Phantoms of the AATA." We showed historic old slides taken by Aina Nucho, and I rewrote the lyrics from "The Phantom of the Opera," which my students sang and played on the piano and violin. We had a hilarious art therapy fashion show put together by Randy Vick and Deb Behnke and modeled by our students, and we also gave tribute to our pioneers.

But perhaps the highest light in AATA for me was being awarded Honorary Life Membership in 1992. In my acceptance speech, I said that art therapy was my professional home and that AATA was my professional family.

CAREER TRAJECTORY

During my years in Chicago, the prophesy of my decision drawing about moving from Washington materialized. My career did take off. In addition to developing and directing a prominent training program, I was launched on the international circuit. I moved to Chicago shortly after the publication of my first book, *Art Psychotherapy*. I had already published many papers on my NIH work and presented some of it nationally. I often encouraged my students to write, telling them of the unexpected rewards that could come their way as a result. Certainly, that was the case for me in 1981 when I was invited to give a keynote speech at an arts therapy conference in Sydney, Australia. I fell in love with that country, made some wonderful friends there, and stayed for three months, traveling to its hinterlands. I have visited three more times since, teaching and giving workshops in Sydney, Melbourne, Perth, Brisbane, and New Castle. Each time, I have stayed several months and traveled extensively. If I did not have so many ties in the United States, I would move there.

During the last two decades, invitations to many more countries followed. Because art therapy is so much more developed in the United States, there is much interest abroad in learning from us. In addition to presenting to many training programs and local art therapy associations throughout the United States, I have taught and/or presented in Mexico, Canada, the UK, Germany, Italy, Yugoslavia, Denmark, Greece, Korea, and Japan. For the past 10 years, I have taught annually in Sweden and frequently in Finland, where I was made an honorary member of their art therapy association.

In 1995, I led a delegation of 80 for a professional exchange in China under the auspices of People to People International. That was followed by delegations to Indonesia and several to Bali to study arts and healing. In 2003, I took a group of art therapists to Sweden to celebrate the Summer Solstice and to make art there. These travels have added brilliance to the colors of my life, and I have made some wonderful friends throughout the world.

Writing has also been a very important part of my career. Many of my students have hated to write, but I love it. Writing helps me to think, to put my thoughts together, to formulate my beliefs, and to send them out into the world. Many times I have been thrilled and immensely gratified when strangers have approached me at AATA conferences to tell me that they entered art therapy as a result of reading one of my books.

I began writing at NIH because that is what everyone did there. And I have continued to publish papers, though they have moved from descriptions of my work in the beginning to the formulation of my ideas since becoming immersed in teaching. To date, I have published 68 papers, initially in psychiatric journals, and more recently in art therapy journals. I've also authored nine chapters in psychology and art therapy texts. After *Art Psychotherapy*, which is mostly descriptive, was published in 1980, I wanted to write a book about why we do what we do. Through teaching, I found myself wanting to explore these issues and discuss them with students. That book,

The Dynamics of Art Psychotherapy, was published in 1987. Next came an edited book, *Advances in Art Therapy*, in 1990 with co-editors Jean Durkin and Dorine Perach. On the occasion of its publication, I was awarded a Resolution of Commendation from the State of Illinois Legislature for training people to help the needy citizens of the state. Nevertheless, I vowed never to do another edited book–it was far more work than writing it all myself. But I didn't listen to myself. I was Research Chair of the American Art Therapy Association and felt guilty for not doing enough work in that position, so I acted on Judy Rubin's suggestion to put together a research manual. I also felt that since I had derived much from AATA, I wanted to give something back. What developed was *A Guide to Conducting Art Therapy Research*, which was the first book published by AATA, coming out in 1992 with all the proceeds going to the association. Nancy Knapp, the next Research Chair and a much better diplomat than I, helped to navigate it through the sometimes treacherous shoals of AATA Board approval.

I waited a long time before attempting another book. I had repeatedly encouraged my students to publish their thesis work. Some did, but most were eager to move on to greener pastures once they graduated. Several years ago I looked over the thesis work of the past decade and was struck by its variety and meatiness. I decided to put some of it together to cover the impressive spectrum of the diversity and creativity in art therapy, *Art Therapy Practice: Innovative Approaches with Diverse Populations*, published in 2000. I was pleased with most of the content and proud of my students.

And guess what? Despite difficulties with previous editing, when Maxine Junge suggested that the two of us edit a book of memoirs by prominent art therapists, I didn't hesitate at all. We decided to invite all Honorary Life Members to contribute a chapter, so here I am!

ART

Art has threaded its way through the fabric of my life in many textures and gradients. I made art constantly as a child and adolescent. When I was married and had children, I entered art shows spurred on by my painting partner, Adele Wynne. I won some prizes. The most significant was a first prize from the Smithsonian Institution in Washington. Once I started work as an art therapist, my artwork dwindled. With young children as well, there was little time. But there were fits and starts–periods of collage, light boxes, clay. More recently, I've made lots of masks, and in the last few years, I've fallen in love with watercolors–their fluidity, transparency, and clarity. I've started work in glass for some of the same sort of beauty and hope to develop it further. In my teaching, I have enjoyed making art in the company of my students. There is a kind of mutual stimulation and sharing that builds community among us. But my attitude toward my art has remained essentially the same. For me it is a misnomer to call it "artwork." It is play. I do it for enjoyment, release, expression, beauty. Creativity can be encompassing for me and challenging, but never drudgery.

APPROACH TO ART THERAPY

My life has been of a piece. It has not been compartmentalized. I have seen this in–of all things–my clothes. I have not worn one outfit to the office and changed when I got home. I wear comfortable clothes all the time. The values I hold in art therapy are the values I hold in my life.

I want to sum up my own principles of art therapy, but it is difficult, even though I have taught them for 35 years. So often in teaching they arise organically, and there is no necessity for a prepared lecture. But I will try to capture a few.

Children draw and paint naturally. When they are young they are not judgmental; as they grow older they learn to judge and may find their art inadequate. If we leave them alone, they will continue to draw. But we don't. In art therapy, we can help people to find that nonjudgmental place and simply enjoy their own self-expression. We can help them to become curious about their expressions, especially in noticing patterns that may lead to new insights. Of course, this is possible only if we are nonjudgmental about them and their art and if we are curious about their expressions. The client must lead the way in determining what is important, what gets expressed, and how it gets expressed. So what is important is one's own experience of the art, not what it means to the art therapist.

Students can learn how to encourage art expression and the curiosity about it. Although I refrain from interpreting the art and try to encourage my clients to explore it without interference of my reactions, I tell my students to "listen to the music, not just the words." These are the subtle perceptions that are hard to define, the empathy that helps to connect. In group work I try to foster the connections that can be seen in the images as each member speaks to the others through the art.

I believe that most emotional problems are rooted in low self-esteem. The therapeutic relationship itself is often the healing balm that helps people to feel accepted, understood, and valued. For many, this is a unique condition, not previously experienced. It is important to establish support and build trust, and sharing images offers a unique opportunity to build a trusting relationship. These are simple guidelines, and yet it is amazing to me how many reports I have heard from clients or seen in action myself of therapists (usually not art therapists) who are harsh, remote, and overly interpretive. I have seen some with prestigious training belittle patients. I have seen some set up power plays.

Recently an adolescent client asked me if it was "weird" hearing all about so many people. I told her that this work enables me to enter many "worlds" I would not otherwise see as I come to learn of lives of people from backgrounds very different from my own. The work expands me. I am licensed to practice what I call "plain therapy" (not art), but I prefer to use art if the client is willing. More happens. More gets shown and said. But people must work at their own pace. I sometimes acknowledge to them that it took them many years to become who they are, so they cannot change overnight.

When I was a child, I liked to hear stories and look at pictures. As an adult, I have gotten people to pay me to hear their stories and look at their pictures. I feel fortunate to have found work I love and to have had the opportunity to teach it to others. The work of art therapy is a creative endeavor that fosters the creativity of others. The work itself can be wonderful, but the institutions that support it are sometimes less than wonderful.

RETIREMENT

In 2003 I retired from University of Illinois at Chicago after 23 years, and 2004 was the last year of the Summer Institute at Lake Geneva, Wisconsin, that I had run for 20 years. But I missed working with students, so I started up a post-graduate art therapy program at Northwestern University. It is directed toward those who want to add art therapy to their practices, such as social workers, counselors, and teachers. Many such professionals had attended the UIC Summer Institute, so it seemed to me that there was a need for such training. As I write this, the program is one year old and has been well received.

Sometimes people question whether I am really retired, but I think retirement is a state of mind. It is no coincidence that Northwestern is only five minutes from my home, whereas UIC is an hour away. Retirement is doing what I want, when I want. If Northwestern becomes a hassle (as universities can), I'll turn the program over to someone else. I'm glad I have traveled a lot, because my hope to travel more in retirement has been restricted by my recurring back problem, this time in the form of spinal stenosis. Writing and making art are at the top of my wish list. I am deeply immersed in writing a novel about the relationship between two artists, one a student and the other

writing and making art

a teacher. I find that I love writing about making art. The text is very visual, painterly even. And I am painting more.

ART THERAPY IN THE FUTURE

Art therapy's future will surely be calibrated to the future of our society, and I have no predictions for that. (Thirty years ago, I never would have predicted that our lives would be run by computers.) My hope is for change in our values, away from greed, acquisition, and power, towards a world that recognizes the beauty around us and the possibilities for each individual's self expression. In such a world the arts would become a major mode of expression, not just a modality for artists, but for everyone. Art therapists would become primary facilitators for reflection, expression, and action in ways we have not yet imagined.

CONCLUSION

Being a part of an emerging profession, growing up with it, co-mingling with the creative colleagues and students it attracts, feeling like one of its "architects," though at times a difficult path, always made my work an exciting adventure. This profound new territory we explore together has offered many creative opportunities that would not have been available to me on a more traditional professional path. I am grateful for every minute of it.

In Houston I had a student who was a professional astrologer. She begged me to tell her my birthday so she could plot my horoscope. Then she was reluctant to show it to me, because she was afraid for me to see all the fire and conflict it contained. She could read 200 horoscopes, she said, without ever seeing one like this. When she told me she believed that in the karmic cycle people choose the lives they need, I asked her why anyone would choose a life like this. She replied, "Harriet, when you came into this life, you said, 'Give it all to me in this lifetime.'"

When my Mother used to say, "In my day. . . . ," I guess she was referring to her youth or a time when she thought she had some influence. I am still living "My Day." It has been a long day with much sunshine, rain, and storms. There have been moments when I have wished for a more peaceful life. It has been unpredictable. I never expected the rich opportunities I have been afforded, nor did I anticipate some of the painful difficulties. I expect that in another 15 or 20 years I'll be ready to write a new memoir. But today is My Day.

[handwritten margin notes: Student. Professional astrologer. Saw lots of fire & conflict in her horoscope.]

[handwritten margin notes: In reference to her mother saying "In my day..."]

Judith A. Rubin

Chapter 9

JUDITH A. RUBIN

AN UGLY DUCKLING FINDS THE SWANS OR HOW I FELL IN LOVE WITH ART THERAPY

PREHISTORY

The roots of my interest in art are deep and old and personal. And even after years of therapy and analysis, I am still not sure of all of the meanings for me of facilitating, making, and viewing art. Just as my sometimes insatiable hunger felt appeased when receiving brand-new art supplies, so viewing art had a nourishing quality as well. It was a taking-in, a drinking-in with the eyes of a delicious visual dish. To see an exhibit of work I liked was at least as fulfilling as to eat an excellent meal. (It still is.)

If looking at art was validated voyeurism, the making of products was acceptable exhibitionism. So, too, the forbidden touching, the delight in sensory pleasures of body and earth, put aside as part of the price and privilege of growing up; these were preserved through art, in the joy of kneading clay or smearing pastel.

Not only was art a path to permissible regression, it was a way to acceptable aggression as well. The cutting up of paper, the carving of wood, the representation of hostile wishes; these were available to me as to others in the many symbolic meanings inherent in the creative process.

Many years ago, I found a drawing made when I was five. It was developmentally appropriate, allowing me to articulate what I knew about the human body and to practice my decorative skills. Perhaps more important, it represented the fantasized fulfillment of two impossible wishes: to be my king-father's companion as princess-daughter (or even queen), and to be *like*

Note: You may recognize some of the writing in this chapter, as part of it is from previous publications. However, the recycled portions have been modified and amplified with new material. I hope I will be forgiven for not writing the whole thing from scratch, but it seemed foolish not to use excerpts when they could tell the story just as well.

him, to have what he had (the phallic cigarette) that I lacked (note the missing legs on the girl). The drawing was also done *for* him, a gift that was probably praised for its very making and giving.

Judith A. Rubin drawing with Daddy watching.

Sometimes art became for me, as for others, a way of coping with trauma too hard to assimilate. When I was seventeen, my friend Peter suddenly died. Numbly, I went home to the funeral from the camp where I was an arts and crafts counselor. Numbly, I returned, then succumbed to a high fever. When I awoke, I felt a strong need to go to the woods and paint. The painting was not of Peter, but of a person playing the piano, making music in dark reds, purples, and blacks. It was a cry, a scream caught and tamed. It was a new object in the world, a symbolic replacement for my friend who was lost, a mute, tangible testament. Doing it afforded me tremendous relief. It did not take away the hurt and the ache, but it did help in releasing some of the anguished tangle of feelings that held me in their grip.

Judith A. Rubin's father-king & daughter, age 5.

Not only the making, but also the perceiving of art was vital when I was growing up. As a young child I stared at a Van Gogh reproduction in our living room. The "Sunflowers" were so big and alive, so vivid and powerful, that even in a print they seemed to leap forth from the canvas. As a teenager, I recall the drunken orgy of a whole exhibit, room after room of original Van Goghs. Each picture was more exciting than the last–the intensity and beauty of the images, the luscious texture of the paint–like the "barbaric yawp" of Walt Whitman, another of my adolescent passions. Surely much in art feels "therapeutic" to the viewer, as well as to the artist.

So the roots of my interest in art lay deep in the soil of my childhood before flowering in a variety of roles–provider of art to neighborhood children, arts and crafts counselor at summer camps, art major in college, art educator (of children, then teachers), art researcher, "art lady" (on TV), and–eventually–art therapist.

Judith A. Rubin's self-portrait, age 14.

When I first discovered art therapy, I felt like the ugly duckling who found the swans and no longer felt like a misfit. As an artist, I had enjoyed being the art editor of the yearbook and the advertising editor of the high school newspaper as well as making the drawings and paintings hanging on my relatives' walls. I especially liked doing portraits, some of which reflected my adolescent self-preoccupation.

But even though I had always thought I would be an artist, by the time I graduated, I realized that I wasn't talented enough to make a career of painting and that the commercial art path followed by my cousins didn't appeal to me. So I decided to get a degree in education, because I loved children and expected to love teaching art.

As a teacher, although I did enjoy working with the children, I never fit in with my colleagues. When I declined to accept the stencils offered to me by the teacher next door, she was hurt. When I reorganized the furniture in the classroom, my supervisor was upset. In fact, I was told that I would have been fired from the Cambridge Public Schools in 1958, had we not been moving to Pittsburgh. My "crime" was that I had naively brought a "dirty book" of photographs into the classroom—*The Family of Man.*

As an art teacher in Pittsburgh I still got in trouble for unacceptable acts, such as wearing flat shoes (heels were as essential as skirts in those days); or not eating lunch with the other teachers, who were so critical of the children and their families that I preferred to eat in the park. My supervisor chastised me for not writing detailed lesson plans, and for showing slides of artwork—which was not in the curriculum.

At a different school the following year, I disturbed neighboring classrooms with too much singing. I was also called into the principal's office to be criticized for not using the paddle, and thereby undermining other teachers' discipline. No wonder I decided that the time was ripe to get pregnant and didn't mind leaving the classroom.

But one day in 1962, visiting with a friend while our little girls played together, I admired the paintings in her kitchen. When I asked where they had been done, she told me about this great preschool her youngsters attended, where they were collecting and studying the children's art. I was excited to hear of such an interest, as it was one that had been stimulated in me during both college and graduate school.

PRIOR GLIMPSES OF ART IN DIAGNOSIS AND THERAPY

In college, I had taken Child Psychology from a woman named Thelma Alper. While I was in her class, she was collecting data for a study about the effect of child-rearing practices on finger paintings by preschool children. I'll never forget her excitement, as she held up paintings that vividly showed the differences between youngsters from different socioeconomic groups. Then when I did the required observations for her course at the Wellesley Nursery School, she allowed me to focus on their behavior with art materials. I was fascinated.

In a graduate seminar on Human Development at Harvard, where we were invited to choose a topic for our presentation to the group, I read everything I could find in the library about "The Psychology of Children's Art." I discovered articles by child therapists and a few books, including a collection of Margaret Naumburg's early papers. At the time, I thought that using art in child therapy was a great idea, but I was not in any sort of clinical training and had no such plans. I did expect, like most art educators of that era, that I would be able to do many therapeutic things with art in the classroom. After all, Viktor Lowenfeld's third edition of *Creative & Mental Growth* had just come out, and there was a chapter on the "Therapeutic Aspects of Art Education" that was even longer than in the second edition. And Florence Cane's *The Artist in Each of Us* had a whole section on "The Healing Quality of Art," including a chapter on "A Modern Psychotherapy." Sadly, my teaching experiences turned out to be less satisfying than I had hoped, though I could see that many children benefited from making art.

BACK TO THE KITCHEN

So when my friend told me about the nursery school where they were studying children's art, I decided to call the Director and volunteer my services. I met with Dr. Margaret McFarland, and it was love at first sight. She not only knew Mrs. Alper and her research, but she herself had participated in a landmark study of Alschuler and Hattwick's, published in *Painting & Personality*, one of my favorite discoveries in the Harvard library. Best of all, there were funds available, and she had some appealing ideas.

The program in Child Development & Child Care at the University of Pittsburgh, which was in the Psychiatry Department, ran the Child Study Center, which was founded by Erik Erikson and Benjamin Spock. Dr. McFarland asked if I'd like to try doing "art therapy" with the schizophrenic children on an inpatient unit run by the program at Western Psychiatric Institute & Clinic (WPIC). When I said I had no clinical background, she said that she would be available for consultation.

Well, if I fell in love with Margaret McFarland, I was even more infatuated with art therapy. The children responded positively, and though I didn't know why they were improving, it was very exciting. Doing art therapy was more stimulating than any art teaching I had done, largely because it was an even greater challenge. And my work in art with the school-age children at the Child Study Center was also rewarding, since what I did was welcomed and valued for the first time since graduate school. This ugly duckling had indeed found some swans.

Doing art therapy was immensely gratifying, both emotionally and intellectually; but I needed advice about becoming a "real" art therapist. Therefore, I sought the guidance of Margaret Naumburg and Edith Kramer, whose first book had come out by then. Both gave generously of their time, meeting with me and allowing me to visit their classes when I could. Their willingness to help me is something I always think of whenever people ask me for guidance.

Indeed, their kindness lasted a long time. Both gave consultation freely when asked; and I would meet with them when I went to New York to see my parents. I will never forget visiting Margaret in her apartment, seeing artwork from her books, being told about the *Bulletin of Art Therapy*, and learning that Florence Cane was her sister. I remember some elegant cocktails, followed by dinner at a nearby restaurant.

I will never forget attending Edith's classes at the New School for Social Research, feeding her lunch in my parents' apartment across the street, and following her around the Jewish Guild for the Blind and Jacobi Hospital, where she let me observe art therapy sessions. In 1983, she helped me revise my 1978 book *Child Art Therapy*. She suggested changes on every page and spent a whole day going over them with me in her studio.

Although Margaret's and Edith's ideas about art therapy were quite different, their advice about what I should do was identical. Both suggested that I learn about myself through personal therapy and that I learn about being a therapist through supervised work under an experienced clinician. For therapy, I went for two years twice weekly to psychiatrist Naomi Ragins, who later became a beloved supervisor, teacher, colleague, and friend.

For training, despite Dr. McFarland's thoughtful consultation, I soon felt that I needed to learn more about what was happening with these children. At that point, I met Professor Erik Erikson of Harvard. My contact with him, while brief, had an impact that lasted for years. It was affirming, but also delayed my training for almost a decade.

As a consultant to the Psychiatry Department, Erikson visited annually, commenting on a child case at a Grand Rounds. In 1964, I was asked to present the artwork of "Dorothy," whose art was as articulate as she was unintelligible. The director of the unit and Dorothy's psychiatrist discussed her history, diagnosis, and treatment. I showed her artwork and described her behavior during our sessions. Professor Erikson critiqued the material and noted possible future interventions.

Afterwards, he complimented me warmly. I told him I felt I could help even more if I understood better what was going on and that I was longing for training. Much to my surprise, Erikson was adamantly opposed. He suggested that it might well ruin—or at least interfere with—something of value in the intuitive approach I was, by default, forced to follow. So I tabled my explorations of further study, at least for a time.

In 1966, Fred Rogers, whom I had met through Dr. McFarland, invited me to be on his new public television program, "Mister Rogers' Neighborhood." As the "Art Lady," I used my ad-libbed segment to communicate the therapeutic value of art to parents and children. Because of that experience with the power of the media, I developed a desire to teach about art therapy visually as well as with words, and have been making films since the early seventies. During that same year, I also began teaching courses in Art Education at a local college, including an elective on the "Therapeutic Aspects of Art Education."

In 1967, I was asked to start an art program at an institution for physically-handicapped youngsters. Shocked by how few children were seen by the professionals, I designed a rudimentary "Art Assessment," to determine who might benefit. All were found capable of making art, though many required creative adaptations.

In 1968, my therapist suggested that I meet with child psychiatrist Marvin Shapiro, who was interested in the arts in therapy. He invited me to join an Expressive Arts Study Group he had recently started at the Pittsburgh Child Guidance Center (PCGC), the outpatient clinic of Child Psychiatry. When I was offered a job on an adolescent unit at another hospital, Dr. Shapiro thought the time had come to start a program at PCGC like the one Ellie Irwin had initiated in drama therapy. Fortunately, the director of the clinic agreed to support a one-day-a-week pilot program in art therapy.

We knew we needed to prove—to those in the established disciplines of psychiatry, psychology, and social work—that art therapy could offer something unique. I was fortunate to have such an enthusiastic mentor, who was also a child analyst. Dr. Shapiro's supervision was frequent and intensive. He watched sessions through a two-way observation window; and when I went to half-time, we met for two hours a week.

ABOUT PROFESSIONAL PARENTS AND SIBLINGS

For a "Festschrift" in Margaret McFarland's honor, I wrote something about the unique quality of her consultation. I called her a "creative catalyst," a concept also applicable to a good art therapist. Some caregivers have a gift for helping others to access their creative potential. Such individuals, through their very presence and the ambience they provide, are able to create conditions in which another can grow—like rich, moist soil, in which flowers can get bigger and brighter than in a less nurturing milieu.

I have come to think of such people as creative catalysts, in whose presence the expressive potential of others is able to become manifest. Although Margaret McFarland was supportive, her effectiveness was based on much more than a belief in the other's potential. Her role was like that of a catalyst—a substance in the presence of which something new transpires.

Advice, when requested, was offered in the form of relevant associations—ideas, memories, facts—which led you along your own problem-solving way. Margaret inspired people to find themselves, but not by showing, telling, or guiding like most mentors. With a deep respect for others' uniqueness, she never sought to impose her own ideas. Not needing to compete or challenge, she was able to use her own creative thinking capacities in the service of another's self-actualization. In helping people to live in ways isomorphic with their inner selves, Margaret McFarland made possible an outpouring of expressive work which not only enriched the lives of its creators, but others as well. Fred Rogers, the most famous of those who sought her counsel, has affected millions of children and families through his "Neighborhood."

I have always felt extremely fortunate to have entered her space at a critical moment in my young adulthood and know that she affected my life far out of proportion to the actual time spent in her presence. But that is, after all, how it is with a catalyst, isn't it? Once the transformation is set in motion, the newly emerging substance (self) goes on to develop, without necessarily requiring further contact with the catalytic agent. On the rare but critical times I turned to her for help with an important life decision, I always felt emotionally and intellectually "refueled"—recharged, energized, better able to cope. She was a wonderful role model for the delicate task of helping others.

If Margaret McFarland was my professional mother, Marvin Shapiro was my professional father. He guided my development as a therapist with a firm but loving hand, and pointed me in the direction of psychoanalytic training—which I eventually decided to pursue, and which proved to be helpful in my clinical work and my personal happiness.

I have been exceptionally lucky to have also had a professional sibling in Ellie Irwin, my friend and collaborator for almost 30 years. We began working side-by-side, then jointly at PCGC, running "Art-Drama Therapy Groups." In 1980, we started a Creative and Expressive Arts Therapy program (CEAT) in a psychiatric hospital (WPIC), and later left for full-time private practice. We have jointly produced and nurtured many creative "offspring"—research studies, articles, films. We still turn to each other frequently, to consult about problems, and for personal and professional "refueling." Ellie has been the sister I had always wished for.

MEETING ART THERAPISTS AND OTHER RELATIVES

While it was great to talk with Ellie about drama therapy, I hadn't met art therapists except Naumburg and Kramer, and knew no one in the psychology of art or art education. Since I was teaching art education courses, I decided to take a 1968 workshop sponsored by the National Art Education Association on developing behavioral objectives. There, I met an editor who asked me to write my first article, suggesting that I put down what I had said in our discussion group about helping elementary teachers offer art.

I had noticed that Rudolf Arnheim, whose 1954 book I admired, was one of the speakers, and since Margaret Naumburg had told me he was interested in art therapy, I asked if we could have lunch. To my surprise he said yes, and it was a meal I will always remember. A brilliant and compassionate man, he was supportive as well as stimulating.

Another person I met at that meeting was Lambert Brittain. I asked him why he had omitted the "Therapeutic Art Education" chapter from the fourth edition of *Creative & Mental Growth*, which he had published after Lowenfeld's death. He explained that it was partly due to its length, but mostly because he felt that art teachers didn't have sufficient psychological background to understand and use it properly. There was some truth in that idea, but it was a loss to both art education and art therapy that it was no longer in print.

In 1969, I attended a Boston meeting of the American Society for Psychopathology of Expression (ASPE), a group founded by psychiatrist/psychologist Irene Jakab. Carolyn Refsnes, another art major from Wellesley, was also there; and she invited me to join her, Hanna Kwiatkowska, and Elinor Ulman for dinner. It was thrilling to exchange ideas with these two women, whose articles I had read and whose work I admired.

I was also lucky that Asher Bar, one of my husband's students, asked me to accompany him to a party at Irene Jakab's apartment, where I met Elsie Muller and Marge Howard, midwestern art therapists who described their work with children. In 1970, after another ASPE meeting in Houston, Texas, Felice Cohen invited me to visit her Child Guidance Center, observe her doing art therapy, meet her supervisor, and come to dinner. Recalling how friendly and generous people were to an unknown newcomer, I feel doubly fortunate to have entered the field when I did.

In 1971, the ASPE meeting was on Staten Island. I got to know Irene Jakab during a long ferry ride and gave a paper about the "Diagnostic Art Interview" I had developed at PCGC. Ernest Harms, who was about to start a journal called *Art Psychotherapy* (now *The Arts in Psychotherapy*), asked if he could publish it in the first issue. I was flattered, for I had read and liked his articles on expressing feelings in line drawings and on using art in therapy. During my next New York trip, I visited his apartment for a most stimulating evening.

Meanwhile, in 1970, an event had occurred which dramatically changed the landscape for me and for the field of art therapy. The first meeting of the newly formed American Art Therapy Association took place at Airlie House in Virginia. There were 100 present, and I will never forget the tension of all those passionate people trying to find solutions to thorny problems. One thing they agreed on was that Margaret Naumburg, who had written four books and had spent years promoting art therapy, deserved the first Honorary Life Member (HLM) award.

I met some people who remain friends to this day, like Harriet Wadeson, Bob Ault, Arthur Robbins, and Millie Lachman [Chapin]. I presented a paper on a Mother-Child Art Therapy Group I had been running at PCGC. Afterward, Elinor Ulman came up and asked if she could publish it in the *Bulletin of Art Therapy*. I often wonder if I would have written any articles—or books, for that matter—without the encouragement of those who invited me to publish early in my career. I really don't know.

What I discovered after the paper was published was that sometimes another art therapist—like Helen Landgarten—would tell me that reading the article had stimulated her to do something similar. The idea that putting things in print could help other people in their work reminded me of how vital the writing of others had been for me.

I also discovered that I liked to write and was finding out that I liked making films too, since words often seemed inadequate for describing art therapy. I made a film in 1972 "We'll Show You What We're Gonna Do," about work with blind children, and another in 1973 "Children and the Arts," based on work with at-risk children, highlighting the therapeutic values in all of the arts. I had less time for painting, except on vacations, but writing and filmmaking satisfied my need to create.

FURTHER TRAINING

Even though I had three child psychiatrist supervisors and attended the in-service training available at the clinic, I still felt a need to learn more. Fortunately, Dr. Shapiro was as encouraging as Erikson had been discouraging. After consulting with Dr. McFarland, I decided to pursue psychoanalytic training rather than a Ph.D. since my best supervisors were analysts, and psychology doctorates were heavy on research and weak on clinical work.

Halfway through my training analysis, I discovered that the idea that I didn't "need" a Ph.D. had neurotic roots–that the degree represented a penis, which I didn't "need" in order to be recognized. While it is true that I didn't require a phallus to be a therapist, I was also denying the realistic benefits of having a Ph.D.

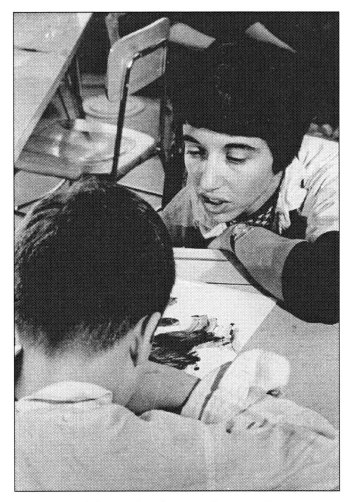

Judith A. Rubin doing art therapy, 1971.

After that insight, I found a program in the School of Education in Counseling, where I could obtain credit for my masters' degree and for some of the coursework I was taking at the Pittsburgh Psychoanalytic Institute. And I was able to meet the dissertation requirement by writing a book about art therapy with children (*Child Art Therapy*). Ironically, the most useful fringe benefit of the degree was not even a goal—qualifying to sit for the Psychology Licensing Exam. The credential was a great asset when I went into private practice.

Since finishing adult and child analytic training in the early '80s, my learning has been informal. But I still attend meetings of the Child Analysis Study Group, teach for the Psychiatry Department and the Psychoanalytic Institute, and go to presentations.

MY LIFE IN AATA

My friend Ellie says I identify too strongly with AATA. But what she doesn't understand is that it really is my professional extended family. I still enjoy the meetings as a kind of family reunion, a "gathering of the tribe" (a phrase I think was coined by Shaun McNiff). I've not yet missed a conference, though attending them is costly since I retired. Never having been a club or organization person, my involvement in the association was a new experience.

When I was elected to the Nominating Committee in 1973, I had no intention of running for office. I had three young children and had just started my training analysis in addition to full-time work. But I was so flattered by Hanna Kwiatkowska's seductive persuasion and assurance that the work was minimal, that I ran for Constitution Chair. In 1974, my father had just died, so when Elinor Ulman and Bernie Levy asked me to run for President-Elect I said yes because I knew it would have pleased my dad. I must have been crazy to take on the presidency, since my home was the "central office," the work was endless, and the pressures were immense. Fortunately, I had a supportive Board, which helped me weather many of the stresses.

Over time, many people with whom I worked in AATA became personal friends as well, an unexpected fringe benefit—one I continue to enjoy with people like my conference roommate for the past 20+ years, Laurie Wilson. Over the years, I have had the pleasure of hanging out with many art therapists—too numerous to name—but one of the most valuable aspects of my involvement with AATA.

Sometimes a friend outside of AATA was able to help further the goals of art therapy, like Phil Hallen, head of the Maurice Falk Medical Fund, who had supported art, dance, and drama therapy in Pittsburgh. I ran into Phil on a plane trip to Washington. He invited me to join him in First Class (an experience I wish I could have more often), asked what he could do to help art therapy when I was President, and by the end of the trip we had planned a conference to be held at the American Psychiatric Association, which led to the formation of the National Coalition of Creative Arts Therapy Associations (NCCATA). Phil also got me invited to be a consultant to the Task Panel on the Arts & Environment of the President's Commission on Mental Health, where I could help to write recommendations that included art therapy.

"RETIREMENT"

In 1996, I retired from full-time private practice and became a "snowbird," although I still see patients occasionally when I'm in Pittsburgh for half the year. I haven't said much about my clinical work, perhaps because I've written about it so extensively in books and articles, but I have enjoyed it tremendously. Although there have been plenty of stresses, doing art therapy has always been a fascinating challenge. I enjoy working with people of all ages, and I love having my own office, because I can treat individuals in the way I feel is best for them without having to justify or report it to others. After working for so many years in institutions, I appreciate the autonomy.

The best thing about retirement has been the freedom from schedules and the availability of time to do what I want, whether it's playing with my grandchildren or traveling, often in relation to art therapy. Actually, since ending my full-time practice, it sometimes feels as though I'm busier than ever. As one of my first liberated acts, I took up tap dancing, something I'd always wanted to learn. It's a new and humbling experience to be the slowest student in the class, but I love tapping, and when I'm in Sanibel (Florida) for the winter, I get to do it four times a week.

Sanibel Island is beautiful and peaceful (70% wildlife preserve) and a wonderful place to create. There I finished *Art Therapy: An Introduction*, and revised *Approaches to Art Therapy*. I revived an idea for creative drawing books mimeographed in the 60's; and APA wanted one on divorce/separation: *My Mom & Dad Don't Live Together Anymore*. I'm considering revising *The Art of Art Therapy*, and if I ever write another book, it might be one about using art and imagery in psychoanalysis.

I've also been bitten by the filmmaking bug. I had worked with photographers, musicians, and sound engineers to edit my earlier films. By the time I began work in 1999 on a video to go with the introductory text (*Art Therapy: An Introduction*), I had to learn how to edit on the computer. After collecting 300 hours of art therapy footage and spending more time and money than I could ever have imagined, I was finally able to finish a 50-minute overview of the field: "Art Therapy Has Many Faces." I also did a short film for AATA: "Beyond Words: Art Therapy with Older Adults."

I find editing films to be quite addictive. I think it's such an appealing creative format because I can say something I care about visually as well as verbally and can also try to do it artistically. I just finished revising *Child Art Therapy* for the second time as well as writing a book for nonart therapists on the use of art and imagery in their work (*Artful Therapy*). For both I made DVD's with many still and video images on them—to be played on computers. I found the writing to be easier and faster than the editing which was, however, more fun.

Oddly, while I like the books, I love the films. So far I don't mind watching them repeatedly. Perhaps it's the long gestation period, or maybe being able to watch the reactions on viewers' faces, which an author doesn't get to do.

Although I enjoyed making the films, the marketing part—distribution through a nonprofit Ellie and I had to form years ago in order to take our films and tapes with us when we left the hospital—is one I dislike. I reluctantly learned enough Photoshop to make an ad for the AATA Newsletter, and I followed the directions of the ISP to put some information on a Web site. But I really hope that we can sell enough films to pay someone else to do the commercial part of the work, since I'm not very good at taking orders, depositing money, or mailing packages.

At this point, one of my wishes is to live long enough to make all of the teaching films I'd like to, using the wonderful footage I accumulated for "Faces." I'd really love to get some funding, so I can rough them out and someone else can refine them, but so far I haven't had time to look for money. As usual, since art therapy is a hybrid, it's not easy.

PROBLEMS AND PREDICTIONS

I realize that I haven't written much about struggles, but the truth is that there really haven't been very many. For the most part, I have been lucky, I think best of all, entering the field in its infancy when it was easy to invent things and to meet the kind of people who are pioneers. They were a rare breed, and those of us who followed in their footsteps would never have been able to do what we did without their courage and perseverance.

There have been stresses, of course. It was good and bad to find a field I loved so much at the time in my life when I discovered art therapy. My two little girls were just toddlers in 1963, and my son was born in 1966. Although I started out working part-time, by 1970 I was working full-time; by 1973 I had entered analytic training, and by 1974 I had begun a doctoral program. On top of that, from 1973 to 1979 I was on the AATA Board, for the last two years as President.

It wasn't easy juggling the multiple demands of family, work, and school. Oddly, however, my enthusiasm about all of them and a naturally high energy level somehow carried me through. It was many years later that my husband confessed that he wished I hadn't gone back to work when I did, though at the time he was very supportive. And it was only as adults that my children let me know how hard my involvement in job and studies had been for them, when I wasn't as available as they wished.

I wasn't terribly torn at the time; I was so "turned on" about both motherhood and art therapy that, despite being in therapy and analysis during those years, I denied whatever problems existed. When my husband Herb didn't want to come with me to the AATA meeting where I received the HLM in 1981, I felt hurt and disappointed. Only later, did I realize how hurt and disappointed he was, and how much my involvement in my career had intruded into our lives.

Later, realizing that my family had felt neglected and that my youngsters' childhoods had passed all too rapidly, I wished I had continued part-time work until they were older. I am relieved that my children are better parents than we were; although at the time my husband and I thought we were doing a pretty good job (and we were, compared to our own rearing).

There were stresses at work because of my involvement with AATA too. Even though I had checked with the Director of the Clinic before accepting the nomination for President, I was cut to half-time for a while because I was so busy with the organization. And within AATA, there have been a few difficult moments and personal hurts. I remember threatening to resign, for example, if the members voted to negate a contract the Board had signed with Elinor Ulman continuing the *American Journal of Art Therapy's* affiliation with AATA. I also recall being called "the leader of the wolf pack" by my friend Don Jones several years later, after a heated debate on the same issue.

But despite the personal and professional stresses, especially during the seventies, for the most part my life in art therapy has been wonderful, and I consider myself a fortunate person to have found a field in which I feel so at home. My friends have often teased me about being a Pollyanna, but I do generally tend to see the bright side, and to be a half-full person, which makes therapeutic optimism easy.

Art therapy has matured greatly since I began. Two of my books were written partly because I was distressed by the ignorance and confusion evident in some papers and presentations. That would no longer be true. In fact, when I revised *Child Art Therapy* this year, I was astonished at how many new books were in the References. And most of them were good! Art therapy has indeed grown in sophistication, as well as in size.

My predictions for the future are wishful. I hope that the field and the organization continue to grow and to develop in increasingly open and flexible ways. I think that the possibilities are limitless, if we can work with our natural allies in the arts and mental health, and if we have the courage to seize opportunities when they present themselves. I believe strongly in the healing power of making art, and while I expect that we will be able to prove it scientifically some day, I have also become convinced that one Grandma Layton is as good as several outcome studies for convincing others.

I believe that art therapy has been such immensely satisfying work for me because it calls on all of my resources–feeling and intellect, heart and mind. Despite the challenges and complexities of doing a good job, unlocking someone's creativity is always a profoundly gratifying experience. This is especially true since I love to watch people–as well as the unique images they create–being (re) born. When art therapy works well, it feels like a birthing, a kind of miracle. I believe art therapy will continue to thrive for similar reasons–because art truly involves the whole person, and finding their creative potential allows people to come alive, to flower more fully.

The need to make the healing power of art available to all is more urgent than ever, for art is a universal language, which enables us to speak to others and to hear them, regardless of cultural difference or distance–something sorely needed in this troubled world. If I've accomplished anything in my working life, I hope it's to advance the cause of art therapy, of which I am still as much enamored as I was when I first discovered the swans, some 43 years ago.

Felice Cohen, 1974.

Chapter 10

FELICE COHEN (1919-2002)

THE DYNAMIC TEXAN

Myra F. Levick

Felice Cohen and I met in 1968 when she flew in from Texas to Hahnemann Medical College and Hospital for the first meeting to establish a national art therapy organization. Bob Ault described her as a "big presence" and she was. Felice immediately captured everyone's attention. She was articulate, friendly, and mesmerizing with her deep Texas drawl. The arrival of Felice Cohen the morning before that meeting was the beginning of a personal and professional relationship that I treasure.

Felice was born in Galveston, Texas in 1919, but after her marriage to Aaron Cohen she moved to Houston, Texas, where she lived until her death in 2002. Like all of us who were "art therapists" before there was an art therapy association or art therapy programs, Felice came into the field through the back door. Her friend Irving Kraft, then Chief of Child Psychiatry at Houston State Psychiatric Hospital, had read work by Margaret Naumburg. He invited Felice to work with him and introduce art media to the patients. She had been interested in psychology in college and had completed two years of medical school. She described herself as a "Sunday painter," but was also a talented craft artist. Her interest in research reinforced her commitment to the art therapy field. By 1968, she was Chief of Art Psychotherapy at the Family Service Unit at the Texas Research Institute of Mental Sciences. She continued there when the institute became associated with the University of Texas, Mental Sciences Institute, Houston, Texas.

She was very excited to be at the formation meeting in Philadelphia and her enthusiasm permeated the group. Her stature as a leader was immediately obvious, and it was no surprise to anyone when she was elected to the Ad Hoc Committee to form a national association. For Felice, this was a connection she had longed for. Like so many of us at that time, she was the lone art therapist in her community, feeling isolated in a profession that we weren't even sure existed. She subscribed to Elinor Ulman's journal and had read whatever Margaret Naumburg had written. She told me that she was so excited to meet Elinor Ulman, Margaret Naumburg, Edith Kramer, and Hanna Kwiatkowska that she maneuvered her way into having dinner with them. She also told me that somehow they maneuvered her into paying for everyone. In what I came to know was typically Felice, she thought it was funny and loved every minute of it.

Felice was elected secretary at the Ad Hoc Committee meeting in Louisville, Kentucky, to form AATA. My husband and I invited Felice and Aaron to visit us in Philadelphia and travel together to the first annual meeting of the American Art Therapy Association. One hour out of the city, Felice and I realized we had both forgotten the plaque awarding Margaret Naumburg the first Honorary Life Membership. We returned for it as this presentation to Naumburg was to be the highlight of that meeting.

Over the years, we planned time together at the annual conferences. These grew into peer supervision sessions for both of us. Her work was demanding and exciting. She began to write about some of her extraordinary cases. When the federal government passed a law that mandated states to mainstream children with mental and physical handicaps, Texas was the first state to adopt this law and Felice was called upon to introduce art therapy in the school system in Houston. She started working with children and in a very few weeks realized that teachers were in need of guidance and even therapy before they could accept this challenge to mainstream. In 1976, she published a paper on the diagnosis and treatment of a transsexual male. In 1977, Schaefer and Millman edited a book, *Therapies for Children*, and invited Felice to contribute a chapter on childhood depression.

Felice met Loretta Bender in the early 1970s at a conference and became interested in her work with abused children. Dr. Bender had identified what she considered incest markers. Felice was intrigued because she, too, had a number of abused children in her patient population. Along with Randy Phelps, Chief of Family Studies at the Texas Research Institute of Mental Sciences in 1985, she designed a study looking at incest markers in children's artwork. It is an interesting study and an important contribution to the field. Students in the Hahnemann Medical College program and the Wright State University program served as sophisticated raters.

Years later at one meeting, Felice confessed she was very anxious about doing family art therapy. She loved working with children and even drawing with them, but felt inadequate directing art tasks and possibly drawing with adults. I wanted to help and finally asked her if she would draw with some of us, thinking that working with her peers would give her more confidence. She agreed, and I was able to gather Don Jones, Janie Rhyne, Carol Carrino (my assistant) and Sandra Kagin (now Graves-Alcorn). Together we collected a huge piece of white paper and boxes of craypas. We spread the paper on the floor and sat down around it. We all began to draw and somewhere in the process Don Jones drew what looked like a barrier across the page. Spontaneously, we all encouraged Felice to literally draw through the barrier. She did, and years later—when she shared this experience with students, she described it as the most incredible art therapy experience of her life. I think that was true for all of us who experienced this with her. I remember afterwards, Carol went to the gift shop and came back with a box of chocolates which we sat around munching like a group of happy, but exhausted people who needed an energy fix. And Felice did work with families.

Felice became the third president of the American Art Therapy Association and in 1989 was awarded Honorary Life Membership. It was she who initiated having a parliamentarian present at board meetings and annual business meetings. This was an important step in professional development and one AATA continues today. Over the years she attended all the meetings she could until her health failed and her beloved husband died. She was an invited lecturer around the country and served on the editorial board of the *Arts in Psychotherapy Journal.* For several years she was the "News and Notes" editor of that publication. But whether at a meeting, on the internet, or in writing, Felice's voice was a powerful advocate for our field. She was an early pioneer in shaping the American Art Therapy Association. She was loved by colleagues and students, respected by all, and as Don Jones said, "we should celebrate that she was among us." And we do.

Myra F. Levick lecturing in Texas.

Chapter 11

MYRA F. LEVICK

SERENDIPITY AND SYNCHRONICITY

As far back as I can remember I was creating something. In fact, my mother often told the story that as a toddler she found me pulling up corners of wallpaper, pulling out the plaster underneath and trying to mold it. She and my father wisely bought me large crayons and paper and subsequently any art materials I asked for. Until the days before she passed away at 95, my mother also denied that the reason she removed me from an adult art class at age 10 was because we were drawing a nude model and one senior male student was preoccupied with rendering the model's breasts.

But the loving support for my interests and talents continued. As I was about to enter high school, we learned that one school in Philadelphia had made the decision to include art as a fifth major in the academic track for qualified students. I qualified and my parents arranged for me to attend even though it was not the high school closest to home. I did well both academically and in art and was recommended for a scholarship to Moore College of Art in Philadelphia. Fate intervened. My boyfriend was entering his first year of medical school and we wanted to marry. It was my choice to forego the scholarship, go to work and support us while he completed medical school. But we made a deal. When he completed his training and we were financially stable, I would go to Moore College of Art, and in the interim, I would take art courses whenever I could. My wonderful husband kept the deal and shared responsibilities at home, long before either one of us had heard the term "liberated women."

In 1958, at 34 years of age, the wife of a successful physician and the mother of three daughters, seven, eight and ten years, I applied to Moore College of Art and was accepted. There was no continuing education at that time, and I was required to complete the first year and fourth year as a full-time student, but could extend the second and third years. I graduated in five years with a Bachelors of Fine Arts Degree in painting. The girls and I did homework together and as a mommy/college student, I was "show and tell" in their classes.

While painting was what I wanted to do most, I recognized that my family came first and I could not commit myself to the isolation of just painting. I applied to Bryn Mawr College for a Master's Degree in History of Art. I was accepted and my family was very pleased.

But fate intervened again. This time, the director of the first open unit for mentally disturbed patients in a general hospital in Philadelphia posted a notice on the bulletin board at Moore seeking a graduate to work as an "art therapist." I had no idea what an "art therapist" was, but I was intrigued and decided to apply. Leaving that interview with the late Morris Goldman, I knew I wanted that job. I got it, gladly relinquishing my acceptance at Bryn Mawr. This time, my family was disappointed and confused and my husband was angry. He had envisioned me becoming a teacher and possibly a college professor. Little did either of us know that I was on my way to becoming just that. I started working as an art therapist at Albert Einstein Medical Center North in June, 1963. Serendipitously, I was launched on what would become a lifelong career.

The milieu in which I found myself at that time was the psychoanalytic community in Philadelphia. Within weeks I was part of an exciting, stimulating experience. There was no limit to the art supplies I was able to order. There was no restriction on art projects I offered the patients. I was considered a full-time member of the staff of this 29-bed inpatient unit. And as a member of the staff, including psychiatrists, nurses and aides, I attended three one-hour lectures a week. These lectures were on abnormal development, psychoanalytic/Freudian theory, and child psychiatry. Our lecturers were all psychoanalysts with specific specialties in the field and rotated throughout the year. For this artist who had one undergraduate psychology course, it was exhilarating. Within a year, the staff and I were looking at drawings, evaluating art projects and creating our own definition of art therapy. It all began to synchronize.

But looking back, one must wonder how art therapy developed within an established psychoanalytic group. Credit must go to one man—the late Morris J. Goldman, who was "Murray" to all of us. He quickly made two major decisions. The first was to create an open unit, the first in the city, barring all restraints and limited sedation based on the theories of Maxwell Jones (a psychiatrist in the United Kingdom, who in 1947 founded the Democratic Therapeutic Community). Briefly, this approach created an environment in which patients and staff processed together patient progress, regression, crisis and disruptions. For example, if I planned a group art therapy session and someone decided not to attend, I, a staff member and all the patients would gather in that patient's room and have the session there. Later on that day, a group therapy session would be led by one of the staff psychiatrists to discuss this event in relation to the philosophy of the unit and goals for all patients.

The second decision was made several months after the unit opened coinciding with my graduation from Moore College of Art. In staffing the unit, Dr. Goldman had hired an occupational therapist but began to feel this modality did not fit with the Maxwell Jones approach. He decided that he wanted an "art therapist." This led to his posting the notice that caught my eye. I must add that it caught the eye of some of my classmates who also interviewed for the job. Several years later, I asked Murray why he chose me. My classmates were much younger, prettier and just as talented. He told me he liked the fact that I had been a Brownie and Girl Scout leader of troops our daughters belonged to. He thought this indicated I was not only caring for others, but that I would do more than was expected. Who knew that wearing that uniform for years, being teasingly called "Captain" by my husband, would get me the job I now most wanted?

The four years that I was at Albert Einstein Medical Center were something like the first five years of life. We all know that as individuals we normally grow more physically in those first five years than we do at any other time of our life. For me those first four years symbolized major giant steps in my professional career. I went from being a painter and thinking medium and product, to thinking medium, art making and process. And most of all, I learned about the psychological implications in that creative process.

During my third year, Dr. Goldman decided it was time I moved beyond the weekly seminars held on the unit. He suggested I apply to Temple University for a Master's degree in adolescent psychology and education. I did, and Dr. Goldman arranged for the staff to cover for me when I was away for classes. During this time, he and Dr. Paul Fink, who had joined the psychiatric staff, suggested we begin to write what we were learning about art therapy and how it impacted on this psychiatric unit. We began to meet at specified times to write articles separately and together that we would later submit to journals. I remember those sessions filled with brilliant exchanges between us and with humor. One of our residents was known to be a writer and she was asked to join us to help structure our format. Her conclusion was that Dr. Goldman had "constipation of the mouth;" Dr. Fink had "diarrhea of the mouth;" and I was "somewhere in between." We did finally get it together and published several articles.

My family, of course, did adjust to my unexpected choice of profession. The first year, my husband frequently dropped in to the unit to make sure I was OK and still wanted to do this. Our oldest daughter, Bonnie, became a candy striper and worked on the unit. She loved it and at one point considered becoming a psychiatric nurse. Our other two daughters became intrigued with dinner table talk about medicine and psychiatry—discussions that surely influenced their individual career choices.

The nursing staff at the medical center consisted mostly of working moms and we made it known that our families were our first priority and covered for each other if we were needed at home. It was not unusual for one of my children, or someone else's, to spend the day at the hospital if school was closed. As art therapist/artist I soon became the decorator for the walls and rooms. I got to pick the colors and hang the paintings, many of my own. Making these selections grew into a therapeutic activity as patients and staff told me how certain colors made them feel and how certain images affected them.

Ad hoc committee to form AATA, clockwise, Robert Ault, Don Jones,
Elinor Ulman, Myra F. Levick, Felice Cohen, 1968.

My actual teaching career began in 1965 when Dr. Goldman suggested I meet with the Dean at Moore College of Art and propose that we teach five evening lectures on psychology and art. The Dean thought this was a very interesting idea and agreed to offer it as an elective for one credit. Four members of the Psychiatric Staff and I participated and much to the surprise of everyone, over 100 students attended each lecture. The following semester I was offered a scheduled time each week to continue this subject under the heading of "Introduction to Art Therapy." This, too, was an elective and many students applied. I taught each session and thought the class was very successful. I was disappointed when I was not asked back, but learned from one of the students that the Dean was not happy—more students were asking for this elective than those offered by him and other faculty. That seemed to be the end of my teaching career.

But fate stepped in again. That year Dr. Fink became Director of Residency Training in the Department of Psychiatry at Hahnemann Medical School and Hospital, and the next year Dr. Goldman was appointed Medical Director of the Hahnemann Mental Health Community Center. While we at Einstein were happy for Dr. Goldman and Dr. Fink, we felt abandoned. But Dr. Goldman's energy and innovative ideas knew no bounds. Within weeks after assuming his new position at Hahnemann, he invited himself for breakfast on a Sunday morning and appeared with Dr. Fink. They informed me I was going to Hahnemann as the Activities Director for the Mental Health Center. I would also receive an appointment as a senior instructor in the medical school and would begin to develop a graduate art therapy program in the Hahnemann Graduate School. I would not be alone. Many of the nursing staff and psychiatric staff would be joining us in this new embracing environment.

When I look back, almost 40 years later, I realize how amazing my becoming an art therapist and an art therapy educator really was. Changing approaches to mental health, the emptying of state hospitals and the opening of mental health community centers all came together. And a few extraordinary men determined that an art therapist was an integral part of this change and therefore professional training in this field was essential. I was certainly challenged, but by then, I knew what I wanted and had learned how to go after it.

The then Chair of the Department of Psychiatry, Dr. Van Hammet, welcomed me as an equal member of the staff. Dr. Mede Bondi, Chair of the graduate school, welcomed me as a faculty member. While Dr. Goldman held the title as Director of the program, Dr. Bondi made it clear he expected me to design the curriculum in keeping with the graduate school requirements. As Dr. Bondi confided, few practicing physicians are interested or able to address course credits, required hours, etc. And he was right. That task was mine until the day I retired.

We advertised and accepted six students in the fall of 1967. Two art school graduates accepted were two young women who had attended my class at Moore College of Art. A good question would certainly be how did I determine the requirements for admission and the required courses? There was no national association, no defined criteria for what an art therapist is. What I did have were all the articles and books written by Ulman, Naumburg,

Kramer, Kwiatkowska and those published in Ulman's journal. The lectures I had attended and taken notes on at Albert Einstein Medical Center for four years were invaluable. My master's degree curriculum at Temple University introduced me to behavioral theory and theories by Carl Rogers and Fritz Perls. In addition to psychoanalytic theory, I had learned there was another whole psychiatric world out there and our students needed to know that. And, of course, I was becoming aware of the diverse approaches to art therapy, some based on these different theories and some based on no theory.

That first semester we obtained a small grant for a guest lecture series and invited Elinor Ulman, Hanna Kwiatkowska, Margaret Naumburg, Edith Kramer and Harriet Wadeson to speak to the students. These lectures were open to all faculty and students in the Medical School and, surprisingly, were well attended. This helped spread the word about this new program at the college and paved the way for me to develop a cadre of graduate school faculty to sit on thesis committees.

That first semester we felt we were on a roll. Then tragedy struck. After we returned from our Christmas break and were beginning our second semester, Murray Goldman died suddenly of a massive coronary. He was 39 years old. It was devastating to us all–his wife and children, whom my family had come to know so well, to the staff, faculty, residents and students, who had all come to love him in that short time.

I remember Paul Fink telling us we had to go on. And we did. In the midst of our grieving, there was an ironic, funny twist. Dr. Bondi called a meeting of the graduate school board to appoint a new director of the art therapy program. I was invited and will never forget that meeting. Dr. Van Hammet, Dr. Fink, Dr. Jules Abrams, Director of the Ph.D. psychology program, and chairs of the different departments in the graduate school were all present. Dr. Bondi asked those present from our department who was going to take Dr. Goldman's title and responsibility for the art therapy program? And each answered he knew nothing about art therapy and couldn't possibly do it. A few commented that I was the only one that did know anything about art therapy. Finally, Dr. Bondi faced our Chairman, Dr. Hammet, and informed him that contrary to tradition, he would simply have to promote a woman with a Master's Degree to assistant professor and appoint her Director of this program. Dr. Hammet agreed immediately and everyone was relieved. I was overwhelmed. And so, again, because of a sudden tragedy, I was serendipitously launched on another career track.

The art therapy program grew and attracted students who have gone on to make a difference in the field. It also attracted psychiatrists interested in teaching in this milieu, thus creating an impressive faculty. Dr. Fink, always supportive and encouraging, proposed that we now present what we had written and what we were learning about the field and art therapy education at American Psychiatric and Psychoanalytic Association conferences. In 1967, at one of these meetings in Boston and later in Florida, there were other art therapists also presenting. These included Elinor Ulman, Edith Kramer, and Hanna Kwiatkowska. Over lunch, hosted by Paul Fink, the question of how to start an art therapy association was raised. I suggested hosting an organizational meeting at Hahnemann. Dr. Fink concurred and immediately sought out Dr. Hammet, who was in attendance, to approve such an event. We left that meeting promising to make all the arrangements for such a meeting at Hahnemann the following year. We did and it happened. Helen Landgarten, whom I had met in Florida, helped prepare that first list. We had 50 art therapists attending, including Margaret Naumburg. An Ad Hoc Committee was elected to develop a constitution and structure for an American Art Therapy Association. The committee was Don Jones, Robert Ault, Felice Cohen, Elinor Ulman and me. We were given a year to prepare this material and locate art therapists working in the United States and Canada.

Myra F. Levick with a patient.

The adoption of the constitution in Louisville, Kentucky in 1969 and the establishment of the American Art Therapy Association is history that is well documented. But there are some interesting, some hair-raising and some funny anecdotes that are part of my story. Even before we met in Boston and there was talk of starting a national organization, a movement I strongly supported, editorials pro and con appeared in Elinor Ulman's journal, the *Bulletin of Art Therapy*. In one such article I was described as that "redheaded upstart at Hahnemann" who was moving too quickly. I was already a grandmother and loved that description. But I couldn't help wondering why there should be such resistance to moving forward in a direction that could only benefit this nascent field. Needless to say these dissenters joined us in Philadelphia.

A most memorable event was my first meeting with Don Jones and Robert Ault–the marvelous short and tall of art therapy. The three of us have told the story in different settings, but I want to tell it again in my story. I was sitting at my desk, the morning before the meeting, waiting for people to arrive, when these two gentlemen came marching into my office. Before we could even get into any pleasantries, Mr. Jones was pounding on my desk, pointing a finger, telling me that we either get it together now or forget it. I was taken aback and wondered what had I let myself in for. But getting to know Don Jones and Bob Ault and working with them over the years has been one of the great pleasures of my professional life. And making life-long friends like Helen and Nate Landgarten and Felice and Aaron Cohen has enriched my personal life.

At that meeting we did begin to get it together. Ms. Naumburg thumped the floor with her cane in agreement and disagreement; the Ad Hoc Committee was charged to put it in writing for the next year; and we adjourned. Everyone was on their own for dinner and I invited everyone back to our home for coffee and dessert. A number of guests came and it was the first of many social evenings I would spend over the next 37 years getting to know my colleagues outside of the arena we just erected.

We met in Louisville the following year as planned. The meeting was intense, but the American Art Therapy Association became a fact. I was elected President. Would this have happened if a small group of us had not been at the same American Psychiatric Meetings in Boston and Florida? I think so, because there were others as committed as I was to this mission. But for me it was another marvelous coincidence that led me in yet another direction. The important thing is that the American Art Therapy Association has grown from the first 100 members we identified to over 4000. The road has been anything but smooth and we still have much to accomplish. But I am very proud of this organization and grateful to the many art therapists who have given their time and energy to serve as officers and board members to improve our professional credibility.

First AATA board, 1970, l to r (standing) Robert Ault, Ben Ploger, Bernie Stone, Marge Howard, Don Jones, (seated) Elsie Ferrar Muller, Sandra Kagin (now Graves-Alcorn), Felice Cohen, Myra Levick, Hanna Kwiatkowska, Helen Landgarten.

Our training program continued to invite art therapy pioneers to scheduled seminars and we were most fortunate to have Edith Kramer as an Adjunct Professor and supervisor for two years. At her invitation, we took the students on a field trip to her apartment in New York. She introduced us to goat cheese on toast and showed us her marvelous paintings. The psychiatric residents were required to join us on field trips to the National Institute of Mental Health (NIMH) where we observed Hanna Kwiatkowska behind a two-way mirror do art therapy evaluations of families.

During the years that followed, an esteemed faculty member who became a good friend remarked that I was always walking uphill. We survived three department chairmen and seven university presidents and the program moved forward. My shortness of breath was more often from excitement than "walking uphill." And surprisingly, wonderful things happened along the way.

In the early 1970s, I attended a conference in Boston, sponsored by the Society for the Psychopathology of Expression. During a presentation focusing on teenage drug addicts and their families, never one to be shy, I offered

an observation that seemed to meet with some agreement from other participants. As we were preparing to leave the room, I was literally accosted by a
short little gentleman who shook his beard at me and announced that he
liked what I said and I was coming to lunch with him and his companion.
My curiosity compelled me to follow. The gentleman and the elegant lady
with him were the late Dr. Ernst Harms, founder and editor-in-chief of the
Journal of Art Psychotherapy, and his then editor, Dr. Edith Wallace. Dr. Harms
questioned me at length about our program and the orientation of the
Department, now called Mental Health Sciences. He had read our articles
and informed me he was coming to visit me and Dr. Paul Fink. Within weeks
he arrived at a prescheduled time. We spent a most pleasant few hours
together, discussing art therapy, psychoanalytic theory and current literature
in the field. When he left, he made another pronouncement: he told us that
when he died, Dr. Fink and I were to become Editor–In-Chief and Editor to
insure, with Edith Wallace, the continuity of the Journal. We agreed, not
anticipating Dr. Harms to leave us for some time. Within a few short months,
Dr. Harms was gone. As Dr. Fink later said, Dr. Harms confirmed his prior-
ities and went home and closed his eyes. And so, serendipitously, I became
an editor of an international journal. The years working on that journal were
memorable and invaluable to my own growth as a writer.

    During that period, Dr. Van Hammet stepped down as Chair of the
department and we were professionally enhanced by his replacement. Dr.
Israel Zwerling was a psychoanalyst, a Ph.D. psychologist, a family therapist
and nationally and internationally known. He was also a staunch supporter
of art, dance/movement and music therapies and had employed all three at
Bronx State Hospital, New York City, where he had been Director. He could
also be a very autocratic leader and was known to rant and rave when he was
crossed. I remember his first budget meeting in which he announced everyone was to cut their budgets. I decided to do a little ranting and raving on
my own, making it clear it did not make sense to cut a successful program,
and if it was to stay that way an increase in budget was needed. I won and
each year that followed we played the same game and each year I received
an increase. I treasured him as a boss, colleague and friend.

    When Dr. Zwerling was settled in, I told him I had been approached by
the music therapy association to start a graduate program in that field. In
fact, we had engaged Nancy May to introduce music therapy to our art therapy curriculum. He thought that was a great idea and told me to develop a
proposal for all three modalities and I would now be the director of all three.
I balked and instead proposed three separate tracks, under an umbrella
degree, with a qualified therapist as director of each discipline. I would serve
as the director/coordinator of all three. He balked, saying there was no
money for more professional staff, but I prevailed and he finally agreed this

was the only way to go. I could now hire my directors. Of course, there was a condition–we would have to write a grant. The Creative Arts Therapy Program became official in 1975. Carol Carrino became the director of the art therapy program; Dianne Dulicai, who had worked at Bronx State Hospital when Dr. Zwerling was there, became the director of the dance/movement therapy program; and Cynthia Briggs, a young music therapist, was approved by all of us to become director of that program. We were a great team. With Dr. Zwerling over my shoulder, I did write that grant and was awarded $250,000 for three years. The three programs continue to be approved by their respective associations. We also received the commendation from the NIMH that this was the model program for the country. That was worth walking uphill for. In keeping with our new identity, Dr. Fink and I received permission from the Board and the publisher of the *Art Psychotherapy Journal* to change the name to *The Arts in Psychotherapy, an International Journal.* We held a contest for a new cover design. The cover of the journal has never been changed.

There was more serendipity and synchronicity. In the early years of Dr. Zwerling's tenure, he learned that Anna Freud was having financial difficulty supporting her clinic in Hampstead, England. He contacted her and arranged for a psychiatric resident, a psychology and an arts therapy student, to spend a year in training with her and that year's tuition for Hahnemann students would be paid to the clinic. This was a most exciting and productive partnership for all parties involved. I first met Ms. Freud around 1976. I had attended a conference in Israel and Dr. Zwerling arranged for me to stop over in London to visit the clinic and our students. After spending the morning with our students, my husband and I were invited to attend a weekly seminar that afternoon. Ms. Freud arrived early to meet me, took my hand in both of hers and said "you have come to see the children." And that is exactly what Dr. Zwerling had sent me to do.

Ms. Freud's greeting gave me the impetus I needed to confront a troubling issue on my return to Hahnemann. As our art therapy program grew, it was inevitable that there were times when I was involved in personal as well as administrative issues concerning students. My mentor and coffee break supervisor, Dr. Michael Vaccaro, strongly cautioned me about wearing too many hats---program director, teacher, advisor and sometime confidant. Taking his advice, I appointed the head social worker in the department to be our student advisor. From then on, I kept my distance from the students, but this did not feel right. Ms. Freud's reference to the students as my children felt right. On my return home, I met with Dr. Vaccaro and told him "no more distance." The students were my responsibility while they were in the program and I had an obligation to let them know I cared about them.

Myra F. Levick with students in Israel.

By 1978, I had demonstrated my own academic scholarship and was promoted to a full professor, the first woman professor in our department. My
forte as a teacher was mechanisms of defense and I co–taught a course with
Dr. Vaccaro examining patient drawings and showing how these defenses
were manifested developmentally in graphic images. In discussion about this
process, several faculty members suggested I put this in writing. Because of
the relationship we had with Ms. Freud, I asked Dr. Zwerling if he would
help me obtain her permission to illustrate her book, *The Ego and Mechanisms
of Defense.* He readily agreed, then proceeded to add that this would make a
great dissertation for a Ph.D. program and I was to plan on going back to
school. I was flabbergasted and went home to inform my husband that Dr.
Zwerling had lost his mind. I was certain he would agree with me as we had
decided some years earlier that one doctor in the house was enough. Again,
I was in for a big surprise. My husband, too, thought it was a wonderful idea
that I pursue this degree. I had little choice but to think about this and where
and how I would do it. I was assured at work that I would continue as
Director of the three programs and would be free to arrange my teaching
schedule and school schedule in whatever way was necessary.

I considered applying to Union Institute, an approved psychology program without walls, but was encouraged to apply to Bryn Mawr College in

the Department of Child Development and Education. I thought it was unlikely that I would be accepted, but made an appointment with Mrs. Ethel Maw, the then chair of that department. She was intrigued with my profession and liked my idea for a dissertation. However, she asked me first if I would consider including cognitive development and second, what would I do if defenses were not seen in the drawings of normal children and adults? I actually thought the idea of looking at the relationship between cognitive and emotional development interesting and important and told her so. I also said it would be important to know if defenses could not be identified in drawings of normal individuals, although I believed they could be. Mrs. Maw handed me an application, told me to complete it and return it the next morning. And to consider myself accepted. Past fifty, and a grandmother, I was now a Bryn Mawr girl.

I placed out of courses that I was teaching in our program, but still had to do the required reading, which was thirteen hours a week, and take the exams for each one. The good part was that I was able to take courses in normal development and learning theory which I now considered to be an essential part of the Creative Arts Therapies curriculum. I completed the course work and written exams in two years–probably the most grueling two years of my education. The approach to teaching at that hallowed institution, at least back then, was archaic. Some of my professors were uncomfortable with the fact that I was a full professor in a medical school and they were still only an assistant or associate professor. Statistics were a nightmare. There were no personal computers available yet, and we attended a computer lab to learn how to enter and retrieve data. When my computer printed out "myra study can't spell," I almost quit. We were required to develop a research design for which the instructor would give us the data. I had been collecting drawings for years from art, dance and music therapy students I taught in an introductory course to group art therapy for all three modalities. I informed the instructor that I had my own data, would create a design and if he approved it, the statistician in my department at Hahnemann would do the data entries and retrieval and I would interpret the results. He was not happy, but did think my design was good and agreed. The paper was published in the *Arts in Psychotherapy* journal in 1980.

Though there were no grades at Bryn Mawr, the instructors wrote comments on the students' progress. The note by the statistics professor was both hilarious and gratifying. I quote, "there were times when I wished Mrs. Levick would withdraw from my class. But she stuck it out and did well." I think he summed up my two years succinctly. Graduation at Bryn Mawr is like a Polish wedding. It goes on for days. At one reception, Mrs. Hoopes, the incoming Chair of the Department, told one of my daughters she must be very proud of me. My daughter, Karen, in turn asked her if she knew how many graduations of mine they had been to. That summed up the family's feeling about my education. Enough!

My years at Bryn Mawr were not only grueling, but difficult. Keeping up with my position at Hahnemann and school work were minor in comparison to becoming a member of the "sandwich generation." The week I was taking my written exams, I was confronted with impending surgery for my husband, a heartbroken daughter in the throes of ending a long relationship and my mother preparing for a knee replacement. After the third of four exams, I told my husband I didn't think I could make it. After a couple of drinks and a lecture from him, I took the final exam. My husband and mother did well, my daughter recovered and I graduated.

Dr. Zwerling kept his promise and arranged for me to work with Ms. Freud for six weeks and gave me two months off to complete my dissertation/book. As one member of my committee predicted, it went from the oral defense (which was another nightmare) to the publisher, who asked only that I change the title, *Resistance: Developmental Image of Ego Defenses, Manifestations of Adaptive and Maladaptive Defenses in Children's Drawings* to something more "reader friendly." Taking words from a poem written for me by a nurse I worked with, the title became *They Could Not Talk and So They Drew*, published in 1983. The poem is included in that book.

My experience working at Hampstead Clinic with Ms. Freud and her staff is certainly one of the highlights of my career. I was introduced to the children as the "art lady" and they were encouraged to draw with me in all free periods. I also kept a diary in which I wrote daily observations and sketched Ms. Freud, her staff and the children. I was very pleased when Doris Arrington asked for experiences some of us have had abroad for an article she was writing. I loaned her copies of some of the sketches I made and words I wrote.

In 1984, my husband retired and in 1986, I, too, resigned. I remained as a consultant to the program. After I resigned, my husband Len and I moved to Boca Raton, Florida. Rudolph Arnheim once told me that in retirement he was doing all of the things he never had time for and now had little time to do things he should do. He was right. I wrote a book with Edith Zierer about the provocative theories she and her husband developed. When she died the executor of her estate could not decide if he liked it and considered editing the manuscript. It is still sitting in his office. I have taught graduate courses in mental health tracks and loved it. I have had no administrative responsibilities. I was invited by my former student, Janet Bush, to develop an art therapy assessment for the art therapy staff at Dade-Miami School District for the clinical art therapy program she founded and directed for over 20 years. I am still working on the *Levick Emotional and Cognitive Art Therapy Assessment* (LECATA), norming and revising, and a book on this assessment is in process. Thanks to Diane Safron, I was qualified in five states as an expert witness and have had many amazing experiences in the courtroom. One of my students in the drug addiction track opened a dual diagnosis rehabilitation facility and invited me to provide art therapy there one morning a week. I have been doing this for four years. Serendipitously, I have written two more books. Twelve years ago I was an invited speaker at a Moore College of Art Homecoming. Another alumnus introduced herself as a Boca Raton neighbor and on our return sponsored my acceptance in the National League of American Pen Women as a dual member. This is a professional group of artists, writers and composers with whom I am painting more, exhibiting and writing more. It is wonderful. Two years ago, I was asked to consult with a group of nurses and college faculty at Florida Atlantic University, here in Boca Raton. They were in the process of writing a grant for an institute for health and wellness using the creative arts. Reading their philosophical approach, I was disturbed to learn that they were suggesting that professionals in the field of health, if so inclined, could and should introduce the arts into their practice. I naturally objected and did a little educating in terms of needing to respect other disciplines and seeking the appropriate credentials. They prevailed on me to incorporate a future training program in art therapy in the grant. The grant was not awarded, but a year ago, the nurse in charge of the holistic nursing program in the Christine E. Lynn College of Nursing asked me to make a proposal for a Post Master's Certificate Program in Art Therapy. I did and am looking forward to this new experience.

I have received many honors over the years for which I am very grateful. Among the most surprising was being selected alumnus of the year at Moore College of Art, and a year before I retired, made an associate member of the Alumni Association of Hahnemann Medical College and Hospital. Don Jones's tribute to the founders of the American Art Therapy Association and the young exciting members is an event I will long remember.

Finally I am reminded of a statement made by a family therapist when he completed his evaluation of a family group presented for therapy. "You just might get what you wished for." Well I wished for some things that never happened and some things happened that I never wished for. But it all came together in one glorious day, May 7, 2005, in Philadelphia. Last year, I visited that city to see our children there and give a lecture on the LECATA for the students in the Creative Arts Program. At breakfast with Ron Hays, current director, during that trip, we realized that 2005 would be the thirtieth anniversary of this program. Ron and his faculty wanted a celebration and the Dean said go for it. I was asked to be Honorary Chair. There were over 200 people there—over 150 graduates from all over the country and Canada, students and faculty, the Dean and her husband, the provost of Drexel and his wife. All but one granddaughter and great-grandson came. Looking back, I define my personal and professional journey by looking at my family and students. One daughter became a specialist with learning disabled children, the second an art therapist, and the third is a lawyer renowned for her work as a juvenile advocate. My children/students defined their own journeys and made a difference. Saying goodnight to friends, I was hugged by one who said, "there was a lot of love in this room tonight." And there was.

Helen B. Landgarten and her husband Nate.

Chapter 12

HELEN B. LANDGARTEN

THE MISSION

EARLY AND MIDDLE AGE HISTORY

On my fathers lap I jump, put my skinny arms around his neck and look into his twinkling blue eyes, "Daddy tell me again about the day I was born." He hugs me tight, pushes away my bangs and bounces me on his knees.

"Okay, sweetie, it was like this. The day you came into this world the whole United States celebrated with big parades. There were marching bands with leaders who wore red uniforms with sparkling gold buttons and tall hats with a big white curly feather in the front. They twirled silver batons high up in the air. The happy crowds stamped their feet and clapped their hands in time to the drums." Daddy touches my cheeks and smiles, "The day you were born was a day of joy. A day we will always remember."

I visualized that event over and over again until I was eight years old when I found out that the marching parades did indeed happen on my birthday, but the celebration took place for President Harding's inauguration!

But you can imagine what the message of being "special" did for a child growing up. Perhaps that played a part in my being an outgoing person. I was always the lead in the elementary school plays. I took toe-ballet lessons, even did tap dancing on my toes; my older sister also signed me up for elocution and piano lessons.

Even when I spent my seventh year in the Cincinnati Children's Hospital because I was dangerously anemic, I knew I was special because when my doctor felt my side, he told the other doctors and the nurses that my spleen was the BIGGEST one he had ever felt!

It was in this hospital that I performed every weekday, at one in the afternoon. The nurses rolled the patients in their beds into the solarium where I put on a half-hour show. I would always begin with my theme song, "Button up your Overcoat," with gestures that matched the words, pointing to someone as I continued, "take good care of yourself because you belong to me." Then I danced, did some little acting number, and ended with a smile and a bow. Of course, I loved the applause from the other children and the nurses.

I remember that a number of artists and art therapists also were ill as children. Perhaps turning into an artist is in part due to our childhood when we had to spend a great deal of time in bed. It gave us a chance to make more intense observations, a chance to lay quietly to fantasize, visualize, and to draw.

In high school I took all the art classes that were available. After graduation, I attended Wayne University as an art major, transferred to School Society of Arts and Crafts, then attended New York's Grand Central School of Art.

When I was going to school at Wayne University, my locker was six lockers away from a boy I did not know. His name was Nathan Landgarten and as he pointed me out he said to his buddy, "See that girl, someday I am going to marry her." In 1942 his prediction came true.

The following year he volunteered to go into the army because that war was going to save the world for democracy. He was sent to China, Burma, and India. Two and a half years later my husband returned and we moved from Detroit to Los Angeles, where we were lucky to have a daughter and a son. As soon as my youngest child went into second grade, I went back to school in a community college. I began with night classes (I had to take three buses to get there) and found myself to be the oldest student at age 37. At that time it was unheard of for women to go back to school. As our children got older I started taking day classes. There were five other women close to my age at Santa Monica City College. We received a lot of attention. The youngsters wondered why women their mothers' age were willing to study. After awhile, they stopped projecting their mothers onto me and I was accepted as a "regular person." The only complaint about the older women was that we were "curve raisers."

After three years I transferred to the University of California at Los Angeles (UCLA) and graduated in 1963 as an art major. I felt privileged to be accepted into the Graduate School of Fine Art because women older than twenty-five were almost always excluded.

For a year and a half I was fortunate to have the visiting artists Nathan Olivera and Elmer Bishoff as my instructors. Then I decided that I needed to prove myself as an artist. Though it was a scary move, I took a leave of absence. I painted in our garage, submitted work to juried shows, and was elated when my paintings, sculptures and etchings were exhibited in galleries and museums across the country.

THE SEARCH

It was wonderful to be a working artist. However, I felt something was lacking in my career. What I needed was unclear. Coincidently the answer came through my husband Nathan.

In the sixties, the UCLA School of Business offered a course for persons in upper management titled, "Sensitivity Training." It claimed to give the participants special skills in working with their employees. The course was composed of two weekends in a retreat, one at the beginning, the other at the end of the course, plus ten two-hour sessions in-between. At that time Los Angeles was sky rocketing with many approaches to therapy. All of them focused on "finding oneself." To be normal meant being in therapy. Ofttimes the emphasis was on group work.

This was thought to be essential because confrontation and feedback were necessary to understand how others perceived you. Participants had to wear a coat of armor in order to protect themselves from the projections that were thrown at them. Crying was also a form of protection since it proved one's vulnerability (apparently, a positive attribute).

The answers to the question, "Who am I?" often left people with an image that they would rather not have. There were many times when members left the group because they could not, or would not, take the outspoken negative comments that were directed toward them. The sensitivity part of the course which participants were promised to acquire, had often gone astray. Nevertheless, the huge deluge of different experiential therapies (some of which should have been labeled "experimental") gave those seeking therapy a large choice to choose from.

My husband, an outgoing personality person, was amazed at what went on in his Sensitivity Training class. To his astonishment, he reported that people cried and quickly confessed their sins and desires. They revealed their frustrations, their anger, their hatred, their lust, and their disappointments. Many betrayed themselves in hopes of learning "who I am." The newfound freedom of expression encouraged members to act-out and to be sexually seductive.

So dear reader, you might wonder what this course had to do with the well-known Business School? Was it a ruse of some sort? Should upper management become more sensitive to their employees? Perhaps, but how did "getting to know who you are" help business executives?

Still, the sensitivity idea fascinated my husband and me. When the school offered this course to the spouses of the participants I signed up.

After a few sessions it became apparent that participants often referred to me when they spoke. To my amazement I became the quasi-leader of our group. When our sensitivity training sessions were over, the person in charge complimented me for my honesty and my responses to the other members.

I wondered how I could combine my major as a painter, my minor in psychology and this "insight-oriented" format. I could see how art as therapy could be a way to "Self Realization" (a most popular catch-phrase).

I spoke to my friends who were therapists about my ideas. As a result I got the chance to work in a County Hospital with hospitalized adolescents. I was limited in what I could do with patients through the art. Though I believed it to be a therapeutic experience it was not art therapy as I envisioned it. Several months later, a social work agency gave me the opportunity to do more intensive work with geriatric women. The results were amazing and I became convinced that art therapy worked as a modality in its own right for clinical treatment.

CLINICAL WORK

It was by chance that I met Ellen Ruderman, a social worker who worked at the well-known Thalians Mental Health Clinic, a part of Sinai Hospital (later Cedars-Sinai Hospital). I told her about my ideas. She was impressed and arranged an interview with Dr. Saul Brown, the Chief of Staff of the outpatient Family & Child Division of Psychiatry. I told him what I had in mind and, as an art enthusiast, he could foresee the possibilities of the art format as a means for treatment. We agreed that I would volunteer my services during the summer, working with groups as an adjunct to their primary treatment. If the clinic was impressed with my performance then I would be hired in the fall.

It was fortunate that I had much success with my groups. Thus, in 1967, I was the first art therapist in the field (at that time I thought I was the only art therapist, only to discover in 1969 that other art therapists were in Louisville, Topeka, Philadelphia, Dallas, New York, and Washington, D.C.).

At the clinic I attended the many seminars given for the psychiatrists, psychologists, and social workers. I owe my knowledge and my skills to the Thalians staff who taught me how to become the primary therapist. It was also lucky that in this setting I worked with clients as individuals, couples, families and groups. I am thankful for all the opportunities they granted me. Without them I could never have written my first book, *Clinical Art Therapy: A Comprehensive Guide and Case Book*, plus numerous other publications. The Chief of Staff encouraged me to have my work videotaped. Those tapes were used as a teaching technique. Not only were they available to our staff and my students, with written permission they were also used at conferences and by other art therapy graduate programs.

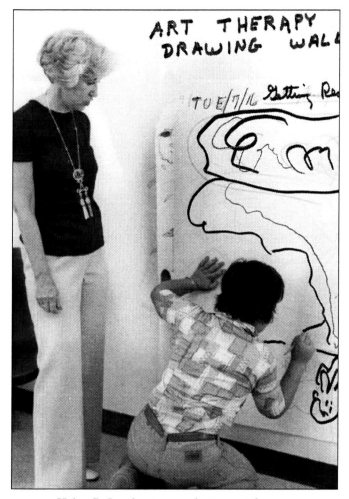

Helen B. Landgarten conducting art therapy.

I held my art psychotherapy position for twenty-three years. During that time other art therapists were added to the staff as well as interns and fellows who were graduates of Immaculate Heart College and Loyola Marymount University.

UNITED FRONTS: ART THERAPY ASSOCIATIONS

The American Art Therapy Association (AATA) was started in 1969. I served on the first board as Publicity Chairperson, was Treasurer several times, and held many other positions. In 1975 I became the sixth person to be awarded the Honorary Life Membership.

American Art Therapy Association Board 1974:l to r (standing) Mary Lee Hodnett, Christine Wang, Helen B. Landgarten, Mickey Rosen, Mildred Chapin (formerly Lachman) Elinor Ulman, Sandra Kagin (now Graves-Alcorn), Myra F. Levick, Don Jones; (seated) Judith A. Rubin, Elsie Ferrar Muller, Felice Cohen, Bernard I. Levy, Katherine Martinez.

Shortly after AATA was formed, also in 1969, Christine Sharpes, an art therapist from Virginia moved to Los Angeles. She and I formed the Southern California Art Therapy Association, in hopes that the future would bring one in the northern part of our state.

ART THERAPY TRAINING PROGRAM

In 1971, I began to teach art therapy classes at Immaculate Heart College and in 1973 began a certificate program which acknowledged one year of study in Art Therapy. When the certificate program was completed, only seven of the original fifteen students were selected to enter the newly formed Masters Degree Program in Clinical Art Therapy. This was the first degree to have the word Clinical included as a way of clearly defining the type of training that was being offered (as opposed to Art as Therapy).

The goal was to have my graduates in primary therapists' positions. In 1973, single-handedly I designed the entire program, wrote the syllabi for every class and functioned as an expert quick-change artist, wearing different types of hats as I went from teaching Child Art Therapy, to Adult Art Therapy, to Family Art Therapy, to Case History, to Group Dynamics. My more elaborate chapeaus were worn as Director, Field Placement Coordinator and Supervisor.

Dr. Saul Brown and his staff came to my rescue. They taught the Psychology and Child Development courses. In 1974, I hired my first faculty member, Leslie Thompson, a newly graduated student from Hahneman Hospital and College. Shortly thereafter, I turned over several of my hats to Maxine Junge, a social worker whom I trained at the Thalians Clinic. Luckily they fitted her and she wore them with excitement and pride functioning as my Field Placement Coordinator, Instructor, and Supervisor.

In 1975, with so few Master Degree graduates in the country, experienced instructors were not to be found. Therefore, I selected our former students Suzanne Silverstein, Bobbie Stoll, Judy Pastel, and Shirley Riley to team teach. As time passed, Shirley Riley, in addition to teaching and supervising, became the Field Placement Coordinator, a position she held for many years.

Our well-established program was transferred to Loyola Marymount University in 1980.

A ROUGH TERRAIN

When the Clinical Art Therapy program got started in 1974, a war broke out. There were two fighting factions. The first was composed of women identifying themselves through the Southern California Art Therapy Association (SCATA) as art therapists. They wanted to teach in my newly formed program. But, did they have degrees? NO! Did they understand academic requirements? NO! Did they see me as the enemy? YES! As a result they joined forces with a very angry person who was rejected from the Master's Degree Program. This woman's wrath was boundless. She and her husband phoned me and tried to get me to falsely acknowledge the reason for her rejection. They threatened to sue me and Immaculate Heart College for denying her entrance to the Master's Program. This person plus the others who wanted to teach formed a badmouthing chorus. Rounds of insults were cast upon the program and me. I would get calls from our field placement directors and other clinicians who were concerned, asking me, "Is it true that your program is failing and about to come to an end?"

Although I felt vulnerable, I was stoic and truthfully denied the malicious rumors. I never explained why the rumor mongers were spreading poisonous accusations. My weight loss was not due to bulimia, but I did vomit up the lies that were strewn upon me.

To illustrate the jealousy and the determination to defeat my goals, my students were invited to a SCATA meeting. They were curious about the way the art therapists were negatively directing their questions toward the program. One of my students was horrified to find a tape recorder under the table. When she confronted this unethical group, they merely made some lame excuses and changed the subject. Thoroughly disgusted, my students saw how jealousy could turn people into unfair and cruel opponents.

In spite of the war mongers I persisted and forged ahead. I was determined to make art therapy a known modality because I often witnessed my clients' gains.

The Immaculate Heart College Presidents Sr. Gerald and Sr. Helen Kelly, Sr. Margaret Rose, head of the Psychology Program, and Elizabeth Broom, Director of the Marriage and Family Counseling program, plus the Field Placement personnel were very supportive. I felt proud of our accomplishments. I kept telling my students that they were pioneers and were helping to blaze the trail for the newly founded profession. Such peptalks were a motivating necessity. They paid off since our students were beginning to get jobs and proved that our innovative approach had therapeutic value.

I managed those difficult times because I was on a mission. The more evidence I gained about the value of art therapy the more determined I was to take it out of the adjunctive category and to have our graduates acknowledged as primary therapists. With our former students getting positions, I knew that our healing method was proving itself.

Amongst my roadblocks were the Thalians clinic's social workers. The majority could not understand how I was allowed to do treatment. They seemed threatened and complained that I had no previous training as a clinician and resented the attention I was getting through newspapers and television. The art my clients produced was a media attraction since it was concrete evidence of their feelings and demonstrated the work they were doing on serious life issues.

The social workers concerns were right; although I had minored in psychology, I was not trained as a therapist. I therefore legitimatized myself by getting a degree in Marriage and Family Counseling, then went on to acquire a license to practice.

To prove my ability, I held sessions in an observation room where staff members could watch me working with my clients. It took several years before I was fully accepted by the entire staff. During those difficult early years, Chief of Staff Dr. Brown, Social Workers Ellen Ruderman and Helen Reid, and Psychologist Dr. Jan Sperber, were the colleagues who encouraged and helped me to feel confident about my work.

As if I didn't have enough boulders interfering with my journey to success, yet another gigantic one got in my way at the American Psychiatric Association Conference. Initially I was thrilled and honored to be invited to such a prestigious event. Myra Levick and Dr. Paul Fink invited me to present.

I asked one of the psychiatric fellows whom I was supervising to be my discussant. When I read her speech she claimed that she was supervising me on a case. This was opposite to the truth. It was bizarre. The Chief of Staff and I corrected her. I should have recognized that something was very wrong. Because I thought she was straightened out on the matter, I failed to remove her as my discussant.

When I was about to present at the conference I was nervous and excited. I looked at the audience which was overflowing with psychiatrists, many of them famous. I presented a fascinating and successful case about an elective mute. It was very well received. I was thrilled!

My talk was followed by my discussant getting up on the stage. Her first words were "HELEN LANDGARTEN IS A LIAR! She does not know what she is doing." She went on to quote from an article that Elinor Ulman wrote in an early edition of *The Bulletin of Art Therapy* stating that the field of art therapy was not yet defined.

The audience was aghast!

I wanted to crawl into a hole in the floor!

Better yet, to drop dead.

The saving grace was that my discusssant was obviously decompensating as she went on to talk about animal therapy and rambled on making statements that were out of a reasonable range. Can you the reader imagine how demolished I felt?

In spite of the held-back tears I held myself high. I was fortunate in knowing who I was. Certainly not the dishonest person the psychiatric fellow claimed me to be. I was an art therapy clinician who was proud of her work. I was Helen Landgarten, a good person. And though I was beaten up by an unworthy discussant I would put salve on my wounds and remain at the conference. But I did need to be consoled. I phoned long distance to my Chief of Staff and amidst my tears managed to choke out what happened. He said he would take care of the matter when we returned home.

The Thalians' clinicians who heard what happened were dismayed and tried to comfort me. Even after 35 years, it still pains me when I think about the humiliation that I experienced so long ago.

Enough of the hurts. I can now tell you that bringing Clinical Art Therapy to a known and respected place was worth it many times over.

ARTIST

Before I founded art therapy education on the west coast, I was and still remain an artist, except for a period of five years. During that time I was busy doing my various duties as director of the program, presenting at conferences and doing professional writing. There was no time to paint or sculpt.

I longed for that part of my life and felt guilty because I failed to pursue it. My biggest worry was that I would lose my talent. I spoke to Hanna Kwiatkowska about this concern. She understood about my guilt and to allay my feelings she said, "While we are not making art we are collecting images for the future." Her response did not comfort me since my art always spilled itself out on the canvas. My unconscious did the work for me.

For those five years I tortured myself. I feared I would lose something so valuable to me. I was scared that when I returned to my art it would lack the spontaneity I once possessed. My talent would be gone. Being an artist would not bring me the same satisfaction that it had in the past.

To my utter surprise and delight, that five-year hiatus never affected my work. If you viewed my paintings you would never know which works were done before or after that empty art period.

I want you the reader to know, if you ever get into a time bind, that talent is never lost. It is merely stored away until you have the time to bring it back out. Please remember this, especially students who are pressed for time and have the same worry that I once had.

When strangers find out I'm an artist, their usual question is, "What do you paint? Do you have a theme?" I am tempted to say, "Life is my theme." But that would be evasive and impolite. Therefore my answer is generally, "I most often paint woman in the interior or in a landscape."

"Where do you get your models?" they ask.

"All my models are right here in my head. I have seen my mother, daughter, my own body and spent years painting models. When I come to a canvas the female form is simple to create. It is sort of a magical experience that is hard to explain. Aside from painting the full figure, there are also times when members of my family and even the face of Maxine Junge have sprung up in my work."

The not-knowers look at me puzzled. But other artists knowingly shake their heads.

Those "not knowers" and even some of the "knowers" frequently want to know what my pictures MEAN. I want to say, "It is none of your business." But to be nice, I ask them, "What do you think it means?"

Without realizing it they give me their free associations. As a result I learn more about them than they learn about me.

Helen B. Landgarten painting.

Since I seldom reveal the meaning behind my work, I was surprised to find that I stated more than I intended in the video film, "Art and Art Therapy with Helen Landgarten." Lilli Young created this tape as her research project for her Loyola Marymount University Art Therapy degree. Her husband, a famous film director, helped her by being the photographer and on the side asked me pertinent questions. I answered him in the video. When I viewed the film it surprised me that I shared some intimate thoughts.

WRITER

In 1980, my first book *Clinical Art Therapy: A Comprehensive Guide* was published. It took me several years to write. I believed it was essential to create a book which explained the various areas in which art therapy was effective, a book that explained where this modality could be utilized with case examples to demonstrate the process and results. Fortunately, I worked with persons of all ages in individual, conjoint, family and group therapy. Although I was in the Family Child Outpatient Division of the Thalians Mental Health Center, I had opportunities to work in the psychiatric in-patient division as well as in partial hospitalization. In addition, I was invited by other clinics and hospitals to do short-term treatment for demonstration purposes.

It was my wealth of experiences that gave credence to writing a book that was an informational resource for mental health agencies.

The text on family therapy was easy for me to write since the Thalians Clinic was a forerunner in this form of treatment. In 1967, it was natural for me to convert this type of therapy into another book, *Family Art Psychotherapy*, again, to educate the mental health agencies about the work we art therapists can do.

Education, education, education, that is what writing books is all about. For this reason I went on to write *Magazine Photo Collage: A Multicultural and Assessment Tool*, and co-edited (with Darcy Lubbers,) *Adult Art Psychotherapy: Issues and Applications.*

I am making a plea for art therapists to record and publish works which describe their practice. Publications help agencies better understand what we do. It is also inspirational for art therapy professionals to gather new ideas and examine deeper thoughts about their practice. Books are also a motivating vehicle for persons who are considering art therapy as a career.

PRIDE AND GRATIFICATION

How very fortunate I have been. When I look around and see what my graduates have accomplished I swell with pride. The graduates who have done exceptional and innovative work are too extensive to list. They work in every type of agency imaginable. Three are directors of their own art therapy programs. Some have become directors of mental health agencies. From the original seven graduating students three are well-known for outstanding clinical art therapy contributions: Suzanne Silverstein established her own Psychological Trauma Center; Bobbie Stoll traveled world wide to serve disaster victims; Shirley Riley had many publications to her credit.

In 1973, I had a Clinical Art Therapy (CAT) baby.

In 1975, I became a mother CAT to my first batch of kittens.

I mothered many kittens until I retired from LMU in 1988.

In 1998, Vermont College of Norwich University awarded me the Honorary Degree Doctor of Art Therapy.

I had a small dream and now it has turned into a gigantic one, for the best is yet to come! An Art Therapy Clinic is in the planning stage at Loyola Marymount University. It will serve the underprivileged in the community who for a single dollar will receive art therapy treatment.

Janie Rhyne

Chapter 13

JANIE RHYNE, 1913–1995

VIJA B. LUSEBRINK

Janie Rhyne was one of the pioneers in art therapy who used art as expression and communication in the 1940s. But she is best known for her own approach to art therapy–Gestalt art therapy. In her life Janie followed her own path; her life styles and professional development worked in tandem.

Janie was born in 1913 in Tallahassee, Florida. She received her Bachelor of Arts degree from the University of Florida, Tallahassee in 1935, with a double major in art and social science. After a brief study in Heidelberg, Nazi Germany in 1938, Janie settled in Philadelphia. There, she raised her family while teaching art and using art as communication in different settings, including working with children with emotional problems and paraplegics at a Naval Hospital.

Janie's life and involvements changed after two years of pychoanalysis and divorce. She received a Master of Arts in art and cultural anthropology in 1956 from the University of Florida in Tallahassee and began what seemed to be her "here and now" experiential period. She lived with her second husband in Mexico from 1956–1960, where she was training Mexican boys in crafts. From 1962–1964 she lived in an experimental commune in Fauquier, British Columbia, Canada. Upon returning to the United States, Janie trained at the San Francisco Gestalt Institute as a Gestalt therapist with Fritz Perls from 1965–1967, and became a Senior Trainer Therapist there from 1966–1972. During part of this time she lived in the Haight Ashbury area of San Francisco and had a private practice, including working with hippies on drugs. Later, Janie moved to a ranch-style house in the redwoods in Pescadero near the California coast, where she conducted Gestalt art therapy groups.

Janie's intellectual explorations began after she finished her book *Gestalt Art Experience* in 1973 and moved to Santa Cruz, California, where she enrolled in doctoral studies in psychology at the University of California,

Santa Cruz. For her dissertation project, Janie designed her own approach of looking at visual expressions as visual constructs, based on Kelly's personal construct theory. Janie's strong point in imagery was kinesthetic imagery and Gestalt art therapy as well as her work with visual constructs. She emphasized the kinesthetic aspects in the perception of visual expression.

Janie received her Ph. D. in 1979 and joined the Expressive Therapies faculty at the University of Louisville, Kentucky, 1978–1980. She was visiting professor at the art therapy program at Vermont College of Norwich University from 1979–1992, and, after moving to Iowa City, Iowa, she taught courses annually at several art therapy programs.

Janie was active in the American Art Therapy Association (AATA) and was awarded Honorary Life Membership in 1980. As Chair of AATA's Research Committee, she emphasized the importance of art therapy research. Janie questioned, though, the validity of art therapy as an independent discipline and deplored the lack of internal agreement among art therapists on their vocabularies and descriptions of perceptions.

In her last decade, Janie integrated many aspects of the latest developments on emotions and existential psychotherapy and synthesized these into a systems framework with emphasis on the individual. In her last presentation before her death, at the 24th Annual Conference of the American Art Therapy Association in 1993, Janie summarized her different interests in psychology, art education, and anthropology.

Discussing different "dramas of transition" in life, Janie stated: "There are always alternative roles that can be tried on for size. Who knows... how... persons will perform in their own individual actual everyday dramas of transition." Throughout her life, Janie remained true to herself and honest and searching in her comments. She never lost her interest in people, her love for stimulating and challenging discussions, and her gracious hospitality.

Gwen Gibson

Chapter 14

GWEN GIBSON

LIFETIME EXPERIENCE, AN INTERNSHIP

My early life experiences were the keystone for this my budding art therapy professional adult self. Born in 1923, my consuming pleasures from third grade on were reading and violin lessons; two years later I added saxophone lessons and joined the marching band that toured Pennsylvania towns plus annual trips to Virginia's Apple Blossom Festival. Beginning in the eighth grade, I blended my alto voice to form a traveling trio–Hometown's Andrews Sisters! Early public performances finally cured my troublesome childhood shyness.

As a small child, I helped my country doctor Dad. I started "playing" receptionist to patients entering the outer office when Dad was busy in the inner surgery tending wounds, broken bones, or counseling patients with medical or mental diagnoses. I had learned to speak in conciliatory tones to calm incoming patients, recognized "code red signs" as times to interrupt Dad if a presenting emergency need outweighed the treatment in progress in Dad's back room surgery. On rare occasions, he counseled one or two depressed patients by listening for an hour. Then he dispensed sugar pills, which he dubbed "pink pills for pale people." Our family house rule was "never divulge names of persons who come for medical attention." I learned early the patient's rights for privacy, upheld Dad's medical training, and his vow in the Hippocratic Oath to respect each patient's privilege to receive the best care possible.

Hometown friends and classmates were children of merchants, farmers, coal or iron ore miners, railroad men, and lumbermen. Nationalities were "freckles" on the world's countenance: German, Italian, Polish, Jewish, Scotch/Irish. Religious mixes were varied–a wonder how one small community could afford the varieties of churches! In school, we mixed.

When the 1930s Depression years hit, the bottom fell out of everyone's purse. Coal miners, especially if on strike, were frequently out of work.

Families existed on a pittance. I watched friends who resented their second-hand clothing. Walking into their kitchens I smelled cabbage and eyed the mound of mashed potatoes (no meat) on their dinner tables. I noted the single communal toothbrush next to the kitchen sink pump handle. Parents then had eight, 10, or 12 kids!

Even as a child, I recognized hopelessness, depression, envy, and the retaliating anger of "I don't give a damn!" My parents, products of small towns, explained to us kids the concept of extended family. They revealed ways people help each other, stressing each person's need to "save face." Dad's financially-stressed patients knew they could pay him a bushel of apples, a "side" of bacon, a basket of tomatoes or peaches for canning, or the loan of a teenage son to help weed our garden The lady whose kids brought a wagon each week to pick up our laundry, delivered the ironed, folded items from the week previous. These intimate glimpses of my early experiences helped me relate in my adult role as family therapist in a blue-collar neighborhood.

My last three years of high school were on scholastic scholarship at Grier School, near Tyrone, Pennsylvania. New friends there were from wealthy (some famous) families, daughters of diplomats or missionaries from Korea, India, etc. I was the weekend houseguest in worlds that dazzled, with persons who opened their arms to me. I met one New York City mother who had bipolar illness–the reason her son and daughter lived in boarding schools. She was a sweet, lovable lady who read her own poetry at dinner. In 1940, I dated a college student who described family therapy to me. His wealthy father had taken his wife, son, and daughter to Vienna for two months one summer. Father and Mother had individual sessions with Sigmund Freud; my friend and his sister were counseled separately by two Freud trainees.

In the 1930s, the wife of a hometown high school teacher suffered depression after her second child's birth. She resumed normal life in two months. My Dr. Dad, wise beyond his time, had counseled, "No more children!" Despite my father's words, the couple had a third child and the wife was institutionalized with a poor prognosis. In the 1930s, mental health treatments were primitive or nonexistent.

My maternal grandmother suffered a psychotic depression when her husband, Grandfather Comerer, died. She stayed with us through the worst phases of her affliction. Young friends avoided coming into my home, fearing my "crazy Grandma."

I relate these life experiences because they provided learning that does not come from textbooks. There are no Ph.D. degrees in *fundamental knowledge.* Personal experiences helped me work with all levels of society, indigent to most wealthy.

In the summer of 1940, I joined four Quaker youths who came to town to put forward peaceful interventions to conflict rather than the violence of war.

For two months, we met in the Methodist Church basement with youths from the town and countryside. This pursuit involved using art materials for self-expression. It was my entrance into art as an everyday work tool, to visualize humanitarian messages from others' points of view. The following summer, 1941, my father died. In the same year, my Grandpa Locke, a widower, died (he had lived with us for 15 years). Grandma Comerer (who also shared our home) suffered a returning depression and was admitted to the Harrisburg State Hospital. Mother withdrew my college entry to sell our home to an incoming doctor. We moved to an apartment in Huntington, Pennsylvania. Pain and loss overturned my life.

The local hospital's Chief Surgeon, Dad's best friend, "rescued" me. He found an opening at the University of Pennsylvania Graduate Hospital where I could learn on-the-job laboratory technician skills. Though not my career choice, I traveled to Philadelphia where I rented a third-floor rear room in the home of a Jewish widow and her two maiden daughters, both older than I and each one employed in different doctors' offices. "Mama" Cohen, Pearl, and Eva "adopted me." I was honored, fully accepted and loved.

World War II struck in December. Reviewing my entries in a journal I kept, four years later I realized the depths of grief and hurt I had "forgotten." I had existed on automatic pilot in those first months after the family deaths and displacements.

I accompanied my "new family" to the Hebrew Y. We folded bandages, donated blood for the soldiers, and helped at their canteen for servicemen. The Cohens also informed me about student tickets for the Philadelphia Symphony Concerts. What a thrill for a country girl-music lover! Music has always been a healing experience for me. My two years with the Cohens helped me to relate with Jewish patients in my care.

I completed laboratory technician training in two years. My first placement was Wills Eye Hospital. The excellent training I had assured my high performance ratings with lab procedures, but I lamented the fact that so few moments of my day involved direct patient contact. Yearning for higher education and a career more personally connected with people, I began a night class at the University of Pennsylvania and at the same time I met my spouse-to-be. One and a half years later, Bob and I married.

I postponed college, needing to continue as a wage earner until my husband finished medical school and internships which paid "zip" in the mid-1940s. Later, Bob earned $100 per month as a psychiatric resident in training. This was big money then.

A therapist's life experiences can be a valuable tool, providing empathy when working with distressed individuals and their families. My past hodge-podge experiences, my own personal successes and losses, plus work in a general hospital milieu, allowed me to understand other persons' afflictions, to help them mend or assuage their bruised emotions.

My 33-year marriage to Robert W. Gibson provided many opportunities to audit courses in psychology, psychoanalysis, and psychiatry. When Bob was in the University of Pennsylvania Medical School, I attended Saturday lectures the semester he studied general psychiatry. Between his January graduation in 1948 and July medical internship, we worked six months at New Jersey State Hospital. I witnessed mental patients before "wonder drugs," shouting curses through barred windows, tearing their clothes, and tossing them onto the parched lawn below. Although I was hired as an office typist, I met a few concerned families of inpatients. The New Jersey State Hospital System provided some weekend lectures for psychiatrists and trainees. Again, senior staff members welcomed me to attend and learn with them.

Twelve years later, my husband Bob Gibson became Director of Sheppard Pratt Hospital near Baltimore. He scheduled evening and weekend training sessions for psychiatric residents in our home. I reaped the advantage to "audit." Official trainees, resident psychiatrists, requested I be allowed to join the discussions; bless their hearts! My spouse replied, "Only if Gwen reads the papers or books assigned for study." During these sessions, I met senior psychiatrist Gertrude M. Gross, M.D., who later opened a charter psychiatric all-day treatment center on North Charles Street in Baltimore.

In 1962, I had enrolled at Towson State College, Maryland, as an art major, English minor, with electives in psychology and sociology. In 1967, I graduated with my Bachelor of Arts Degree. The ink wasn't dry on my diploma when Dr. Gross approached me, saying, "You have all the makings of an art therapist. I want to hire you." I stammered, "I'm a painter, a potter. What would I do?" Her departing art therapist, who had been drafted into Army service, invited me to sit in on one of his last sessions. Still unsure, I visited another pioneer art therapist who worked at Johns Hopkins Hospital; he had invited me to observe a session with his inpatients. His role was more like that of art teacher. I wanted to offer suggestions but kept silent. Afterward, I met with Dr. Gross at Baltimore City Psychiatric Day Center's pilot outpatient program. I agreed to take on the challenge if I could work hours that fit my kids' school routines. In 1968, Bob Ault traveled from Menninger's to visit our center. He sat in on a couple of my sessions with patients and asked where I trained. I laughed and explained, "I'm self-taught in many ways." He informed me that art therapy pioneers were organizing a national art therapy association and invited me to be involved in their Louisville meeting. I had a prior commitment and couldn't attend.

The same year, Bob Ault and I met again. We had lunch at a Miami Conference of the National Association of Private Psychiatric Hospitals. The

Menninger Foundation and Clinic sponsored an art therapy display; Bob was there to inform psychiatrists from other areas about this new treatment modality, art therapy.

Gwen Gibson's "Weary Me."

Life experiences were my pathway leading to art therapy training and practice in the years from 1967 up till my 1996 retirement. For the first three years, I worked in a community-based pilot program, Baltimore City Psychiatric Day Treatment Center, an historical attempt to provide intensive care while keeping patients in their home settings. Later, the staff moved to Baltimore City Hospital's Adult Out-Patient Department, with our same goal for patients to sustain home base. Johns Hopkins University system purchased the city institution, provided further benefits and enriched our out-patient department goals. For example, I was one of four practitioners selected to train as a family therapist. Henceforth, I blended this modality with art therapy when it fit the treatment plan.

As a pioneer art therapist, I vowed to expand my body of knowledge. In the years 1970–1975, I earned the Master of Liberal Arts Degree at Johns Hopkins University, evenings. I studied abnormal psychology, sociology, and other courses to augment my career needs. In the meantime, I became active in the newly-formed American Art Therapy Association by serving on committees and giving annual presentations and workshops. I was Treasurer, President Elect, and President.

Early in my practice, Dr. Gross prescribed art therapy for a reluctant, depressed woman; reluctant because she was unable to continue her career as an art teacher and felt like a failure. I was told she had refused art therapy. I listened to her reasoning and offered a possibility. On my studio bookshelf, there was a book of haiku poetry; at the margin of each poem, there was a small black design with Oriental flourishes—all nature themes. Each member of the art therapy group she was in read aloud a poem "which spoke to him or her." Then in the next session, I recommended we create a group haiku; after that, the challenge was to "write your own haiku." Some group members chose to add a symbol that related to their subject. The artist became intrigued in spite of her earlier reluctance to join in. She liked her poem so much, she said, "it deserves a pair of exotic leaves in black ink." This experience broke the ice; she asked permission to bring from home her unfinished painting, which, she said had sat facing her studio wall. Not wishing to overreact in my own pleasure at this hoped-for breakthrough, I discussed mundanities: "How big? Do we have okay lighting?" We ultimately decided to align two or three easels for support. I provided brushes, oils, etc. The next session, she lugged in her painting. Then she reviewed anew her recent conventional ink design. She compared it with her wild "hippy style" of the painting. "I have been out of control. It is there in front of my eyes. What am I teaching my students! Mrs. Gibson, do you have a fresh canvas here?" At the next staff meeting, the artist's psychiatrist told me that his patient felt that art therapy, which she feared and negated at first, had really provided a healthy turning point midst a troubled time in her life. Insecure, obsessed with a former mentor, commuting to ever more classes in New York, she was draining energies necessary in her challenging Baltimore job setting. The haiku experience, along with other therapies, helped this young professional to focus on basics in thought and design. Tapping inner strength, she resumed her position.

Dr. "Gertie" was hoping to explore a young male's sense of physical identity, insisting he draw himself head to toe. This was to take place in a private art therapy session. The doctor said she would be nearby with her office door open. (That was my cue to proceed with care.) On one page he placed his head; I gave him another larger size art paper "for the rest of your self portrait." He got to his waist, using all of the paper length. I had the sheets tacked in a row on the art room wall. I reached for an additional extension, because Dr. Gertie wanted full body. While I taped more paper on the wall, I felt the hair rise at the back of my neck, primitive animal warning signal. I turned around to find this ordinarily droll, amiable youth with hands extended as though prepared to choke me. Ducking away, I went to the opposite side of a sturdy table and spoke with him firmly, hiding my fear and trepidation. "Will you talk with me and tell me what you are feeling?" (I knew from studies that if a therapist shows fear that the patient may lose control, the disturbed person is more likely to act out and fulfill the perceived expectation. On the other hand, if I trust my patient to curb his need to attack, he will image himself capable of control.) From across the table, I invited my patient to put into words what he was feeling. He said, "You were invading my privacy. You wanted to expose me." Tears came to his eyes, "You reminded me of my mother." He calmed down and looked at me with apology. "I would never hurt you. My happiest times are art therapy sessions." I said, "Sit down now; draw what you choose." He drew an Indian mother with a papoose on her back, outside a teepee. There are many interpretations to this scene. Afterwards, I went to Dr. Gertie's empty office. She was entering and looked at me and said, "Oh, I forgot you had this session with Ted! How did it go?" I just glared at her, my friend!

Ted was functional, though a diagnosed schizophrenic. He relocated to a group home where he learned to live within a secure urban setting, minus contact with his widowed mother who was suspected of molesting her son. He sends a holiday card each December from "Miss Kitty," his cat, "and me" and writes that he is still drawing and writing snatches of poetry.

It is in my nature to be a team player, to dub myself a facilitator rather than a healer. I have studied various brands of treatment: behavioral, analytic, psychiatric, and chemical for starters. But I am not a "cardholder" in a specific brand of therapy. I view my therapist self as an artist with paintbrush or steel blade in hand, a rainbow on my palette; the space before my eyes, the problem—a breathing canvas.

In the early days, 1950s–1960s, psychiatric units hired art teachers to provide hobbies for their patients; playtime, if you will. They served under Occupational Therapy departments. Pioneer artists honed their skills and sought training appropriate for the psychiatric work setting and its treatment goals. We learned to focus on the whole person, for example, to note in our sessions both physical and mental changes in the patient. We learned to check mounting tensions within the group, note member-to-member interactions, be cognizant of medication side effects, and report unusual sweating, rashes, thirst, etc. We also learned to give timely feedback to other members of the treatment team and not to attempt to shoulder complete responsibility which may soothe the therapist's ego but may short-change the patient as a result.

When patient drawings reflected suicidal ruminations, even "how-to" plans, I advised against patient discharge. In the early days, some staff scoffed, "You're reading tea leaves; where's the crystal ball?" Sadly, two departing patients soon committed suicide; a third had threatened to murder an allied health official. When he died from a heart attack, I sighed with relief. Staff never again ignored my warnings. It is unfortunate; it took two deaths to convince them!

At Hopkins Bayview Medical Center, we shared in-service training speakers and sessions with (1) staffs of the outpatient clinic, where there were scheduled weekly or monthly aftercare sessions, prn, (2) out-patient day care, and (3) the inpatient psychiatric ward. As staff in three departments, we overlapped some of the same patients and used every opportunity to confer re: persons ready for referral. The physical proximity of the three departments enhanced lines of communication with patient/family plus staff. Team effort!

Working with the Johns Hopkins Allied Hospital System offered me ongoing education privileges to grow professionally. Mentioned earlier was my selection for family therapy training, with two psychiatric social workers and one psychiatric nurse. An expert came to our facility where we had a pair of two-way mirror rooms for educational purposes. The trainer selected appropriate families from our outpatient waiting list. We scheduled evening sessions in order to include families from our working class neighborhood whose presenting problems would merit total family involvement. Sessions were evening hours; laborers could not schedule afternoon times despite need for total family involvement. When my months of training ended, I began to schedule families for combined art and family therapy. The language of art, color or lack of color, the equally primitive efforts of adults and children cut through generational differences in language. The graphic expressions were equally primitive, so often the family communicated better through their art than they communicated verbally. Despite age spans, the picture "said it all" and leveled the playing field, so to speak.

Adding family therapy to my skills provided increased services to my patients and additional job security for me. Also, in the early years of my career, I was pressed into the teacher's role. I mentored graduate level college students whose major studies were art, music, and dance therapy. This provided mutual exchanges, which were beneficial to my patient groups, the trainees, and me.

I first retired at age 70 in 1993. However, I was inveigled to return part time. I worked another three years and quit again in 1996. When staff invites me back for special occasions, I'm "hustled" anew. Apparently I still pass the Mini-Mental exam.

In retrospect, I let the changes related to divorce and working full time impact my professional painter and potter self. Ending a 33-year marriage, moving from a large house I left behind my former lifestyle, my third floor art studio, the basement pottery room/electric kiln. Newly established as American Art Therapy Association (AATA) President in 1979, in those "old days" when AATA lacked an established, efficient office staff, pioneers handled their own correspondence, typed, scheduled commitments, and liaisoned with other national associations and individual AATA chapters. We contributed more service hours for the American Art Therapy Association than one can fathom.

Gwen Gibson's "Fragmented Me."

Peggy, my youngest, was a college freshman at the time; my apartment office/den studio couch and guest bathroom were hers. Son Christopher was in the South Pacific, Navy; Gibby was married and a lawyer.

In many ways, vicariously I experienced creative fervor when my patients used art materials to shape forms of *their* self-expressions. I never grieved my own turning from oil and clay. They demanded too much time: shows, cost-ly media, networking, marketing. Fortunately, I had won my share of blue/red/white ribbons at shows; my pottery had been accepted into the Baltimore Museum of Art (every five years they jury Maryland artists for a month-long show). In my new apartment, I chose to create pastels for personal pleasure — no marketing.

Gwen Gibson's stoneware pottery.

Post Script: The patients' spiritual background beliefs were never ignored or discounted. It can be an important tool in the healing process. Many priests and ministers in today's world have had training in counseling, and recognize ways to guide the hyper-religious or extremist members in the congregations. If necessary for patient well-being, my advice is to welcome a liaison with the cleric, extend family therapy this way, if needed. (I am Unitarian by membership, with an affinity for Quakerism. I never was a proselytizer.)

In my years of practice, it has been a privilege to work with afflicted persons who sought understanding of their pain and misery. When patients trusted me with their confidences, innermost hurts and fears, I felt humbled to be considered trustworthy and reliable.

In retirement, I have time to compose poetry and attend classes for senior citizens at the College of Notre Dame at Baltimore. Each week, I take a piano player plus 10 men and women volunteer singers into a retirement home, lead sing-alongs, and encourage the residents to exchange anecdotes from their lives, witticisms, and repartee.

A wise therapist once said, "If your ex-patients do not seek you out to provide "blow-by-blow" descriptions of their lives, you've done a good job." Help them through the crisis, with feet set on solid ground, *set them free* to engage their own destinies.

Bernard I. Levy

Chapter 15

BERNARD I. LEVY, 1924–1984

A FORMIDABLE PRESENCE

Harriet Wadeson

Bernard Levy was one of art therapy's more flamboyant pioneers. Prior to serving in the army during World War II, in which he was wounded and received a Purple Heart, Bernie studied watercolor painting and ceramics at Pratt Institute. Following discharge, he received his Bachelor of Arts Degree from New York University in 1948. In 1952, he was awarded a Ph.D. in psychology from the University of Rochester, after which he served as a research psychologist at several Air Force training centers. In 1956, he and his wife Claire and their children moved to Washington, D.C., where he lived for the rest of his life.

Bernie became Chief Psychologist at D.C. General Hospital, where he met Elinor Ulman, who was the hospital's art therapist, at a time when only a handful of people were practicing art therapy. They became lifelong colleagues and close friends. During this period, Bernie was also an Assistant Professor of psychology at Georgetown University Medical School.

In 1963, he joined the Psychology Department of George Washington University (GW) and served as its Chair from 1967 to 1971. It was in 1971 that he and Elinor founded the Graduate Art Therapy Training Program at George Washington, one of the first art therapy graduate programs in the country. Bernie directed the Program until his death.

Additionally, Bernie had a private practice in clinical psychology, was a member of the D.C. Psychological Association and a Fellow of the American Psychological Association. He was a member of the American Art Therapy Association's Executive Board for eight years during the early years of the

---

Note: Some of this information is from Galbraith, N. (1984). Bernard I. Levy. *American Journal of Art Therapy, 23*, 41.

development of the profession. Bernie was a strong support in Elinor Ulman's creating the *Bulletin of Art Therapy* in 1961 (later named the *American Journal of Art Therapy*) and served on its Editorial Board until his death. This first journal in American art therapy paved the way for the organization of the few practicing art therapists during the 1960s into a professional association. His publications centered largely on the use of art in diagnosis.

Bernie remained an enthusiastic watercolor painter and exhibitor, for which he won a number of awards: from *American Artist* magazine, the Cayuga County Art League, the Washington Watercolor Society, and the Arts Club of Washington. For the 15 years prior to his death, he taught watercolor painting at the Chevy Chase Community Center. He offered an occasional watercolor workshop for art therapists. Bernie continued work in ceramics as well, and for many years played in a recorder group.

I remember Bernie best for his wry wit, outspoken opinions, and the strong leadership he provided AATA as we were becoming a profession. He did not shy away from controversy and sometimes seemed to relish it. I was always struck when I met GW students and graduates that they spoke of their teachers as Elinor, Hanna, and Edith, but always "Dr. Levy." He commanded a kind of respect that was his alone.

Frances E. Anderson making a People Pot.

Chapter 16

FRANCES E. ANDERSON

A REMEMBERANCE

We have no word for art,
We do everything as well as we possibly can
--Pueblo Indian saying

I am an inveterate lover of cats, the ocean, walking on the beach, scuba diving, tennis, hosting dinner parties, clay, making people pots, photography, sun hats, improvisational theater, dry humor, the Dead Bug Society, the psalms, initiating things, grant writing, art therapy, problem solving, and visualizing the big picture. I took early retirement so I no longer have to leap buildings with a single bound, nor publish, publish, publish, nor deal with university politics, sexual discrimination and harassment.

THE SCHOOL YEARS

I remember learning how to write standing behind my father as he "helped" me write a theme when I was 10 years old. He did not actually teach me. He took my ideas and put them on paper via typewriter. I just figured out how to compose by watching him. This kind of problem-solving ability is a thread that goes throughout my life.

I was a preacher's kid and while we moved in wealthy circles because my father's parish was comprised of very rich parishioners, we did not have the material means to really be a part of those strata. I was a scholarship student at a prep school, and my education was marked by a theme of not belonging. I rarely had the right clothes and was not asked to join the best club. I turned to writing to console myself. When my best friend died in the eighth grade, I again turned to writing to help me deal with my loss. I certainly did not fit in. Yet I had to move in those circles.

Frances E. Anderson (in white) with her family the night she became a debutante.

AN EXAMPLE OF PROBLEM SOLVING

Learning languages has always been difficult for me. I struggled with Latin and French in prep school. I somehow figured out a way to survive my Latin final–not by reviewing all the Latin words and verb tenses. Knowing we were going to be given a passage from Caesar's chronicles, I just memorized them verbatim in English. Then I knew I could recall enough Latin to figure out exactly which chronicle we would be given to translate. I passed Latin! However, the way I did it was a bit strange. Most of my life, it seemed I did things in reverse or in strange ways.

COLLEGE AND THE DISCOVERY OF THE
BULLETIN OF ART THERAPY

One of my father's parishioners paid for my college education so I was able to attend Agnes Scott College, a prestigious women's college in the Atlanta, Georgia area. When I started college, I thought I would be an English major. However, I found it difficult to keep up with all the reading in my freshman and sophomore English courses. (This difficulty will be explained later.) So having had an art studio course as a freshman and having done very well in it, I decided to major in art. I remember when I came home after my sophomore year and declared that I was going to major in Art. The first thing my Dad said to me was "What are you going to do with THAT? How will you support yourself?" "Teach, I guess," I said.

I had an incredible psychology professor and ended up taking every course taught by Dr. Miriam Ducker. In doing a library search for one of my psychology papers, I discovered the *Bulletin of Art Therapy*. As an art major at a liberal arts college and one whose family had imbued her with a commitment to giving back to society, I seized on the idea of becoming an art therapist. However, there were no training programs in existence at the time.

In my senior year I commenced thinking about how to get qualified to teach art in public schools. (As a liberal arts college, Agnes Scott offered no courses in teacher preparation.) I applied to the School of Education at Indiana University/ Bloomington (IU/B), which was a two and one-half hour drive from my home in Louisville, Kentucky. I received a tuition waiver from IU/B and decided to attend and work on both a Master's Degree and teacher certification at the same time. I completed my degree in 1964 (less than a year after receiving my Bachelor of Arts degree).

TEACHING ART IN PUBLIC SCHOOL AND THE DISCOVERY OF CHILDREN WITH DISABILITIES

My first job was teaching art to students in first through twelfth grades in a small southern Indiana school district. This was where I encountered children with mental and emotional disabilities for the first time. Nothing I had been taught had prepared me for this challenge. I had 13 children in one class with an age range of 6 to 15 years. The six- year olds were twin brothers and both were extremely hyperactive. At least once a week one of the brothers would literally freak out. I would have to catch him and carry him up three flights of stairs to his classroom, leaving the other 12 children alone. (I am very lucky that they did not kill one another while I was gone.) Years later, I figured out that both boys were autistic.

DOCTORAL STUDIES AT INDIANA UNIVERSITY/ BLOOMINGTON

That summer, I received a phone call from one of my IU/B professors who offered me an assistantship if I would return to work on my doctorate in art education. So I did. At the time, IU had its own entrance examination, which I had to take. I had never scored very high in any standardized exam. In fact, when I took the Graduate Record Examinations (GRE), I did poorly. So I decided to take the GRE over. Guess what? My scores were even lower on the second GRE!

The IU/B admissions sent me a letter stating that I had not performed well on their admissions test and my status as a graduate student was contingent upon my grades that first year. The fact that I was the top doctoral student in my class three years later belies the credibility of this kind of entrance examination. And the fact that I became the 17th Distinguished Professor in the history of Illinois State University years later is further testimony to the lack of validity of entrance examinations and the GRE.

In my last year of study at IU/B, I wrote a seminar paper on art in mental hospitals. I visited the activity therapy department in the largest mental hospital in Louisville, Kentucky (Our Lady of Peace). I saw patients working on various art projects. I thought perhaps I could become an activity therapist. In that same seminar, I learned about occupational therapy; this field excited me so much that I wrote to several university training programs. One occupational therapy program's response stated that it would take three more years of study and advised me to remain at IU/B and complete my doctorate. That is what I did.

THE ORGANIZATIONAL MEETING TO FORM THE AMERICAN ART THERAPY ASSOCIATION

In the summer of 1969, my father, who was aware of my interest in art therapy, found out there was going to be a founding meeting of the American Art Therapy Association (AATA). He called me and suggested that I might want to be there. So I drove up from the University of Tennessee/ Knoxville, where I was teaching, and attended the meeting. It was held at the University College of the University of Louisville. I remember that there were about 50 people in the room. I sat next to Dorothea Lange, Director of the Activities Therapy Program at Our Lady of Peace Hospital, whom I had met while doing my seminar paper on art therapy the year before. She was the only person I knew in the room.

After a few minutes someone got up and said, "We all know why we are here—to form a national art therapy association." Then a discussion followed as to who would fill what office. Myra Levick was selected as President, Bob Ault, President-Elect, Margaret Howard, Treasurer, Felice Cohen, Secretary, Elsie Muller, Constitution Chair, Helen Landgarten, Public Information,

Don Jones, Publications Chair, Ben Ploger, Professional Standards, and Bernard Stone, Membership. Sandra Kagin (now Graves-Alcorn) was chosen as Education Chair. She was not at the meeting, but someone said she was applying for a job at the University of Louisville at that very moment. When the list of board members came to Research Chair, Dorothea Lange wanted to nominate me because of my earlier research and interviews at Our Lady of Peace. I quickly declined, and Hanna Kwiatowska became Research Chair.

It seemed that the group had already discussed these offices and who would fill them. When all the offices were filled, there was a vote. Then the meeting was adjourned. I offered to provide transportation for anyone who needed to go to the airport, train, or bus station. One person did want a ride to the bus station. Her first name was Edith and she was an older person with dark hair who had ridden 24 hours on the bus from New York City to Louisville for the meeting. She spoke English with a German accent. Three years later when I first saw Edith Kramer, I thought that was the person whom I took to the bus station. Years later, Myra Levick told me that the person I had taken to the bus depot was Edith Zierer. (I still like my version of the story, although Myra was right I am sure!) The next day, June 30th, there was a small notice in the *Louisville Courier Journal* announcing the formation of a national art therapy association.

In 1972, AATA was just starting the registration process and the country was divided into regions. I became the first Midwest Standards Chair. What surprised me was the intense interest AATA members had in getting registered. This interest was so intense that I was heavily lobbied at national meetings, and I received phone calls at all hours of the day and night.

The first several AATA Conferences were truly memorable. The business meetings were highly charged and there was intense debate. It seemed to me that these pioneers, including Edith Kramer, Elinor Ulman, and Myra Levick, each believed she had THE only "true" approach to the practice of art therapy. I saw little room for consideration of diverse approaches. I suppose these pioneers had overcome many obstacles in their efforts to establish art therapy as a valid treatment modality in mental hospitals and treatment centers, so they were very passionate.

ILLINOIS STATE UNIVERSITY, 1970–2002

In 1972, Helen Landgarten and I teamed up to conduct a survey on the status of art programs in mental health facilities. We found there was real interest in art therapy and in adding art therapists to facilities in the Midwest and in Southern California. Helen and I presented our results at the Fifth Annual Art Therapy Conference in Columbus, Ohio, and subsequently published our results in both the *Bulletin of Art Therapy* and *Studies in Art Education*.

Even though Helen and I were able to document the need for art therapists, it took from 1972 to 1989 for the Illinois State University (ISU) Art School to approve a graduate art therapy training program. The name of the game in academic circles was, and is, politics, politics, politics. Until my retirement in 2002, I ran the program and obtained grants for assistantships and tuition waivers. Financial support was available to every art therapy student who wanted it. From the beginning, I firmly believed that it was (and is) unethical to have only one art therapy faculty person teaching in a program. Students should have the benefit of several teaching styles and perspectives. Further, no one person could have all the knowledge to teach nine or ten different graduate art therapy courses. So I obtained external funding to bring in art therapy educators to teach in the program. Marcia Rosal, Doris Arrington, Valerie Appleton, Sister Jean Carrigan, Laura Cherry, and other nationally recognized art therapy educators came to teach weekend courses. These teachers, who had to have doctorate degrees to teach a graduate course at ISU, provided important alternative perspectives and clinical experience to the courses.

At the 1990 International Art Therapy Educators Convocation at the University of New Mexico, I made a presentation on the qualifications for art therapy educators. As part of this presentation I offered this sample job description. While not totally true, aspects of being a program director seem very close to the advertisement that follows:

Wanted: Art therapy program director. Responsibilities include: Program administration, fundraising, directing master's theses, teaching four courses per semester, practicum site development and supervision. Qualifications: doctorate in art therapy or closely related field, ATR-BC status, 7 years clinical work (with special populations, geriatrics, clients with eating disorders, chemical dependence, physical and sexual abuse); 5 years administrative experience; publications sufficient to qualify for university graduate faculty status; and an exhibition record as an artist. Also needed is more energy than a speeding locomotive, ability to leap tall buildings with a single bound, ability to repel bullets and colleagues' slings and arrows, x-ray vision, mind-reading capacity for dealing with college administration and students, ability to walk on water, live with no sleep, write like Shakespeare, paint like Picasso, the luck to land grants and pick winning lottery numbers, the political acumen of a Boss Tweed or Richard Daley, the diplomatic skills of Henry Kissinger. It would also help if the applicant were independently wealthy, as we have no resources for student help, secretary or travel, etc. Applicants with no family responsibilities are encouraged to apply as there will be no time for family on this job. Salary: $12,000 per year. Timbuktu University is located in the beautiful countryside in the far outskirts of Civilization City, the state's cultural center, which is 2 hours away by airplane or 2 days by mule.

(This was published in *Art Therapy, Journal of the American Art Therapy Association* in 1993 as part of an editorial by Cathy Malchiodi.)

Frances E. Anderson scuba diving, having made over
100 dives since 1980.

A DOG-EAT-DOG WORLD

The world I encountered at Illinois State University in 1970 was a fiercely competitive academic environment. Moreover, I remember that my first attempt at promotion from Assistant to Associate Professor was denied because I had refused to welcome the male advances of one of the committee members. Unfortunately, discrimination continues to this day, but it is much more secretive now.

This was not the first time I had encountered discrimination. My first full-time academic teaching when I finished my doctorate in 1968 was at the University of Tennessee, Knoxville. I taught ceramics and craft design. I remember interviewing at five universities and being offered jobs at all of them. Even in my first year of teaching, several universities tried to entice me to come teach at their universities. I remembered during one interview the interviewer stated, "You have three strikes against you. You are young, single, and female; why are you interested in this position?" I replied that none of these "three strikes" had kept me from completing my doctorate in record time. Yes, this was the era of discrimination and sexual harassment of women in higher education. During one job interview, I was even "hit on." In another incident at the University of Tennessee, Knoxville, one of the workmen literally grabbed me. I was saved only by a student knocking on the classroom door. When I reported the incident, my boss replied. "Oh, we have one administrator that is so bad they had to put a window in his office door." That was the extent of the response to my complaint!

ILLINOIS STATE UNIVERSITY MERIT EVALUATION SYSTEM

There were 50 faculty members in the Art School and every year each person was rank ordered in terms of his or her teaching, service, and scholarly productivity. I hated the system because it was so competitive and demoralizing. So I started volunteering in the lab school and working with Larry Barnfield, the art teacher there. (ISU has a very large Special Education Department and a special school for children with and without disabilities).

LAB SCHOOL

The Illinois State University Lab School served children with hearing, visual, physical, and emotional handicaps. We also had children with learning disabilities and mental challenges. All these children taught me an incredible amount about themselves and their abilities. I loved being a part of a treatment team. Our common goal was helping these children learn about themselves and the world around them. Being able to communicate was a major goal for these children, especially those who had hearing impairments.

MY MENTORS

We all need mentors. I was fortunate in having two. Dr. Mary Rouse at Indiana University gave me a passion for research and the model for publishing at least two articles a year. Larry Barnfield was (and is) the other mentor. Larry had a profound influence on me. He was an exceptional teacher and clinician and always shared information and methods of working with the children. Two of the most important art directives I learned from him are the Starter Sheet and the Life-Size Body Trace.

ART EDUCATION AND ART THERAPY

Those of us in the American Art Therapy Association who came from an art education background felt the strong anti-art education bias held and expressed by other AATA members. At the Seventh AATA Conference in 1977, I was on a panel titled "Art Therapy: An Exploration of Values," led by Roberta Shoemaker. Others on the panel were Elinor Ulman, Edith Wallace, Mildred Lachman-Chapin, Robert Wolf, and Edith Kramer. When it was my turn to discuss the topic, I spontaneously asked those in the audience who came from an art education background to raise their hands. Two-thirds of the audience did just that. I had dramatically made my point that art education was a major content area of art therapists. Soon after that, Sandra Packard and I published "A Shared Identity Crisis: Art Education or Art Therapy?" in the *American Journal of Art Therapy* to point out some of the roots and overlapping areas of the two fields.

My art education background included a doctorate in Art Education and Curriculum and Instruction at Indiana University. A major part of that doctoral program was devoted to developing research skills and methodologies. It was this in-depth study of research and ways to conduct research that enabled me to obtain many grants to conduct many studies. These studies were in art education and the so-called "grey area" (art for persons with disabilities) from our identity article. I kept to the rubric that my major doctoral advisor had set–publish two articles a year. My research shifted towards work with special populations and traumatized adults and children. Continually, I have advocated the need for systematic research and for quantifiable and qualitative data in many of my publications.

One of the things I quickly learned as a new academic (especially in the competitive ethos of Illinois State University) was to work "smartly." Grant final reports became conference presentations, which then were translated into journal articles. I never thought of myself as a writer, and writing was not easy. However, only one time was I asked to revise an article before it was published. Perhaps that explains how hard I worked when I wrote. I think the lessons I learned from my Father added to my skills as a writer. Finally, practice does make perfect.

Because I was writing so many articles and grants, the work became easier for me. I had completed a major research study funded by the National Committee on Arts for the Handicapped (NCAH, now Very Special Arts), Washington, D.C. The study was a review including summaries of all the published research articles using quantifiable data in art, music, dance, and drama for persons with disabilities. The study was commissioned because NCAH needed quantifiable data to support its premise that the arts are a viable means to educate and to increase the quality of life of its constituency. The study resulted in a review of the published research literature on arts for the handicapped, 1971–1981. Quantifiable data are always helpful in establishing rationales for programs. I also conducted a critical analysis on the published research on the visual arts section for persons with handicaps. To include as much cogent information as possible, I developed a charting system. It was the only way I could conduct a critical analysis on the research results. Soon after this article was published, researchers told me that I had written what was known as a "meta-analysis." I think this is another example of my "creative" problem solving/coping ability.

FINALLY FINDING OUT I AM LEARNING DISABLED

After an auto accident in 1981 that required a complete neurological evaluation, I discovered I was learning disabled, not from the accident, but as a generic condition. I was told I would have qualified for special education services had I been identified while in elementary or junior high school. Being learning disabled explained my slowness in reading and a number of other things, such as my inability to follow verbal directions, and my inability to navigate in unknown surroundings (i.e., getting lost all the time when going to unknown places). It also explained my difficulty in learning language (remember how I passed 8th grade Latin).

It also explained how focused I had to be on any endeavor. No matter how long a task took, I always completed it, even if it took two years longer than the funded scope of a project. I think that is why my credo is summed up in the saying at the beginning of this chapter: "We have no word for art, we do everything as well as we possibly can," a Native American saying.

THE FOUNDING OF *ART THERAPY, JOURNAL OF THE AMERICAN ART THERAPY ASSOCIATION*, AND, IN 2000, EDITING THE JOURNAL

Not being privy to the background details of this event, I can only say that apparently AATA was negotiating with Elinor Ulman, Editor and owner of the *American Journal of Art Therapy* (AJAT) so that this publication would become the official journal of the association. When negotiations broke down, AATA decided to establish a new journal. A committee was formed that included those art therapists who had experience with publications. We met several times and finally in 1982 in Washington, D.C., we established the journal. We decided that the first issue would be edited by Linda Gantt and Millie Chapin, thus getting the journal launched and permitting time for the search for an Editor.

This first issue was a landmark for our Association and the field of art therapy. Since Margaret Naumburg died soon after our journal-founding meeting, a special tribute to Naumburg was the lead article in this issue.

In 2000, I was named the Editor of *Art Therapy, Journal of the American Art Therapy Association.* This was both an exhilarating experience and extremely hard work. (Remember I have learning disabilities.) The work was made more difficult because I had just been diagnosed with breast cancer. The entire time I was Editor, I was also dealing with surgery and chemotherapy. Few know how hard that struggle is. Even many who knew my situation "cut me no slack" (including members of the AATA Executive Board), nor did I ask for it. I also did suffer the "slings and arrows" of other AATA members. One member telephoned me about publishing a letter. After she asked how I was, she proceeded to cuss me out using a string of profanities because we were not able to accommodate her in what she considered a timely way.

It is unfortunate that the American Art Therapy Association has to rely on volunteers to fill both the editorships and the journal editorial review board.

Note: Ulman's journal the *Bulletin of Art Therapy* had become, in 1970, the *American Journal of Art Therapy* (AJAT).

Few have the time to devote to this extremely important publication. It was especially rewarding to help unpublished authors and important research studies get into print. My most memorable issue was the one in which I published interviews and stories from art therapists who were involved with 9/11 and its aftermath.

Just before I became editor, a new journal structure was instituted. A Journal Executive Board (JEC) was added that served an important function in developing journal policies and in providing an objective sounding board for the editor. The JEC also had the responsibility to provide oversight for the editors, a much needed check and balance system. The JEC was an enormous help to me, and it presented a real "brain trust" because its members represented art therapy educators and researchers with strong academic credentials from traditional universities. With the exception of one, all had doctorates. The JEC approved my proposal for my Associate Editor, Richard Carolan, to take over while I was away for four months due to my forthcoming Fulbright in Argentina. However, the AATA Executive Board refused to accept this arrangement and I was asked to choose between continuing as Editor, or accepting my Fulbright Award. In the 2002 editorial for the journal issue that followed my resignation, Richard Carolan, Associate Editor, wrote:

> It is important to note that if Frances Anderson had been met with grace and art and, yes, even therapeutic understanding she would not have resigned as editor. It was not Dr. Anderson's intention to resign. The Journal could have continued in the direction that she was leading even while she fulfilled her additional professional contributions in serving as one of art therapy's first Fulbright Scholars. I know that it was Dr. Anderson's intention to integrate this international scholarly work with her commitment to the growth and development of the Journal. It is unfortunate that we have lost her hand in guiding the Journal. Gracious thanks are due her for her willingness to hold the Journal with passion and care.

CLAY GROUPS WITH ADULTS MOLESTED AS CHILDREN AND THEIR INFLUENCE ON MY WORK

In 1990, one of my former students, Karen Deske, contacted me about a grant project for women who were adult survivors of childhood sexual abuse. This began my eight years of clinical work serving a clientele with whom I would never have imagined working. I have to note the importance of my Christian commitment, as it was essential to this difficult work. I felt I was where God wanted me.

This was the hardest clinical work I have ever done. Karen's idea was to find funding for a special nine-week clay group with these women. That began the first of six special clay groups all of which were funded by grants. I felt and still do, that in this work one is confronting evil and that there is a spiritual aspect to healing. In fact, I never started a group without prayer and the staff, the clients, and I were on several prayer lists the entire time. This work had a profound effect on me spiritually and on my artwork.

THE ORIGIN OF "PEOPLE POTS"

The evening of our first clay group, one of the directives was to create a simple clay sculpture of a pet or other animal. We heard horrendous stories about parents killing or torturing pets. Because of the emotional content of these stories, I was literally propelled into the clay studio at school the next evening. I began making small pots with people and animals on them. I titled these "people pots." Gradually the pots and the figures got large, and they began to touch each other. I realized that this was a metaphor for what was happening in the clay groups. The women were connecting with one another.

Frances E. Anderson's People Pot.

We found that clay was an especially powerful medium for art therapy with these women. Intellectualization is one of the ways they survived their abuse. They literally stopped feeling. It is almost impossible for a client to remain emotionally frozen when she manipulates clay. We had reports from the clients' individual therapists that they were making major progress. (All the participants had to be in ongoing individual counseling while in the clay group.) They started dealing with feelings that had been locked up inside from the time of their abuse. One client reported she had been in therapy for 20 years and was making major emotional breakthroughs as a result of her participation in the clay group. Our success also generated jealousy from several of our participants' individual "talk" therapists. The outcome projects for these grants were a monograph, *Courage Together We Heal*, a videotape, four conference presentations, and a journal article.

Our final funded project had a research component to document, with quantifiable data, the effects of the clay group on the participants. We used pretreatment drawings, current treatment drawings and post-treatment drawings of "A Person in the Rain." We also used paper and pencil measures of self-concept, anxiety, and depression. It took over a year to set up the groups and to begin collecting data. Everything went wrong with the data collection, from using the wrong paper and pencil questionnaires as multiple measures to the wrong glazes.

This experience underscored how very hard it is to conduct art therapy research. In spite of all the problems, the clients improved. Positive outcomes for the clients were far more important than any data or documentation.

WRITING A BOOK

In 1970, inspired by my mentor Larry Barnfield and the fact that no book existed on art with children with disabilities, I began photographing and collecting information. Over the next seven years I worked on my first book: *Art for All the Children: A Sourcebook for Impaired Children*, which was published in 1978.

Do not believe anyone who says writing is easy; it is not. Nor is it easy to find a publisher. I sent out a sample chapter to three publishers (one at a time, as it is unethical to send out chapters at the same time to different publishers). One publisher rejected the prospectus, and another publisher kept asking for more chapters (which sort of kept me writing). Finally, when I had written five chapters, I asked for a decision, and the publisher decided not to publish the work. I then sent a letter and my resume to Charles C Thomas, who had published several books on art therapy by Kwiatkowska and Nucho and many books on special education. In the midst of a faculty meeting, I recall opening the reply from Thomas. This publisher did not ask for chapters. Instead, a book contract was enclosed in that initial letter.

Sometimes things come easily (but most often after many efforts). After my book was published, I was at a National Art Education Conference, and in a crowded hotel elevator, a representative from the publisher who had finally decided not to publish my work looked at my name tag and remarked, "We regret not publishing your book." What vindication that statement carried for me!

Some think one can get rich by writing books. I have to say in my case, I never recouped the investment of time and money I put into that first book. The same has been true for my other books.

In 1988, I was in line for a sabbatical from Illinois State University. Knowing that authoring a book was one sure way to be granted a sabbatical, and knowing that my publisher had been after me for several years to revise my first book, I applied for and received a leave to write a second edition of *Art for All the Children*. My next hurdle was to find a host university at which I could spend my sabbatical.

Because I was a member of the prestigious Council for Policy Studies in Art Education (CPSAE) limited in membership to 50 of the best art education scholars in the U.S. and Canada, I had important academic contacts in a number of universities. I had already spent semesters at the University of Illinois at Champaign, University of Arizona, University of Texas, Boston University, and Harvard University at the Bunting Institute. Florida State University (FSU) came to mind. I knew Dr. Jesse Lovano Kerr through my membership in the CPSAE, so I called her up and asked about the possibilities of spending the fall semester at FSU. She immediately began the process for me to be named a Visiting Professor there.

FLORIDA STATE UNIVERSITY AND THE EXPANSION OF THE ART/SPECIAL POPULATIONS PROGRAM

So I began my residency at Florida State University (FSU) and my book revisions. Had I been smart, I would have made revisions five years after the publication of my book, but because I did not, I had a decade of information to assimilate for this project. At the same time, the Chair of the Art Education Department at FSU asked me to help evaluate the efficacy of the master's degree option in art therapy/special populations with emphasis on art for individuals with disabilities. (I think he wanted to eliminate these courses and the related student service activities.)

I had just been appointed to the American Art Therapy Association (AATA) Education Program Approval Board (EPAB). We were reviewing art therapy training programs and were able to hold our spring meeting near Tallahassee. As I reviewed the AATA guidelines for training and the renewal and approval documents that had been submitted for review, I realized that FSU could expand the art therapy/art special populations master's option to meet the AATA program training guidelines. This could be accomplished with the addition of several courses while utilizing some existing courses in research and clinical experience.

I made a proposal, which was given administrative support. Betty Jo Troeger, who was Coordinator of the Art /Special Populations Concentration, had strong ties to the FSU Center for Professional Development (CPD) and had begun the Very Special Arts, Florida organization. She was able to get some funding from the CPD to initiate a special art therapy course the next spring, 1989. When she called me to tell me the news, she asked me for suggestions for guest faculty. I recommended Myra Levick, Doris Arrington, Marcia Rosal, and Larry Barnfield. For the next 10 years the program grew, and I, along with other visiting art therapy faculty, including Vija Lusebrink, helped teach in the summer.

Meanwhile, I struggled with my book revisions. I remember a conversation I had with one of the visiting art therapy faculty in 1990 as I was in the throes of the writing. She said, "I've learned one thing from watching your struggles, never write a book." And I agreed with her! At any rate, I delivered my manuscript in 1990. I had been working on chapters and had never stopped to figure out how long the book would be. My publisher said, "This will be 1,000 pages, but we will honor our contract with you." Realizing that a 1000-page book would not be financially viable for students, I decided to split the manuscript. It then required additions of chapters to each of the manuscripts. In 1991, I delivered the revised version of *Art for All the Children*. In 1994, I completed the other book, *Art-Centered Education and Therapy for Children with Disabilities*. It was published in 1998. It was the hardest work I have ever done.

THE AMERICAN ART THERAPY ASSOCIATION EDUCATION AND PROGRAM APPROVAL BOARD

Beginning in 1988, I served for six years on the AATA Education and Program Approval Board (EPAB). The workload and serious responsibility of evaluating training programs were almost overwhelming. I was able to bring my decade of experience serving on university-wide curricula committees. I also had a broad understanding of curriculum development because of my doctoral studies in art education and curriculum and instruction. The EBAP was (and is) an important oversight entity for the profession and for many programs that did not have the advantage of more formalized curriculum evaluation structures so evident in a large university. Being able to see both the small and the big picture as far as curriculum development is concerned helped me see the viability of the expansion of the FSU program in 1989. I must also add that those who served with me on the EPAB were some of the hardest working professionals I have ever met. We worked as a team for the common good of the profession. Through this board, I met Marcia Rosal, Valerie Appleton, Patricia St. John, Nina Denninger, Mari Fleming, Julia Byers, Mary St. Clair, Lynn Kapitan, and others.

PROFESSIONAL FRIENDSHIP

One of the strengths of being a part of the AATA organization has been the professional friendships and contacts that have been established over the years. That is how I met Judy Rubin, Cay Drachnik, Doris Arrington, Marcia Rosal, David Gussak, Lynn Kapitan, Paula Howie, and many, many more colleagues. Because of my meeting Doris Arrington at an AATA preconference course in 1988, in 1995 I was invited to spend a semester as the Sister Julie Cunningham Professor at the College of Notre Dame (now University of Notre Dame de Namur, UNDN). I have returned every summer since then to teach in the UNDN art therapy program. Doris and I became co-presenters, and co-authors. Doris taught me many things. She told me that it was very important to work with colleagues who share the same values. That wisdom explained many of my conflicts with my colleagues at my university. Few there shared my values. It also explained my friendship with Doris. Among other things, we share a core value as Christians and a core value of hospitality. The parties at AATA conferences given by Doris have been memorable and legendary.

We have shared some unusual moments in putting together those parties. At one conference we tried to drive the wrong rental car. Another (with the permission of the grocery store) took a grocery cart filled with food for the party into the hotel and up to our room. Another value we share is a pragmatic approach to art therapy education. Doris was the first art therapy educator to offer her students the option of writing a grant instead of a thesis. Because I had written and implemented many grants (about 40 then), Doris and I teamed up to offer AATA conference presentations, preconference courses, and a regional symposium on grant writing. These efforts underscore another sage axiom that Doris taught me: if you are going to work together on something, be sure you enjoy your other team members. It was this spirit of teamwork and fun that resulted in one of the most enjoyable pieces of co-authoring for me.

The article on grant writing began with a list of truths (good news and bad news) about grant writing and grant implementation, most of which at least one of us had experienced. We wrote:

- Grants are political!
  PROMISES, PROMISES, PROMISES.
- Grants can be unbelievably easy!
  You've heard about the Oldest Profession . . . and the Second Oldest Profession.
  Grants are a combination of both. You prostitute your mind, your body and your soul.
- Grant writing can be Painfully Disappointing!
  The submission date is THE DAY AFTER you receive the guidelines and the forms.
- Grant writing is knowing your Buzz Words.
  From the time you submit your grant until the time it's reviewed, the buzz words have changed.
- Doing a grant can be a Wonderful Group Experience!
  If you don't do it, it doesn't get done.
- Getting a grant is Ego Building!
  After the first month, you realize that you really need five times as much money to do half as much as you promised!
- A successful grant can give you High Visibility and Professional Integrity!
  Three quarters of the way through the grant you KNOW you should have lied about your budget . . .YOU'RE OUT OF MONEY!
- Grant writing can be a good way to create a Job.
  Grants are like puppy love . . . they don't last.
- Doing a grant is a wonderful Professional Experience.
  Implementing a grant is like jogging–IT FEELS SO GOOD WHEN YOU STOP.

SMILE, THIS IS ARGENTINA

Another life-changing contact that I made through AATA was Marcello Gonzales Magnesco. As AATA's Publications Chair, I led an open forum at the 1990 AATA conference. Marcelo was in attendance and said that there was a great need for art therapy information in Spanish. I took this to heart and with the help of Marcia Rosal and Virginia Minar, AATA translated it's membership brochure into Spanish. Three years later, Marcelo, on behalf of his university, Instituto Universitario Nacional del Arte (IUNA), invited me to come to Buenos Aires to lecture for two weeks.

In June 2000, when I arrived in Buenos Aires and entered the IUNA lecture hall for my first lecture, I noticed that the room was very large. This worried me more than a little. I then was told that there were to be psychiatrists, Jungian analysts, music therapists, teachers, psychologists, artists, and students at my lectures. Just about then, I found out that my videotapes were in the wrong format and could not be shown.

As I gathered my wits, Adriana Fares, the Director of the Art Therapy Program at IUNA, came up to me and said, "Smile, this is Argentina," which I did for the rest of my lectures. The phrase "This is Argentina" was also used by one of the technicians that night, when we could not get the overhead projector to work (apparently a frequent occurrence). So "Smile, this is Argentina" had a double meaning.

In spite of these "glitches" the lectures were well received. There were several hundred attending every night. After every one of my lectures, I received an ovation (sometimes a standing ovation). I would like to think it was totally because of my efforts, however, I think it might also be an Argentine courtesy.

FULBRIGHT SENIOR SCHOLAR AWARD

Upon my return from Buenos Aires, I began the application process for the Fulbright Senior Scholar Award (FSSA). William Fulbright, a U.S. Senator, spearheaded these international exchanges of students, teachers, scholars, and artists over 60 years ago. Since then several types of Fulbright awards have been established. Some awards are for brief summer studies and exchanges. Others fund students from the United States to study abroad and students from around the world to study here. There are also awards for public school and university teacher exchanges and for university research. In the 60 years since these exchanges were established, 250,000 Fulbrights have been awarded.

To receive a Fulbright award, especially an FSSA, is one of the highest honors an academic can achieve. I had been told that there were two major hurdles in achieving the FSSA. The first was a screening by academics in the United States to determine one's qualifications as a researcher and scholar. Then having passed that hurdle, the second was being approved by the Argentine Fulbright Commission. I had been told that the most important aspect of the application for Argentina was the applicant's ability to teach.

It was significant that I was a Distinguished Professor of Art at ISU, had many publications, and had a doctorate from a major research university. These credentials helped me scale the first hurdle. I also had to propose a research project. Having just given two weeks of lectures for the IUNA in Buenos Aires helped me scale the second hurdle, the excellence in teaching.

The review process takes seven months. It was not until April of 2001 that I heard I was (to my knowledge) to be the first art therapist to receive a Fulbright Senior Scholar Award. My tenure in Argentina began in 2002.

The four months of my Fulbright in Buenos Aires were fantastic, memorable, and overwhelming. I had 104 students in my "Art Therapy with Children" course and 40 in my "Art Therapy Research Course." Students had come from Ecuador, Peru, and Brazil to study. The students were exceptionally enthusiastic. I had questions ranging from, "What is your theoretical approach?" to "Can you go through an art therapy session minute by minute?" I also trained the research class to assist in collecting children's drawings that were a part of my Fulbright research project. My research proposal was to establish a benchmark for Argentine children's drawings, ages 7–9. We collected house-tree-person drawings (HTP), and A Favorite Kind of Day (AFKD) drawings as well as Pictures of Someone Picking an Apple from a Tree. In one of the schools, all the students from all the grades wanted to do drawings for us. I now have a huge number of drawings. But then my Indiana University advisor always said, "Get as much data as you can, just in case something goes wrong." That is exactly what I did. In fact I have enough drawings to keep me busy researching for the next 20 years!

The Fulbright Specialists Grant (FSSG) is a new program that started in 2002. The FSSG is limited to professionals who have terminal degrees in one of 12 specific disciplines. As with the FSSA to Argentina, there is no teaching discipline specifically noted as "Art Therapy." Doris Arrington was the first art therapist to be awarded an FSSG. She qualified under the education category and went to teach in Kiev for four weeks in 2003. Inspired by her example, I decided to apply for an FSSG. Because I (like Doris) have a doctorate in education from a research university, and because of my record as author and teacher, I was able to qualify under the education category. The FSSG permits one to travel to any academic institution in any country that participates in the program. The tenure is for two to six weeks.

I received an FSSG and in November 2005, I traveled to Taiwan to be a Fulbright Senior Specialist at the Taiwan Municipal Teachers College and assist Liona Lu with the establishment of the first art therapy program in Taiwan. It seems once again I have become a pioneer!

POSTSCRIPT

Frances E. Anderson (center) receiving the HLM award,
with Marcia Rosal and Doris Arrington.

Like all Honorary Life Members (HLM) of the American Art Therapy Association, I have served the Association in many capacities. The following comments are based on these experiences and my 35 years in the academic world

Need for Systematic Research

For most of my academic career, I have called for systematic research in art therapy. It is absolutely essential that AATA and art therapy's training programs focus on research that addresses issues using quantitative as well as qualitative data. Our survival is tied to this kind of research, and it often is the only research to which other mental health professionals and administrators listen. Training programs need to focus on one or two art therapy issues, and several students need to study various aspects of those issues so that a body of research is built. Our survival depends on good systematic research.

Missed Opportunities

In the mid-1970s, with important federal legislation supporting the placement of children with disabilities into regular school classrooms, there was a tremendous potential for art therapists to gain access to children in this context and I noted this in four publications. That opportunity was seized by Janet Bush in the Florida Dade County Public Schools (and a few other art therapists in other locations). Because of Janet's efforts there have been about 15 art therapists working in the Miami public schools since 1980. Imagine what might have happened if art therapists had been able to gain footholds in other public school systems? Art therapy as a related service was included in the landmark special education Public Law 94142. However, in 1992 these words were dropped from the reauthorization legislation. A major opportunity was lost when this happened. AATA and its members needed to lobby state education departments for a special certification for art therapists so they could work in public schools. In 1988, I argued for this at the national AATA conference because I felt, and still feel, art therapy in public schools is a major growth area for the field. Given our current budget problems on local, state and federal levels, it may be too late for this to happen.

Two other missed opportunities have been in the fields of play therapy and child life. These two areas have gained footholds in mental health and in general hospitals. It would be important to study how child life and play therapy accomplished this. I think we have lost crucial opportunities here. If nothing else, we should have developed special (fairly easily achievable) certifications in art therapy for play therapists and child life specialists.

An Emerging Opportunity

There is a huge tsunami coming. As our service personnel return from Iraq, a huge number will have Post-Traumatic Stress Disorder (PTSD). Art therapy can play a major role in treating these veterans if we can inform the powers that be. At least one treatment team has developed a model for treating trauma, and an important part of that model includes art therapy. I am speaking of the work of Linda Gantt and Luis Tinnen. They have developed the model over the past 30 years, and they have the research data to document the efficacy of their approach. AATA should be lobbying heavily for the inclusion of art therapy in the treatment of PTSD in returning Iraq War veterans. Will this important use of art therapy be another example of a missed opportunity? I hope not.

Rawley Silver

Chapter 17

RAWLEY SILVER

LOOKING BACK TO 1962 AND THEREAFTER

My interest in deafness began when I was deafened accidentally in mid-life. Although most of my hearing eventually returned, I have relied on hearing aids ever since. Being deaf made quite an impression. Painting had been my vocation before the accident; afterward, it became a consolation as well. I began to wonder about the importance of studio art in the lives of others like me and visited art classes in schools for deaf students. In one, I saw teenagers take turns with a single brush, dipping it into a jar of paint and filling in shapes outlined by their teacher. In another school, children were copying their teacher's drawing of a Christmas tree ornament, step-by-step, and adolescents were not allowed to model clay, only pour it into molds.

Outraged by such low expectations, I volunteered to teach art in a school that did not have an art teacher. My offer was accepted conditionally: I must be a graduate student doing research approved by the New York City Board of Education. I enrolled at Teachers College, Columbia University, and wrote a proposal about art for the deaf, my motivation in undertaking graduate studies:

> I believe that art can have greater value for the deaf than creative experience alone. It offers a ready means of communication with those whose channels are already concentrated on the visual. If it can be used to stimulate imagination, spontaneity, abstract thinking, and vocabulary; if it can be developed as a channel of communication whereby feelings and ideas are expressed in pictures and their meanings interpreted, then it can have additional value both for the deaf and those who work with them. The exploration of these possibilities is my purpose in undertaking graduate study and my request for the opportunity to teach at this school.

The proposal was accepted and I began to teach. I received a Master's Degree, and then a doctorate in Fine Arts and Fine Arts Education. In addition, I took courses in Special Education and the only course in art therapy I could find in the 1960s, taught by Margaret Naumburg at New York University during one summer.

The deaf children assigned to my first art class had been diagnosed as emotionally disturbed. Since only one could lip-read or speak and I could not sign, we pantomimed and communicated through gestures at first. Then I made a quick sketch of my husband, two sons, and myself, then pantomimed an invitation to sketch in reply. A girl, age 14 and tall, drew herself as the smallest in her family, isolated from others by a tree. This drawing clearly had psychological meaning for the girl beyond her visual reality. The deaf children's drawings awakened the therapist in me.

Rawley Silver and her family.

Although I loved painting in college, a career in fine arts was considered impossible for women in the 1930s. After graduating, I went to the Smith College School of Social Work. Employed in hospitals at first, I switched to the American Red Cross where I chose work in Europe or the South Pacific during World War II. However, motherhood foiled my plan to follow my soldier husband overseas, and while my children were young, I stayed home, as expected in the 1940s. I took some classes at the Art Students League in New York and began to exhibit paintings in juried group shows. I had my fourth one-person show before the accident when I went deaf, and my 14th in April, 2005.

As a child, I loved to draw, and when art classes in my school ended in the seventh grade, I took the train to New York City on Saturday mornings for classes at Parson's School of Design. There, and later at Cornell, art education consisted of learning how to draw, paint, and model clay "from life." In college, I was impressed–imprinted–by the aesthetics of tenth century China, particularly the painter, Ching Hao, who wrote that the goal of an artist was to capture the essential qualities of the chosen subject.

Rawley Silver as a child, "Up a Tree."

Neuroscientists today seem to agree. According to Zeki, the preeminent function of both art and the visual brain is to acquire knowledge about the world by selecting what is essential and discarding what is superfluous. Neurons in the brain's visual pathways search for constancies, just as artists search for the constant, essential features of objects and situations.

Posing for art classes was a way to earn tuition then, but by the 1950s, students had to find other ways because recognizable subject matter had become taboo. For example, Clive Bell, a venerated guru, proclaimed that "To seek behind form, the emotions of life is a sign of defective sensibility always," and that "the representative element in a work of art may or may not be harmful; always it is irrelevant."

After teaching deaf students in four schools while attending graduate school, I realized, despite Clive Bell, that representation in art was pertinent and that seeking "behind form" the emotions of life was the way to go for me. The findings of my doctoral project supported several conclusions, among them that art symbols can serve as instruments for organizing thoughts, recalling, generalizing, imagining, and evaluating; that studio art experiences can provide opportunities to exercise control, experience success, and express anger and fear in acceptable ways; and that drawings and paintings can be used to assess knowledge, abilities, interests, attitudes, and needs.

In 1963, I received a letter from Elinor Ulman, the editor of the *Bulletin of Art Therapy*, asking me to contribute an article to the journal I had written on art expression and education with the deaf. I had submitted the article previously to a journal for educators of deaf students, and after waiting three months without a reply, asked for its return. I then sent it to another journal in this field whose editor rejected it promptly. When I tried a journal for art educators, however, it not only was published and listed in Elinor's journal, but also abstracted in *Rehabilitation Literature*. The abstract prompted a letter from a journal for educators of deaf students, asking if I could write another article on the same subject. Yes, indeed, I could, and did.

The year our oldest son received his Bachelor of Arts Degree., I received my Doctorate in Fine Arts Education (Ed.D.) and a grant from the U.S. Office of Education: I was to demonstrate (if I could) that deaf children and adults had aptitudes, interest, and vocational opportunities in the visual arts. Although the Board of Trustees of the sponsoring organization had approved the project, its administrators had doubts. One warned that anyone who came to my art class would expect to be paid. Another advised that my biggest problem would be finding anyone interested in art. They were mistaken. After announcing that art classes were available, we received so many applications that we added a second term to accommodate the 54 students who applied.

One of the adolescents, "Charlie," seemed highly intelligent even though he could not talk. For example, when his art class visited a museum, he led the way because he could read a map of the museum galleries held upside down in my hand as we walked. I tried to interest psychologists in testing his intelligence, but failed. I wrote to three specialists: One did not reply and another advised me to have Charlie tested, but the third, E. Paul Torrance, sent copies of his *Torrance Test of Creative Thinking* and offered to score the results.

I gave Torrance's test to 11 deaf children and adults and sent their responses to him. Torrance wrote:

> While the records were being scored in my office, several visitors saw it [sic] and were immensely impressed. This occurred both among those sophisticated about testing and those not so sophisticated. All felt that his performance [Charlie's] reflected a high order of ability to acquire information, form relationships, and in general, to think.

I tried again: I sent a copy of Torrance's letter to the psychologist in Charlie's school, but he was not impressed. He replied that Charlie's performance on the Torrance Test "changes nothing" because "language comes first, and there is a limit to what you can do without language."

"What are the limits?" I asked. I began a search for answers in a demonstration project. I invited teachers to observe the art classes and then respond to questionnaires. Most found the deaf students were as independent, sensitive, original, and expressive as their hearing students. The only observers who thought otherwise taught deaf students only. Perhaps they believed art activities resembled sign language. During the 1960s, manual communication was forbidden in most schools for deaf students. It was claimed that students must learn to lip-read and speak or else remain isolated from the hearing world.

When the demonstration project ended in 1967, the adults formed an art club to continue visiting museums together. Three enrolled in art classes. One was given a one-person show. Another went on to study sculpture in college and continues to maintain a pottery studio. A fifth returned to his home in India where he initiated annual art exhibitions of drawings and paintings by deaf children, at first in India, then expanded elsewhere in Asia. My correspondence with some members of the art club still continues.

SMITHSONIAN TRAVELING EXHIBITIONS

In 1969, the Smithsonian Institute began to circulate an exhibition of artwork by my deaf students and extended the tour until 1976. The exhibition was an attempt to demonstrate that studio art experience can be especially helpful in the education of children with hearing impairments by providing opportunities to express thoughts and feelings that cannot be put into words. Like the demonstration project, a second aim was to demonstrate that these deaf children have aptitudes, interests and occupational dreams that were largely unexplored. Explanatory texts accompanied the drawings and paintings, which were presented in groups to illustrate Abstract Thinking, Imaginary Play, Personal Involvement, Emotional Outlet, and Clues to Interests and Concerns. The Smithsonian showed the exhibit at art centers around the United States. Then the exhibit was shown by the Metropolitan Museum of Art, which published a catalogue, *Shout in Silence, Visual Arts and the Deaf,* and invited the exhibitors to an opening reception. We had a grand reunion and agreed to continue the exhibition. This second tour of the exhibit began at the Kennedy Center in Washington, D.C., and continued until 1987.

The Smithsonian also circulated a second exhibition from 1979 to 1983. It concerned art procedures used to assess and develop cognitive skills, nonverbally if need be. Eventually, I donated both exhibitions to the Junior Arts Center in Los Angeles.

During the 18 years of the traveling exhibitions, many letters, photos and newspaper clippings came in. These were given to the archives of Gallaudet University (a university for the deaf).

BEGINNINGS OF THE AMERICAN ART THERAPY ASSOCIATION (AATA)

In 1968, a group of art therapists met to discuss the possibility of establishing an American society of art therapists. I learned of the meeting because someone sent me a copy of its May 14th minutes stating that those present had agreed that the society "would do much to help establish Art Therapy as an important ancillary psychiatric modality." Challenges followed: In a letter sent me in September 1968, Elinor Ulman and Edith Kramer proposed instead that art therapists "look to an independent place in the broad field of special education and rehabilitation rather than limiting their sphere to that of an ancillary psychiatric discipline." I agreed with their statement, but in 1970, was among those who presented papers at a conference of the American Art Therapy Association, and became a Registered Art Therapist (ATR).

FROM OBSERVATION TO EXPERIMENTATION

Although much can be learned from observation, described in words and illustrated by drawings and paintings, I began to realize that they were not enough: I had to conduct successful experiments if I hoped to convince doubters that art procedures could be used to develop and assess cognitive skills.

I applied for and received a grant to conduct a New York State Urban Education Project in a school for children with language and hearing impairments. As stated in my proposal:

> The purpose of this project was threefold: first, to help an experimental group of children develop mathematical and logical ideas; second, to develop procedures for teaching these ideas through drawing and painting; third, to develop procedures for evaluating cognitive achievements through drawing and painting.

The children who participated had impairments caused by damage to the brain rather than the ear. They included 68 children and adolescents. The experimental group attended art classes while the unselected students remained with their classroom teachers, and served as controls. After the project ended, I asked a psychologist, John Kleinhans, Ph.D., to analyze the data. He found highly significant differences between experimental and control groups in favor of the experimental group. In addition, I gave the pretest to 60 unimpaired students in a public school. To our surprise, Kleinhans found no significant difference in pretest scores of impaired and unimpaired groups, but significant differences in post-test scores in favor of the impaired experimental students.

"Burt," age 13, one of the students in the experimental group, had receptive and expressive language disorders, severe hearing loss, and an I.Q. of 43. Before the art program began, I asked his homeroom teacher to rate the abilities of her students. She gave Burt the lowest score for his ability to select named objects, combine words into sentences, group objects into categories, or associate new information with what he knew. She rated her students again after the three-month art program, and again six months later at the end of the school year. Burt's total pre-test score was 36 points; his post-test score was 66 points of the maximum 70 points.

THE ART THERAPY PROGRAM AT THE COLLEGE OF NEW ROCHELLE, NEW YORK

Sister Justin McKiernan was head of the Art Department at the College of New Rochelle when we met in 1974. She decided to establish an art therapy program in the graduate school where I served as Adjunct Associate Professor until 1980 when I retired. One of the courses consisted of a series of lectures by prominent art therapists. The art therapists included Elinor Ulman, Myra Levick, Edith Kramer, Bernard Levy, Hanna Kwiatkowska, Elaine Rapp, and others. I sketched them while they talked.

STRUGGLES AND ACCOMPLISHMENTS

A major struggle for me was trying to persuade educators in schools for deaf students that the visual arts could be useful to them. In 1961 and also in 1995, I submitted manuscripts to a journal addressed to educators of deaf students. Although the 1995 article described two research studies which showed that deaf students had significantly higher scores than hearing students, and a Russian study by Kopytin in 2002 showed that deaf students had equal abilities to "normal" children, the editors of these journals were not interested and eventually I withdrew the manuscripts. I published these results in my book, *Three Art Assessments: Silver Drawing Test of Cognition and Emotion; Draw a Story, Screening for Depression & Stimulus Drawings and Techniques.*

Another struggle has been my own hearing impairment. The accident left me with "recruitment," a hearing disorder that leaves a small window between sounds loud enough to hear, and sounds too loud to bear. The strain of trying to hear across classrooms and trying to hear what is said from a distance can be tiring, particularly when there is background noise. After teaching art therapy courses for six years at the College of New Rochelle, I retired. On the other hand, being hard-of-hearing has compensations, such as escaping some noise. Missing the key word in a sentence can be hilarious as well as confusing. Suddenly realizing you mistook a key word for a word that means something else, can be like the punch line of a joke.

As for accomplishments, they include the Honorary Life Membership award from the American Art Therapy Association (AATA), research awards from AATA and my three art assessments. About the Honorary Life Membership award, it was written:

Rawley Silver, Ed.D., ATR, has substantially broadened the scope of art therapy by her research dealing with disability due to neurological deficiencies, communication deficiencies, or both. Starting with her work in 1966 with the deaf and language impaired, she became the first person to develop the systematic use of art for a wide range of children and adults with cognitive deficits. Application of her innovative evaluation procedures and remedial techniques, particularly in the field of special education, is helping children acquire conceptual skills often denied them in an overly verbal educational system.

Dr. Silver has published many articles and presented several exhibits. She summed up her findings in an influential book, *Developing Cognitive and Creative Skills Through Art*, published in 1978. Recently, Special Child Publications has published *The Silver Drawing Test of Cognitive and Creative Skills*, a nonverbal instrument for assessing individual progress.

The HLM plaque has hung on the wall beside my desk ever since.

In 1976, 1980, and 1992, I received the American Art Therapy Association research award for research with deaf students and those with learning disabilities. I also received the AATA research award in 1996 for my art assessment the *Silver Drawing Test of Cognition and Emotion.*

In November 1976, AATA's annual award for research went to my paper first presented at the 1975 Conference, and then published. The paper described two studies that used art procedures to assess and improve the cognitive abilities of children. It reviewed findings of the New York State Urban Education Project and a second study, which found that the teaching and testing procedures developed for students with hearing impairments could also help students with learning disabilities. A second study asked the question, "Would the teaching and testing procedures developed in the State Education Project be effective with students who had an opposite constellation of skills-verbal strengths and visual–spatial weaknesses?" The study results found that graduate students could also use the procedures.

In 1980, the American Art Therapy Association's research award went to a project, funded by the National Institute of Education, in which six art therapists, including myself, worked with 84 children who were performing at least one year below grade level in reading or math. The aim was to assess and develop the children's cognitive skills using the same techniques developed in the previous studies. In each school, individual children made dramatic gains in all test scores.

In 1992, the American Art Therapy Association research award went to my study "Age and Gender Differences Expressed Through Drawings: A Study of Attitudes Toward Self and Others." The responses included drawings by 531 males and females in five age groups of children and adults. The 338 drawings of human subjects matched the genders of those who drew them. This tendency peaked in childhood, and then dropped to its lowest level among younger adults. Among older adults, however, gender differences emerged. Most of the older men drew male subjects, reversing the decline from the sample of boys, whereas the decline continued among older women. A small percentage of men drew female subjects, The older adults expressed more negative attitudes than any other age group. On the other hand, they drew more humorous fantasies than any other age group, often self-disparaging humor. More older men drew fantasies about stressful relationships than any other age or gender group whereas the smallest proportion emerged among adolescent girls.

As for gender differences, the proportion of drawings about assaultive relationships changed with age among females but remained stable among males. That is, the older women drew the most assaultive fantasies surpassing not only their male counterparts but also all of the male age groups. In drawings about caring relationships, almost no gender differences emerged, but the converse age and gender interaction was found. Almost half the number of younger men drew fantasies about caring relationships, surpassing not only their female counterparts but also all other male and female groups. In 1996, the research award was given to the *Silver Drawing Test of Cognition and Emotion.*

THE ART ASSESSMENTS

The three assessments present different sets of stimulus drawings but the same "Drawing from Imagination" task. The directions are: choose two stimulus drawings, imagine something happening between the subjects you choose, and then draw what you imagine. Respondents are encouraged to alter the stimulus drawings and add their own ideas. As they finish drawing, they are asked to add titles or stories; and when appropriate, talk about them. The test is based on the theory that choosing from a limited set of stimuli is more likely to trigger associations with personal experiences than unstructured tasks

The first assessment, *Stimulus Drawing & Techniques in Therapy, Development, and Assessment*, includes 56 stimulus drawings. It was first published in 1981. This assessment is for children or adults who had brain injuries, learning disabilities, dementia, sexual abuse, or psychiatric disorders.

The second assessment, *The Silver Drawing Test of Cognition and Emotion* (SDT), has 15 stimulus drawings presented in test booklet form. Drawings from Imagination, Drawing from Observation, and Predictive Drawing are each designed to assess one of the three concepts said to be fundamental in reading and mathematics. This assessment is based on the premise that cognitive skills can be evident in visual as well as verbal conventions and that these skills which are traditionally identified, assessed, and developed through words, can also be identified through drawings.

The Silver Drawing Test was standardized on approximately 1,000 children, adolescents, and adults in the United States, 2,000 in Brazil, and 700 in Russia. Regardless of culture, cognitive scores increased with age and level of education. Adults were the same across cultures and no significant gender differences emerged.

Suicidal fantasies appeared in some responses to the "Drawing from Imagination" task, raising the question whether it could be used to screen for depression. The test is based on the premise that responses to the drawing task may reflect depressive illness. Several investigations led to the third assessment, *Draw a Story, Screening for Depression* (DAS). DAS has been administered to 1,028 children, adolescents, and adults by art therapists in various parts of the country. A recent study asked if DAS could be used to screen for aggression as well as depression. Results indicated that aggression was significantly related. Significant gender differences also emerged.

Most recently, the study's findings were expanded when it was found that DAS could be used to identify children and adolescents at risk for aggression as well as depression. My edited book, *Aggression and Depression Assessed through Art, Identifying Children and Adolescents at Risk*, presents responses by aggressive students in the experimental group and a control group, as well as subgroups and individuals. It also compares respondents and genders in Russia as well as in the United States, and examines changes and consistencies in emotional states after therapeutic interventions.

Questions about self-images in responses to the DAS have also been explored. Fifty-three boys, ages 13–18, incarcerated in California, drew responses, talked about their drawings with an art therapist and identified a self image in them. The findings suggested that discussion was not essential for identifying self images, and can be bypassed, particularly in urgent situations such as suicide when circumstances or time limitations make interviews impossible.

BELIEFS ABOUT ART THERAPY

I believe that research in art therapy should be objective as well as subjective, quantitative a well as qualitative. Unless we can combine art experiences and psychological insights with scientific evidence, we convince only ourselves of the contributions art therapy can make to knowledge about human intelligence, emotional needs, and behavior.

In addition, I believe that qualified art therapists can make contributions that artists and psychotherapists cannot provide, that subtle meanings elude artists with no background in psychotherapy as well as psychotherapists with no background in studio art. On the other hand, I also believe that art therapists, psychotherapists, artists, and art educators, should be partners rather than adversaries. We all know the redemptive power of drawing, painting, and modeling clay; that art experiences invite contemplation, and that children and adults use the arts to express thoughts and feelings about themselves and their worlds. We also know that these expressions provide access to fantasies and emotional states.

Rawley Silver's drawing of Dame Edith Sitwell.

Looking into my crystal ball, I see art therapy becoming a handsomely paid profession that interweaves the visual arts with psychological and neurological sciences, contributing not only to psychotherapy and rehabilitation but also to the education of typical students in elementary and secondary schools as well as in college and graduate school programs.

Gladys Agell celebrating 10 years at Vermont College of Norwich
with President W. Russell Todd.

Chapter 18

GLADYS AGELL

MY PAST, YOUR FUTURE

CHILDHOOD: NEW YORK

Evenings, my father returned home bringing me legal pads for drawing. I relished the long yellow pads with pale blue lines. I carry in memory a drawing of my father I made on these magical pads when I was about three years old. It was a full length, frontal view of him in a suit and oversized fedora. I think that picture was the origin of my enduring fascination with figurative work.

People-watching, also, has been a lifelong pursuit learned early. My early life was nomadic. My parents often said it was "cheaper to move than to paint," so move we did. I was born in New York City; we then moved to Freeport, Long Island, home of the Dolly sisters, and when I was seven we moved to Brooklyn. Among my favorite activities was to sit at our living-room window and watch the human parade. I fantasized about each person outside, taking clues from the clothes they wore, the gestures they made, and the people they were with. I spent so much time at my window watch that I finally put a pillow on the sill so my elbows wouldn't continue to get scraped.

My family moved back to New York a few years later, when my interest was taken by royalty. I had multiple paper dolls of the English princesses, Elizabeth and Margaret, so it followed that I drew multitudes of beautiful princesses with long blue dresses and long blond tresses. I never could get the princesses quite right. I used reams of paper trying, usually in arithmetic class. My passion for drawing those figures helped me to understand perseveration.

Soon after, I was captivated by Sonja Henie and thought ice skaters were made for graphic investigation. My fifth grade teacher voiced admiration for my drawing and instructed me to make a linoleum cut of my best skater. My lack of cutting skill destroyed the dynamic quality of the original drawing, but taught me a valuable lesson: When invention bears fruit, recreating the image in another medium may result in a second-rate imitation. Such is the case in the American Art Therapy Association's (AATA's) recent counseling debacle, which demonstrated that art therapy cannot be art counseling. Art therapy would have much to lose if ever such a transition would occur.

But back to the more distant past, in high school I fell in love with Daumier and tried mightily to paint and draw as he did. Human foibles of ballerinas, orchestra conductors, and outcasts attracted me. My art-making history has been the foundation for my interest in people and visa versa. I'm certain that visual vigilance and art making of people influenced my becoming an art therapist and psychotherapist. It seemed the natural outcome of my proclivities, however, not to be realized for decades. I was a college dropout.

Gladys Agell in adolescence.

HOW I ENTERED THE FIELD: COMMUTING FROM ROCKLAND COUNTY

The consequence of my early marriage was that I didn't complete my college education. As it turned out, I didn't complete the marriage either. I divorced after I had three children. A psychologist friend recommended I return to school for a degree so that I might find a job and be independent of my ex-husband. Though I had moved to Rockland County, an hour from New York City, I nevertheless decided I would be a commuting student at New York University (NYU). I had been volunteering at the Museum of Modern Art's Peoples Art Center. Victor D'Amico directed the program and had been my high school advisor. I therefore called upon him for advice once more. He recommended NYU's art education program. (Coincidentally, Margaret Naumburg had recently been offering a course in the department but not the year I enrolled.)

Psychology and art were the focuses of my Bachelor's degree. Soon after I received my degree, I enrolled in courses with both Margaret Naumburg and Edith Kramer. Margaret Naumburg taught at the New School for Social Research. Edith Kramer was teaching at Turtle Bay Music School. Antipathy between them, I felt, made my position precarious. It proved increasingly unnerving when Edith also took up teaching at the New School. I feared my duplicity would be discovered, nevertheless, I continued to take courses from both. I'm amused now to recall meeting with a psychologist who remarked that I was overqualified when I told her about the four art therapy courses I had completed. Years later I found out Edith was indifferent to my being in Margaret's class as well as hers. I never told Margaret, who was less open-minded than Edith. (ATR, ATR-BC, HLM, the AATA credentials and award hadn't been developed yet.)

D'Ann Fago, an artist, was leaving her position at St. Agatha's residential school. Under the auspices of Catholic Charities, the school predominantly served children who were court referrals for one reason or another. The position was part-time but I grabbed it. A social worker acquaintance was developing an out-patient program for formerly hospitalized patients of the county psychiatric hospital. The program, under the umbrella of Rockland County Community Mental Health Association, was one of the country's first community mental health services. Thus in no time, I found myself with two part-time jobs, one with troubled children, the other with troubled adults. Life was perfect!

When I think of my career, I realize how fortunate I was in the people I knew. Many shaped my perception and provided me with opportunity.

ACCOMPLISHMENTS: VERMONT

Elinor Ulman and Edith Kramer had presented a workshop at Goddard College which stirred the interest of the summer dean, Francis Voigt. I had been Chief of Activity Therapy at the Vermont State Hospital when Francis Voigt asked me to recommend an art therapist to develop a program at the college. Working at the hospital was thrilling and I was loathe to leave. I recommended the only other art therapist in Vermont, Mary Willmuth. As chief of activity therapy at the hospital, I was responsible for art, recreation, and occupational therapy departments. Three terrific department supervisors and twenty-six therapists served a population of approximately 1,000 patients. Amongst us, we developed a service that included every conceivable and inconceivable modality.

Mary Willmuth declined the Goddard offer. I took the position and with Fran, developed the program . . . nights . . . days were filled. I continued to work full-time at the hospital until the day the Goddard art therapy program opened. I gambled on establishing a program that was like no other. Edith Kramer questioned my judgment, believing the schedule was too demanding and that the program wouldn't survive. However, we attracted students from all over the country, as well as foreign students. They survived and so did the program. This program enabled students who had established lives to remain in their geographic areas for internships with the exception of three months in the summers. Foreign students were required to secure an internship in the United States or Canada so that I or another full-time faculty member could site-visit them. Coursework was full-time in the summer. Mornings, students were in classes, in the afternoon they were at fieldwork sites in central Vermont. Because between summers students would be in internships far from the college, I reasoned that a summer fieldwork experience would prepare them for their internships and inform us if there were problems in fieldwork that would adversely affect the internship. Unique to the program were visits by another faculty member or myself to each person at the intern site to observe students conducting both individual and group therapy, as well as their on-site and off-site supervision sessions.

I collaborated with Dean Voigt in program development beginning in January 1976, and in June 1976 we opened at Goddard College with 25 students, three summer faculty, and me. Three years later I was disenchanted with the Goddard rhetoric. Thus, after a summer of negotiations, and the art therapy graduation, Fran Dodd, assistant director, and I stuffed easels and drawing boards into her station wagon and drove the 10 miles to Vermont College of Norwich University (VC). That was in 1979. In 1981, five Goddard programs joined us at Vermont College.

The program thrived at Vermont College. I had great faculty. Bernie Levy, Janie Rhyne, Robin Goodman, Linda Gantt, Carol Cox, Rachel Garber, Paula Howie, Barbara Sobol, Katherine Williams, Josie Abbenante, Marcia Rosal, Kay Stovall, Nancy Humber and Millie Chapin were some of the instructors who taught multiple summers. Elinor Ulman was an annual guest lecturer who presented the *Ulman Personality Assessment Procedure* (then it was a diagnostic procedure).

For several summers, new courses were added, field placements multiplied, and internship sites were developed. Each time we admitted a new student, a new site was found. And lo and behold, when we had finally become a 60 credit program, we were closed. Sixty credits was unattractive to enrolled students who could get a Master's degree with 48 credits. The candidate pool of potential students who would spend three summers in Vermont lacked swimmers. In my opinion, my decision to become a 60 credit program was premature. In 2002, Norwich closed the program.

It was a gorgeous program. We had wonderful faculty, supervisors, and students. I enjoyed every moment and there were billions of moments.

THE AMERICAN JOURNAL OF ART THERAPY

In 1984 Elinor Ulman was considering closing the *American Journal of Art Therapy* (AJAT) (formerly the *Bulletin of Art Therapy*). The *AJAT* was in financial straits. This was the first professional journal in art therapy, founded and published by Elinor beginning in 1961, at which time it was largely responsible for bringing art therapists together and establishing a "field." Informing artists working in mental health agencies and special schools that what they were doing was art therapy was enlightening.

The demise of the *American Journal of Art Therapy* was intolerable to me. I convinced Norwich University to buy the *AJAT*. I became coordinator, a prestigious gopher until 1986, when I became editor and Elinor became executive editor and trained me. She was in Vermont in the summers and on other occasions during the year. I would also visit her in Washington. I adored working with Elinor; she had wit and wisdom that were remarkable, irreplaceable, and sometimes irrepressible.

As an art therapy educator, I was accustomed to questionable grammar and syntax. To find this was also the case among colleagues long respected in the field was shocking. I was also surprised at the boldly bald statements made that were uncorroborated by research or even common knowledge. Assumptions were made about art therapy outcomes that were inaccurate. In the eyes of authors, art therapy was the "promised land." In some instances,

I believe art therapists were governed by their enthusiasm for their work. In other cases, I suspect, they were governed by their aspiration to be accepted. In either case, we edited like mad. Within the first five years of *AJAT* at Norwich, we were able to operate in the black and though Norwich didn't get rich from the journal, we were able to show a modest profit for most of my tenure with the journal.

Finally, getting my Ph.D. (1990) in clinical psychology was a great, but wearing experience. I worked full-time at Vermont College, did homework 'til the wee hours, and left many a statistic exam running to catch a plane to make a site-visit. But it was worth it to hear my mother call me doctor.

Working toward my doctorate supported my clinical work, teaching, and my responsibilities as *AJAT* editor. I had to examine my assumptions carefully. I will never forget when I added my "insights" to a drawing that was being considered by an assessment class on projective techniques. The drawing was a portrait of a woman with a broad grin that revealed several teeth. I was expansive in my analysis of the face and particularly the teeth. My peers pointed out the difficulty of concealing teeth when mouths are open. That and other comments brought me abruptly to my senses, and I became careful to have reliable confirmation when venturing an interpretation. That and other-like experiences when writing papers and especially when writing my dissertation shaped my editing.

In the last years of the *AJAT*, I was disappointed in the many articles we received that were poorly written and lacked substantive ideas. We were also receiving submissions from practitioners in other mental health fields who were using art in their clinical work and had a confused idea of what art therapy was about. But the articles that were the most difficult were those that presumed to be empirical studies, from art therapists and other mental health professionals as well. Therefore, though I regretted Norwich's decision to close the journal, my feelings were mixed. I was disheartened by the articles I read and was sometimes uncomfortable when compelled to publish a few, often from authors of prestige.

STRUGGLES

When I became President of the American Art Therapy Association (AATA) in 1983, I, with my board of directors, inherited an association on the brink of bankruptcy. As a board, we had to move offices, find an administrator/manager, and cut costs unmercifully. We had been renting space from the American Counseling Association that we could no longer afford. Dissatisfaction with our executive director required that we find a way to manage the day-to-day business needs of the association. Helen Landgarten was the new treasurer. She and I were hardly on speaking terms, but in no time, collaborating to ward off disaster brought us together, and we became close associates and closer friends. Helen had a plan. Her plan was to give up the national office and for me to handle all the association business out of my home. I had just started my psychology internship at a Veteran's Association Medical Center on Long Island and was renting a small apartment. The internship was an eight-to-four position that gave me more time than I had administrating the program, but I couldn't visualize myself as "girl Friday." Fortunately, I convinced Helen that her plan would make everybody crazy, and AATA would surely go "down the tubes" if we were dependent on my filing. We formed a search committee who found Cate, a management firm.

I recall four or five of the board members going to George Cates' office with me to interview him. It felt like a crowd and we were fairly green in our negotiations, but we were able to strike a satisfactory deal. Because we were in dire straits, the first year Cate gave us bargain rates, and we needed that.

That was a difficult time for all of us. We had major battles, left over from the previous board, and the organization, that never got resolved. We all struggled to keep the association afloat, though we had conflicting ideas about how to accomplish that.

Gary Barlow held three "e" chair positions: ethics, education, and editor of our new journal. The *American Journal of Art Therapy* had been the official American Art Therapy Association journal, but during Georgiana Jungels' presidency, she represented a group who was dissatisfied with Elinor Ulman's editorial position and policies, and successfully disenfranchised the *AJAT* and created *Art Therapy, the Journal of the American Art Therapy Association.* I did everything I could to persuade Gary to give up at least one of his positions. I thought he was overburdened and would not be able to do it all, and I was right.

Bobbi Stoll sat at the opposite end of the board table (we were a larger board then, I think we were 12 members, so it was a long table) and stared at me. I never could figure out what she was thinking, but when she spoke she presented a significant point of view that was usually not mainstream, but original and worthy of regard. Nina Denninger was briefly secretary of AATA, but resigned in midstream. Through it all, the Cate organization performed well and provided us with the stability we needed. Additionally, George Cate trained Sandy Graves [Kagin, Alcorn] president-elect, and me in strategic planning, and our first strategic plan was developed.

It was either our first conference or first new board meeting, when George Cate surprised us. He sent a chauffeured limousine to the airport to pick up Sandy Graves and me. This was in contrast to our cost-cutting practices of doubling-up in modest accommodations and dining at Pizza Hut[8].

When we received our next management contract, lo and behold, the management fee was considerably higher than our first, and we believed we couldn't afford the fee. So once again a search committee was formed, and we found our present management firm, Stygar Associates.

It all looks easy now. Hindsight helps. But those were a "hard day's night."

Gladys Agell saying "Listen Ladies."

BELIEFS

Art therapy is a therapy for people who are able to use art materials in a psychologically productive manner. Art therapy is not for everyone. I'm stating the obvious because many art therapists commit to the belief that art is necessarily a creative enterprise that has intrinsic value for most people and is a "nonthreatening" therapy. Some go so far as to say that art therapy is for everyone. Are we going to coerce clients into using materials? I hope not. There is no doubt in my mind that art therapy is unattractive to some; materials don't entice them. On those occasions when a patient who lacks both interest and skill in art making is referred to art therapy, the venture usually serves to generate feelings of frustration and inadequacy, not only for the patient, but for the therapist as well.

Guiding people in becoming aware of their expectations for themselves and in determining whether those expectations truly represent what they wish or, for that matter, are even realistic is generally my focus for outpatient therapy. I anticipate therapy with adults will yield information that bolsters constructive decision-making, promotes open-mindedness, and neutralizes pernicious affect. That it cures people is humbug. Cure is a byproduct of the medical model. Except in cases when actual organic symptoms precipitate dysfunctional behavior, I have difficulty accepting the sickness model. In my mind, mental illness has been a curious and destructive term.

I believe art therapy, like many human undertakings, includes a struggle among conflicting needs of the client, but more often than not, between the client and therapist.

There is an unvoiced mandate for the client to relinquish familiar ground or ways of thinking or being. Giving up habitual behaviors that lack purpose, and even may be toxic, may leave a feared void. Sometimes that struggle bears unsatisfactory results. I certainly have had sessions when the client uses art materials to avoid discussing substantive but unsettling material. Those are the sessions when the picture is unusually pretty!

On the other hand, if all art therapy sessions involved resistance, I wouldn't continue to practice art therapy. Thus, in the times when a picture will emerge that is "unbidden" (a term used by Pat Buoye Allen that I find perfect), I am filled with admiration for art therapy and find it magical. That event signals a breakthrough, and therapy thereafter often moves swiftly and successfully.

There are times, as well, when progress happens, but not only in the art therapy session, although it may begin in art therapy, but it is an ongoing process which, if the therapy is successful, may continue long after sessions are terminated.

ART THERAPY'S MEANING FOR ME

Art therapy has provided me with a satisfying, multifaceted career in teaching, in editing, and as a clinician. It hasn't changed my life, but it certainly has added to my life.

Because of art therapy I had an entrée into the mental health field. I worked in special schools, residential and day schools, for community mental health programs, in a state psychiatric hospital, in a Veteran's Medical Center, and in private practice.

My doctoral internship at a VA hospital was a psychology internship in the psychology department with psychologist's for supervisors. I used art therapy part of the time, and it was appreciated by patients and staff. It worked well with people, especially several combat veterans who didn't have the language to express their daytime nightmares but who could use art materials to get their message across. I have drawings by veterans of Vietnam, Korea, and World War II.

One World War II veteran had worked with many therapists at the Veteran's Administration with little success. Our sessions were going poorly, as well. He had told his story so many times that it angered him to repeat it to me. One day, for no reason that I can think of then or now, I decided to try the Winnicott Squiggle technique. "Norman" drew a linear pencil figure that reminded me of a bifurcated molar. My job was to add to the figure so that it was a recognizable image. I resisted completing the squiggle and tried to find/see another image in the lines. I gave up finally and drew the one short line that would identify this as a tooth. Nothing was said by either one of us and the session ended soon after.

The next day, I had an early morning appointment with "Norman." I waited but he didn't appear. Soon after, I received a call from a nurse on his unit. During the night, he had an abscess rupture and was sent to the dentist that morning. I never did find out whether it was a molar.

Art therapy paved the way for me to be an art therapy educator, to work with colleagues and students who stretched my mind. And it provided me with the opportunity to wheel and deal in an interesting, complex institution. The military and middle-of-the-road and progressive/liberal civilians [at Norwich] were quite a mix for a university.

DO WE WANT A FUTURE FOR ART THERAPY?

Because we don't have licensure, employment is in jeopardy. Over thirty years ago, Bernie Levy passionately warned us about the imminence of third-party payers and the need to secure licensure to be able to work. The program approval process and the ATR and BC credentials (Art Therapist Registered and Board Certified, respectively) were developed as forerunners for professional credibility and licensure. Presently art therapists are turning to other licensed professions for credentialing. Once licensure is secured, many art therapists affiliate with the licensing profession and abdicate from art therapy. This, in part, reflects the decrease in American Art Therapy Association membership and regional associations.

Aside from a few state associations, most states lack art therapy licensure. Interesting that Mississippi, a state that has a minimum number of art therapists, has licensure. Clearly they did something right. Has AATA learned from them? AATA has dragged behind.

AATA's legislative consultant Matt Dunne recommended two years ago that we undertake efficacy research. He also recommended that a psychiatrist be the lead researcher, a serious mistake, in my estimation. It's time we demonstrated our competence, rather than attributing successful outcomes to patronage. Certainly, art therapists can include psychiatrists, psychologists, and underwater zoologists as collaborators, but the lead author must be an art therapist. In any event, it is a moot question, squabbling amongst ourselves and irresolute leadership have impeded beginning research.

Indeed, in general our research showing is poor. Rather than admit we don't know how to do research, we continue to play at it, rather than get adequate research training or find researchers who know what they are doing and are willing to guide us. We waste money on consultants who give us information we could have figured out ourselves. We pursued the American Counseling Association (ACA), hoping they would admit us under their umbrella. Our membership was told what we were doing before we knew whether we could do it. We were turned down. ACA wanted no part of us, thank heaven. It seems that not only are we slow (30 years), but we are also bunglers.

It is time we really look at what art can do, do some good research, and begin to think seriously about the field. We can no longer afford to look to the one-size-fits-all model, and neither can we afford negligible results of consultation. The AATA committees, as they are presently composed, are unable to meet the demands of time and expertise required by the task.

AATA must develop a team of experts who consult with each state and work with states to meet their specific requirements. There is something to be learned from the success of the few states that have licensure. If we want a future, we must get licensed. Pronto.

Part III

EXPANSION: ART THERAPISTS WHO BEGAN IN THE 1970s

Shaun McNiff teaching in a studio session, early 1990s.

Chapter 19

SHAUN MCNIFF

CREATING A LIFE WITH ART THERAPY

A DIFFERENT WAY OF PRACTICE

It intrigues me how even some close colleagues respond to the way my work has developed over the past 35 years by saying, "You've left art therapy." They say this perhaps because I have left clinical practice to explore other socially relevant applications of what I see as the core process of art and healing.

I started my career within a traditional psychiatric environment at Danvers State Hospital just north of Boston, learned a great deal there and shaped my core methods and philosophy within this context. I used clinical training in a wide variety of settings as the basis of the graduate program I founded at Lesley University in the early 1970s, but always knew that I aspired to something that could reach all people.

In no way have I left art therapy. I just try to bring the essential process to places where it has not been. Like James Hillman, I take the liberty of viewing "psychotherapy" as attending (therapy) to psyche. In my professional work I have an unbroken commitment and record of attending to psyche through art in all sectors of life and I have been very fortunate to have people from different parts of the world invite me to do this with them.

I have always believed that the work of art therapy applies as much to healthy people as it does to those afflicted by severe emotional disturbances. I approach art therapy as a mode of public health; a way of dealing with existential angst and crisis; a companion to medical treatment for physical illnesses; a spiritual practice; a way of enhancing creativity and well-being in communities; an essential component of every school and child care setting; a sympathetic and resourceful aid in dealing with painful losses, crises, and death. There is no end to the range of possible applications.

How can I leave art therapy when it is my orientation to life?

My approach is no doubt different from many people active in the field because I encourage the blurring of boundaries, especially between the different forms of artistic expression, and I believe in an ever-increasing variety of applications. From my perspective, the relationship with art therapy gets stronger as my experience expands. As someone who has always approached the work from the perspective of both art and depth psychology, I find that these practices immerse me in processes that cannot be neatly separated from the complete complex of life where everything is interconnected. The deeper I go with the work, the more it opens to every aspect of experience.

I work with people in groups, communities, and retreat settings in various regions of the world and do "the work" as completely as I can. These people come with many different goals that shape what we do together—training, healing, artistic renewal, the need to revitalize therapeutic practice, and so forth. I support some form of clinical and psychological training as the foundation for every person pursuing art therapy practice, but I believe we can be more creative and less literal-minded in encouraging a wider range of applications.

GETTING STARTED

Art therapy's lasting power in my life is closely tied to how the relationship began. The first moments of my art therapy experience were a kernel that contained everything from my personal and family past that would unfold in a social context that was ready to embrace and explore how art heals.

As contrasted to those in our professional community who selected art therapy as a career and then prepared themselves through systematic education and training, I had a more abrupt, totally unplanned, and almost magical start, becoming an art therapist completely by accident in March of 1970. These beginnings no doubt had a tremendous effect on my orientation to a large view of what art therapy can be.

I never would have set out to be an art therapist. Everything about my upbringing, although focused on service, was directed toward a more established professional role—being a medical doctor, or a lawyer like my father. But as a member of the undergraduate class of 1968 I became part of a transformative era when people's lives took radically unexpected turns. On April 4th of my senior year at Fordham University, Martin Luther King was killed. Shortly afterwards Bobby Kennedy was to be our commencement speaker, and he was shot just before the event, which literally became a memorial service. Two years earlier, at my father's suggestion, I applied to the Marine Corps officer training school and discovered that I had a detached retina which ultimately kept me free of the draft and the moral dilemma of whether or not I would go to Vietnam. High ratios of Marine Platoon Leaders were killed, either by the other side or their own soldiers, so it is surreal to imagine myself on that track.

The first major step toward my ultimate career path happened during my senior year in college when I had the opportunity to study painting with the eminent abstract-expressionist Theodoros Stamos. Although I was a history major, I took every painting course available and my teachers arranged for me to do advanced study at the Art Students League of New York.

Stamos was a powerful and physically imposing man; he howled in response to the first paintings I brought him–"They're terrible, fussy"–and I think he may have said "get them out of my studio." I recall trying out his class because there was lots of room and the more conventional sessions were packed. It soon became clear why the group was small. Stamos could be harsh and demanding but he was just what I needed. I committed myself to painting, and he started to admire my work and selected one of my large paintings for his student show. This support from a major figure in the New York art community and my fascination with how artists lived focused me on painting as a life work.

I got a job after graduation as a welfare social worker in Brooklyn and made minimalist paintings in a Soho studio with one line on big canvases. The paintings were proceeding toward the absence of form. I called my father around the beginning of August and asked if he could help me enter law school in Boston in the fall. I went to law school for a year and a half, enjoyed it, and worked in my father's law firm as I had done during the summer while in college. I liked the day-to-day legal work, but I could not envision doing it for the rest of my life.

Impulsively, I dropped out in December of 1969, just before taking final exams, for which I was pretty well prepared. I felt that if I finished the exams and made it halfway through the legal studies, it would be too difficult to leave. I had never thought seriously about leaving law school before that day, but the course work during the second year was tedious and of little intellectual interest to me. I was in a community meeting being run by the Dean when something about the session was upsetting to me, and I just walked out. At key moments in my life I have made bold decisions and radical changes, trusting that they will bring creative renewal.

I worked for three months in an iron works for minimum wage with the dream of being like David Smith and having my own welding studio. I needed to make more money and heard that the local Massachusetts state mental hospital hired social workers without graduate degrees so I thought that maybe my New York welfare experience could help. It turned out that a Master of Social Work (MSW) was required. But the personnel director and former head of volunteer services revered my grandmother Margaret Tyndall's twenty years of volunteer work at the hospital, and he said to me, "The art therapist just moved to Hawaii. Are you interested in the position?"

I had never heard of art therapy, but I walked out of the hospital as an art therapist. The idea of using art to help people fascinated me, and that incident became my life's most defining moment. The primary decision that I made was one of choosing art over the more traditional professions for men. Art therapy came in response to this decisive step in the form of a job opportunity.

At the start of my art therapy practice I had no idea where I would be going or how long it would last. Everything seemed right about making art with people suffering from serious afflictions. The work was in sync with my vision of art being something much more important than what I do alone in my studio. I was intensely committed to art, but with a more revolutionary sense of what it could do within the world.

The work in the mental hospital was immensely challenging, and perhaps the most important feature for me was all the new learning I gained. The hospital was a training site affiliated with Massachusetts General Hospital, so there were ongoing seminars, an excellent library, and many opportunities for supervision. I received a major practical and human education in the mental hospital where I worked full-time for four years before starting the expressive therapies graduate program at Lesley University.

Soon after arriving at the hospital I began to work closely with Christopher Cook, the Director of the Addison Gallery of American Art at Phillips Academy in Andover, who wanted to involve the art museum in community mental health services. We organized an exhibit of the patients' art works in the museum and then received a grant from the Massachusetts Council for Arts and Humanities to enable the show to travel to leading museums and university galleries throughout the Northeast.

The Addison Gallery collaboration reinforced my belief that art therapy can be connected to serious art making and that the general public will show great interest in the images produced within art therapy environments focused on positive manifestations of the human spirit. The Addison Gallery program used all the arts and experimented with new portable video technology. When I left Danvers in 1974 to start the Lesley program, I continued for four years at the Addison coordinating a nationally recognized art and video therapy program in the museum.

The Addison Gallery experience was one of the first of many that reinforced how what I was doing in art therapy had social significance. It was so easy to lose confidence, vision, and a sense of personal value when working within the often pathological systems of a mental hospital. I realized early on that I was there as an artist who was offering something different from the more general bureaupathology of the institutional environment and the tendency to rely exclusively on drugs to treat severe emotional disturbances. The Addison Gallery is a premier art center in one of the world's leading educational institutions, and recognition from Christopher, his staff, and students at the academy, kept me going in a transitional period. I realized how art therapy could cross over into the mainstream of the artistic and educational communities and ignite people's interest and imagination. The Addison connection resulted in favorable reviews and stories from the *Boston Globe* and other leading newspapers, and these affirmations increased my confidence and commitment.

In addition to the work at the Addison Galley, my relationship with Rudolf Arnheim provided a crucial stimulus for sustaining my early involvement with art therapy. Arnheim was at Harvard and the leading authority on the psychology of art. He agreed to supervise my Masters Degree studies at Goddard College from 1970 to 1972, and the close attention and interest I received from him reinforced my vision that art therapy could be integrated into the larger social purpose of art.

The Goddard Graduate program combined field experience and individualized study coordinated by a Goddard professor and a mentor selected by the student. I wanted someone with expertise in the broad philosophy, history, and psychology of creative expression. I wrote to junior and senior professors teaching art, aesthetics, and art history at Boston College, Boston University, Brandeis, Harvard, The School of the Museum of Fine Arts, Tufts, and Wellesley, but only Arnheim, the foremost authority on the psychology of art, replied. Arnheim told me that he was willing to put in the time with me because he could learn. He was keenly interested in what I was doing with patients, the art I brought to our meetings, and my efforts to apply his theories to art therapy.

The next two years of our work together solidified my emerging academic and research interests. Rudi Arnheim wrote a letter introducing me to Margaret Naumburg and encouraged me to meet with her in New York. When I showed an interest in Hans Prinzhorn's *Bildnerei der Geisteskranken*, which was not yet available in English, Arnheim reread the original German edition, published in 1922, and gave me summaries of chapters in our meetings. My doctoral studies at the Union Institute, completed in 1977, focused on the psychology of art, and my dream was to teach, publish, and lecture in the tradition of Arnheim's work.

My interests expanded to cross-cultural art and healing practices, and I began to see the indigenous shaman as the archetype of the artist-healer. I knew that the art and healing were connected to an historical pattern of creativity, spirituality, physical medicine, and community well-being, and should not to be understood solely as an adjunctive aspect of contemporary mental health systems.

As I examine my work over the past three decades, I see that everything I do grows from my first years of art therapy practice and my original vision of what art therapy can be. I have always felt that art therapy is for all people and that those whom I encountered in mental institutions were teachers who demonstrated new possibilities for the use of art. The patients helped me to paint in more authentic and imaginative ways. I developed my style of expression with them and began to paint figures in a more kinetic and expressionistic manner in response to their influences. They taught me how to integrate the separate realms of "abstract" and "representational" art. My New York city training with Stamos laid the foundation for painting life via imagination and my most natural ways of moving.

When my oldest daughter was recently faced with a major career decision, I spoke to her about how I believe there is a mainstream, or direction, running though all of our lives that we cannot always see. For many years it may flow underground undetected, gathering all of our interests and experiences and mixing them into the treasuries of our psyches, what I call ecologies of creation that generate imaginative offspring unique to our natures. I realize when describing this process how fortunate I have been to have fallen into a life work that gathers together all of my interests and continuously presents new areas of challenge and opportunity.

The work of art therapy is itself a deep mainstream of human experience that has flowed throughout history in different ways. The greatest challenge that I face continuously in my work is the tendency to compartmentalize that exists within both art therapy and most social institutions, and even in the programs that I have founded based on a vision of connecting the arts to everything. There are so many forces at work in the world that attempt to block and restrict the pure flow of art and healing that manifest themselves in so many different ways.

I have been greatly influenced by figures like Friedrich Nietzsche, D.H. Lawrence, and Charlotte Salomon, who strove to integrate art with every aspect of life. I have tried to do the same thing with art therapy.

LESLEY

I was a generation younger than my art therapy educator peers (Helen Landgarten at Immaculate Heart College, Myra Levick at Hahnemann

University, Arthur Robbins and Joseph Garai at Pratt Institute) when I started teaching graduate courses at Lesley University (then Lesley College) in Cambridge just after my 26th birthday in January of 1973.

My first wife Karen Gallas had just finished a Lesley masters program and provided the contact with the school. I taught an experimental January term course that enrolled close to 50 students and was invited to teach again in the following two semesters. The Dean saw how there was considerable interest in the arts in therapy and supported my proposal to found the Institute for the Arts and Human Development in March of 1974. We offered studies in both the expressive arts therapies and what we then called "integrated arts in education."

Karen, who taught young children in the 1970s, has since written many books, including *Languages of Learning: How Children Talk, Write, Dance, Draw, and Sing Their Understanding of the World*, published in 1994. As a result of her influence, I gave as much attention in the early years at Lesley to integrating all the arts into the school curriculum. At the very beginning, my vision was not restricted to circumscribed clinical practice. I wanted to apply the creative process to every sector of life and selected the general title of "Arts and Human Development" for our institute. This was as much of a business decision as a philosophical inclination, because I wanted to make sure the Institute succeeded, and I did not want the arts to be restricted to one particular application. Interestingly enough, the education offerings that I started in 1974 grew into what is now Lesley's Creative Arts in Learning program, which has for many years been the largest program of study at the university, involving thousands of teachers at off-campus sites throughout the country. We called our place the Arts Institute because it was more than a collection of programs. It was a community within Lesley with a unifying philosophy of the arts.

Since Lesley in the early seventies was focused almost exclusively on child studies, I worked with children in Karen's classroom after leaving Danvers to gain experience beyond the realm of art therapy with adults and adolescents. Many of my early publications during the 1970s were focused on children and the burgeoning area of learning disabilities. At Lesley where the mission was then focused on "the world of children," we kept our work with adults closeted and low-key. In time, the Expressive Therapies program, which was the first Lesley graduate program to attract talented students from throughout the United States and the world, helped to change Lesley in a major way and expand its mission to address the needs of people in all stages of life.

While exploring the prospect of starting programs at Lesley, I was also involved with serious discussions with the Dean of The School of the Museum of Fine Arts in Boston about establishing an art therapy program there. I had just organized an art therapy exhibition at the school that the Boston Globe art critic, who wrote a wonderful review of the work, selected as one of the best small shows of the year. The links with The Museum School grew naturally from the Addison Gallery, but I felt that art therapy would have to fight art academy battles about the differences between "serious art" and art therapy and "art not being therapy." I had difficulty then and now with the narrow thinking that permeates the art world as much as certain sectors of art therapy.

Christopher Cook, who had just spent a year directing the Institute of Contemporary Art in Boston as a "work of art," was active in the Boston conceptual art community which included leading figures like Doug Huebler, who later left Boston to be Dean of the School of Art at California Institute of the Arts, and Don Burgy, who was on the cover of *ArtForum* when we were all working together. The group involved me in their art events, participated in a show I organized at the Massachusetts College of Art, and viewed what I was doing as a vital aspect of "art" in the world. Maud Morgan, the *grand dame* of Boston painters, also joined our art events and supported my work. Close collaboration with these important artists affirmed my vision that art therapy was part of the core healing function of art. However, there are many forces within art institutions and art therapy itself that hinder this vision. In my conversations with faculty at the Museum School it was clear that turf and *guild meister* issues would be intense.

Lesley, on the other hand, was progressive, committed to experiential learning, the integration of disciplines, group work, and field training. Perhaps most importantly, Lesley did not have established art values and prejudices, so we were free to create on a clean tableau. My experiences at Danvers also affirmed the importance of working with all the arts, and I wanted to start the first truly integrated arts therapy masters program, just as we did in education.

The first time I encountered the words "expressive therapy," was in 1973 when I was appointed to the Massachusetts Commissioner of Mental Health's Advisory Committee. William Goldman, the Commissioner, was a progressive psychiatrist and a leader in the community mental health movement from the San Francisco area. He was brought to Massachusetts to reform the system by Francis Sargent, a Republican Governor whose unprecedented initiatives in mental health, corrections, and youth services were undone by psychiatric vested interests after Michael Dukakis was elected.

Our advisory committee was charged with examining the ways the Commonwealth supported mental health training. At that time, virtually all

---

Note: The description of the origin of the term "expressive therapy" is adapted from "Interview with Shaun McNiff" by Stephen Levine (1995).

of the training money went to psychiatry. Goldman saw that other mental health professions were unacknowledged and unfunded so he established a plan to distribute resources across the spectrum of professions, which he called "multidisciplinary training." He believed that specialized training did not serve the new community-based needs and initiatives.

In addition to nursing, psychology, occupational therapy, and social work, Goldman recognized all of the individual creative arts therapies–art, dance, drama, music, and poetry. But because I was one of the only arts therapists working in the state at that time, and because we were such a small entity and all sharing a creative arts base, he appointed one person to represent all the arts in a collective discipline that he called "expressive therapy." His staff probably did not spend long hours coming up with the term. It no doubt came spontaneously as a way of articulating a shared essence. This early experience established my ongoing belief that art therapy must collaborate closely with the other creative arts therapies in professional development efforts.

Psychiatry was incensed since funds were being taken away from some of the world's pre-eminent psychiatric residency programs; they ultimately prevailed, and William Goldman went back to California. But he had a lasting impact on me and my vision of expressive therapy practice.

I had worked with all the arts at Danvers and at the Addison Gallery, and when the state adopted the term, "expressive therapy," it fit my experience. Goldman's "multidisciplinary" philosophy was revolutionary. He was really taking on the specialized systems and they won, but I was able to make something from it. The same dominance of narrow specialization continues today in art therapy and the general mental health field, and I am convinced that it has more to do with the controlling interests of institutions than with the needs of people.

I adapted our Lesley program to fit the state's multidisciplinary orientation, and we received one of the first training grants that enabled us to train expressive therapists together with other mental health professionals. There was a clear incentive to include as many disciplines as possible. Our hope was that the psychologists and social workers would be as interested in expressive therapy as the art-based trainees were in psychological training. But they were not. The creative arts students were eager to study verbal therapies, but the verbal therapists were not committed to the arts. The multidisciplinary vision goes contrary to our specialized world, but the work took hold within me and other people at Lesley, and my well-received book *The Arts and Psychotherapy*, published in 1981, embraced all of the arts.

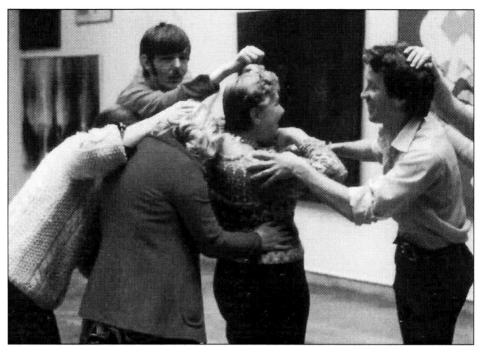

Shaun McNiff, right, in a group body sculpture, mid 1970s.

THE BEDROCK OF ART THERAPY

In my practice I consistently strive to engage people in the most complete process of creative expression, believing that the art experience will bring something of value to them. This approach is perhaps best captured in my 1998 book *Trust the Process: An Artist's Guide to Letting Go.* Little has changed with regard to my fundamental values and goals since the first days of my art therapy work at Danvers State Hospital.

My early art therapy work was focused on chronic mental patients and others suffering from acute disturbances, so it was clearly necessary for me to develop therapeutic credibility in order to be effective within the clinical milieu. This form of art therapy work demanded the ability to accept, understand, and engage acute psychological problems and disturbed behavior. Art was the anchor of my therapeutic approach and the humanizing factor that brought dignity, release, insight, and meaningful interpersonal contact to people severely isolated by their emotional condition.

At Danvers I welcomed the opportunity to work with the most withdrawn and difficult patients, and the significant progress that people made in the arts drew considerable attention from inside and outside the hospital. I experimented with many different creative and therapeutic methods and developed approaches to the work that have been documented in my writings. My philosophy was shaped by a belief that all people share a common humanity and creative resources that can be likened to a pulse.

As I became more involved in training art therapists and offering workshops for other mental health professionals and educators, I discovered in the experiential sessions how the methods shaped through my therapeutic practice had a strong personal impact on the people that I was training. The future direction of my practice emanated from these experiences in a thoroughly organic way. I did something, people responded, and I have been continuously invited by people to work with them in an ever-expanding range of settings. The ongoing response keeps shaping the context of my practice, and I stay with the essence of the work, doing similar things but in varied settings.

The transformations, in keeping with my entry into art therapy, were not planned. I went about engaging people in the process of making art with sensitivity to emotions, relationships within our groups, depth psychology, and the soul—all of which emerged from art therapy practice and the orientation it gave me. I could not do these things unless I had been educated and experienced in the different domains that comprise the profession.

The work within the Lesley University community from 1973 through 1995 was the primary basis for all of the changes and expansions that happened in my work. As I engaged students in experiential training sessions, their needs and artistic inclinations carried me and the work to deeper and more culturally universal places. Expressive arts therapy informed everything I did then and continue to do now. There is an unbroken continuity in my development within the discipline which has been the vehicle for everything I do.

My focus shifted from thinking about art experiences in relation to different clinical settings to exploring and researching the core processes of art and healing. I felt that the work was being dominated too much by the variables of clinical application, and the overall "clinification" of art therapists as described by Pat Allen, and not enough attention was being given to the essential dynamics of art making, creative and insightful ways of interpreting and responding to images, and the soul life of creation that holds us all. Like C. G. Jung, I became immersed in the process of studying how the psyche and the creative process work.

There is no question that what I do with artists in my studio sessions evolves directly from my experience as an art therapist. I also engage them as another artist, and I endeavor to create an environment committed to serious expression, but one that offers something very different from the traditional art academy. Although I am an art therapist, I am not doing conventional "therapy" in my studios, yet every aspect of the work is permeated by therapeutic values, sensitivities, and goals for more creative and enhanced living. I focus on the person together with the image and the process of creation. This is what I learned through my formative art therapy experience.

In order to engage this threefold interplay of person, image, and process of creation, I need the experiences, knowledge, and skills that can only be provided by the art therapy discipline. The person is a complex phenomenon as are images and the process of making art. Those of us who work primarily in groups and communities engage a four-fold and even more challenging interplay of dynamics. Art therapists do not do enough to acknowledge and affirm the ambitious nature of our work and the breadth of skills that it requires. Each of the domains integrated by the art therapy process can be life-long professional pursuits.

I do marvel at how some think that I have left art therapy when I continue to research how art heals and how people can engage it as effectively as possible. This to me is the bedrock of art therapy. As I say to my students, clinical and professional applications are endlessly variable and tied to the particular conditions where you work and the needs of the individual people that you serve.

My work has taken me to diverse places and settings where the soul is in need. Suffering, human needs, difficulties, and desires for the creative expression of these conditions are not and should not be confined to clinics. It is a great inspiration to see today's art therapists working on the streets of communities, with children and families in different parts of the world suffering from political conflicts, in hospices, the workplace, schools, museums, art centers, churches, and many other kinds of places.

When working with a person, group, or organization to enhance their creativity, a guide needs to have an understanding of people; the complex of creative expression; the nature of psychological wounds, resistances, and fears; group and organizational dynamics; culture; the depths of the psyche; and other domains of expertise that form the basis of the art therapy discipline, all of which require a never-ending educational process for the art therapist.

How can a profession assume to help people with their creative expression without dealing with their psyches? I do not know of any other model for training people to achieve this integration of skills outside of the expressive arts therapy domain. However, since the area of creativity enhancement is so important to the world, new educational and professional models will emerge if art therapy fails to take advantage of this opportunity.

PERSISTING

Art therapists who are pioneering new ways of serving others have unique and strong needs for support. Considering how little funding art therapy has received from mainstream health and governmental systems, I conclude that art therapists who persist are sustained by the following factors: (1) the continuous appeal of the vision and practice of art and healing; (2) the positive outcomes that tend to consistently characterize the practice of the work, ranging from the satisfaction of participants and therapists to the transformations in people's lives; (3) the enjoyment, continuous challenge, and creativity that characterize the work; (4) the dedicated and imaginative community of colleagues in the profession; and (5) most importantly, the realization that people and the world truly need the services we provide.

My identification of these factors springs from my own experience and the opportunities I have had to meet with so many other art therapists on a regular basis. In my experience, the enthusiasm of new people entering the field has been a primary source of renewal and inspiration. During difficult periods in the 1970s and 1980s when I had doubts about what I was doing, I was cured and transformed by group interview sessions with aspiring graduate students at Lesley University. Year after year, I was in awe of the talent and passion that people brought to expressive arts therapy, and I felt privileged to be a transmitter of the process. Young people with outstanding academic records, who could have done so many things with their lives, were choosing to work with the arts in therapy. I also interviewed countless professionals with graduate degrees and sometimes doctorates in the middle of their careers or in senior positions, who desired to become involved with art and healing.

Teachers, professors, clergy, nurses, medical doctors, social workers, psychologists, financial analysts, business people, a professional tennis player, a fire-fighter, and many others were exploring how their lives could expand into the work I do. The way in which this complete spectrum of people was drawn to expressive arts therapy affirms, in reverse, my inclinations to bring the work to wider communities of practice. My experience with this diversity of backgrounds and the richness it brings has strongly supported my commitment to keeping art therapy education open to those who have done more than study art and psychology before entering the field. Again, art, psychology and clinical practice are prerequisites and foundations of art therapy, but our community can also expand to include other contributors to the life of the imagination.

My life-long immersion in this work has also been sustained by integrating different art forms in creative expression. This multiarts focus was first introduced by the patients at Danvers who moved naturally from one mode of expression to another. I have become increasingly involved in this work of "total expression" each year, and I need the variety of challenges and different inspirations that it generates.

The most decisive factor in sustaining my work in expressive arts therapy has been the responses I receive from others and the fact that what I do may be of value to them. My mentor, the historical novelist and political radical, Truman Nelson, often said something like this to me: "I want to be of use to people. That is my dream. Here I am with all of the things I have studied and I want to make it available to people. I am waiting here, but no one comes." Truman was, however, profoundly useful to me, Jonathan Kozol, and a relatively small group who took advantage of his generosity and entered into sustained relationships with him.

Paradoxically, the aspect of art therapy that has been most useful to me is the one that has disturbed me the most. When I first started work in art therapy I was appalled by the way a person's artistic expression was routinely reduced to psychopathological clichés that were often outrageous and absurd projections of the interpreter. My response to this serious problem became the defining quality of my work, and I like to think that any success that I have had has helped to turn the tide. I am delighted to see how intelligent and influential contemporary authors and art therapists, like Bruce Moon, have joined me in addressing the peculiar practice of labeling images. The need that many feel to "explain" images and the lack of validity attached to these practices have been a primary impetus for my efforts to understand the true motivations of art and to experiment with more creative, fulfilling, and precise ways of engaging images. The problems of art diagnosis persist and they still offer me a lively platform for the presentation of my own views about the way in which art heals.

What intrigues me most about my art therapy history is the way in which the work has informed and shaped my art. I never imagined at the start of my art therapy work that it would have such a significant impact on my personal expression.

First, it was the Danvers patients who taught me how to paint more organically and with my own natural gestures, and then over the years my studio participants have kept me immersed in the primal qualities of gesture, color, and form and the connections between images and soul. Art therapy keeps taking me into the essence of art, year after year, integrating everything I value.

Through another unplanned synchronicity, I was invited last year to present a retrospective exhibit of over 70 of my paintings at Gallery 1581 at the Boston Graduate School of Psychoanalysis. After exhibiting actively during the 1970s and early 1980s, I began to incorporate my art in my books, especially *Depth Psychology of Art* (1989) and *Art as Medicine* (1992), and I exhibited paintings only in response to invitations that I received from college and university galleries. Even though I created a number of well-received "art therapy-oriented" exhibits at prominent galleries and museums during the 1970s, I was not satisfied by the separation of my art from my art therapy work that seemed to be required by the conventional gallery culture. It was only in my collaboration with the conceptual artists that I felt a complete acceptance and assimilation. I have always searched for ways to integrate my artistic expression and art therapy, and the focus on book publication also brought the work to a much larger international audience.

Shaun McNiff with his paintings, 2004.

When I decided last year to work seriously on exhibiting my painting, I had to once again deal with the split between art and therapy worlds. I felt that I had to package myself as a "painter" and minimize my expressive arts therapy background. I am grateful for the way in which the Gallery 1581 show enabled me to present my art in a venue that recognizes the unique features of what I do. The exhibition avoided the alienating split that happens when we feel that we have to take on the one-sided roles of artist or therapist rather than thoroughly integrating the two. The retrospective exhibit has catalyzed other exhibitions and I am becoming involved once again with gallery life, but feeling more secure in my identity. Just as the inclusion of my paintings in my books and my methods of art-based research have encouraged others to do the same, I hope I can now do things with galleries that will make it more natural for art therapists to exhibit from the basis of who they really are.

In keeping with the sentiments of my mentor Truman Nelson, I believe that my ability to persist in art therapy is closely tied to the degree to which I am useful to others. Helping art therapy colleagues and institutions keeps me going on all cylinders. In addition to my long and productive relationship with Lesley University (1973–1995, and returning again to Lesley after seven years as Provost of Endicott College to serve as the first University Professor from 2002 to date), I have been invited to teach at many colleges and universities, and I have enjoyed working closely with colleagues at these schools to build their programs. I am especially attached to the schools that invite me back year after year and to the traditions I have established with Mount Mary College through four successive program directors and Ursuline College. Close involvement with these traditionally Catholic institutions and the sisters who lead them, and especially Sister Kathleeen Burke at Ursuline, has been a meaningful way of staying connected, and better yet "of use" to the primary religion of my family. In 1993, Mount Mary gave me an honorary degree for the work I did in helping Lynn Kapitan establish their Masters Degree program. Other ongoing affiliations in the United States include The Institute of Imaginal Studies in Petaluma, California; The Rowe Conference Center in the Berkshires; and Prescott College in Arizona.

Another of my unique experiences as an art therapist is the way in which I have worked for many years outside North America. A most significant turning point of my career was the founding of the Arts Institute Project in Israel in 1979 with a Lesley graduate, Vivien Marcow Speiser, who was the first director of the project and now the Lesley professor who directs the University's work in Israel with 600 students. I served for many years as Chair of the Board of Trustees and I continue to work closely with Vivien and teach at least once each year in Israel.

My other primary international connection was established through my close relationship with Paolo Knill, who brought me to teach on a regular basis at various institutes in Switzerland and Germany while he was working with me to establish Lesley programs in Cambridge and Europe during the 1970s and 1980s. Paolo and I have lived like two wings of one flight for over thirty years, and our collaboration expanded to a network of intimate colleagues including Steve Levine with whom I have collaborated on many projects. A second major doorway to Europe was opened by another Lesley alum, Phillip Speiser, who established the Scandinavian Institute for

Expressive Arts in Sweden and Norway, where I became a frequent guest faculty. Phillip also connected me to Annette Brederode in the Netherlands, who invited me regularly to teach in training programs in Amsterdam and Helsinki.

Shaun McNiff (right) with Paolo Knill at Lesley Israel
Colloquium, early 1980s.

During the 1980s and early 1990s I spent at least two months of every year working outside the United States, and this involvement had a wonderful impact on my family life and my four children. When my son Liam was six or seven and accompanying me on a trip, I became irritated about something related to the work. He said, "Stop complaining Daddy. You have it pretty good." Liam grasped the essence of it all.

My life and more importantly the life of the family have been formed and enriched through art therapy. I am painting more than ever and with increased optimism about the ultimate place of the art's healing function in the world. As another close mentor, Vincent Ferrini, the Poet Laureate here in Gloucester, Massachusetts, says, "Life is the poem" and "let's see where it takes us."

Shaun McNiff's painting "Summer Beginning," 2005.

Arthur Robbins

Chapter 20

ARTHUR ROBBINS

MOVING IN AND OUT OF THE SANDBOX

My story begins in a dark, gloomy house located in the Bay Ridge section of Brooklyn. My mother, a hard-working woman obsessed with cleanliness and order, kept the shades drawn, fearful that the sun would fade the plastic covered furniture. The windows were closed, creating a stale and musty feeling. Yet, paradoxically, everything I conceived of as art came from this stifling atmosphere. The aesthetics of the house can best be described as neat, orderly and, without the plastic covers, modestly appealing. My mother and sister spent endless hours decorating and redecorating this house. My sister later majored in interior decorating and became a successful professional in Canada. My father manufactured artificial flowers for hats and dresses. Memories come to mind of him bringing home his newest creations for his wife and daughter to offer their critique. An early conception of aesthetics, then, was drawn from these surroundings. Art was something pretty, neat, orderly and clean. These notions affected me, and in a very convoluted way laid the groundwork for my interest in becoming a sculptor and an art therapist. Not surprising, one of my earliest dreams turned out to be a nightmare consisting of my crying out in my sleep, "I don't want to take art classes."

My backyard served as a retreat, prison, and fortress from the outside world. My mother worried about contamination from other children; she kept a watchful eye and locked the gate, giving an illusion that I was safe from the dangerous outside world. In this enclosed little box I built my playground, where tunnels and castles intertwined with each other and I devised plans for hiding out. Intermeshed, however, were also plans for escape from something that was threatening yet quite incomprehensible. I did not understand why I was frightened of people; I was simply labeled shy. Certainly I had little opportunity to test my fears about people. There were, however, many advantages in having this safe retreat. Here was a place where I could roll in the dirt and pour water in the sand, and create the most interesting kinds of structures. I'd tear them down and build them up again as if I were trying to master something that was indescribable. Occasionally, I was aware of my curiosity about the outside world, but at the same time that world seemed very strange and forbidding.

My parents kept a watchful eye as I played in my sandbox. When their attention was drawn to other things, I would rush to the drain and plug up the drainpipe. Perhaps I was just curious to see what would happen; I suspect, however, that I had deeper motivations that were completely dissociated from my consciousness. I never thought of myself as a rebel, but rather as a timid, shy little boy. Also, I could never manage to get things quite right. Clothes were always a problem for me. Invariably my shirt hung out, and if one would take a good look at me, nothing seemed to be quite put together. To this day I rarely wear clothes that fit, and my shirts still hang out. To add insult to injury, at least from my parents' perspective, I rarely stood up straight. I still can hear their words ringing in my ears, "Stand up straight, Arthur, you are a *schlump*. Stop schlumping." They even resorted to a back brace, but that didn't help. And so the term *schlump* stayed with me, and my students to this day still see me schlumping in my chair as I teach my courses. On my 60th birthday, I recall with a certain degree of pleasure, being presented with a clay sculpture created by some of the students in my class of me schlumping in my chair. Schlumping had become my identity and trademark.

Perhaps as a means of survival, or even as a way of bringing attention to myself, I became exceedingly diligent in breaking order wherever I found it. Order seemed to surround me at every turn, yet, for the life of me I could never make order out of anything. My teachers could not understand my handwriting in spite of all their efforts. They insisted that I write my schoolwork over and over again. I hated art classes, for I couldn't copy anything in the way it was presented. Slowly, a character formation arose that had both positive and negative aspects, and ultimately became a bridge to my becoming a professional art therapist. Without really understanding the genesis of my anger, I became contemptuous of the conventional and glorified the nonconventional. My anger was usually expressed in passive-aggressive terms, although I had my explosive moments. Again, all these early determinants became an important basis in my becoming an artist, a sculptor and, later on, an art therapist.

In all fairness, my parents were good people; they did care about what would happen to me. They were really worried that I would not survive in the world. They did the best they could to give me material comforts, and I am very thankful to them. They sent me to camp, and I recall with a good deal of fondness and a debt of gratitude that they would save every penny they had to provide for the tuition. Maybe, I thought, they needed a respite from me. The camp was heaven; I was able to find my own space. To this day I still have a picture of myself that I have saved from those early camp days. I am lying under tree in a blissful and contented daze. Later on, when I underwent a series of important operations, that picture provided me with a feeling of hope and guidance that there might be peace and safety in the world.

There was much more to my so-called "badness." The stove was an object of fascination. When my parents were not looking, I would turn on the gas and experiment with fire, mixing different potions, like wax and spaghetti. My grandmother, who was blind and living with us at the time, would scream out, "He's at it again!" Perhaps there was a future alchemist in the making. Indeed, much later on as an adult, a number of my theoretical assumptions about therapy had much to do with alchemy. Of course, this was not the whole picture, for there was a rascal in me who was crying out to be seen and gain recognition for my own particular, distorted, creative talents. I still recall riding on my bike and suddenly shooting away from my mother, leaving her far behind. When I spotted a fire alarm, I would get on top of my seat and pull the handle down. An alarm offered me so much pleasure and fascination. I cannot say the same for my mother, who would whisk me into a shop, hoping no one had seen the culprit who was creating the mayhem.

In school, I was not a very good student, nor very neat, and tried to hide in the back rows. My marks were at best borderline. This was in contrast to my sister, who could do no wrong. She won medals in school and was an outstanding student. I barely got by. My parents and teachers could not understand what made me tick. My mother encouraged me to read books, but rarely do I remember her reading stories to me. I have no memory of snuggling up next to my mother while she read me a story. Now, as I look back at this picture of my childhood, it remains one of gloominess, conformity and living somewhere on the edge of terror. All these elements had the potential for transformation as an adult. To be truthful, there was a burning part of me that wanted to better understand myself, particularly during adolescence. However, I must confess that I was on a search to find out about sex, and Freudian literature seemed to be a logical place to discover this information.

Looking back now at how I was raised, it is very hard to blame my parents. Both of them were orphans. My mother was bandied about from one uncle to another. She had lost both parents at a very early age. Her father had abandoned her and was seen as a n'er-do-well. I suspect, indeed, that I was the recipient of many of her projections regarding men that held their genesis in her father. I rarely met my grandfather, for he was not invited to our house. I suspect that somewhere in her unconscious, she held the conviction that no good would come of me and I would turn out like her father. There was no question in my mind that my mother did not trust men and held no hope for my salvation. Men were seen as evil and usually up to no good; I suspect that I was living out her perception of this image. And yet, she did marry a very good man who tried to please her and be a good provider. Their backgrounds were similar in this respect: he was also psychically an orphan. He lost his mother at a very early age, and his stepmother treated him as an outsider. I knew nothing about his stepbrothers and stepsisters until I grew up. Ironically, they became pivotal figures in my life. My father's family was viewed as the enemy. Cloistered in my backyard where I was left to rely on my own resources, my security in making new relationships was at best marginal. In fact, the idea of new relationships gave me a good deal of anxiety. I was shy and had few friends, and I slowly developed the identity of a lost, inadequate loner. Yet, underneath all this, I craved to be recognized and master some of my fears about the world. These early influences are threads that would ultimately weave their pattern in determining the person I became as an adult and a therapist. Mess, chaos, nonconformity, shyness, aloneness and a hungering search for recognition–all were important influences that laid the basis for my adult professional life. When I was young, however, my life looked pretty dim and dismal.

Other factors in my early background became important determinants in shaping my professional career. Like so many adolescents I was preoccupied with sex, and I found it very hard to discover any information about what was plaguing me. At that time there was no such thing as *Playboy* magazine, and the best I could do was to go to the library and search for pictures that would illuminate the differences between men and women. I thought that women had a little penis, which I couldn't detect. Avidly, I would search out professional psychology books that I hoped would give me answers about life and sex. I was rather ashamed about all of this and kept it to myself, for indeed it was all a very dirty business. I did stumble across some books on Freudian psychology. They didn't make much sense to me, at least at first, but it was the best I could discover that would give me some information about sexual development. Slowly and imperceptibly those books began to whet my appetite for finding answers about myself. It was not just the pictures that I was looking to find, I was trying to find out what made me so unhappy and confused.

In my later adolescence I discovered my father's stepbrothers and stepsisters, who were indeed a very interesting group of people. I rarely saw them, for they were seen as the enemy. Yet, interestingly enough, four of them were psychoanalysts, which was very unusual for those times. My mother, however, saw them as ne'er-do-wells. For how could a therapist be a professional without an M.D.? My mother simply did not trust them, and I was protected from their very bad influence. They also, I believe, threatened her, for they were intellectuals. So as I saw it, on one side of my family were the psychoanalysts, and on the other side were the artists, and I didn't seem to belong in either place, I simply lived in no-man's land. The analysts on my father's side were never invited to my home. Yet, when I married I made it my business to seek them out. Little did I know that one of them was a pioneer in psychoanalysis and had been directly trained by Theodore Reik.

Psychology seemed the best path to follow when I went to college, as I continued to be interested and curious about people. I must confess, however, I wanted to further my understanding of sexuality as well as my place in the world. But formal academic psychology seemed dry and sterile. Nevertheless, it was the best path to take. I majored in psychology and went on to take my doctorate at Columbia Teachers College. What I learned about psychology left me unfulfilled. There was a good deal of emphasis on behavioral reinforcement and sometimes a smattering of Rogerian theory. I still recall my major teacher in the doctoral program. He would start at one end of the board and wind up at the other end with a whole complicated, schematic outline of what made people tick. It was both cognitive and behavioral in nature. I was cynical about such theory, but I knew this was my meal ticket out of the morass and jungle I lived in. I therefore played ball, learned the material, and received my doctorate at the early age of twenty-four.

The years of completing my doctorate were full of stress and anxiety. I was twenty-four years old and had but a short time to finish my dissertation, for the Army was breathing down my neck. At the point of beginning my doctorate, I could at best be considered an average or mediocre student. Then, something very important happened in my life. I met my future wife. Characteristically, she presented a profound acceptance and love for me. Rarely had I felt so completely understood, accepted and appreciated. I knew that even if I failed, she would stand beside me. Now I sometimes think, how did I not repeat the mistakes of my early childhood and marry someone like my mother? Maybe it was clear to me who my mother was. And it was even clearer that I wanted to meet someone who was very different, even though women like my mother had an enormous magnetic pull for me. Those women who reminded me of my mother always seemed to smell nice, look good, and were pretty, but somehow they were untouchable. My better judgment prevailed. Whatever possessed me, I made the right choice. I chose a very earthy, sensuous woman who was the embodiment of the Earth Mother. She became my first healer. I still recall in our relationship her warm, bright smile, and her willingness to help me out and do whatever it took for me to get where I was going. When I qualified for doctoral status at Teachers College, I had but three months to start and finish my thesis before I would be inducted into the Army. This indeed was a formidable challenge, but something I desperately wanted to do. You see, I had a good chance of becoming a psychology officer in the Army if I received my doctorate. At that time there were no computers, so my wife became my typist and took down verbatim the material that I was putting together for my research. You can imagine, everything required six duplicates, and corrections had to be made through five carbons. I vividly remember her nodding approval as I espoused my thoughts regarding my thesis topic. Occasionally she would stop typing and say to me that I could do better. "What do you mean?" I would say. "This is my thesis." But there she was, saying, "I'm behind you, but you really could do better." That profound sense of approval and encouragement, love and respect for my abilities opened everything up to me academically. Suddenly, my reports were receiving A's. My material seemed to flow out from me and, lo and behold, within a three-month period from start to finish I had received my doctorate. I still recall the committee's comment: "It may not be the most brilliant thesis, but it is one of the quickest completed in the history of Teachers College." That sense of complete acceptance from my wife became very important to my understanding of what makes people grow. It became, in fact, an important framework for all the types of therapies that I started to put together.

As it turned out, there were no available commissions for psychologists in the army, at least in the Northeast corridor. And so I was sent down South and began my difficult but short career as a private, enlisted man. One day, I happened to view on the bulletin board an opening for first lieutenants in the psychological field. At that point I had little hope of getting anything from the army, but I applied anyway. At least it was a good way of getting out of K. P. In spite of all my anxieties, I received my First Lieutenant commission. There were 100 psychology officers in the U.S. Army, and the great majority were career men. I had the unique distinction of being someone who had volunteered, or applied for a two-year "hitch." The Korean War had begun. I'm not sure if there was any relationship between my not being a career man and my being sent to Korea, but I was the only psychology officer who was stationed right behind the front lines. I had very little experience except what I learned in my internship. And here I was in an extremely important backup position behind the front lines. I learned quickly and, indeed, experience became my best teacher. My colleagues were twenty-five psychiatrists, all of whom were friendly and warm. They easily volunteered to teach me some of the basic principles of short-term psychotherapy, and I in turn, as the chief diagnostician, would help them understand the ins and outs of the "Rorschach." Our job was to either send the patient back to a hospital located in either Japan or the States, or return the soldier back to the front lines. If we felt it was a chronic condition, we would recommend evacuation to the States. We learned our lesson from World War II and worked on the principle that if the person could go back to the front, the less chance there was of reinforcing secondary gains and emotional trauma. Another job was to spot soldiers who were malingering and feigning psychosis. Thus, as a psychologist in the front lines, I was learning by the seat of my pants and making important decisions.

At night I poured over books and went over case studies until I developed a feel for the various issues that came through our services. I encountered many soldiers and required a whole slew of technicians to administer the tests. Soon, I found myself going from room to room where the technicians were administering the tests, and I in turn would offer my impressions of the symptoms and personality organizations that were being manifested in the different psychological tests. Little did I know that I had begun my training as an art therapist.

The "Rorschach" test offers a profound exposure for developing a frame for the interaction of color, space and form related to personality organization. The sequence of material, the way images are perceived on the inkblot, the organization of these images, the originality, the bizarreness, all seem to have powerful threads that contribute to personality organization. The usual "Rorschach" analysis takes four to six hours to reach any understanding of what is going on in the examinee. I simply didn't have that much time to devote to each protocol, for many soldiers were referred to us for immediate determination. As a result, I developed a capacity to gain quick and intuitive impressions about soldiers and their manner of experiencing the inkblots. These experiences also provided a basic training for my profession as an art therapist.

In 1955, the Korean War ended and I received an honorable discharge from the Army. Becoming a therapist was very much on my mind, and I found my first job in a family service center. In this setting I learned the very basic principles of therapeutic relationships. I was required to do intake, short-term and long-term treatment, and was introduced to child group therapy. I was taking over for the original therapist of this group who was leaving for another job in Texas. He had experimented with the group to see what would happen if he allowed the limits to be very loose. There was chaos and mayhem when I walked into the room. The therapist simply said to me as he walked out the door, "Take over." I found myself confronted with 11 and 12-year-old children who were either acting out or extraordinarily withdrawn. I felt as though I had entered a snake pit. Blocks were being thrown left and right, some children came up and started to shove me, others voiced contemptuous comments to me, and many just shrieked and yelled. It was all too much for me. I still recall my Wednesday group night. My wife invariably knew that I would be beside myself when I got home. She prepared chicken soup and gave me her special form of healing.

Thank goodness I was in analysis. I remember telling my analyst, "I don't belong in this field. I hate these children. I think I should get trained in market analysis." He prevailed and said, "Stick with it." I owe him a good deal of thanks for helping me to stay with it. I survived the first month as best I could. I will confess that my behavior did not always fit the usual ethical standards and rules that we have today. Here I was, a middle class guy who, frightened of his own hostility and not very emotionally related, offering rather standard interpretations to these children. I remember saying, "Yes, you miss your old therapist. You don't want to work with me. You are just hoping I'll get scared and walk away from you. You are trying to show me how tough you are." None of these interpretations worked. And then one boy, who it seemed was in the middle of a homosexual panic, jumped on me and started to hump. I got hold of him by the scruff of his neck and said, "Don't you ever do that again or else you will really be sorry." By today's standards that does not sound very ethical. After all, we are not supposed to touch our clients, but it was the best thing I could have done. It had an immediate impact. Suddenly, the room became very quiet; everyone understood they had discerned the limit of my personal boundaries and had witnessed a demonstration of my aggression. That was a very important experience for me, for I had begun to understand the centrality of limits as well as the ability to be comfortable with one's aggression as basic underpinnings of a good therapist.

To be sure, I understood that patients needed to be seen and to be recognized, but also at times they required confrontation in order to make choices in their lives. In this group, kinetic impulses poured from every corner. Behind me, when my back was turned, one of the children would pour hot wax down the pipes and plug them up. Once again, I was back in the sandbox in my backyard, returning to my experience of stuffing up the drains. Were these patients acting out my own unconscious or being very sensitive to some of my own impulses? I began to suspect that there was a subtle smile behind my consternation as I witnessed the adolescents creating such a mess. This experience was vital to my understanding of the power of the therapist's unconscious being communicated to patients. I recall one of the children making feces out of clay and then running downstairs to put it in front of the door of the bank that was below us. Was he acting out something that was inside me? I wondered about this. Were they at all sensitive to the rebel inside of me? In some way we were in collusion. Slowly, I began to understand the profound impact of the therapist's unconscious in working with patients, and the use of countertransference, which later on became a very important cornerstone in my future work as a therapist. Much later I would write articles and books about this subject.

Learning the fundamentals of group therapy with children was a form of basic training for competence in the field. In this very unique setup sponsored by the Eastchester Family Service Center outside New York City, our caseload consisted of the children of servants who worked for very wealthy families, as well as children of members of its Board of Directors. This was all part of the mix. I still have a very vivid memory of a child from a very wealthy family taunting a black child in the group, calling him, "Nigger, Nigger, Nigger." The black child began pummeling the provocateur. I confronted the boy and said, "If you don't want to get your head kicked in, don't call another member of the group names." Again he challenged me to see what I would do. He provoked again, calling out, "Nigger, Nigger, Nigger." I said nothing. I believed that he had to take responsibility for his provocation. I had to restrain the black child from kicking the daylights out of the young provocateur who now was frightened. Ultimately, these two children became best friends. Thus, another cornerstone was laid down in those early days of group therapy: help patients take responsibility for their actions. I learned not to be a savior or a rescuer. This principle became a very important aspect of my work as a therapist, particularly with masochistic, sadistic, and borderline personalities.

I entered the National Psychological Association for Psychoanalysis Institute in 1958 and began the long and arduous journey of becoming a psychoanalyst. As much as I yearned to be an analyst, I was very frightened of entering analysis and projected all types of fears onto my analyst. It took me six months to lie on the couch. Long, hard hours followed in order for me to face my suspicions about the world, my fears and my hostility towards authority. In about the third or fourth year of my analysis something very important erupted in the therapeutic dialogue. Like a sudden wave coming from a very deep and private part of myself, I expressed a wish to go back to the sandbox. This time, however, it was to learn how to be a sculptor. I was already a practicing psychologist as well as an analyst, but I somehow felt very incomplete. I wondered out loud if this was another way of putting my mother and father together, for there seemed to be such a division in the family. I enrolled in a sculpting class, and was terrified to join in. I remember standing at the doorway and peeking in, and viewing this very old and wise Russian teacher who caught me in the act of looking. "Vell, vhat are you vaiting for? Come in!" she would say. She invited me in, and thus began my long love affair with sculpture. I played with clay and created all types of outrageous figures. I remember my first piece, a sliding pond on top of a pregnant woman. Soon, however, clay became less of a challenge for me and I began to work in stone. Always in the background was this wonderful teacher who delighted in my creations and maintained a very encouraging and positive attitude towards my work. Much to my surprise, I did not encounter any criticism or shame, but indeed, a celebration of my creativity and my ability to see the world in a different and nonconventional way. The aesthetic ideas that I was exposed to very early in my life were thrown out the window. I could be as unconventional as I wanted to be, I could enter into the mess, and I discovered that disorder and chaos were often the fore-runners of something creative. No longer did I feel like a dirty, messy boy, but found, indeed, worth and value in chaos. I still remember my early days working with stone. I felt as though I was giving birth to a baby; it took too much out of me. Yet there was something about working with stone that was akin to the basic axioms of therapy. For instance, you don't fight the stone, you go with the flow of the stone, you take advantage of all accidents while working with the stone, and you try to feel the energy of the stone by touch-ing it and feeling its rhythm. All this became an important underpinning to my understanding of art therapy. But most important, I learned not only about resistance and flow and accident, but indeed, about the very special role of a supportive teacher.

At forty, my private practice was quite successful. Yet, I became increas-ingly restless, yearning to find something different outside the private office. I wanted to discover a new way of expressing myself. It is an old adage that when we are ready for something to happen, the opportunity presents itself. For me it was a part-time teaching position at Pratt Institute. I was teaching psychology to artists, and I was quite intimidated with the whole notion of standing before a class and lecturing about psychology. I recall requesting an evening class, for I thought evening students would be less challenging. I was truly afraid of standing before this group and being frightened and vulnera-ble. I would prepare voluminous notes before each class, but I soon learned that my outlines did not help–I had to go with the flow. Those art students were quite different from any type of psychology class I ever encountered. They experienced life more from a perceptual than a cognitive level. They were creative, challenging, and they enjoyed the whole flow and dialogue of understanding relationships and images. But much to my dismay they were also anti-psychology. After my first class, I became despondent as to ever finding a way to work with these students. I had to find a new way of com-municating–not through the head, but through the body and through the art.

It was the end of the '60s, when there was a good deal of excitement in the atmosphere. At that time one felt that anything was possible and there was room for plenty of experimentation and the breaking of old structures. I approached Joe Garai, the head of Pratt's psychology department, with my new idea. What would he think of combining psychology and art? And rather matter-of-factly his answer was, "Sure, why not? I have been thinking about it myself. Why don't we become partners?" Joe had a vision that matched my own, and we became close and creative buddies, sharing the same values of anti-conformity and speaking out one's mind and not being frightened of the consequences.

Joe was a part-time photographer and I was a sculptor. His interest was in developmental psychology and mine in psychoanalysis. As our excitement mounted, we sent a proposal to the Dean's council for a new and innovative program called "Creativity Development." At that time psychology and psychiatry were not very accepted in the art community, and therapy was viewed with a good deal of suspicion. We thought that the title "Creativity Development" was much more palatable and politically acceptable to the faculty. With little resistance, our proposal was passed. Later on, when we had our foot in the door, we changed our name to "Creativity Development and Art Therapy." Three other art therapy training programs all started in 1970. None of them knew that the others were inaugurating a program, and as a result each began to develop in its own particular orientation. Available were books by Margaret Naumburg and Edith Kramer. But neither of their formulations, in my mind, offered the true promise of what art therapy could potentially offer. I must admit there was a good deal of arrogance behind this stance. Joe and I were critical of the art therapist being only a secondary member of the therapeutic team. A more traditional, psychoanalytic approach to art also did not make sense. Kramer's sublimation hypothesis ran counter to everything I understood as a psychoanalyst. The split of one therapist working out the conflicts and the other therapist attending to the sublimation process seemed to me unnecessary, unwieldy and unintegrated. Furthermore, when you tap material of a very profound nature through the art, it makes no sense then to bring it to the primary therapist. The message of the art was really meant for the art therapist and not for other members of the team. Naumburg, on the other hand, seemed too intellectual; her approach made art therapy a very cognitive affair. From all her illustrations and texts, patients seemed to leave treatment abruptly—I suspect, from over-interpretation. I had strong reservations about applying a traditional, classical notion to art therapy.

In the meantime, the psychoanalytic field was undergoing its own revolution. Object relations, self-psychology and ego psychology became very prominent on the professional scene. For many therapists, the therapeutic process was still viewed as facilitating the emergence of the unconscious to consciousness. However, for many other professionals, therapy became a matter of relationships, creating holding environments, and a mirroring of the self. All this seemed very adaptable to what happens in art therapy. Once again, as in my Army experience, we learned by doing. Our students and teachers developed their own particular framework that emerged from their clinical experience. I still recall some of our newest applicants in the program. They were food service majors who were interested in art therapy. Joe and I mused to ourselves, "Why not?" We invited them into the program and developed a catering unit run by veterans. Was this art therapy? We felt so, though a former president of the American Art Therapy Association protested that it was a far cry from her conception of art therapy. I still recall at a meeting her statement, "My grandmother makes bagels, but I don't call that art therapy." However, we didn't mind at all being called the "Bagel Art Therapists of America."

In many quarters our program was viewed as wild and unorthodox, and perhaps, the rebel in me who was a nonconformist interfaced with the development of a theory of art therapy. Linda Sibley, a first-year graduate student, approached me and said, "You know, our program lacks a basic textbook. How would it be if we would work together to develop an introductory text?" This seemed exciting to me, and so our first book emerged, *Creative Art Therapy*. That first textbook set forth the basic principles of our approach to art therapy, which then subsequently developed into many different branches. The underlying premise of our approach still holds today. Our emphasis was on creativity and the artistic utilization of the therapist's abilities in making contact with patients. Yes, we believed in the importance of art, but there was equal emphasis on the creative interventions that made art therapy a very exciting affair.

My theoretical development emerged from experiences with patients and students. This development is still unfolding. I have authored six books attempting to deal with the changes and my evolving notions of art therapy. Back in 1970, I viewed art therapy as a creative way of building communication between patient and therapist. Art was a means of organizing symbols in a cognitive framework, which ultimately would enhance therapeutic communication. Slowly, I included the notion of expressive therapy, where different modalities could all work hand-in-hand under a common framework. This evoked a good deal of controversy, for some art therapists wanted to the keep the frame of art as the central core of their profession. But then I thought, what about the patient who needs to be met through poetry or drama? Or what about the adolescent who needs a drum to express himself through hip hop music? Why should we as art therapists, if we have the talent and interest, become limited by a visual arts role? Object relations soon filtered into my work. The concept of the holding environment and the art as a transitional object became pivotal points in the therapeutic process. Art became a means whereby patient and therapist might create a third space. In this space, there was a combination of unconscious material emanating from both partners of the relationship, which ultimately blended into its own particular mix.

In the '70s my son Michael became interested in spiritual work and brought to my attention the work of Carlos Casteneda. In one of my earlier articles I drew parallels between the spiritual teachings of Casteneda's Don Juan and a therapeutic orientation that basically encompasses both healing and psychotherapy. To this day, there is a spiritual thread that runs through my various conceptions and theories of the role of the art therapist. From my viewpoint, a healer works with a much broader perspective than a therapist, attempting to help the client find his or her place and acceptance on a universal level. In some respects, it starts with the community, and I believe that there is an important function for what I call the community art therapist. In short, what I have seen are evolving roles that encompass a broad continuum of healing, adaptation and psychotherapy.

As my own career was developing, my wife pursued a career in children's theatre. Along the way, she also became very involved in psychic healing. As often occurs between husband and wife, there is much sharing, both on a conscious and unconscious level. The concept of energy that is so basic to a healer soon became an intrinsic part of my own theoretical framework. I became interested in the manner in which energy flowed in any particular piece of art, where it stopped, if it presented a ground and a center. These are also the working notions of a healer, at least from my wife's perspective. Did the art piece lack cohesion, did it have a soul, and what was the interplay between form and space and movement? All these are concepts related to energy. And, indeed, energy is central to my understanding of how healing can be adapted to an art therapy framework.

Art therapy, likewise, was struggling as an organization for definition and professional recognition. I recall the second meeting of the American Art Therapy Association in 1970; it was one of the rare times that Edith Kramer and I agreed. We both expressed great reservations about starting a registration so early in our profession. We both felt that any definition was premature and that we needed space to find our own direction. Of course, the push for professionalization could not be stopped and registration was adopted in the second annual meeting. In the meantime, Edith Kramer and I maintained a long and argumentative dialogue about our different conceptions of art therapy. Our ongoing argument often represented the varieties of splitting that were taking place in the Association. Transference became a hot issue. Some art therapists believed that transference belonged in the psychotherapist's ballpark, while others, like myself, believed that in some instances art therapy could offer a very deep and meaningful transference experience. I also believed that transference was inevitable in an art therapy relationship. The notion that transference was always acted out in the art form did not make sense in terms of our actual experience. Students were overwhelmed with primitive projections that touched some of their own conflicts. I was aware that we could not work out transference issues. However, the mere recognition and articulation of these conflicts was often accessible and could lessen anxiety on the part of the student. I also added the notion that countertransference occurred when the student lost his or her presence. To this day, I have not regretted formulating this position for it dealt head-on with the reality of the student's experience. Certainly, with so many traumatized patients in one's caseload, the possibility of induced trauma was both frequent and significant, even though much of the process was communicated on a nonverbal level.

I still recall one of Edith Kramer's famous phrases at an annual meeting: "Some people are content to tend to their rose gardens, and others must deal with the whole forest." She implied that my aspirations for art therapy were a wee bit too grandiose! I in turn responded that her notion of art therapy sounded closer to art education. This split regarding the definition of art therapy became an overriding topic in the early '70s and '80s. But this soon died down for, indeed, all of us were struggling to find a meeting ground between these opposite polarities. Ultimately, I arrived at the perspective that studio art offered something very important and vital to patients. Not all patients required or were able to utilize psychotherapy. Slowly, saner heads prevailed and we were able to live with our differences and share our commonalities. I now give greater credence to cognitive behavior therapy as a way of working with depression and affect regulation. Brain research supports these notions. At the same time, I am constantly dealing with the intersubjective, while self-psychology approaches can become very central in my work with patients. Thus, I believe, the subjectivities of the artist and the therapist, as well as their perceptions of the artwork, all meet in a very complex interaction. From this perspective there is really no one reality. In time, Pratt's reputation as the "Touchy-Feelers of the East" changed. For, indeed, our program was recognized as presenting a very solid psychological and psychodynamic base. However, from the very first day of classes, students are placed in internships without too much background or preparation, for we believed that learning by doing was the quickest way to master such a complex field. Along the way, however, we started to build up with our students a theoretical structure that was based on their actual experience. Perhaps this reflected the paradoxical state of a schizoid teacher such as myself, who on the one hand sought out aloneness and yet created circumstances where there were intense communications in his classes.

In this turbulent period when we all were struggling for our identity, I was suddenly confronted with a very personal impact on my life. My father died. I felt lost and saddened by his passing and requested a session with my former analyst. I carried with me a sculpture that expressed my feelings regarding his death. It was a clay piece of a skull that symbolized emptiness and hollowness. We spoke briefly of my feelings about the loss of my father. He then took hold of the piece in his hand and said to me, "You know, the eyes and the whole organization of the piece look just a little too balanced. Are you sure that you are not trying to keep something together through an artificial balance?" Soon this discussion led to my feelings about my father's death. His cancer was a long and difficult trial for the whole family. Now, I was ready to move on with my life, and I struggled to allow this realization into my awareness.

Much more could be said about my relationship with my father. He simply was no match for my mother and in terms of power she was the dominant one in the family constellation. There was much disappointment on my part for his inability to support me in my separation from my mother. One of my most surprising insights evolved from a dream. As I recalled the kiss I received from my father in this dream, I became aware of the love and care I held for this man, and this man held for me. Inherent in this new awareness was a basic void that I struggled with. Male identification is fortified by an ego ideal that is reinforced by a coherent value system. Out of my experience as an artist the values of individuality, creativity and humanism became part of the fabric of my self. Slowly in my own analysis, the lost sense of values and the struggle for what was important for me in life started to evolve. In many respects, this process seemed to solidify a very important male identification that gave me insight into the struggles of identity formation.

In reviewing some of the important experiences of my analysis, I realize that some of them were highly nonverbal in nature. I still recall one day in my analyst's office when I discovered a bronze sculpture of a very sensuous woman reaching out in a most erotic pose. My immediate reaction was one of revulsion, but he challenged me to touch it. Slowly and with much anxiety, I followed his instructions. The act of touching opened up a whole arena of experiences regarding eroticism and closeness. There was something very frightening about this very new experience in my life. Art, then, even in analysis, became a very action-oriented experience.

As for the session with the clay skull, my analyst taught me a very basic lesson. He was not an art therapist, but he possessed a very intuitive and sensitive feel for art. This became a very important principle in how I taught art therapy. Not everything is an expression of the true self. It is important for us to look at resistances and protections that are a part of the art, as well as to discover the underlying affects and feelings about the self.

In my search for the definition of art therapy, something else was happening on a very deep and personal level: the male part of me as well as the feminine stopped warring with one another. The artistic and analytical parts of my self came together. I discovered the rhythm of going deep inside one's self and then reaching out to the world to make some sense of one's intuitive experiences. In many respects art therapy created for me a wholeness, an integration that I was searching for all my life.

Over my fifty-three years of practice in the mental health field, my development has been marked by an evolution characterized by an expanding, letting go, and reorganizing of concepts and experiences that have led to a new synthesis of material. As a psychoanalyst, psychologist and art therapist as well as a sculptor, I have witnessed tremendous cross-fertilization that has occurred in my perception of each profession. During the course of this long career I have trained analysts and art therapists as well as psychologists. I have held faculty positions in psychoanalytic institutes as well as art therapy programs. In each of these areas there is a good deal of cross-fertilization that occurs from one profession to another. Each one of these fields holds a commonality of the intuitive as well as the linear, of understanding the importance of body communication, and the recognition that the visual-motor is our first byway into awareness and sets the stage for cognitive integration.

As a teacher I often hear the lament, "What can you do with so many patients in such a short time?" From my perspective, if we give up a goal orientation to therapeutic growth, and appreciate what occurs from moment to moment in therapeutic time, we are no longer thrown into a demoralized state of chaos. Each moment, then, becomes important. This approach ultimately led to one of my last books, *Therapeutic Presence*. Here, grounding, finding your center, an awareness of body communication, all are a part of doing deep work, even within one solitary session.

As I review my professional development, the artist who played a central role in my foundation was not an art therapist but a sculpting teacher called Lilly Entie. In many respects, she was my role model for what an art therapy relationship could ultimately present. I started to write about the love relationship between a teacher, the artist and his material, where touching, sensitive intonations and sharing of common space become very important. I soon learned in my own art pieces that early attachment issues seemed to permeate and determine the kind of work I did. My work was full of touch and symbolic communication around the deepest part of contact between mother and child. I started out with clay but soon moved on to stone. Being, however, a rather impatient person, stone simply took too much out of me. I then discovered metal, and was back at the stove, finding my first love, being an alchemist. I loved to see how metal could dance under fire and how it concentrated and demanded all my energies to be focused on the art process. For me, becoming a junk sculptor was discovering a lost piece of myself. As part of being a sculptor who wanders in junkyards, I found the art process starting right there. As I wandered around discovering lost pieces, it was like finding lost pieces of my self that needed healing and finding a new home to live in. Now as I look back at my experience in welding and the pleasure I discovered in finding new meanings and connections with discarded pieces, I suspect that this had much to do with both my parents feeling like orphans.

My introduction to welding took place at the New Hampshire Festival of the Arts. Here, musicians and dancers, artists and sculptors worked together in harmony. I recall first discovering the festival; it was like entering a magical community. I was excited by the melding of different artists, musicians and dancers. After my first year of attendance, the American Art Therapy Association held its annual conference in Virginia Beach. I recall the faculty and myself standing at the edge of the ocean, carrying with us sparklers that we threw into the air. As we played with the sparklers the whole beach lit up, and I remember the full moon adding light that seemed to encompass all of us. As we watched the sparklers burst into dancing lights, I shared with my fellow faculty the experiences of the previous summer in New Hampshire. I remarked how excited I became when I was part of an artistic community that had in residence a ballet company, a symphonic orchestra, and sculptors working in the background. "What would you think," I proposed, "if we created a resident summer arts therapy program in New Hampshire?" We all thought it was a great idea and approached the building of this program with an involved sense of enthusiasm. The kernels of our summer program, then, really started with the sparklers of Virginia Beach.

This summer program evolved into a unique conception, even though there were other summer programs already in operation. Ours was a melding of artists at work who intermingled with art therapy students. An exciting new form of teaching developed. The program was very intensive. People from all over the country met for a few weeks in the summer, and the sunsets, the mountains, the artistic atmosphere and the symphonic music with its melodic sounds inspired them. Here was the ideal teaching circumstance, where nature and art and music seemed to find their place and formed a very exciting mosaic of expression. During the summers that followed, I devoted a good deal of time to welding, creating exciting new pieces that were placed all over the lawn. In time the festival closed and left for greener pastures, and we were left by ourselves. Soon, the owner sold the grounds to developers. I was informed during the winter that my pieces were gathered up and sold to a junkyard. Many of my colleagues were upset when they learned of this. As for myself, I thought that I had the best of it. I'd had the experience of creating, and that was most important. Of course I missed my old pieces, the protectors of the lawn, but it was an important lesson that one learns and relearns: nothing lasts forever. For letting go and discovering something new is a basic axiom of life. I still have pictures of my sculptures, reaching up twenty to thirty feet high. It was very important for me to move on. I recognized the loss but was ready for a new mixture of experiences.

Within this very complex pattern of work, I also began teaching in Europe; I have returned there to teach for over twenty-five years. One of my closest colleagues in Europe, a glass sculptor, offered me the opportunity to work with glass. I created glass lamps and tables. Working with glass was like creating a giant pizza. I would put my creations in the oven and experienced the delight of the new forms that would come out by accident. There was something glorious in the interplay of light and glass and color. There again, I was reaching back to my old fantasies of fire. It was like returning to an old love affair and discovering it in a new form.

Arthur Robbins creating a sculpture.

In the meantime I was growing older, and my body was showing signs of wear and tear. At the ripe old age of seventy-three, I became a candidate for open-heart surgery. I required a new aortic valve. I was told that the operation had a very good success record, albeit the procedure was a very complicated one. When I learned of the statistics of a 95% recovery rate I entered the operation with a good deal of confidence. However, I failed to fully understand the complications that could arise after a successful operation. On the second day I was diagnosed with pneumonia. I was hooked up to all kinds of tubes and basically found myself in no-man's land, hovering somewhere between life and death. I spent seven days in the ICU room, living on the margin between darkness and light. The family was gathered around me. My youngest daughter, a pediatrician, was part of our advance patrol, letting us know the newest medical developments regarding my case. Standing on one side of my bed was my wife and on the other side my son, both of whom were schooled in the basics of applying healing energy. I felt their love like a rich cradle of holding. Frankly, I don't remember much about this experience, for I lay there in a semi-comatose state. Yet, I do recall the light that seemed to be emanating from both sides of me. This light became my personal beacon of hope, giving evidence that there was a world out there. The beacon held a steady light, even though I was being tossed back and forth in a stormy sea.

That experience created a lasting impact on me. I could offer you such words as transcendence, or transformation, but perhaps this story will give you an insight into my personal experience of light. Eight days after the open-heart surgery procedure was completed the doctors attempted to take the tubes out of my body, but my body simply could not handle it. I was throwing up, and much to my dismay they placed all the tubes back inside of me. When my wife entered the room that day, she carried with her a copy of *The New York Times*. I motioned to her that I wanted to see the *Times*. She began to open it up for me. With much effort I motioned to her that I wanted to hold it in my own hands and turn the pages myself. Half conscious of what I was looking at, I began to read and get some sense of what was going on in the world. Politics had become a very important part of my life. Slowly, as I read the paper, something very interesting happened. As my involvement and attention to the articles in the *Times* increased, the numbers that were monitored by my machines started to move towards normal. The doctors gathered around me, wondering what was going on. Something didn't compute. Here was a man holding up *The New York Times*, and hooked up to every tube you could imagine. His numbers were now normal! I was immediately unhooked from the life support systems. As I look back on this experience, I still remember that light that was my guide—my guide back to reality. Yet, the full articulation of the light still eludes me. Certainly, artists have painted light that surrounds religious figures, and writers have alluded to the light that emanates from very special healers. The light, for me, holds its own unique mystery, touching the deepest recesses of my unconscious. Perhaps it was a way of making contact with the deepest, darkest part of my existence. Certainly I can say that it held some degree of hope and connection. But it was much more. To this day, I cannot give it form or shape.

After thirty-five years as a pioneer, teacher and mentor, I have further thoughts about the future of art therapy. I believe that the masters training programs must be devoted to imparting the fundamentals to new students that would help them find entry-level jobs. I believe that profound and basic research belongs on a doctoral level, where adequate training and methodology can prepare practitioners to deal with very complex problems. From my perspective, the major job of a masters program is one of helping students move into the world of work. Doctoral programs are needed to develop leaders with knowledge of research and leadership skills.

This leads me to a much broader concern of mine regarding the institutionalization of art therapy. I accept the development of standards, both for art therapy programs and the certifying process. Yet I am constantly preoccupied by the developing bureaucracy of art therapy, which may be more concerned with regulations than with imparting room and space for creative expression and exploration. I am truly worried about the preoccupation with meeting the letter of the instructions for annual meeting proposals, at the cost of originality and freedom. It is also sad to me that our students will now take additional courses so that they can meet licensing requirements. I fear that the very creative may move to other fields that are not so restrictive. Is it possible, I wonder, to maintain standards and still make room for the experimental and the nonconventional? To function outside the box is an important dimension of good art therapy. Can't we have our regulations and criteria without stifling someone who needs to follow his or her own voice?

Along different lines, I am saddened that the entire field of mental health has not addressed the increasing polarization of society. Art therapists have something very unique to offer a conflicted world where groups of people are set against one another. Nonverbal expression cuts across social boundaries and may offer a new commonality of connection among diverse populations. As an organization, we need to sponsor workshops that take place throughout the world and offer a meeting ground that cuts across the linear as well as our prejudices and biases. In the recent film "Born into Brothels," a young photographer teaches children whose mothers are prostitutes the very basic elements of photography. Their world opens up, and a few even leave the ghetto and see the world through different eyes. We art therapists have a very powerful tool that can facilitate an understanding of different cultures and their commonalities. I know some of this work has already begun between Israelis and Arabs.

As I close this chapter, some important truths now seem to be reaffirmed over years of professional work. An art therapy relationship is an intersubjective one. Truth holds no one form of reality, and what works for one situation does not necessarily apply to another. Individualism and the ability to listen to one's body are important to the development of an intuitive feel for one's work. As part of my acceptance speech upon receiving the American Art Therapy Association's HLM award, I stated that I am proud to be a member of an association that offers me this highest award, one that respects individualism and honors someone who needs to go his own way. I am grateful to the association and all my students and colleagues for providing so many enlightening experiences that have contributed to a broader vision of what art therapy can potentially offer our patients as well as ourselves. (Parenthetically, art therapy has provided a new sandbox for play and a permeable border for the transmission of ideas, feelings and new horizons.)

I have just come from a new doctor, who is schooled in oriental medicine. After taking my pulse, he commented that I have too much fire and not enough water.

Vija B. Lusebrink, center, with Sandra Graves-Alcorn and Marcia Rosal.

Chapter 21

VIJA B. LUSEBRINK

PER ASPERA AD ASTRA OR THE PATH OF
AN ART THERAPIST

INTRODUCTION AND BACKGROUND

Looking back over my life from an eighty-year perspective brings to my mind the question: what are the seemingly mysterious ways that give us the ability to face life challenges and ultimately focus on a path innate to our strengths and yearnings? There seems to be a continuous thread that weaves through seemingly unrelated experiences and builds on these to help us find inner fulfillment.

I was born in a physician's family in Riga, the capital of then independent Latvia. My best memories of those years are from my grandmother's farm, where I spent summers during my first ten years and returned again in my middle teens. My interest in drawing started early. As the story goes, one time when I could not find a flat surface to draw on, I placed my drawing book on my stomach and continued drawing. This came to an abrupt end, though, when I was six or seven years old with the arrival of a governess who insisted that I learn to draw perspective. The mechanical aspects of drawing were further reinforced in my drawing classes at school and drawing from gypsum casts. These activities effectively killed the rest of my ability for self-expression at that time. I still would look longingly at the beautiful art materials in store windows, and later at the bright colors of French paintings in museums.

The history lessons in school prepared us for the difficulties of being born in a small country which had been overrun and occupied for seven centuries by its powerful neighbors, including German crusaders and Swedish and Russian armies. At the beginning of World War II, it was my generation's turn to follow the path of history. Latvia was annexed to the Soviet Union in

1939, followed by mass deportations to Siberia in 1941. My aunt, uncle, small cousins, grand-aunt and grand-uncle, and later my grandmother, were among those deported. My parents escaped deportation by seeking refuge under a false name in an insane asylum, where my father's friend was the director of the institution.

Vija B. Lusebrink, age 6, and sister Maija, age 2.

The advancing German armies pushed the Russians back for three years, but with the collapse of the Eastern front in 1944, it was obvious that our lives were in danger. My father had died already in 1942, and our car had been confiscated. My mother organized a horse, buggy, and a cow from her brother in the country and, along with my younger sister, we joined the long lines of refugees fleeing to the west from the approaching armies. As the front came closer to the west coast of Latvia, we were able to get on a German transport ship carrying refugees as workers for German war factories. Our destination was unknown to us at that time, but we found ourselves in Breslau (occupied Poland) in a concentration-like camp, surrounded by high barbed wire fences and guard towers with machine guns. Part of this camp housed Polish forced labor workers who were so starved that they could not stand up; they crawled on the ground, begging food from us through their barbed wire partition. When we were transported, again under guard, to a barbed wire enclosed camp in Erfurt in the middle of Germany, I had a clear idea in my mind that we had to get out of this situation as soon as possible. Our opportunity came when the Allied forces bombed the camp and the refugees were readied for another transport. In the ensuing melee at the train station, we were able to escape the transport. We melted into German everyday life with its nightly aircraft attacks by the Allied forces. We were looking forward to our liberation by the Allies while at the same time fearing for our lives. Even after the Allied forces occupied Erfurt, we had to face new difficulties, since this area was supposed to become part of the Soviet zone. We set out again, this time with our few belongings in a handcart, walking towards the west to a town where the Allied forces were gathering refugees and foreign workers for evacuation to the American zone.

I had had a year of training after high school in Latvia as a medical technician, and I ended up working in this capacity in a refugee camp. Being young and restless, I tried to apply to universities. My first choice would have been to apply to a medical school, but in post-war bombed-out Germany, I was lucky to be admitted to the chemistry department in Frankfurt a. Main. I studied for three years until the possibility came for refugees to immigrate, first to England, then to Australia. I had made my decision that I only wanted to go to the United States. President Truman had set up special quotas for immigration to the United States for "displaced persons" who could not return to their home countries as a result of World War II. We had obtained sponsors in the United States through the International Refugee Organization (IRO), but it took us two years to be considered for immigration because my sister had contracted tuberculosis as a result of living in the unsanitary conditions in the German camps.

Eventually, in 1950, I ended up on a Sunday morning in June at the Sandusky, Ohio, train station with $5 in my pocket and nowhere to go. The minister of the local Lutheran church and his family took me in and provided a job as a nurse's aide in a hospital. I had already applied through the International Refugee Organization for a scholarship, which came through and in fall 1950 I enrolled in the University of Nevada at Reno Chemistry Department. I graduated with a Bachelor of Science in chemistry in 1951 and married a fellow chemistry student, a born Californian. After a detour to graduate school at Pennsylvania State College, I was ready to settle down, this time in the San Francisco Bay area in California, where we had three daughters.

I returned to my first love, art, and received a Master of Arts degree in painting in 1964 from the University of California, Berkeley, Department of Art and had a solo show "People by Windows." During this time my husband finished his Ph. D. in physical chemistry. Brief stays in Santa Monica, California, and Morris Plains, New Jersey, gave me the opportunity to explore museums and galleries and attend "happenings" in Los Angeles and New York. We returned to California in 1968. I had been trying to establish myself as an artist, but I realized that I did not have a successful artist's size of ego and that I lacked the self-promotional skills to succeed as an artist. At this point in my life—in my middle forties—I felt lost and disoriented about my direction and goals after the many moves and trying to build a new life for myself and my family. A license to teach art in Junior Colleges gave me the opportunity to teach landscape and figure-painting classes, but I needed a larger challenge and commitment than that. Luckily for me, I was back in California amidst its Human Potential Movement.

SELF-EXPLORATION AND BEGINNINGS OF
MY ART THERAPY CAREER

In my search for direction to follow in life, I participated in a 24-hour "marathon group" led by a psychiatrist and a dance therapist who incorporated nonverbal modes of expression. During this session, I became aware of how much people's expressions and communication through drawings supplemented their verbal communications. Similar to the stories of many art therapists, my transition to art therapy was a calling that took me by surprise and force. That night I decided to become an art therapist, even though I did not know what it would entail to become one. As I embarked in 1969 on my search for information about art therapy, I was lucky to live near Stanford University and its Medical School library. I found there back issues of the *Bulletin of Art Therapy* and other material on art therapy, including Plokker's *Art from the Mentally Disturbed*. I enrolled in selected psychology classes at the local state college and started to volunteer at Agnews State Mental Hospital in San Jose, California, offering to the patients groups in art expression.

During that time a group of mental health professionals had obtained a large research grant from the National Institute of Mental Health to open a research ward at the Agnews Hospital. Their research was designed to inves-

Vija B. Lusebrink's "People by Windows: Ted in Berkeley."

tigate the effect of the reconstitution of schizophreniform patients with or without using psychotropic drugs. I was able to join the team as a research assistant/art therapist. The four years working with the research project was indispensable experience for me as an art therapist. I worked daily with floridly psychotic schizophrenics, and their visual expressions provided me a window into their experiences. Often the patients perceived their environment and the people who worked with them in a symbolic context. I was the "cat woman" with a third eye since I could relate to their visual expression. At one time I was also a "Russian spy" because of my foreign accent. Some patients used the whole ward for their art work, making assemblages by using furniture and posting signs on the walls to express their inner journey.

I compiled stacks of patients' drawings and paintings with their comments and dates of completion. Their comments gave me many insights into their visual expressions, supplemented by the research data and follow-up interviews collected a year later. Among many books on symbolism, therapy, and altered states of consciousness during this time, I also read Kramer's *Art as Therapy with Children* and Horowitz's *Image Formation and Cognition.* The latter book gave me good insight into understanding imagery, its formation, and different levels, including imagery evoked through electrical stimulation of different parts of the brain.

Living in the San Francisco Bay Area in the early 1970s gave me many opportunities to explore and participate in the Human Potential Movement. I explored workshops dealing with guided imagery, Sufi stories, dance/movement therapy, Jungian symbolism, psychodrama, and sand-tray therapy, among others. Through the Agnews State Hospital research project, I was able to participate in Gestalt therapy workshops at the Esalen Center in Big Sur, California. I also joined two groups of women therapists, one of which was interested in using art in therapy, the other in transpersonal psychology as therapy.

In the early 1970s, a group of San Francisco Bay artists, art educators, and therapists who used art in their approach to therapy started meeting to discuss the formation of an art therapy association in Northern California. The first meeting included people with very disparate views and needs. From these meetings eventually emerged a group of committed individuals using art in therapy that became the core of the Northern California Art Therapists Association (NCATA). We continued to meet at each others' homes, sharing our observations on art therapy and leading workshops. Among the early participants were Janie Rhyne, Gestalt art therapist, Virginia Goldstein, artist and art therapist, and Janet Long, who was volunteering and working with me in art therapy at Agnews Hospital. A dynamic addition to the group was Cay Drachnik, an artist who had been teaching art in a mental health clinic in Washington, D.C. She had obtained my name from Elinor Ulman from the list of subscribers to the *Bulletin of Art Therapy*, which Elinor edited.

Janie Rhyne had studied Gestalt therapy with Fritz Perls and was conducting art therapy workshops at her home in Pescadero, California, located in a redwood setting. Janie's directness and openness to others and their art work provided an inviting environment for self-expression and exploration. Janie eventually moved to Santa Cruz, California, where she enrolled in the Ph.D. program in the Psychology Department at the University of California, Santa Cruz. Her home in Santa Cruz became a special place for me to visit; Janie and I had long discussions about art therapy, creativity, and humanistic psychology.

Ted and I divorced after our second return to California. In retrospect, it seems that we both were going through a mid-life crisis at that time, and five relocations in eight years had left us depleted and unable to give each other the emotional support we each needed.

In 1973, the NIH research grant at Agnews State Hospital finished, and I had to look for a new job. I wanted to teach art therapy and to share my acquired knowledge and experience with others. Virginia Goldstein and I started looking into the possibility of establishing an art therapy program and submitted a proposal to the Lone Mountain College in San Francisco. Our efforts, though, were premature, and we could not get funding because of economic difficulties at that time. I taught two courses in art therapy through the Adult Education program at San Jose State College, but I was not successful in finding employment as an art therapist in the San Francisco Bay Area.

TEACHING AT THE UNIVERSITY OF LOUISVILLE, KENTUCKY

In 1974, I saw an advertisement in the *American Journal of Art Therapy* (formerly the *Bulletin of Art Therapy*) for a faculty opening for an art therapist in Louisville, Kentucky, at the University of Louisville. The decision to move to Louisville was a hard one for me, since my three daughters, who had started their college educations, had just lost their father. My departure for Louisville in summer 1974 was another loss for them. I cried half-way across the country grieving for my ex-husband as I was driving from Palo Alto, California, to Louisville.

The Louisville Art Therapy Graduate Program was directed by Sandra Kagin (now Sandra Graves-Alcorn), a dynamic woman who had been instrumental in organizing the first art therapy meeting in Louisville in 1969 to form the American Art Therapy Association (AATA).

I enjoyed teaching and sharing with the students my knowledge and experiences as an art therapist. In elective classes, I introduced topics such as imagery and the use of different expressive modalities in therapy, based on knowledge I had gained from the many workshops I had attended in California. My personal response to living in Louisville, however, with its anti-busing protest marches, was a shock after living in California. My reservations about living in Kentucky were mollified by its beautiful springs with blooming dogwood, tulip, and redbud trees, plus the Derby.

Attendance at The Annual American Art Therapy Conferences in late fall was part of the curriculum of the Institute of Expressive Therapies (IET). My first conference in the fall of 1974 took place in New York, and I enjoyed meeting art therapists there about whom I had heard and whose works I had read: Eleanor Ulman, Bernard Levy, Edith Kramer, Hanna Kwiatkowska, Helen Landgarten, and Felice Cohen, among others. At the conference, I gave a presentation on my work with schizophrenics; it was my first entry in a long list of my many presentations at these conferences for 21 years until my retirement. The next conference was in Louisville, and the organization of the event rested on the shoulders of IET faculty and students. One of the highlights of the conference was the excitement created by an experiential workshop where the participants had set a fire in a trash can, which prompted the arrival of firemen in screeching fire trucks.

In the fall of 1975, a family therapist, Joe Griffis, joined the IET faculty. Joe had studied family art therapy with Hanna Kwiatkowska, and as an ex-marine he had the ability to move quickly in unusual circumstances. This ability came in handy one day when I was in our offices alone at lunchtime and was cornered by a stranger who had walked in unexpectedly through the unlocked front door. Fortunately, Joe returned and, assessing the situation in an instant, pulled out his gun, escorted the intruder to the lab and asked him to draw his Kinetic Family Drawing on the blackboard while Joe was waiting for the police to arrive. During that semester I also had a chance to demonstrate through action the skills I had learned in psychodrama work in California. The students had been dissatisfied with some of the actions at the Institute of Expressive Therapies and they were holding long meetings that ended up interfering with my class time. At one point I decided that I had had enough of interferences with the classes, and for a "Methods of Art Therapy" class I took a large sheet of brown paper, laid it down on the floor and covered myself up with it. The students came in, but for a time did not react to my unusual behavior. As some of the students started to leave the class, I rose up from the floor and declared that I failed the whole class for the day for not responding to my body language.

In the summer of 1976 I took a leave of absence from the IET. My mother, who lived in San Francisco, was getting weak and had difficulties with walking. In addition, I had discovered an area of skin cancer on my back. At Sacramento State College in Sacramento, California, Donald Uhlin, the Director of its art therapy program, was on a sabbatical leave for the upcoming fall semester, and I took his place. At the end of the semester, I was exhausted from the aftereffects of the radiation therapy; I did not have enough strength to deal with the challenges which I would have to face moving back to Kentucky, and I resigned from my position at the IET program there.

As I started to look for an art therapy position in California, I still had access to the library at Sacramento State College. I pursued reading wide-ranging subjects, directly and indirectly related to my different interests in art therapy. At this time I started to formulate the different levels of expression and information processing involved in art therapy and how these were activated through interaction with art media. My studies of the different facets of art therapy included symbolism, the Gestalt approach, and formal aspects of visual expression, cognitive information processing, and creativity. These different aspects of knowledge aligned themselves along a developmentally based sequence of kinesthetic/sensory, perceptual/affective, and cognitive /symbolic levels. This insight became the basis for the concept later defined as the "Expressive Therapies Continuum." In spring 1977 I reapplied for the art therapy faculty position at the University of Louisville, since I had not been successful in my job search in California.

SECOND SOJOURN IN LOUISVILLE

I arrived in Louisville in the summer of 1977 rested and looking forward to teaching again. This time I was ready to expand my teaching based on the knowledge I had accumulated through my studies in Sacramento and my own theoretical formulations. I also wanted to pursue a doctorate degree.

In addition to teaching and supervision, I saw some pro-bono clients in the laboratory room with students as co-therapists. One time we dealt with a depressed young man whom I encouraged to throw clay at a target pinned on the wall in the laboratory in order to help him express his pent-up anger. He picked up a large hunk of clay and with all his might threw it against the wall. With a crash, the wall gave in and instead of a target there was a gaping hole in the wall. The poor young man had a terrified expression on his face as he looked at the consequences of his action. I started to laugh in surprise, as I was not concerned about the building which had already been designated for demolition. I reflected the client's feelings and the harmlessness of his actions in this case back to him. This incident seemed to be a turning point for the better in his therapy.

Upon my return to the Institute of Expressive Therapies, my work there was made more upbeat than before due to three factors. I shared with Sandra my concept of different levels of expression and interaction with art media in art therapy. Sandra's Master's Thesis in 1969 had been on media dimensions in art therapy, and she was able to elaborate on my ideas from this and also from cognitive viewpoints. Sandra had a facility with words and writing, and we had many creative laughs working on the project of producing a paper on the Expressive Therapies Continuum (ETC). Second, while in California I had decided already that I wanted to work towards a doctoral degree. The University of Louisville at that time was offering an interdisciplinary doctoral degree. I designed a program incorporating psychology and psychiatry courses related to therapy and imagery, and my specific interests in these areas.

Lastly, my endeavors were also buoyed by the arrival of Janie Rhyne as a faculty member at the IET in 1979. Janie was just finishing writing her own dissertation on a study of visual dynamics. Janie, Sandra, and I used to meet together for discussions of our different viewpoints about art therapy. Janie was solidly grounded in Gestalt psychology and visual dynamics, whereas Sandra and I had been teaching the different levels of the Expressive Therapies Continuum based on a developmental sequence of visual expression. My special interest was symbolism, and in the heat of one of our discussions Janie declared emphatically: "I do not get into dragons, I get into lines." The main area of differences of our opinions was that Janie saw art therapy as consisting of different approaches related to different psychological schools of thought. According to her, art therapy did not have enough substance in what could be called a theory. My view was that art therapy had something unique to offer through the creative involvement of the whole body in expression through art media and that the theories of art therapy needed to be formulated. Janie was a clear thinker and she presented a good challenge to our thinking. Janie was interested in research and she stimulated and challenged the students' thinking in this direction. We were sorry to see her leave the IET in 1980 in her move to Iowa to be closer to her family.

In 1984, I finished my Ph. D. degree in Interdisciplinary Studies with areas of concentration in psychology and psychiatry. My knowledge and experience as an art therapist had given me a strong sense of direction for my doctoral studies. My main focus was on imagery, its different perceptual and psychophysiological components, and its applicability in therapy. My doctoral dissertation was *Visual Imagery: Its Psychophysiological Components and Levels of Information Processing.* It showed the significant differential increase in covert muscle activity concurrent with simple images. I was lucky at that time to have available for my studies the facilities of the Perfomance Laboratory at the University of Louisville, directed by F. J. McGuigan. His interests were cognitive psychophysiology and the principles of covert behavior. My ultimate reward of writing the dissertation and publishing the results was the multitude of requests for copies I received from many parts of the world. I expanded my thoughts on art therapy and the brain later in a paper.

After obtaining my degree, I embarked on the writing of a book on art therapy and imagery synthesizing the knowledge gained through my studies, papers and articles. My book *Imagery and Visual Expression in Therapy* consolidated the different strands of my theoretical and clinical knowledge. Working on the several drafts of the manuscript helped me to elaborate on my concept of the different levels of the Expressive Therapies Continuum. I regret that upon my retirement I was not able to follow through on working on the second edition of my book, due to illnesses that curtailed my mobility and energy level.

I had worked hard to pursue my degree while teaching at the same time. I feel that the time span from 1986 to 1995 was a time for me to reap the fruits of my labor. The IET had become the Expressive Therapies Program (ET), and I became its Director in 1986. That same year Marcia Rosal, who was a graduate of our program and had obtained a Ph.D. in Educational Psychology from the University of Queensland, Australia, joined the ET faculty. Marcia's high standards of teaching research classes were reflected in the ET students receiving Elinor Ulman prizes for writing in art therapy. The ET was also able to offer areas of concentration in grief art therapy, group art therapy, and family art therapy.

Art therapy for the most part was well-accepted in the Louisville therapeutic community. The student interests helped to create new practicum locations that in turn became places of employment for art therapists. About half of the ET students came from different areas nationally and also internationally. I find myself enjoying looking back on the more than four hundred graduates of the Expressive Therapies Program and the more than one hundred fifty locations of practicum settings available to the students in Louisville, nationally, and also abroad during my time as a faculty and Director of the Program. In my experience and opinion, these nine years were very successful for the ET program. I regret that I did not have the ability to provide a supportive environment for the Expressive Therapies Program and its faculty within the ongoing restructuring of schools at the University of Louisville. The Expressive Therapies Program has survived, though, in a different location and context at the University of Louisville.

SPECIAL AREAS OF INTEREST

In addition to two core courses and supervision, I taught three elective courses, all of which reflected my diverse interests in the expressive therapies. The "Methods of Expressive Therapies" course, with the help of guest faculty, covered a brief survey of the different expressive modalities of music, drama and psychodrama, dance and movement, bibliotherapy, and the use of guided imagery and dreams in therapy.

Another area of a special interest to me was cross cultural symbolism and the emergence of symbols in self-actualization. I had grown up in a culture that was still close to its ethnic roots, folklore, and folksongs, with their metaphors and symbolism. I was attracted to Jungian symbolism, and appreciated the opportunity to be exposed to John Perry, a Jungian Analyst, and his work with schizophrenics at the Agnews Hospital research project. My work with schizophrenics there helped me understand their states of altered consciousness and their symbolic perception of everyday reality in their quest for the reconstitution of self. In my opinion, to open a door to altered states of consciousness has been a prerogative of many artists, and the willingness to become aware of these states was an important tool especially for art therapists.

My special elective course, though, was the use of imagery and art therapy in the enhancement of healing. I joined the Arts in Therapy group led by Joel Elkes, Psychiatry Professor Emeritus, at the University of Louisville Medical School. Elkes was interested in alternative approaches to medicine and healing and had gathered a group of like-minded faculty members from different disciplines for monthly meetings and exchanges of ideas. I had seen the benefits of art therapy in lessening pain and depression in arthritis patients through the work of art therapist Janet Long, who had worked with my mother in dealing with her severe arthritis. One of my interests was the use of imagery and art therapy as supportive therapy for cancer patients, and I was able to obtain a grant for a study using sand-tray therapy based on the application of sand-tray therapy with cancer patient groups at the Commonwheel treatment program in Bolinas, California. The first part of my research was to investigate and evaluate the elements of sand-tray expressions and their correlations with the personality characteristics of subjects. The second part addressed the use of sand-tray therapy with breast cancer patients to enhance their coping resources.

When I started my research with the breast cancer patients, little did I anticipate that five years later my middle daughter Karen would have to undergo a mastectomy because of breast cancer. Eventually her cancer metastasized to the brain lining, bones, and other parts of her body. By then, I had retired and had returned to the San Francisco Bay Area, where she lived, so I could spend time with her and help her take care of her daughter. Karen was a fighter, and she survived the first attack of the metastases. For the following five years, we were alternating between hope and grief for her life. The suffering my daughter went through in her treatment and her ultimate death from cancer was heartbreaking to watch. While I was taking care of her, the last two months of her life were especially hard for me because there was nothing I could do to save her.

Karen was a professional artist, and her creative involvement in painting helped her to deal with her pain, the effects of chemotherapy, and depressive tendencies caused by the severity of her illness. Karen's use of dance therapy as expressive and emotional release up to the last months of her life showed me again the necessity to incorporate expressive therapies as an alternative and supportive therapy in the management of chronic and terminal illnesses.

INFLUENCE OF ART THERAPY ON MY LIFE AND ACTIVITIES

My involvement in art therapy gave me an increased appreciation of dreams, visual journals, and art. My dream life has always been active, and for the most part I have looked forward to sleeping and dreaming. My dreams also have reflected my anxieties, concerns, and physical illnesses, as for example the scary images of large fast-growing broccoli stems when I had discovered a spot of basal cell carcinoma on my back.

I started to record my dreams in the transitional and searching period after my return to Palo Alto in the late 1960s. During this time, my dreams reflected the internal and external turmoil I felt: I dreamed of stairs leading to nowhere, blocked stairs, stairs overgrown with vines, twisting and turning, and stairs with missing steps. In the summer of 1970 I went to the Esalen Center in Big Sur, California, to learn Gestalt therapy. Upon my return home, I had an important dream. The previous evening I had drawn a dream image of a scary Russian soldier on guard blocking my path. During the night I dreamt that I was sitting on the floor of a ship's deck with a group of women and singing in a "common language." The ship was cruising along a sunlit rugged coast of Greece. The feeling of community and joy I experienced in the dream stayed with me for many years, and I have kept coming back to it in times of emotional need. About a year later, I had a dream that seemed again to be special without references to everyday activities. In this dream two lighted figures were carrying a "light structure" in the form of a small electrical power tower as a spear. They were met by a regular male who had a large hollow sticklike pen in his hand; he had to fill it with the energy from the lighted structure, while he was hiding behind a section of a fence as a shield. These dreams seemed to be very special or "big dreams" with Jungian archetypal components, as compared to regular dreams dealing with everyday affairs. Over the years I have recorded over 1,500 dreams that seemed important at particular times. Dream journals became part of my teaching requirements; I asked the students to write summaries about reoccurring dreams and their development over a period of time.

My other journals in the form of visual "doodle diaries" became especially important to me in Louisville while living by myself after more than twenty years of living with my family and raising children. I would draw my reactions to the events of the day or anything else that was on my mind. Often, I started just with a scribble to reflect my mood and let the images emerge from the tangled lines. At times my doodles and images in the visual journal would become the scenery in my dreams. Expressions in the visual journals also provided for me a way to satisfy my artistic needs and a bridge to the time when I would have a longer period of time to devote to painting. My more than twelve visual journals are also a record of my inner experience of my sojourn in Louisville.

Vija B. Lusebrink's dream image "Light Structure."

Many images were based on my dreams which in turn reflected my inner experiences and reactions to dealing with life. Some of the centering dreams with images of wholeness were very welcome among the other ones of being overwhelmed or facing threats, including some still left over from the war years. The expression of my moods became important to me as did my efforts to center myself through enclosed and/or repetitive forms. The diary helped me to deal with my sadness and problem solving, as I kept on sublimating my experiences and feelings through images of "pulling together."

The challenges of my doctoral studies produced dreams of "rusty pipes" and "energy leakage." It was interesting to me that as I became involved in writing papers for my studies, my expression in the diaries became more verbal than before. The period of six years of working on my dissertation and writing my book on art therapy yielded only one diary book, whereas I had created eleven diary books in the period between 1974 and 1981. Apparently, my creative energies had been redirected into an academic stream.

A real involvement in artistic expression for me required a prolonged period of time, as if I had to step into another state of consciousness different from everyday activities. I joined a group of women artists drawing from a model while still in Louisville, and after retirement I started to paint from models with a group of artists in Palo Alto, California. My major project after my retirement from the University of Louisville in 1995 was building an art studio in the back yard of my house. I had not counted, though, on the deterioration of my spine due to severe scoliosis, and my painting had to slow down considerably because of the pain.

Vija B. Lusebrink's "Descent."

INVOLVEMENT IN THE AMERICAN ART
THERAPY ASSOCIATION (AATA)

Interaction with other art therapists had been very important to me in the early 1970s living in California, in that it affirmed my identity as an art therapist and expanded my knowledge of art therapy. After moving to Louisville, my involvement in the art therapy community expanded to a national level through my different activities in the American Art Therapy Association as a member of its committees. The annual Art Therapy Educators Convocations, initiated by Sandra Kagin (now Graves-Alcorn) in 1978, provided an opportunity to interact with other art therapy educators and exchange ideas and concerns common to all of us. My special interests were the employment or "marketability" of art therapy graduates and the definitions and differentiation of art therapy competencies. As a Regional Chair of the Standards Committee, I conducted a survey in 1981 of all registered art therapists' views of art therapy competencies. While I was the Chair of the Research Committee, I conducted a survey of doctoral work by art therapists with the help of Marcia Rosal and Michael Campanelli. I had hoped thus to encourage a mentor system between the art therapy doctorates and graduate students.

I enjoyed the exposure to other art therapy programs, their faculty, and students while teaching courses as a guest faculty in different programs, such as the College of Notre Dame in Belmont, California, the University of New Mexico in Albuquerque, the University of Florida in Tallahassee, and Marylhurst College, Portland, Oregon, among others. I also became involved in the formation of the Kentucky Art Therapy Association (KYATA) and I chaired two exhibits showing work of the clients of our graduates in Louisville art galleries.

It is impossible for me to do justice in a limited space to all the students, graduates, and colleagues I have worked with over the years. I was deeply touched to see many of them at my retirement dinners in 1995. The crowning point of the retirement dinner at the University of Louisville was a slide show, organized by Henry Gilliam and the 1995 graduating class. The show featured my face in a large straw hat laughing in different art works, such as: Vija as Velasquez' "Infanta," Vija in an Egyptian bas-relief as "Nephrete's daughter," Vija as the "Winged Victory" sculpture, Vija as a Degas Ballet dancer, and Vija laughing instead of screaming in Munch's "Scream," among the 21 slides presented. I had come full circle in my life returning to my first love art, but now as a contributing performer appreciated by others. The award of Honorary Life Membership by the American Art Therapy Association in 1995 was the ultimate validation of my dream of being an art therapist.

FUTURE OF ART THERAPY

Looking at the field of art therapy from more than a thirty-year perspective, I can appreciate the great strides the field has made: increase in the breadth of the field and the application of art therapy in many areas of therapy, rehabilitation, healing, education, and self-actualization; sophistication of the American Art Therapy Association organization, and its interface with other organizations and agencies; professionalism and sophistication of the art therapy literature and presentations.

In order to maintain the status quo of art therapy as a solid base for future growth of the field, several areas need to be constantly kept in focus: acceptance of diversity of approaches and specializations in art therapy; an ongoing dialogue and appreciation of the differences and contributions of clinical art therapy and studio art therapy is paramount to keep art therapy vital and distinctive as a discipline and profession; continuing moral support for Masters Degree programs as the basic training for art therapy as they struggle for survival, often in nonsupportive academic environments; search for viable employment for art therapists, including cross-training with other licensed disciplines; research in the efficacy of art therapy and in the unique basic mechanisms of healing innate to art therapy. The time and means necessary to conduct such studies are more likely to be realized at the doctoral level of training than at the Masters degree level.

Art therapy offers a unique involvement of mind/body/spirit in the process of self-expression and therapy. The distinctive generative and creative qualities of art therapy provide potential for the growth and expansion of the field, despite the restricting environment of regulations and diminishing funds for mental health. Art therapists, though, need to convey information about art therapy, supported by research, in terms understandable to other mental health professionals.

Mildred Lachman Chapin

Chapter 22

MILDRED LACHMAN CHAPIN

LITTLE SHOWOFF BECOMES ART THERAPIST AND ARTIST

Making long-range plans never seems to work out well for me. I form a vision and then stumble along trying to make that vision come to life. Like every other important step in life, my beginnings in art therapy came as an accident or a kind of offshoot of something else.

I think that there were historic forces in my life, and my own personal wounds, that led me to a need to perform, to express myself, to follow the path of the artist. The introduction to the book of paintings and poetry that I published in 1994, *Reverberations: Mothers and Daughters*, tells this story.

Anyway, I guess I have to start at the end of my overseas decade. My husband was working with A.I.D, the Marshal Plan which helped European countries after World War II to recuperate financially. He was assigned to various countries and attached to the United States embassies in those countries. My children and I came along. We were first in Rome, then he was in Laos (but my children and I never got to Laos because there was a revolutionary action). We were "stranded" in Berkeley, California for nine months. Next we went to Ankara, Turkey, then to Paris.

Actually in 1959 when we went to Rome, our first assignment, I could not find anything going on in modern dance. So I immersed myself seriously in my painting. Rome provided wonderful visual experiences that stimulated my work. Other luxuries, like having a full-time maid and an extra maid's room as a studio, were very encouraging. I produced enough good work to have a show there in 1960, my first. As I recall, I sold quite a few works too.

The following years of our overseas life brought us to spend a year in Berkeley, California, then a couple of years in Ankara, Turkey, and four years in Paris. In all of these places I studied and painted. I was very much influenced by the new environments and art scenes. I did much museum-going and studying the current art being made around me wherever I was.

After 10 years of this exotic and profoundly enriching life, and another year remaining alone in Paris to finish my analysis and to study etching and lithography, I returned home to Washington, D.C. After all this foreign living, I was culturally disoriented returning to the good old USA. Shortly after my return, the Martin Luther King assassination occurred and with it the virtual lock-down of D.C. in the wake of demonstrations there. I felt I was a foreigner in a foreign land.

If I was not a diplomatic helpmate, who was I? As a "helpmate," I struggled to learn the languages of the people around me. I related to foreign nationals as an important United States representative. I tried to orient myself culturally in each country, also guiding my teenage children who had orientation problems of their own (aside from raging adolescent hormones). But back at home, what was I to BE? What was I to DO in my home country?

Helping

And so it was that in 1970, I took my first job in 10 years. (As a U.S. diplomat's wife, having a paying job in the host country was frowned upon.) I worked at the now-famous Lab School in Washington, D.C. This was a novel school program for children with learning disabilities. The guiding vision of the school was that artists would be best equipped to teach these children, since artists could use their senses in very inventive ways to achieve maximum empathy and understanding of these strange children. Little was known at that time about learning disabilities. Sally Smith, the founder of the school, had a child with learning disabilities and could not find an adequate school for him, so she developed one herself. She hired me because I was an artist, had a college degree, and had taught children before.

Teaching these six to eight-year olds in "The Gods Club" about the civilizations of ancient Egypt and Greece proved to be a turning point in my life. I was asked to use as much concrete and sensory input as possible, plus anything else I could dream up. I realized that I had a passion for teaching children, for reaching them in all their strange profiles of strengths and weaknesses, for stirring them to curiosity, and inspiring them to learn in whatever way they could.

At about the same time, in 1970, I found out about a class at the Washington School of Psychiatry taught by someone called Elinor Ulman. She was to teach about art and therapy, whatever that was. I took that course and another with Edith Kramer, and then whatever they offered after that. Linda Gantt and Mari Fleming were in those classes with me; we studied together, all getting our first experience with this new field.

Eventually, I met and studied with Hanna Kwiatkowska and Bernie Levy. Hanna was working at the National Institute of Mental Health (NIMH) at the time, as was Harriet Wadeson, whom I met later. Harriet told me about her work and gave me an idea about the art therapy field. Hanna had developed an art assessment procedure for working with families of schizophrenics. She developed this later into a procedure to be used for all kinds of families. With the help of statisticians at NIMH, she designed a research project to examine the results of her procedure. I remember how awed I was when she discussed this research with our class. It was my first experience with this kind of research. I still treasure her research protocols and analyses, and share this material with my students now.

Bernie Levy was Chair of the Department of Psychology at George Washington University. He had been a pal of Elinor Ulman, and together they had initiated art therapy work at a hospital in Washington, D.C. Along with this work and much thinking they both had about this new approach of art therapy, Elinor's passion grew and later she developed a journal: *The Bulletin of Art Therapy.* Theirs was a most productive friendship. Bernie developed a graduate program in art therapy at George Washington University, one of the earliest programs in the United States for training art therapists.

There were lots of firsts in those days. Elinor's art therapy journal was the first one in this country and perhaps anywhere. She found people all over the United States and abroad who were working with art as therapy. She invited them to submit articles. And often she would invite them to come and give classes or workshops in Washington. This is how I met and took workshops with Janie Rhyne, Edith Wallace, and many others.

I was hooked on art therapy. I had found myself and my profession in my home country. And, as it happened with any art field that interested me, I became a passionate teacher and missionary.

ROOTS IN DANCE

Before going overseas I had had a long history as a modern dancer. Actually I started dancing before I started school. I began as a five-year-old doing tap dancing. I remember performing at street parties and such, following my dance performance with the growling crooning of "Some of these Days." I was what they called a showoff. Then in high school I switched to modern dance. Later, between 1952 and 1955, I was a mother of two children in Washington, D.C., and began teaching and performing modern dance. I helped found the Modern Dance Council of Washington and served as one of its first presidents. The Council brought to D.C. such greats as Jose Limón and Merce Cunningham, who performed and gave workshops.

The first president of the Modern Dance Council of Washington was Marian Chase, who was working at St. Elizabeth's Hospital in D.C. Out of her pioneering work using dance with hospitalized mental patients, she developed what we now call dance therapy. She was eager to pass on what she had learned to someone else. She urged me to join her. I went once to participate in a group, was so drawn in and empathic with the patients that it scared me. I said no, I couldn't do this work. Shortly thereafter, a friend brought me to a painting class. Painting became my new passion and the way I found I could eventually relate to mental patients and help them. I never stopped loving dance and movement, but when it came to doing therapy, I found the visual arts to be a more fitting medium for me.

show off → helper (transition)

INTEGRATING MANY CURRENTS: BEGINNINGS IN ART THERAPY

currents

In addition to the reculturation struggles I experienced in returning to the U.S., I see now that I was driven by a need to pull together the many parts of what had become a somewhat fractured, scattered life. I needed and wanted to integrate things. Just as I later wanted to integrate my dance experience with the visual arts in doing therapy, so it was that as a beginning student of art therapy I also wanted to integrate my experience with learning disabilities and dance into this new profession. There was, at that time in 1970, no graduate program in art therapy in D.C., so I proceeded to take my Master's Degree in Special Education.

I remember my interview with Bernie Levy as I inquired about possibilities of getting a Master's degree in psychology. He discouraged me by telling me that it was only at the Ph.D. level that I could actually make this study worthwhile. What was worthwhile for me was my meeting with this fascinating man. At one point, after I had given him a rundown on what I had accomplished so far in my life, he asked, "are you putting me on?" I had never heard this expression. I guess I came off as an exotic globe trotter.

Bernie and Elinor were the most important mentors in my beginnings as an art therapist. Bernie was the academic professor, with knowledge, standing, and power in the university. He spoke with assurance about his beliefs about what art therapy should and should not be. For one thing, he warned against our becoming "assistant psychiatrists." He told us it was important to learn about psychology and hone our clinical skills, but he was passionate and very articulate about the importance of this profession focusing on our unique specialty, which was the art. He knew the psychology world and what it could and could not offer to mental health, so he exhorted us to step out and develop the newness of what artists could offer to mental health. The students loved him. He was witty, very knowledgeable, insightful, and confrontational in an almost teasing way. He introduced us to the importance of research, good writing, and academic skills. He always included art making in his classes. His two favorite media were watercolor and ceramics. He was very accomplished in both.

What Bernie and Elinor shared, and what has endeared them to those of us who were their students and colleagues, and what also drew much criticism and even hostility from other groups of colleagues, were their bone-solid beliefs in how art therapy should develop. They believed only the finest, most disciplined writing and research should comprise our training and our literature. They were both very political. They knew how to throw their weight into the developing organization that was becoming the American Art Therapy Association. They knew how to proceed and were very vocal. Passionate pioneers, they reaped both much criticism and much devotion along the way.

I am surprised as I meet colleagues now who have never known Elinor. She was so deeply embedded in my being an art therapist that I guess I just took it for granted that everyone else had her inside them as I did. Fortunately she has left a monumental legacy in print. She began the publication of *The Bulletin of Art Therapy* (later becoming the *American Journal of Art Therapy*). She also, for the most part, financed it. It was this journal that began to bring us all together before the American Art Therapy Association was formed. Through the *Bulletin*, Elinor developed the original art therapy community in the United States.

Elinor Ulman was an innovator. She developed an art assessment which I use to this day. And even though people sometimes thought of her as dogmatic, she listened to new voices, ran them through her high standard judgments, and then welcomed them in. As a teacher she will be remembered, I think, for the toughest corrections in the writing of papers that any of us ever got. Elinor was editor supreme, heartless and demanding. However, those of us who knew her well and visited her in her rural Vermont home in the summer, loved the tender and loyal side of her as well.

TEACHING

Several years before I began to teach, I went to Airlie House near Washington, D.C. for the first conference of the American Art Therapy Association. There I met Judy Rubin, Myra Levick, Art Robbins, Harriet Wadeson, Bob Ault, Sandra Kagan (now Graves-Alcorn), and many others who became the backbone of our organization. Judy needed a ride back to D.C. and asked if I would take her. That was the beginning of a continuing and deep friendship. I remember with special pleasure the many years we *importance of co-therapists colleagues as friends*

roomed together at AATA conferences, talking into the night, sharing ideas, but also "best friends" kinds of personal stuff.

In 1972, to my surprise and delight, the newly formed graduate program in art therapy at George Washington University invited me to teach. I began with an undergraduate course called "Introduction to Art Therapy." From this class, I was able to single out the most promising students who were applying to the new program. There were very few graduate training programs to choose from in those days. We had long lists of applicants and had to choose carefully for our limited openings. I went on to become a fully active faculty member, giving my input to discussions of needed new courses and other program matters.

I was asked to assist with the group art therapy courses. Since I had been spending considerable time studying group process, especially in experiential groups along the Tavistock model, I came equipped. I was asked to do one class co-teaching with Hanna Kwiatkowska and one with Elinor Ulman. Since neither of them had done any concentrated study of group process, this turned out to be a most unusual kind of teaching experience. One notable class which Hanna and I taught together was presented at an AATA conference in Maryland with all group members presenting their experience in this class. I was proud that we transformed our experience, documenting significant conflict, both between the two leaders and among group members, into an insightful record.

In 1983, Gladys Agell hired me to take over as director of her program at Vermont College while she did her Ph.D. internship in New York City. Those were two very intensive, exhausting, and learning-filled years. Some dear and continuing friendships were made with some students, now leaders in the art therapy profession. Another positive experience at Vermont College was starting a community clinic connected to our program. I was asked also to be the college student counselor. I have great regard for the many issues that a director of an art therapy training program has. In my case, being a "substitute teacher" added to my problems. My hat's off to all the program directors now carrying on so ably.

After leaving Vermont in 1985, and returning to Chicago, where I had moved some years earlier, I began teaching at the School of the Art Institute of Chicago; I specialized in group art therapy. I loved working in an art school environment. Students in the program were gifted artists and interested in the art part of their art therapy identity. It was during those years that I developed a private practice, rented studio space, joined a women's cooperative gallery, and finally concentrated on my own art. I learned about the art world, and had a number of exhibitions. It is not surprising, then, that it was during those years that my published writings were about the artist as clinician, the art therapist as exhibiting artist. My activities in the American

Art Therapy Association became more and more devoted to promoting concentration on our role as artists and how art therapists as artists fit into the art world. Beginning with several consecutive years of conference focus groups on the art therapy interface with the art world, I finally proposed and helped form the current Art Committee. I feel deep pleasure in watching this committee quietly initiate ways of bringing this aspect of our work to the attention of members. Pat Allen, Cathy Moon, and a number of others pioneered the idea of what came to be called "Studio Art Therapy." I believe with this comes a broadening of our horizons as we can share not only the art of our clients but also our own art. The public can know that we are artists as well as clinicians, and that our art making itself can be a source of help and inspiration to others.

I initiated and helped organize shows of art work in Chicago. Later, this was done at several AATA conferences. At each annual art therapy conference there is a slide show of members' art work. There are a number of other art activities at the conferences, as well. Having a history of exhibiting one's art work has become part of an honored resumé in our field.

CLINICAL WORK

Between 1971 and 1974, while teaching at George Washington University, I was doing clinical work with children in the Psychiatric Department of Children's Hospital. This was called Hillcrest and was a training institution, which included both a school and a clinic. It was my first clinical experience. I was fortunate to have a wonderful supervisor, Dr. Ruth Newman, and a rich learning environment. They even had on the staff of the school a full-time videographer, an unheard-of luxury at the time. It was thanks to his videotaping my girls' art therapy group over a period of a year, that we were able to document this group process.

Primarily I worked with groups of adolescents. Ruth taught me much of what I know about group process. There was a succession of professionals in training who joined me as co-therapists. These included psychiatrists, psychologists and social workers, as well as art therapy interns. For all of these, making art in groups was new. Teaching and training them was a great pleasure as I proudly showed them the advantages of using art in therapy.

During these years, I developed a technique of making my own art along with the group members. My co-therapists learned to do this as well. Later, I presented this idea at art therapy conferences and at classes in other institutions. At first this approach was considered to be "impure," that is, possibly influencing group members' art work too much. I believe that now the

making art along with client

many advantages of this technique, properly used, are accepted and used broadly.

At the third American Art Therapy Association conference, in 1972, I was able to accomplish another integrating milestone for myself: bringing my dance/ movement experience together with art therapy. I gave a workshop to demonstrate some of the ways art therapists could use the elements of movement. As I reread the article later published from this workshop, I see that I ended it with exhorting our profession to include all the arts: drama, poetry, music, etc. We now call this combination of the arts "expressive arts."

[handwritten margin note: workshop on movement.]

WORK WITH THE AMERICAN ART THERAPY ASSOCIATION

Also, during these years, I was active in the American Art Therapy Association (AATA). I became the Editor of the *AATA Newsletter.* From 1975 to 1977, I was Publications Chair and a member of the Board of AATA. Before computers, and before we had a national organization office, an editor and her staff actually typed, cut and pasted, proofread, arranged for printing, wrote addresses, and then mailed copies of the Newsletter to all members. We also collected and edited the information. My stalwart helpers were Linda Gantt and Roberta Shoemaker. Usually there were many hours and days of labor on the floor, surrounded by scissors, tape, and mounds of papers. This was labor intensive, to say the least; but we did it, and I'm sure we all remember those times with some amused nostalgia.

In 1976, the Publications Committee also initiated the publication of Proceedings of AATA national conferences. We felt that these important contributions to our field should be recorded and shared with those who could not attend

My experiences at the AATA Board meetings are difficult to describe. Over a number of years, board members struggled to iron out many different points of view, deal with the inevitable politics of strong minded and talented individuals, and form sensible organizational structures. There were endless, heated exchanges that lasted for hours. I remember voting out of sheer exhaustion. And, of course, we did everything ourselves. There was no national office to help.

In 1983, the American Art Therapy Association began planning to have a journal of its own. I was on the committee to organize it. For the first issue, I was chosen Assistant Editor with Linda Gantt as Editor.

A BIG CHANGE

There was a big change in my life in 1974, when I remarried. Elinor Ulman and Bernie Levy came to my wedding in my sister's living room in New Jersey. Thinking about this now, I associate it to my remarks in accepting my Honorary Life Member award in 2001; I said that whatever ups and downs my personal life presented, I could feel a sense of family and steadiness with my career and my dear friends in art therapy.

*friends in Art Therapy.

My new marriage brought me to Chicago where I helped to start an art therapy association there. I brought the experience of D.C. and the East Coast to the Midwest, where there were plenty of people interested in art and healing, but no training courses and very little organization. Don Seiden became the first President of the Illinois group. Later, I became President.

I taught a number of classes in art centers and colleges and had many enthusiastic students who were eager to study for graduate degrees. I tried very hard to start a Master's Degree program in Chicago, but not until Harriet Wadeson began her program at the University of Illinois in Chicago did we get one.

CLINICAL WORK AND WRITINGS

My clinical work intensified when I lived in Chicago. As Chief of Adjunctive Therapies at the Pritzker Psychiatric Unit of Michael Reese Hospital from 1977 to 1978, I worked in many media with hospitalized children and a staff of therapists at this private psychiatric hospital. The administrative experience that I was developing was later enriched as I became Director of Adjunctive Therapies at a private psychiatric hospital in Chicago for adults and adolescents. It was in this last job that I developed my new technique of doing art work along with the patient. This was an extension of what I had been doing earlier with groups at Hillcrest in D.C. In both places, I was emphasizing something I was passionate about: acknowledging and using ourselves as artists. In later years, I focused more and more on the development of the art making side of our art therapist identity. It was at this time that I began a very limited private practice along with my other jobs.

During these years my presentations in Chicago, at art therapy conferences, and at programs around the country focused on group art therapy and learning disabilities using other media along with art and transitional phenomena. (I was a great fan of Winnicott, whose books I had reviewed in 1972.)

*working w/clients both doing art: influenced by having been a show-off? Redirecting?

Mildred Lachman Chapin working with a client in her interactive technique.

Very significant for me during my Chicago years was the publication of my book of paintings and poetry titled *Reverberations: Mothers and Daughters.* This book developed in a period of time in which my daughter was working out her relationship with me. The period was also one of my working out my relationship with my own mother. It came at a time when I was spending many hours painting and print making. Much of this work related to what I was experiencing with my daughter. To my surprise, I found myself writing about the images in a poetic way, beginning what has now become a serious devotion to poetry writing. Patricia Allen, who reviewed the book, called it a kind of personal art-based research. We need every kind of research tool we can find. I consider this as one of them. Along these lines, I think of Alice Miller, Henry Miller, and Marian Milner, whose books of their paintings (or about their paintings) I now reexamine with feelings of kinship and pleasure.

Reverberations: Mothers and Daughters was my first published book. Through this experience I learned a great deal about the publishing world, ended up self-publishing, and then did a second edition with a publisher. My book also entailed an intensive round of book signings and readings.

Having a book out in the world is a defining experience, much like putting a piece of your art work out for public view. It is no longer your inner world;

it is your outer world. As Elinor Ulman liked to say, this artwork became a bridge between my inner and outer world.

One of my most cherished memories is of the performance I did with my daughter and her friend at the American Art Therapy Association Conference in Philadelphia in 1996. It was based on a body of art work and poetry I did called "Sisters in Spirit." While slides of the paintings were projected, I read the poetry I had written and my daughter and her friend danced. This multimedia performance was so exciting that the audience joined in at the end, on the stage and on the floor, with dancing and clapping. The performance represented for me not only a consummate performance piece, but one in which my daughter worked in happy connection with her mother.

Collaboration various expressive media viewer participation

I think my most important contribution during these years was my reporting on Kohut's theories of narcissism and self psychology. I presented a paper about this at an AATA conference, and later, in 1979, published an article in the *American Journal of Art Therapy* (AJAT). Kohut called his new theoretical approach "self psychology." Looking back, I realize that the large body of paintings I did at this time called "Visages" were connected to my own problems with sense of self issues important in Kohut's theories. The interface between my paintings, my own psychic problems, and the topics I was drawn to for research and writing has always fascinated me. This eventually culminated in a presentation I called "Art Odyssey."

During the 1980s, another interest of mine was the theoretician Milton Erickson. I became interested in Ericksonian hypnosis and published an article on it in the AJAT. Although I never used hypnosis in my practice, its study led to my interest in altered states of consciousness, especially during art making.

CONCENTRATING ON PAINTING AND POETRY

I moved to Sedona, Arizona, in 1993. There was virtually no art therapy practice for me during the nine years I was there. I devoted myself to painting, with two Chicago shows and one in an Arizona museum.

During that time my focus in the American Art Therapy Association (AATA) was on governance and fostering the health of the organization in any way I could. I became actively involved in the new e-group. Being on the Nominating Committee gave me an opportunity to help with the selection of fine new leaders.

In 2001, I was awarded the Honorary Life Member Award by AATA. For me this was a confirming, loving thank-you gift, a way of confirming that I must have made important contributions to the art therapy profession that were appreciated. Coming from my deeply significant art therapy family, tribe, circle of life-friends, with whom I had worked passionately for many years, it was particularly supportive. I say "supportive" because I was going through a divorce, another ripping life change. The award came at a propitious moment, giving me a happy little lift into the next life adventure.

2 Divorces?

Mildred Lachman Chapin standing in front of her "Pairs" paintings.

That adventure consisted, in part, in my move to Tucson, Arizona, where I now live. These past few years have given me a new lease on life. I have again been working as an art therapist, teaching at Prescott College, presenting and forming new community connections for art therapy. My painting life is more concentrated than before, as I happily move about in an expanded art world here, painting and exhibiting a great deal.

Since Tucson is one of the important poetry centers in the United States, I am fortunate to be able to study and develop my poetry here. I spend much time now reading, writing, and studying poetry. My present body of paintings, a series of "Visual Haikus," includes my written haikus as well. And the body of my poetry keeps growing, both in quantity and quality, I think.

My most recent body of paintings is a series of 22 "Visual Haikus." I call them that not only because they are small, but because they are meant to give a lightning kind of flash of meaning, as do Japanese haiku poems. For each one I wrote a poetry haiku.

Mildred Lachman Chapin's "Visual Haiku." "Sky Ghosts."

Shift your shapes become
Dream creatures or maybe real
People, you and I.

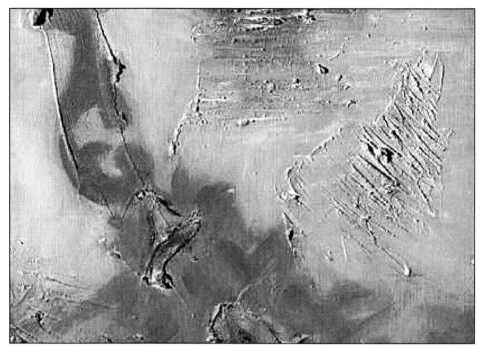

Mildred Lachman Chapin's "Visual Haiku," "Bells Are Ringing."

Bells ring to announce
Delicate, fragile joining.
Plump, pale, juicy wisp.

THE OLD DAYS

I want to talk about my memories of the "old days," when I was among the art therapists formulating who we were and starting the American Art Therapy Association:

- I recall that there were very few books to read and to teach from. I remember the first Kramer and Naumburg books and books by Lowenfeld and Prinzhorn. We had some of the art-based psychological assessment books and not a great deal more. Of course there was the *American Journal of Art Therapy* which provided us with articles from pioneers here and abroad.
- We were making things up as we went along. We decided what courses should be included in a training program, checking out other programs

to see if they had come up with other good ideas. We all thought up new techniques and shared them.

- It was an exciting time of discovery. Nothing yet had been standardized. That, in fact, was what we started out to do.
- There were many prospective students and not enough programs to accommodate their desire for training. When I began, I remember there were little more than half a dozen programs in the United States.
- Everything we did we had to do ourselves. It is hard to imagine now not having an administrative office. In those days, what we did was hard work and very time consuming. We had no computers. You had to be a zealous pioneer, a kind of missionary. We all were.
- It was never a case of fitting a standard or a rule or regulation as it is now. *← freedom.* We were busy trying to develop standards and principles of practice and training.
- And in those days there were very open and tough discussions. Lots of very strong feelings were strongly expressed. There were lots of fights among AATA members. There were lots of personality conflicts, and strong positions taken that lasted for years.
- Pioneering days were tough, but there was a thrill in the creative making of something new. We were shaping our profession. Many of my deepest friendships and affiliations came from that period.

THOUGHTS ABOUT THE FUTURE

We art therapists have succeeded in getting our message out. Our conviction that art making itself can be helpful ("therapeutic" is the sometimes threatening word) to people has caught on. Certainly this is so with institutions of mental health, education, and many other kinds of community groups. Other professionals in the mental health and art communities know we exist. Mental health professionals have paid tribute to the basic theoretical concepts on which our profession is based. That tribute has often been manifested in their trying to imitate, duplicate or adapt what we do. And while this spread of the use of art is flattering, it also poses some questions.

There is a question about people trying to do what we do without rigorous training. I believe there is a fear among us that such untrained people may be undermining our jobs and diluting our professional image. I think it is time to take them into our organization. We can work with them, offer to give them the additional training they need, as well as learn from them. This would not only increase our membership and political clout but offer us the kind of broadening that comes with such openness. I think of the richness from the many ethnic groups that joined our country. There was much fear and prejudice against them at the time too. I think of men's colleges opening to women, psychoanalytic institutes admitting non-M.D.s. There are many examples. Think of being without the jazz that African slaves gave us!

The result has been, and will be, enrichment all around. Art is something anyone can use. It is not ours exclusively. Others will use art to affect people in good ways. Let us enrich ourselves, I say. I think our ideas and actions will spread, as they have already. Let us step out and actively embrace the future which, of course, includes tending to our professional standards, licensures, etc., and making sure we get the jobs and salaries that we deserve.

Aging has many advantages. The disadvantages are obvious. But what I savor now are the many adventures I've had, the good works I can be proud of, the great people I can summon to my side—either in person, or in my thoughts and memories. Life has been good. And my life in art therapy has been essential to who I enjoy being now.

Linda Gantt and husband Lou Tinnin.

Chapter 23

LINDA GANTT

AN ACCIDENTAL ART THERAPIST

Chance favors the prepared mind.
    –Louis Pasteur

Several happy accidents culminated in my becoming an art therapist. Had it not been for those events, I could not have taken advantage of the opportunities for a formal art therapy education that became available just when I was trying to decide on a career.

The year I received my Honorary Life Membership (HLM), 1994, was also the 25th anniversary of the American Art Therapy Association (AATA). I was twice 25 and celebrating my own personal milestone. But I felt the award had some broader significance in that I was the first person with a Master's degree specifically in art therapy to receive an HLM. So, I represent the generation of those who, instead of inventing art therapy on their own, had others to blaze the path.

FIRST CONFERENCES

My first American Art Therapy Association conference was actually AATA's fourth, held in Columbus, Ohio, in 1973. The same year I attended the Boston meeting of the American Society of Psychopathology of Expression, where I got my one and only glimpse of Margaret Naumburg as she received an award. Swathed in a black dress and large hat, she said little to the audience. By then, she showed signs of dementia and I had little sense of her true personality. I think I was really too new to the field to have much appreciation of her importance.

By my reckoning, I am a member of the third generation of art therapists. Although I studied with several of the first generation, there was a second generation whose members (such as most of those represented in this book) were already practicing when I came on the scene. I count it my great, good fortune to have had as my teachers Elinor Ulman, Edith Kramer, and Hanna Yaxa Kwiatkowska.

TEXAS ORIGINS

Getting into the first class of the Master's program in art therapy at the George Washington University involved a chain of events that began in Texas. Both my parents were born there. My childhood in the mid-1940s and 50s was a sheltered, conventional, lower middle class one in one of Houston's first suburbs. Sandwiched between an older sister and younger brother, with a two-year gap on either side (the recommended spacing for siblings at that time), I went to segregated public schools. The Civil Rights Movement did not take hold until I was in college and I had little experience outside my neighborhood except for going to our family farm and to Girl Scout camp. My mother was always embarrassed to pick me up at camp; I never cried when she dropped me off, only when she came to get me. My parents focused on work. They did virtually no socializing with other families and we had few relatives in Houston.

On the whole, I was a shy and quiet child who tried not to be noticed or to be any bother to adults. I was more an observer than an agent in my limited world. Books became my windows to the world—I treasured the libraries in each of my schools (especially those with open stacks) and I frequently thumbed through the *Girl Scout Handbook* and the *World Book Encyclopedia* just to see what I did not know.

My maternal grandparents introduced me to creative pursuits. My grandfather, a union carpenter, built his own house as well as that of my parents and all manner of wooden toys, doll furniture, and playground equipment. My grandmother sewed her own clothes as well as those of the distaff side of the family. I felt sorry for any little girl in my school who had to wear store-bought dresses that might be exactly like another's. Visiting my grandparents, I saw various works in progress. I yearned to use my grandfather's "Yankee screwdriver" and wood planes. My father's parents were "dirt farmers" (sharecroppers who cultivated other people's land) in Dimebox in the Hill Country of central Texas. My rural grandmother had little in the way of material goods or time to pursue anything but housework, cooking, and tending chickens. She did make a few quilts out of feed sacks and inexpensive cloth.

Linda Gantt, age 6.

I moved back and forth between these two sets of grandparents, absorbing a strong work ethic and a pragmatic outlook on life. None of the four had more than a basic education. My mother (Lois) and father (T. K. or Kenneth) had high school educations. Determined that farming would not be his fate, my father moved to Houston to be an apprentice in a drugstore. Having no money to attend college, Dad had to study on his own for the state pharmacy examination. (This was not unlike what happened with some early art therapists who were mentored by others and learned on the job.) Dad worked as a pharmacist for over 50 years, becoming a beloved fixture of the impoverished neighborhood surrounding the drugstore. The Depression forever colored his career. As he told anyone who would listen, his pharmacy license was issued the day after the stock market crashed in 1929 so his fortune seemed to be rising just when many others had lost theirs. He was always on the lookout for signs of the next Depression and never took any financial risk. He did, however, save enough money to buy the farm on which his parents worked. In the 1950s, he was thrilled to be able to replace the unpainted wooden three-room shack of his parents with a brick structure with indoor plumbing and electric stove. The drugstore was my father's weekday life. On most weekends he took us to the farm, giving us a sense of connection to nature (with all the stinging, biting, and snapping creatures that are an integral part of the Texas landscape). Oh, and I got to have a horse or two!

NORTH TEXAS STATE UNIVERSITY

The first substantial link in the chain that led to my becoming an art therapist was in 1962 when I enrolled in North Texas State University (NTSU) in Denton, Texas, where I majored in sociology and minored in history. I did little planning for the future, but I had a conviction I did not want to be a pharmacist and take over the drugstore as my father so ardently wished. Nor did I think I had any artistic talent (although my mother thought so). A good friend in high school was a truly gifted visual artist and the thought of my trying to rise to her level was overwhelming. Instead, I opted to get a liberal arts degree with the idea of eventually becoming a social worker, an appealing alternative to the standard choices for so many Southern women of my time— teacher, secretary, or nurse.

Thanks to the land grant college system in Texas and the oil reserves on university land, the tuition for all state colleges was affordable to a great many lower middle class families. I feared my family could not pay if I tried to get into an out-of-state school and I had no confidence I could get a scholarship. In fact, my parents and I had virtually no discussions about college options since I was the first in my small extended family to consider going beyond high school. A semester's tuition was only $50 and room and board was under $400. Getting into North Texas was relatively easy because most high school graduates wanted to go to the University of Texas in Austin, a much more competitive, prestigious, sophisticated, and somewhat scary place. NTSU appealed to me because it had both an undergraduate and graduate sociology program and horseback riding as a physical education course.

One semester, a friend wanted me to take a painting class. She needed psychological support and asked me to enroll with her. After fighting long registration lines, I got the last place in the class. The next day, much to my distress, I learned my friend was unable to get in. I found myself quite alone, one of only two students who were not art majors. I took several other art classes but could never get into a weaving class because it was off-limits to nonart majors. Looking in the glass doors of the weaving studio was as close as I could get.

Linda Gantt's painting.

Having decided to get an additional minor in psychology, I took a class in abnormal psychology from Dr. Meryl Bonney, a legendary professor on campus. Dr. Bonney stated categorically that one could learn more about the human psyche from the arts than from Freud. To back up his contention, he permitted students to substitute a wide variety of projects such as paintings, poems, and short stories on psychological themes for the usual spate of library papers. I remember handing in several projects–a wood block print of the same face in different colors to illustrate multiple personality disorder and a collage of a crowd scene to show paranoia. Our textbook had some drawings by psychiatric patients. The end papers were full-color reproductions of paintings by a patient who, at first, was unable to speak to her therapist but communicated through her art. This book was Ainslie Meares's *The Door of Serenity*. Meares was an Australian psychiatrist whose books on hypnoplasty and hypnography are probably unknown to most contemporary art therapists but *The Door* was a full-length, illustrated case study. Dr. Bonney's reading list (which I still have) included an article by Elinor Ulman and a book by Margaret Naumburg. This was in 1966, mind you. (I confess I do not recall having read either of them then.) At the end of that course the idea of combining art and psychology took root in my mind.

During the summers between my college years I worked as a camp counselor. Here I got my first taste of applied psychology when I watched a senior counselor help a homesick girl. I did not recognize it then but it was a great example of paradoxical instruction that rivaled anything a master therapist could do. Two assignments in particular deepened my skills–being the Arts and Crafts Director who traveled between three different camps each week and teaching counselors-in-training.

FIRST ART THERAPY COURSES

After college graduation in 1966, a friend and I moved to Washington, D.C., where I worked for the Girl Scouts. This gave me organizational experience and a strong can-do frame of mind. Washington was a fairly sleepy place then. The infamous Beltway had just been completed but most of the surrounding counties were still predominately farmlands. As the suburbs developed I organized the troops at the new schools and learned to navigate the territory. I watched Washington become a more sophisticated and cosmopolitan place and my friends and I enjoyed the increasing number of international restaurants and the newly opened Kennedy Center.

An artist friend suggested that we take a class in art therapy together, and I readily agreed. But, exactly as had happened five years earlier, I wound up in the class and my friend did not. The Washington School of Psychiatry sponsored the class and Elinor Ulman taught it. The following year I took another class with Elinor. She had a heart attack in the middle of the semester and Hanna Yaxa Kwiatkowska served as her substitute. During one session Bernard I. Levy (Bernie), a psychologist and Elinor's good friend, walked in and asked who wanted a Master's degree in art therapy. If there were enough potential students, the George Washington University would start a program. Bernie was the catalyst; as a Professor of Psychology he had the academic credentials to be an administrator. Elinor Ulman had worked with Bernie at the District of Columbia Hospital (D.C. General) and Hanna Yaxa Kwitkowska was at the National Institute of Mental Health in Bethesda, Maryland. As teachers, they seemed polar opposites—Elinor with a stern and demanding exterior who was really quite a softie and Hanna with her lady-like demeanor and iron-straight backbone. I am not certain we are making them like that any more. Elinor's writing and editing became a model for me. When I could afford to I purchased all the back issues of the *Bulletin of Art Therapy* and read and reread Elinor's editorials. Her clear and straightforward writing set a standard I struggle to emulate. It was Hanna's skills with people I hoped to absorb, for she had a marvelous way of helping people without making them feel defensive or ill at ease.

GETTING INVOLVED WITH AATA

It was only a short time after becoming a graduate student that I realized how much work there was needed to develop the field (and how easily one can be roped into doing it). I started my work in the American Art Therapy Association (AATA) as an apprentice to Millie Lachman (now Lachman-Chapin), who was then the editor of the *AATA Newsletter*. Millie and I had met in the classes at the Washington School. One evening we saw each other at a lecture by Anaïs Nin at the Smithsonian; shortly thereafter, Millie asked me to help with the newsletter. The AATA membership was about 600 at the time. We joked that the "national office" was located on the President's dining table while the publications department was located in my living room. Four to six times a year Millie and I sat on the floor, addressing, hand-stamping and sorting the newsletters into bundles by ZIP code (at that time, a relatively new concept from the Post Office).

An actual national office was slow in coming. At first, I watched the struggles from some distance; later, I became involved with several of the moves to different management firms. Ed Stygar (who with his partner Bob Willis took our account in 1984) kidded that Sandra Graves (now Graves-Alcorn), then the AATA President) and I deliberately packed up a mouse when we got the files from the previous management firm because that is what greeted his staff when they opened the shipping boxes in Mundelein, Illinois.

MEETING MY LIFE PARTNER

Of those accidents that led me to become an art therapist the most wonderful one was my chance meeting with my future husband and collaborator Dr. Louis Tinnin. A good friend of Hanna's from Brazil, Dr. Arnulfo Esquebel, was the Chief of Psychiatry at Prince George's General Hospital, just over the Maryland border from the District of Columbia. He welcomed art therapy students on the inpatient psychiatric and the detoxification units. Under the supervision of Heidi Christophel, the occupational therapist, I had the chance to see the psychology textbooks come to life.

Having finished my art therapy degree in 1974, I found that there were few actual art therapy jobs but agencies were starting to hire members of my class. I had already signed a contract to work as a coordinator for group homes for the mentally retarded when I heard that Heidi left her job at Prince George's. The art therapy students who had been placed there convinced the psychiatrists that we had something to offer. When I went to the interview I was surprised to see that Dr. Esquebel was no longer there. The job was now in the hands of Lou, the handsomest man I had ever seen. To say that we were attracted to each other at once is an understatement.

Lou and I found many things in common, including our Southern heritage, our love of the world of ideas, and a passion for our work in mental health. One of the first things Lou did as chief was to reorganize the psychiatric unit to better treat the acutely psychotic patients who comprised half of the unit's population. Most of them could not participate in any form of traditional group therapy sessions so art therapy, occupational therapy, and dance/movement therapy were the mainstays of the program. We, along with Karen Ruback, a talented dance/movement therapist, devised some simple but effective ways of working with people who were temporarily non-verbal. Lou built on concepts from Heinz Hartmann about the autonomous ego functions, and that guided our approach. Eventually, we hoped to write a book about psychosis to offer a more overarching psychological theory about the workings of the human mind. But something interfered with our neat explanations—we started working with dissociative patients. We had only a few (we thought) but their art was a fascinating entrée into their subjective worlds. Two decades later our ideas underwent a radical shift. I will say more about that later.

I worked at Prince George's for seven years, supervising as many as six art therapy students a semester. I had considerable flexibility in assigning them to the extended care facility, the pediatric floor, the orthopedic unit, as well as to the two units where I worked. As a member of the psychiatric consultation and liaison team I received interesting referrals from all over the hospital. Soon I petitioned for a second position. We hired Fran Dodd, a graduate from the George Washington program, to work on the orthopedic unit and to help with students.

POTOMAC FEVER

Perhaps because I had some organizational experience and perhaps because I was infected with "Potomac fever" (the conviction that Washington was the *omphalos* of the universe), I was eager for AATA to play in the big leagues. The mid-1970s were exciting days all around the Washington area because art therapy graduates were creating new jobs. The general expansion of mental health services, along with great optimism about the economy, benefited other developing professions as well as art therapy. National offices for professional associations and advocacy groups for people with special needs sprang up to influence Federal legislation and make health and education programs more uniform across the states.

President Jimmy Carter, strongly influenced by his wife Roslyn, established a Presidential Commission on Mental Health. Judith Bunney, a dance/movement therapist (whose husband at the time was Dr. William Bunney, a well-known researcher at the National Institute of Mental Health) was attuned to the movements and trends within the Federal government. She was able to get an appointment to the Commission's Panel on the Arts and Mental Health and engineer a spot for me by offering my assistance to edit the Panel's contribution to the final report. Through Hanna's connections with Thelma Charon at the newly established National Library of Medicine, Marilyn Schmal and I did an annotated bibliography on the art therapy literature. The Federal government published it in 1974 and distributed it at no cost to medical and university libraries as well as to all AATA members.

At the 1977 AATA conference in Virginia Beach, I made a motion to establish an ad hoc committee on lobbying and Federal job classification (which soon turned into the permanent Governmental Affairs Committee). After the conference Don Jones, AATA President, asked me to chair it. What I did not know, but learned years later, was that a fierce debate ensued among Board members after the motion passed. There was considerable division around the place of "big P" politics in AATA. Many Board members did not see (as I did) the pressing need for such a committee. The Federal job series that includes art therapists (the GS-638 series which exists to this day) was one of the first results of the committee's efforts. We found allies from the other creative arts therapies. Art therapists Patti Rossiter (now

Ravenscroft) and Kristine Jensch, two dance/movement therapists, a music therapist, and I were successful in getting our respective disciplines mentioned in Public Law 94-142 (Education for All Handicapped Children, the precursor of Individuals with Disabilities Education Act or IDEA). Because we were the last to physically put our materials on the stack of public commentaries, ours were the first ones read by the Congressional staff.

As I educated myself about governmental affairs I gathered material on other related professions. I remember visiting the office of the American Psychological Association and being shown the "war room." On the wall behind the desk of the APA legislative director was a large map of the United States with colored pushpins indicating the states where licensing laws had passed or were pending. This methodical approach was an impressive demonstration of what an organization can do when it mobilizes its members and resources. My major frustration with art therapy in general and with the Association in particular has been that relatively few people understood until recently the critical need for such focus on governmental affairs. Granted, the learning curve is an extremely steep one and most initiates do not find the subject exciting when compared to other aspects of the field. At the time, psychologists were licensed in only a handful of states; the same was true for social workers. Virtually no states licensed counselors, and art therapists could work if a psychiatrist decided to hire them. Thus, few art therapists worried about government regulation of the field.

When the President's Commission on Mental Health made its recommendations for improvement in therapeutic services the legislative machinery swung into action. In the September, 1980, *AATA Newsletter*, President Gwen Gibson reported: "Thanks to our newly hired legislative consultant, AATA gained a favorable description of art therapy in the Congressional committee report on the Mental Health Systems Act. Inclusion in this bill will help us ultimately to be recognized as mental health service providers and to receive Federal funds." She went on to talk about efforts to include the creative arts therapies as reimbursable services in Federal programs. Even though the AATA Governmental Affairs Committee was relatively green it had managed a major *coup* to be included in this law. But all of this came crashing down when Iranian students stormed the U.S. Embassy in Teheran and President Carter's administration was demoralized and in 1980, Ronald Reagan was elected President. Suddenly, the enthusiasm for expanding the role of the Federal government in citizens' lives turned sour. The legislative focus for professional organizations went back to the states and the Mental Health Systems Act was gutted; along with it went our hopes for greater professional recognition.

MOVING TO WEST VIRGINIA AND
GOING BACK TO SCHOOL

In 1980, Lou and I married. We had already moved to West Virginia where he got a job as the medical director of a community mental health center. Thinking we might be bringing light to the wilderness, we asked if the mental health center might need an art therapist. But the center was already light-years ahead–they had a fine art therapist, Hilary Gordon, who had come from the Baltimore, Maryland area several years before.

Linda Gantt at her wedding.

Without an art therapy position I had the latitude to pursue a doctorate. Lou even said he would do the cooking when I went back to school. "But, you don't know how to cook!" I pointed out. He replied, "That's no problem—I'll learn Chinese cooking," and he did! For several years, the two of us went in opposite directions, staying away from home several nights during the week and getting back together on the weekends. I chose the University of Pittsburgh's interdisciplinary program that permitted writing one's own course of study. I had begun to feel that art therapy was much too narrowly focused on psychoanalytic theory and that it paid too little attention to research. Other colleagues were discussing getting doctorates and I listened to the arguments pro and con. Getting a doctorate in art therapy was much too narrow a focus for me. By going to a traditional university that nonetheless permitted considerable latitude in carving out a unique path I could get what I thought I (and the field) needed—a shot of ideas from neighboring fields. So, I combed the catalog for courses I wanted to take, not thinking about the specific department. When I saw that the courses fell into three major clumps I weeded and combined. I had to get accepted as a graduate student in two or more departments and write a proposal to explain what end I hoped to reach. I applied for anthropology, communications, and philosophy and got accepted in the first two departments. I would not trade anything for that experience. It expanded my world even more and gave me the confidence to come back to art therapy with renewed energy to tackle some significant problems in the field.

Alternating my formal degrees with real-world experience gave me a pragmatic perspective. I feel comfortable toggling between the poles of the field—art as therapy and art psychotherapy—as well as between the theoretical and the applied, and between art and science. At the end of the doctoral program I came to appreciate the paradox of virtually all scientific disciplines—that the early history of each one swung between opposing and apparently contradictory theories and that at the end of the twentieth century, each had come to some middle ground that retained elements and principles from both ends. It was only a little later that I realized my frustration with most of the art therapy folklore with its emphasis on received wisdom. Perhaps it is my experience on the high school debate team or the added influence of Lou's strongly scientific perspective, but I want to see empirical evidence.

BECOMING A RESEARCHER

I can remember precisely when my interest in art therapy research was born. During a lecture, Hanna Yaxa Kwiatkowska made a statement I carefully noted in my class notebook: "Depressed people draw concentric circles, bull's eyes, tunnels, and vortexes." Next to this statement, I wrote a large question mark. What seemed to me as a flat assertion without qualification or source launched my first "study." At Prince George's Hospital I made notes about every image that could be described as concentric circles. While not all of them were done by people who were depressed, the vast majority were thus supporting Hanna's contention. This little replication of her clinical observations helped me sort out some important principles about research and interpretation.

DEVELOPING THE FEATS

While I attended Pitt I also taught in the Vermont College art therapy program. This challenged me to explain those things my professors never did (if, in fact, they had concepts to explain it). Frustrated at not having all the answers supplied in my own graduate art therapy program, I felt impelled to keep at least half a step ahead of my inquisitive students. When one student presented her case study and I knew she was off-base in her conclusions, I realized I did not have a solid foundation to explain my own point of view. I thought back to classes with Elinor Ulman. When she talked about art from patients she always made perceptive and meaningful comments but she did not tell us her thought process as she looked at a drawing.

When it came to finding a dissertation topic I felt like a shark circling around and around until I caught a whiff of blood in the water. Then, moving in ever-smaller circles, I finally got close enough to a subject to take a big bite out of it. Harkening back to those frustrations in graduate school, I struggled to get some kind of systematic approach to understanding what information was and was not contained in drawings. How did certain aspects manifest themselves? What does one look at first? So I tackled the problem of measuring certain variables in art, trying to combine my clinical experience and the vexing questions from my students. This built upon work Paula Howie and I did. When we graduated from George Washington we immediately became supervisors of other graduate students. Desperate to look as if we knew what we were doing we met regularly, comparing art from our respective patients, searching for common denominators, and trying to figure out what characteristics we thought to be important. This type of "pattern matching" eventually developed into the Formal Elements Art Therapy Scale (FEATS) and the subject of my dissertation.

Carmello Tabone, another GW graduate, moved to West Virginia soon after Lou and I did. He introduced me to the PPAT ("Draw a Person Picking An Apple From a Tree") from his experience in graduate school. In our weekly supervision sessions we poured over the many examples he collected and I brought ideas from Pitt to develop the structure for a systematic study. It took a long time to finally articulate that what we were seeing was the "graphic equivalent of symptoms." Unlike the tack taken by researchers who work with projective drawings, our approach emphasizes variables that interest artists. We hope the FEATS will serve as a model not only for a rating system but also for the focus on the art itself and become a means for studying normal development in art. The core of our approach is observation, not interpretation. It concentrates on what is in the pictures that anyone can see and measure, not on obscure or tiny details.

Such research was impossible to do prior to the third edition of the *Diagnostic and Statistical Manual* (DSM-III), published by the American Psychiatric Association. This watershed classification system made our work possible for two main reasons: it separated the personality disorders from the clinical disorders (making it possible to study a fluctuating clinical course), and it had clear criteria for each diagnosis. We strived to make our approach pragmatic, not speculative. In addition to the quantitative methods I learned at Pitt, I acquired the tools to approach a research question from any angle I want—the ethnographic, art historical, qualitative, or comparative. I think art therapy research needs all of these approaches and then some. I regret I will never have enough years in my lifetime to pursue my research ideas in depth.

WORKING WITH TRAUMA SURVIVORS

In the early 1980s, Lou and I started attending conferences on dissociation and trauma. Recognizing the similarities between the cases described and our previous patients, we revisited Lou's original ideas about psychosis. As we studied emerging ideas on trauma treatment, we saw how art therapy could be an important diagnostic and therapeutic tool. Lou planned to be a psychoanalyst and all my art therapy teachers were heavily influenced by psychoanalysis. But as we learned more about dissociation and about the effects of trauma, the more we questioned the psychoanalytic approach. We now joke that our earlier patients should be subject to a recall as in the automobile industry, for we are certain the vast majority of them had untreated trauma.

In 1984, Lou joined the faculty of the Department of Behavioral Medicine and Psychiatry in the School of Medicine at West Virginia University. He used this position to study art therapy techniques with combat veterans as well as traumatized civilians. Lou took early retirement in 1996 to set up the

Trauma Recovery Institute (TRI) in Morgantown, West Virginia, as an out-patient clinic to treat trauma survivors exclusively. I joined the practice in 1998 and now serve as Executive Director. The core of our treatment is art therapy, both drawing and clay sculpture. We focus on the "thick-chart patients" who have been unresponsive to traditional treatment methods. Our theoretical ideas come from animal studies and brain-based research. The guiding principles are based on what we term the "Instinctual Trauma Response." We have been gratified to hear patients say how the art helps in processing traumas of all kinds, including those in early childhood. We are convinced that art therapy is the treatment of choice for trauma survivors, regardless of age or type of trauma, and hope the data from our outcome studies will eventually support this contention. TRI is the most fulfilling thing Lou and I have done together and we consider it the capstone of our careers.

CREATIVE PURSUITS

My own art has been sporadic but wide ranging–I am really more of a dabbler than a master at any one thing but it gives me great pleasure. Fiber arts and clay sculpture are my primary interests and I have tried a number of different processes in these media. Recently, I started doing watercolor portraits of family and friends. It had been 35 years since I had done any painting. Through the clay program at TRI I have the vicarious experience of working in clay. I have also been involved with Touchstone Center for Crafts (Pennsylvania's only summer residential craft school), serving on its Board and as its President and taking a variety of different classes ranging from painting and flame-worked glass to jewelry and blacksmithing. (I regret to say I cannot seem to coax my inner blacksmith to emerge.)

MY WORLD VIEW

The Texas public schools gave me a broad liberal arts education and solid academic foundation. (I wish I thought that present-day Texas students are getting the same thing.) Being on the debate team (actually, the second string team) in high school taught me to argue both sides of a proposition as well as to question received wisdom, something I hope will be part of my contri-bution to the field. I hope that in art therapy's maturity we will be able to debate ideas without attacking personalities, to question authority respectfully, and to look critically at organizational issues without fracturing into divisive factions as we have in the past. Unfortunately, the arguments about theory (art as therapy versus art psychotherapy) and approach (art versus science) eclipsed the practical and important advocacy issues that were related to our survival.

My science education in high school was rather basic and I took the required biology classes in my undergraduate work. I was not especially scientifically oriented then as much as I was just basically curious. So it did not matter that the subject was science, history, or art; I just wanted to have a broad, general idea of how things were. Because of the fascinating books I found in the libraries, I always knew there was more to learn. When Marilyn and I did the annotated art therapy bibliography we realized that the literature was not especially detailed or sophisticated and if we wanted something really interesting we would have to write it ourselves.

One of my most instructive courses at North Texas State University was on comparative religion. Huston Smith, a superb scholar, wrote the textbook. Having known little about other religions as a child, I took in the common denominators (being kind to one another and living a principled life) and discarded the dogma. This course and my history courses (much of it necessarily focused on church history) gave me a broad picture of the history of ideas, later augmented by my doctoral studies.

My eagerness for new ideas morphed along the same intellectual path as Lou's. Both of us were brought up in Southern Baptist churches. Independently, both of us found the Unitarians in college and then made a radical turn to the left, adopting a healthy skepticism about received wisdom. We are quite content with secular humanism and free thought, especially with respect to claims of authority and belief. While we cleave to the Golden Rule, we do not think a promise of future rewards (or punishment) from a supernatural enforcer is necessary to keep us doing good things.

TWO STEPS FORWARD, ONE STEP BACK

One way or another, as a committee member, on the Board of Directors or as President of AATA, I have been involved in many of the major organizational developments–requiring a Master's degree for registration, protecting the ATR through a Federal law suit, developing national certification, restructuring the Board of Directors, selecting a management firm, sustaining relationships with other creative arts therapies groups through the National Coalition of Arts Therapies Associations (NCATA) [now the National Coalition of Creative Arts Therapies Associations (NCCATA)], licensing in Pennsylvania, and setting up the AATA journal. While these efforts have yielded major advances, it still feels to me that overall we have slipped back almost as much as we moved forward. For example, at one time, AATA had office space in the Washington, D.C., area in the same building as the newly formed American Association for Counseling and Development (AACD) (which later morphed into the American Counseling Association.)

In 1988, AATA President Cay Drachnik and I met with the American Association of Marriage and Family Therapists and AACD to discuss licensing and other legislation pertinent to our common interests. Yet we missed out on many opportunities because we could not maintain forward momentum due to our heavy reliance on volunteers, rather than structuring our national office in such a way to sustain the many connections necessary to promote our field.

Over the last 25 years, the stalwart members of the AATA Governmental Affairs Committee achieved amazing accomplishments despite the limited funding and the other projects that competed for the membership's attention. However, we are now paying for our unwillingness to empower AATA's Governmental Affairs Committee as the chief guarantor of art therapy's survival. Had we not contended that we should be accepted for what we are rather than making some concessions to cooperate with the other developing professions, we could have been in a much better position with respect to state licensing and to jobs. Bureaucrats do not make fine distinctions about definitions and are not interested in nuance. They simply want a minimal standard by which to determine people who are qualified to perform a particular service.

My greatest regret is that I personally did not push AATA hard enough and long enough about establishing a permanent Washington office so we could keep a steady presence vis-à-vis other professional organizations. While we were spending time on our internal debates we could have been learning from other more organizationally sophisticated associations how to raise our credibility and public profile.

CONCLUSION

I matured as art therapy did, developing my interest in research and governmental affairs at the same time the field and the association discovered their importance. What are my thoughts on the future? I have no doubt that the powerful idea of combining art and therapy will outlive us all. In some ways we risk being victims of our own success. Our clinical achievements with difficult-to-reach populations are so appealing to other professionals that they too want to do what we do. Whether we remain a separate discipline or find ourselves defined by others as a modality remains to be seen. To ensure our collective future, I earnestly appeal to readers to apply their best efforts in those areas to which I put most of my energy—publications, research, and governmental affairs. Relatively speaking, not many of our members are involved in these pursuits but I am convinced that this is how we will secure our survival. Each area requires considerable effort for, as a group, we are more visual than verbal, more emotionally attuned to patients and clients than research-minded, and more interested in being alone in a studio absorbed in individual creative pursuits than in the tough and brutal world of political action. Our publications must meet the standards set by the other well-known and older disciplines; our research studies must be rigorous; and our advocacy work must represent us to policymakers at both the state and Federal level.

It is ironic that we live in a time when the sheer volume of information available to us is unprecedented, and yet, there seems to be a backlash against empirical research, rational thinking, and knowledge in general. Our hybrid discipline is both art *and* science, and we must keep it that way. Our task is paradoxical in that it is both easier and harder to be an art therapist in this generation than in the ones that preceded us. To both new and experienced art therapists I say: Do not be afraid of controversy and debate as long as it is centered on ideas rather than personalities or factions, and strive for high standards in all that you do.

I have found art therapy to be both intellectually challenging because there are so many unanswered questions and emotionally fulfilling because of the many wonderful friends and colleagues I have met so far. I would not want to be in any other field. My heartfelt thanks go to my teachers whose accomplishments paved the way, to my students whose questions prompted me to learn more, and to all of those adults and children with whom I have had the privilege of working.

Over thirty years ago I had a dream (which I made into a drawing during one of my art therapy classes) that neatly symbolizes my art therapy career. It was of a field of bluebonnets, the quintessential Texas landscape. I, along with my parents, brother, and sister, picked armloads of flowers. Going from one beautiful flower to the next I did not notice I was getting farther and farther from my family. When I finally looked up I could barely see them. I came to understand that my physical (and emotional) move away from my family was predicated on my interest in the wider world, in the thrill of new ideas and concepts, and in finding a place where I could bloom. Art therapy is my field of bluebonnets.

Maxine Borowsky Junge, 1998 (Photo by Rosalind Beatty)

Chapter 24

MAXINE BOROWSKY JUNGE

THE UNSOLVED HEART

Be patient toward all that is unsolved in your heart and try to live the *questions themselves* like locked rooms and like books that are written in a very foreign tongue. Do not seek the answers, which cannot be given you because you would not be able to live them. And the point is, to live everything. Live questions now. Perhaps you will then gradually, without noticing it, live along some distant day into the answer.

–Rainer Maria Rilke, *Letters to a Young Poet*

Iam an artist, art psychotherapist, writer, teacher, systems person, organizational development consultant, psychotherapist, family therapist and social change agent. I refuse to draw definitional lines or boundaries. While one or another may come to the forefront and be "seen," all have existed in me since childhood and all *are* me as a woman and as a creative person living in this world. It is actually quite simple: I combine the art of creativity and change in people, families, groups, systems and myself in the work I do and the art I make. I always have. Probably, I always will.

I AM BORN AND GROW UP

Before there were televisions, computers, the ubiquitous freeways, or the sprawling housing developments of the San Fernando Valley, I was born and grew up in Los Angeles. Before mini-malls and cement had crept over much of the city, I grew up in a two-story, Southern California Tudor house in Cheviot Hills, on the west side which my parents, out from the east, had first rented and then bought for $15,000 during World War II. In an increasingly transient society, they never moved and forty-five years later, my mother died in that house. Gaston Bachelard, a French philosopher wrote: "The house shelters daydreaming, the house protects the dreamer. The house allows one to dream in peace. . . . The values that belong to daydreaming mark humanity in its depths." And: "Memories are motionless, and the more securely they are fixed in space the sounder they are." I remember looking out my second-story bedroom window into the arms of the Chinese elm tree outside, or lying on my back and dreaming on the cool summer grass of the front lawn looking up through the branches to the big rounded clouds and the changing cerulean sky. The urge to look beyond the obvious has stayed with me.

West Los Angeles then was rural and without the later housing developments which caused my father to call Los Angeles "a suburb in search of a city." Near our house there were ranches with horses and barns and endless lima bean fields. I was ordered by my parents not to go into new houses being built. I ignored them. The neighborhood kids and I dug endless tunnels in the bean fields, which we knew as the "tramps' home." My parents, fearing cave-ins, ordered me to stay out. I ignored them. In the spring, the fields were covered with wild purple loupin.

My best friends were Gussie, Alan, Bing and their older brothers—the boys on the block; there were no girls. We played football on Mosser's lawn and street games, like Kick the Can. Every year, we painted a four-square dodgeball court on the street and shouted at cars daring to disrupt our games. In the summers we played Monopoly. The game went on for days and entailed not skill so much as the players' abilities for longevity. I told my father that I could wrestle all the boys to the floor and sit on them; he laughed and laughed.

In the days before Los Angeles became a formidable city of mean streets, I had tremendous independence and felt safe going anywhere. When I was five, I walked to the bus stop around the corner on Motor Avenue and took the Airdrome, a city bus to Overland Avenue Elementary school, about four miles away. I was in and out of the houses on the block: I badly wanted to play the piano and we didn't have one, so when I found a piano in someone's house, I admitted myself and happily banged and banged. Later on, when we had acquired an old upright with pink rococo angels gamboling across it, I taught myself to play the whole Rogers and Hart songbook, including all the verses. But I never had formal lessons. When I went to a friend's birthday party, age four, and felt teased, I left to walk home terrifying my mother. As a young child, I often went down the block to talk with Benny Black, a judge's wife who worked in her flower garden most days, and her mother Mrs. Arnold, who was bedridden upstairs. Before public health admonitions, Mrs. Arnold told me never to smoke and to tell my mother, who smoked copiously and dropped ashes everywhere, to stop. My neighborhood friends and I went up and down the block, door to door, with my red Little Flyer wagon selling flowers, pillaged from people's gardens, and old magazines first collected from the people we sold them back to. In the summer, we sold lemonade.

Maxine Borowsky Junge, age 2 1/2 with her parents.

But my childhood at 2811 Forrester Drive wasn't all idyllic: At six months, I pulled a sterilizer over on me (a contraption that boiled baby bottles) and got a severe burn that is still visible today on my left arm. When I was eight, my father, age 38, had a life-threatening heart attack. (I have a memory of standing alone at the bottom of our hilly driveway, watching the ambulance pull out.) I shared the disquietude and fears of World War II. At the age of four, during World War II, I stood on the sidewalk three doors from my house and watched while a cross was burned on the other Jewish family's lawn. And my mother bore my younger brother and simultaneously went almost completely deaf. I was a shy and sensitive child.

I adored my father. When he was in the hospital, at age 63, dying from congestive heart failure and bladder cancer, he said, "Good! Now I can eat my ice cream first." When I was a young child, he took me to what was then the combination art and natural history museum in Exposition Park with its unfinished front façade which he said had "umbrella hooks" on it. Using humor, he taught me to look. At the museum, he didn't seem to mind that I preferred the dark cool halls with incredible scenes of huge African animals to the mediocre painting collection. He took me along on his watercolor trips through rural areas and streets of Los Angeles and, with his interest and encouragement, I learned to paint. He inveigled me into playing the cello, so there could be a family trio, with my younger brother on the violin and himself on the viola. And thus introduced me to the pleasures of collaboration and chamber music, both of which I love today. He read to me: *Alice in Wonderland* and all the Oz books–with their female heroines. And he told me nightly stories of the Pushibablas. Their names were E-mouse, (Emmaus,) Macungie, Catasauqua, Hockendauqua and Butsie–my nickname. The Pushibablas, whom I envisioned as kind of sweet and bear-like, remarkably had done everything I had done during the day, so the story was about me and my buddies. (Later, I learned the names of the Pushibablas were the rivers and creeks of Lehigh Valley, Pennsylvania, where my father had gone to college.) And, by taking apart my high school and early college papers line by line, paragraph by paragraph and, on his Smith Corona typewriter, reassembling them so they "worked better," he taught me to write. He told me, "Never be an amateur at anything." It took me a lifetime and many hours of therapy to get over that.

My paternal grandfather, Abe, a Russian immigrant, invented the lock washer which changed manufacturing in this country and made him rich. His motto, which he had printed on everything, was "Keep smiling." My Hungarian grandmother Rae was a glamorous diva before that word was used. She wore hand-crocheted dresses and had regular massages, common with Eastern Europeans. My grandparents came to California on the train every summer and stayed at expensive hotels with large swimming pools like the Beverly Hills and the Beverly Wilshire. My favorite was the summer they spent on Santa Monica beach at the Ocean House–which had been built for Marian Davies by William Randolph Hearst and contained a sweeping staircase suitable for making spectacular entrances.

My mother was born in Albuquerque, New Mexico, and lived the first ten years of her life there and in Denver. My maternal grandfather, Sam Levy, a German immigrant, rode a wagon train to Santa Fe, New Mexico, when he was twelve. Working on the railroad, he learned Morse code and listened in to the stock reports. He settled in Philadelphia after he married my grandmother, Della, who was the judge's secretary in Pueblo, Colorado. They had four daughters and finally a boy, Bobby. It was said that Sam, upon buying stockings for his four girls asked, "Do I have daughters or centipedes?"

I was lucky to be raised by artist parents. My brother, three and a half years younger, wanted to be a football player and grew up to be a gastroenterologist. He was the rebel in the family. My mother, who had gone to the Moore College of Art for Women in Philadelphia and Yale Drama School, was a costume and set designer on Broadway in her twenties. She costumed the first production of "Of Thee I Sing" and was the head of the New York WPA costume shop when she was 21. My mother told fabulous stories of the Mafia bringing cash backstage to get the Broadway productions on. She married my writer father in Baltimore. The story was that he called and said, "Do you want to get married this weekend?" She said, "Yes." So they went to Baltimore where there was less red tape than New York. Her blue wedding suit, faded to uneven shades of lavender by years of strong California sun, still hung in her closet when she died in 1985. When I found it there, after her death, I thought it was smaller than either of us could ever have worn.

My mother came to Los Angeles with my father, pregnant with me. She had suffered bone deafness from a severe sinus infection in New York (before sulfa drugs or antibiotics) and was advised not to have another child. She ignored her doctor's advice and when my brother was born in 1941, she suffered almost complete deafness. (We were a family of "ignore-ers.") Years later, she told me that her deafness at his birth was like a curtain coming down and that what she had to give, she gave to my brother. My mother wore a hearing aid with a five-pound battery pack attached to her thigh. It was the time before the transistor was invented when hearing aids got much smaller. Signing was not known and she took lip reading lessons from Lucinda Moore.

For my mother, painting became a way back to the world from her silence and depression. During my growing-up years, she developed considerable skill as a portraitist. She took this skill into veterans' hospitals with a group of Hollywood artists during World War II and the Korean War, creating bedside portraits of wounded veterans. She painted a number of portrait commissions and later taught painting classes in her home studio. But she never designed costumes again (although the pink satin and tulle ballet tutu she made for me when I was five belies this), and we had a sewing machine with a tension problem that could only frustrate the sewer and make her vow never to sew another stitch. My mother also informally counseled many deaf people who were trying to adjust to their hearing aids.

My father had also been to Yale Drama School. Working as stage manager in New York for the playwright Elmer Rice, he sold a script about King Arthur to Metro Goldwyn Mayer studios. My parents came west to Los Angeles and stayed. First, they rented a small house on South Beverly Drive, down the block, it was said, from the Gershwin brothers, George and Ira. They moved to the house on Forrester Drive after I was born. My father

Note: WPA, Works Project Administration was set up by President Franklin Roosevelt to give useful work to writers and artists during the Great Depression of the 1930s.

worked as a contract movie writer for many years. Not able to get into the war because of his bad eyes and flat feet, he made training films. When gas was scarce he rode his bicycle down Motor Avenue to Metro, and later, in the other direction to Twentieth Century Fox studios. One of his original stories, "Pride Of the Marines" (with John Garfield), about a marine blinded in the war coming home to Philadelphia, earned him in 1945 an Academy Award nomination. As was typical, he didn't go to the ceremony; my parents seldom went to movies and hated fancy restaurants–we went occasionally to the Beverly Hills Brown Derby where the maitre d', named Cobb, invented the Cobb salad. My father always said about a good Cobb salad, "Do I eat it or did I eat it?" After a trip to northern California, he planted four redwood trees in the backyard. When they grew tall, they could be seen from Motor Avenue, two blocks away. When I drive down Motor Avenue, I can still see those trees.

In 1955, my father published the King Arthur story as a novel. Rather than Arthur as a mythological character, my dad wrote about a realistic Arthur, growing old in a dark and difficult world. While he was doing research for the book, the family drove to San Miguel de Allende in Mexico. The Mexican border agents thought my father was a Communist because he had so many books and almost didn't let him go across the border. In his later years, he was a much-loved professor of playwriting and screenwriting, first at the University of Southern California (USC) and then at the University of California at Los Angeles (UCLA).

My father took up painting and became quite good at it; he painted well enough to get into a number of national juried exhibits and to become a member of the California Watercolor Society. He loved the watercolors of John Marin. When he died, I inherited his brushes and painted some pretty good landscapes myself.

I grew up during the Blacklist period in the Hollywood film industry. It is difficult now to imagine the paranoia then, but the Blacklist was an agreement by the studios that certain writers, actors, producers and directors who were deemed "subversives" could not work. They might have been members of the American Communist Party, attended meetings, or had not answered questions put to them by the House Un-American Activities Committee under their first amendment rights; or their participation in anything may have been invented. Many careers were ruined and friendships irredeemably split. Started by Senator Joseph McCarthy, the Committee was ostensibly investigating Communist influence in the Hollywood labor unions. Since my dad was one of the founders of the Screenwriters Guild, he was involved. The "Hollywood Ten" was a group of screenwriters who, citing the first amendment of the Constitution, refused to answer any questions at all. They were cited for contempt of Congress, went to jail and/or left the country. It was a difficult and dark time when few were courageous enough to speak out.

Had it been a different time, I might not have seen my father stand up so often, but as it was, I always knew him as a man who spoke out for what he thought was right and I have tried to do the same. Years later, Carl Foreman gave the Marvin Borowsky Lecture on Screenwriting at the Academy of Motion Picture Arts and Sciences (the lecture my mother instituted after my father's death). Carl had been a blacklisted writer and director who lived in Europe for many years until it was "safe" to come home. He told me this story about my father: Foreman said that during the Blacklist period, he always waited until the lights went down in the theater to go into a movie. He said he couldn't bear to see people turn away from him nor did he want to put his friends in the awkward position of deciding whether or not to acknowledge him. He remembered walking down the aisle of a theater and hearing my father call out to him loudly, "Carl, come sit here." He never forgot.

I BECOME AN ARTIST

I was sensitive and shy. As a child, I was afraid of big dogs, elevators getting stuck, being left in cars that then moved–all of which I had bad experiences with. I was allowed into my parents' life that often consisted of parties where the Hollywood writers–the intelligentsia–plus historians, artists and psychiatrists talked ideas. (For a long time, I thought everyone was as smart as those people.) In my parents' living room, with the old furniture slip-covered in turquoise, yellow and coral and the chairs on wheels ("for a party," my father said), I learned to listen and I memorized a knowledge of cultural history beyond my years. But by the age of ten, I was virtually nonverbal in groups; I feared I would never have anything "smart enough" to say. My paintings at that time often concerned multiples–twins, triplets, quintuplets. Now, I would interpret them as my obsession with intimacy and relationship. I had become a listener outsider.

I entered Palms Junior High School, was given the Iowa test for tracking purposes, did poorly, and was placed in what I knew was the "dumb class." My mother came to school to try, unsuccessfully, to have me moved; she was told that I would do well with "less pressure." At the time when social relationships are chancy at best and often excruciatingly difficult for young teenagers, I took most of my classes with the "dumb" students, whom I didn't know and who weren't particularly friendly to the new person. I sat in the back of the classroom knitting endless misshapen sweaters that could never fit anyone. My previous friends, many of whom I had gone all the way with through elementary school, would make dates to meet me at a certain time or place, and wouldn't show up. I felt like a perpetual big sore and I was very lonely. Increasingly, I stayed home from school, often claiming a physical illness which even I knew did not exist. While my mother might have taken me to a therapist, instead she took me to Eula Long's art class.

Eula taught a children's art class Saturday mornings at the Kann Institute of Art on Melrose Blvd. in West Hollywood. Eula was interested in the psychological aspects of art and the creative process and, in particular, she was fascinated with Gestalt psychology. She believed in a supportive, encouraging environment, that no child's art should be criticized, only praised, and she eschewed the teaching of technique which she felt only hindered art making or stopped it altogether. (She often told us all of this.) She discouraged visual clichés and stereotypes that may represent defensiveness against an inner process of exploration, and she valued imagination, fantasy and the directness of feeling essential to all real artistic products.

Eula Long did not call herself an art therapist, but I am convinced that that is what she was. I loved her class and watched my drawings—mostly of my fellow students—at first stilted and self conscious—become rich, exciting, and even technically outstanding. I painted a mural of my art class at home in the bathroom. It was done in casein paints so it sweated every time hot bathwater was drawn. My younger brother complained that when he peed, he had to contend with my classmates looking at him. With Eula, I found my identity as an artist. In her class, I belonged. With Eula, although I could not name it, I experienced the therapeutic power of art. With Eula, my life was irrevocably changed. With Eula, even though I did not know it then, I became an art therapist.

Through high school, I took two buses down Wilshire Blvd. to Saturday adult classes at Chouinard Art School and Otis Art Institute. I was drawn to the smells and language of art and to the people involved. My artist's identity held me in good stead as I swayed through adolescent surges and years. During high school, I began to win prizes for my art. Three years running, I won more prizes than any other high school student in the Los Angeles area in a contest put on by a national magazine. I was asked to do an illustration for a story in *Seventeen* magazine. I had my picture in the newspaper and went on TV. It was pretty heady stuff. I might have been an outsider, but I was definitely an outsider artist.

Every two weeks, my father would take my brother and me to the Beverly Hills Library and let us loose in the stacks. I pulled out whatever interested me. As a result I received an eccentric self-education and read my way through the boredom of high school. When I found authors I liked, I read everything they had ever written, including any autobiography or biographies about them; for example, Sinclair Lewis. After we went to the library, my father would take us to Martindale's Book Store where my brother and I were allowed to pick out three comic books each and then we went to Wil Wright's on Beverly Drive for a hot fudge sundae.

I read everything I could find on art and decided, when I was about 13, I would be the first really great woman painter. (I figured that Georgia O'Keefe had done pretty well, but I would be better.) I spent hours pouring over art books from my parents' shelves and, as a result, taught myself a good deal of art history before I had ever seen the mystery and majesty of the originals in New York and Europe. In the 12th grade I wrote an essay on "Daumier, Goya and Ben Shahn: Painters of Social Protest."

While I still felt very much the outsider in high school, my artist's identity helped me to manage the hits of adolescent tides. I was "interesting" looking, I was told, but never traditionally pretty, to my sorrow, and I struggled endlessly with weight. My high school boyfriends were a poet and a classical Spanish guitarist who regularly took me to the 50 cent seats at the Hollywood Bowl to hear this or that famous classical musician and to Shelley's Mannhole on Hollywood Blvd. to hear jazz. I still thought of myself as non-verbal.

My parents wanted me to go east to college. I chose the western school I did–Scripps College–because I thought it rained in Claremont (it didn't) and because they served tea every afternoon (they did). Although Scripps, a women's college, had a well-known art department, every year was a crisis for me of "Should I be in an art school?" I stayed at Scripps, taking extra units each semester so I could get what I wanted along with requirements. I took enough units to graduate early.

At Scripps I gained a wonderful liberal arts education and by my senior year had my own studio where I made art most of the time. As a senior, I applied for and received a number of scholarships to grad schools in painting but before settling into one of them, I went to Europe for a year, traveled on a motorcycle and hitchhiked with a college boy friend (whom I later married) and his friends from Cal Tech (California Institute of Technology). No one seemed to mind that I was "living in sin." They minded that I was riding a motorcycle!

We were California kids who knew little of cold and snow. We bought sleeping bags and, setting out in October, planned to sleep in the fields. We nearly froze to death. After many a stay in filthy youth hostels along the road, we put the motorcycles on a boat south and hitchhiked to Italy where we thought it would be warm. I remember seeing the extraordinary Isenheim altarpiece by Grunewald in a tiny freezing church in Colmar. Even the wonders of great art didn't warm the body. In Florence, my boyfriend received a letter from the University of London saying that they were sorry they had lost his letter, but, if he still wanted to go to graduate school there, he should come. Having enough of traveling, we headed for London.

When we arrived, London was in the midst of an unseasonable cold snap and the pipes had frozen. I rented a third floor walk-up flat in the Notting Hill section with a bathtub with "geezer" in the kitchen. I went to the Camberwell School of Art for a short period where I met Sir Frances Rose. Sir Frances kept "accidentally" meeting me on the stairs. He said he wanted to take me to the pub and tell me stories of his days with Gertrude Stein. I never went. I knew he was an old drunk–he smelled pretty bad–and figured he was a liar as well. Later, I learned from reading Alice B. Toklas that it was all true and that he had been part of the Stein circle in Paris. I wish I'd heard the stories.

I married my boyfriend in London. We thought if we could live together under the freezing motorcycle circumstances, we might make it (and did for 28 years). We were married in the South Kensington Registry Office ("births, deaths and marriages"). I wore an old green satin dress and we had an orange cake. We took a red double-decker bus to the Registry Office, because we couldn't get a cab. Two male friends came over from Paris to be our witnesses–one I never saw again. There is only one photograph from our wedding: It is of me and my young husband wrapped together in a quilt we had been given as a present.

I was raised to be intelligent, talented, ambitious and an achieving artist. But, growing up in the '50s and marrying in the early '60s, I was supposed to give it all up for my husband's career. I sure tried. The family story was humorist James Thurber's "A woman's place is in the wrong." While my husband worked for his Ph.D. in neurophysiology, I entered the University of California at Los Angeles' (UCLA) Graduate Department of Painting and supported myself and my student husband as a teaching assistant. (In order to work at UCLA in 1960, I had to sign a loyalty oath to the United States government, stating I was not a Communist.)

At the UCLA painting department, before the Women's Movement gave us language and consciousness, I encountered a heavy and debilitating dose of sexual discrimination. I left after two years before receiving my M.F.A., humiliated and pregnant with my first child. While I did crafts and drawing, I never took them seriously and didn't paint again for ten years. Trying to stay home with my infant, as I was "supposed to do," I nearly went crazy and started "sneaking out" (as I called it) to attend Arnold Mesches' life drawing classes. It is difficult to imagine now because of the Women's Movement–its opportunities and resources–but then without it, guilt about leaving my child in the hands of a baby-sitter became a permanent resident in my heart.

Note: Geezer is a British device for heating hot water.

I taught private art classes to children, adolescents, and adults in the community room of the Co-op Market, classes which my mother and aunt had told me would fail. There, Eula Long's teaching method was now mine. But I discovered and felt a deep kinship with Florence Cane's book *The Artist in Each of Us* and read everything I could find on art teaching and on the horrors of the public school system. I especially loved John Dewey with his philosophy of Progressive Education and Sylvia Ashton Warner's *Teacher*. The sensitive nature of the creative process and its need for a nurturing environment had become all too evident to me. I had decided that when I was 21 I would cease being nonverbal. That didn't happen, so I moved the age to 28.

About 1965, depressed and living in south La Jolla–it had been merely five years before that Jews had been allowed to buy property,–and pregnant with my second child, I found an ad for an art teacher for a children's enrichment program on the bulletin board in the John Coles book store. I applied and began to teach on Saturdays, including one class with a dancer that integrated movement and art and that today I would call "creative arts therapies."

Maxine Borowsky Junge's self portrait, 1967.

And I met Sandy Turner, a Quaker community organizer. Sandy, a Jew formerly from Chicago, was generally the angriest person I ever knew–she was angry at historical and current discrimination, among other things. Sandy later became one of the first draft counselors against the Vietnam War and worked with Cesar Chavez's migrant farm workers. When the middle-class enrichment program would not sponsor our project, Sandy and I went out on our own. She and I put together "Operation Adventure," an alternative education program for minority kids. We believed that learning should be fun. We used three sites, volunteer teachers, rooms contributed by the Methodist church, and a minute supply budget. We painted murals and sidewalks, made movies, wrote poetry and prose and published it in "books." We taught Greek mythology with kids acting out the stories–they especially enjoyed the battles. In art therapy this would be called "Community Arts." In my own art, I did no painting. I was becoming less nonverbal because I had to talk about Operation Adventure, which taught me to speak out for what I believed. I was about 27. By now I had two kids.

Maxine Borowsky Junge's portrait of her daughter, age two.

Moving back to Los Angeles after the first Watts riots with Black Power on the rise, where my husband was now an Assistant Professor at UCLA, I "peddled" Operation Adventure around town and ended up in the East LA barrio of Boyle Heights at the International Institute. One summer, we hired 38 minority college students to teach the classes and I, the nonverbal one, went downtown to beg the Los Angeles City Council publicly for more money to pay them. "How could we enhance self-confidence (a program goal), if we paid so little?" I said. It wasn't much, but we were the highest paid staff in Los Angeles that summer.

Operation Adventure went on for about four years, finally transforming into a project with alienated gang kids from Mexico who thought the powdered sugar I brought with summer strawberries was a large bowl of cocaine. And I, as the white lady boss, learned a lot–I <u>had</u> to. During this time my father died and I decided to go back to school.

In Operation Adventure, I first encountered the power of groups. Our multiracial staff of teachers had so many conflicts with each other, they could not work with kids. Out of desperation and because we couldn't think of anything else, my Chicano assistant director Antonio Gomez and I asked them to sit in a group and talk honestly to each other. Much to our surprise, things got better. At the end of that summer, I decided to learn something about how and why groups work and called the Group Psychotherapy Institute. I was told the group class was already full, but did I want to take the family therapy class? "OK," I said. (By this time, I had my first dose of family therapy as a client and was quite interested in it and in becoming a therapist. I had come up against the myriad environmental constraints of the children of Operation Adventure and felt powerless to change them. I wanted to make a difference and felt I could make more of a difference if I could work with one or two children.) Through the two-way mirror, I watched a talented therapist, Joan Schain, work with a family and was fascinated. At the end of the class, I asked Joan if she would train me–it was the era of paraprofessionals. She said: "I would, but you wouldn't have anything when you finished. Why, don't you go to school?" And so I did.

I had never heard of art therapy then, nor were there any art therapy training programs west of the Mississippi River and if I had known of the few eastern schools, I couldn't have moved because I had kids and a husband with a job. I determined that social work school would give me the "union card" that would allow me to do what I wanted, in the least amount of time

This was the late '60s. The word on the street then was that it was better to go to UCLA's social work school, rather than USC's–there were only the two–because the students at UCLA went on strike a lot and you didn't have to go to school much. But when I went to talk to the white male admissions director at UCLA, he said: "We don't take any white, middle-aged, middle-class Jewish women" (I was 30 years old!). In the meantime, I had become the art teacher at a private therapeutic school, gone on strike to picket on the sidewalk outside the school with the other teachers to protest the inadequacy of resources like books for the students and, over a weekend, written a proposal for our own therapeutic school which opened with 25 students and which is still operating today in Los Angeles.

Because of a variety of circumstances, when the University of Southern California (USC) School of Social Work, after the deadline, asked me to finish my application, I did, was interviewed and admitted. Mental health consultants at the therapeutic schools had both trained at Cedars-Sinai,Thalians Community Mental Health Center and mentioned Helen Landgarten to me because they knew I was interested in art, but I still had no idea of what art therapy was.

I had a wonderful time in my two years at USC. By accident, I met a remarkable African American teacher, Dr. Barbara Solomon, who mentored me, my radical ex-Communist friend and the black students and taught us all about social activism. My master's thesis (with my colleague) was on Jewish mothers, secular and orthodox. There, I discovered one of the great truisms of doing research: That the literature may not have much to say about your subject because researchers hadn't looked there yet and that because it is printed in a book or journal article, does not make it so.

I had gone to social work school to learn family therapy, but discovered that they didn't care much about it there. Nonetheless, I struggled to learn it. In my second social work internship I worked in the Child and Family Psychiatry Department of Cedars-Sinai, Thalians Community Mental Health Center, where they actually did and taught family treatment and there, finally, I met an art therapist, Helen Landgarten, who was on staff.

I always say that Helen was trying to save the world from me because, with no knowledge, I was trying, badly, to use art in therapy. When I graduated from social work school in 1973, Helen invited me to apprentice. Sitting in her therapy sessions, at her elbow, I learned the art of art therapy from a master. After the Symbionese Liberation Army kidnapped Patty Hearst and came to the South Los Angeles area, where most were burned to death by the LA police department, a group of us from Thalians at Helen's instigation went into a local elementary school to help the children who had seen it, deal with their trauma through art.

Although I was a trained artist, previously I was educated as a verbal therapist. It took me most of a year to learn to use art and not fall back on words when I became nervous. Helen put up with my challenging tendencies and my proclivity to think for myself and I put up with her idea that she was always right. I believe we eventually became a good pair because we shared the goal of turning out exceptional art therapists. We believed that our well-trained graduates would be the best salespeople for art therapy, and we were right. We both believed that the people we trained should be <u>primary psychotherapists</u>, art clinicians in mental health settings, using both the ideas of Naumburg and Kramer, by constructing reasoned goals and a treatment plan. Much of my art therapy work is based in the therapeutic relationship with the art being a third and equally-important part, with the client and therapist. Some psychological theories that I was attuned to were objects relations, Erickson's developmental framework and systems theories. Mostly, my interest lay in family art therapy and I developed my own theories.

Helen Landgarten started her Clinical Art Therapy Training Program at first as a lecture series, then a certificate program in 1971 at Immaculate Heart College, a place of exceptional creativity and where Sister Mary Corita (later Corita Kent) changed the face of printmaking and advertising in the United States. The art therapy program was first "approved" by AATA in 1979. It didn't matter that our offices were in the basement with the bathroom pipes running through. (Every time the toilet flushed, we could hear the pipes doing their job.) Leslie Thompson, who graduated from the art therapy program at Hahnemann in Philadelphia, was the first faculty member and I was the second. In 1975, Bobbi Stoll and Shirley Riley were in the first Masters graduating class of six. I thought most of my students knew more than I did about art therapy—and I was right—but I was a quick learner.

Helen was and is an art therapy purist: Our students were trained to be primary clinical therapists and she felt that they should be able to work in paid jobs after graduation. She worried about the students' art therapy identity, but in 1979 when Bobbi Stoll under an "Equivalent Degree" clause gained the Marriage and Family Counseling license (MFC), she supported her and the students who sought the license after her. Art therapy began in an environment of plenty, now money was getting tighter in mental health. The MFC was and is one of only three psychotherapy licenses in California.

Trying to teach my first class at Immaculate Heart, I was so nervous that I had to sit down to keep from shaking. In the door came someone from the administration office with a note for me. It said:"Call your mother." I read it to the class, gave up trying to act like a grownup and went on from there. Before that, I had fearfully given my first professional presentation. Helen criticized that I presented "like a social worker" and my mother whom I had invited for approval's sake, fell asleep and snored loudly. (She denied this, of course.) I mentored a foreign student for her thesis. When she didn't meet the deadline for graduation, she told me "If you won't let me graduate, I'll have to marry a homosexual to stay in the country." Before Immaculate Heart closed, I wrote and had accepted by the college, a proposal for a Ph.D. in art therapy, probably the first in the country.

After our first year of teaching, Helen took Leslie and me to the Art Therapy Educators Conference at George Washington University. I met all the famous art therapy "names" I was in awe of, whose writings had impressed me, and whose theories I had taught. I ate with them, talked to them, and sat in a room with them for two days while I watched them competitively tear each other apart under the guise of "whose training program is better." If this terminal nastiness was the art therapy field, I was sure I didn't want anything to do with it. I didn't go back for five years.

When Immaculate Heart College closed for financial reasons, our art therapy program moved to Loyola Marymount University (LMU), and I became a tenure track professor and Associate Director of the art therapy masters program. I put myself in charge of embedding the program in the school by meeting people. I was still quite shy, but I determined to act like an extrovert. I came to know faculty and administration all over the University. I figured if there came a time when the University tried to shut down the art therapy program and I reasoned it might come sooner or later, they would have a much more difficult time if they knew our faces. And I had something I strongly believed in to talk about–this time, it was art therapy.

Thus, began one of the most creative periods of my life. My "creativity" was the molding of the art therapy program itself and the fancy stepping and quick thinking that kept the program alive, growing and excellent within the wilds of academia. LMU was a men's school established by the Jesuits which had combined with Marymount to make it coed. When, in 1980, I arrived at LMU, a male administrator told me: "The women will be gone soon." I also found out that the accrediting body, the Western Association of Schools and Colleges (WASC) had strongly recommended that LMU have more women and more creative programs. In spite of having a Dean (a priest) who called us "those Jewish ladies" we fit the bill on both counts.

As an art therapy program, we were outsiders in the male-dominated academy and needed to tolerate adversity and to play politics very effectively. When we came to Loyola Marymount, we were offered to art and psychology departments. We were turned down by both. Probably because of WASC's urgings the University made us our own department in the Graduate Division. Graduate education was ignored at LMU, but alone and with no protection, we had a good deal of autonomy. Helen retired in 1988 and after being Acting Chair 1985–1986, I became Chair of the program. Eventually during California's marriage and family licensing problems, the University did try to get rid of the art therapy program. With the help of three students, some organizational consultants I knew, and much understanding of systems and playing politics, I was able to keep the program anchored in the school, even though another department said it was unethical to change our degree title. Although they didn't teach art therapy students, they refused to teach at all if the change was made. This victory came about largely through personal politics and a conscious use of self. Although there were no curriculum changes at all in the program, at the yearly conference, members of the American Art Therapy Association accused us of "losing the art." We had fallen into one of AATA's ongoing arguments: Could an art therapist who had another kind of license, love, understand, and use art? As far as I was concerned, there was no doubt.

During these years, I was involved with AATA in many different ways. I am most proud, as Chair of the Clinical Committee, of writing the first definition of the art therapist, and my years as member and chair of the Educational and Training Board (ETB, now EPAP) to grant "Approval" to educational programs, thereby solidifying standards for training programs.

In 1985, the years of cigarettes finally caught up with my mother and she died of lung cancer. Two years later, on my 50th birthday, having married at age 21 and after almost 29 years, I left my husband.

MY CLINICAL WORK, WRITING, AND ART

Much art therapy writing has been with a particular problem or population, and based on case studies. While this focus has been important in establishing art therapy as a viable profession, to write about clinical work has seldom been an interest of mine. Despite working in clinics and in private practice since 1971, my writing thrusts followed my wide-ranging interests. My published writings are always personal, disguised as idea pieces and often containing and being about works by professional artists.

My internships were in two community mental health centers, at the time psychiatric hospitals were being "deinstitutionalized" and the PET teams (Psychiatric Emergency Team) were beginning. Since 1973, I have practiced clinical work as a primary art psychotherapist in many outpatient clinics: Council of Jewish Women (school groups and family art therapy), Cedars-Sinai, Thalians Community Mental Health Center, Child and Family Department, Ross Loos, Department of Psychiatry and Dr. Michael Scolaro's AIDS medical practice. From 1973 to 2003, I maintained a private practice. Yet, my only clinical writing is a 1985 article titled "The Book About Daddy Dying: A Preventive Art Therapy Technique to Help Families Deal With the Death of a Family Member," about death in a family, and the use of a book to help heal that loss. Presenting a paper at the annual art therapy conferences or giving a keynote address to art therapists has allowed me to think about a topic that interested me in the hope that it would interest other art therapists. I wrote "Feminine Imagery and a Young Woman's Search for

Identity" in which I explored ten years of artwork as developmental touch-stones. I explored conflictual issues of creative women in "An Inquiry Into Women and Creativity Including Two Case Studies of Frida Kahlo and Diane Arbus." One of the questions I asked was about the role of their art in their identity and personality development, was it healing or disintegrating? "Perception of Doors" was a psychological investigation of doors in twentieth century painting. In the area of social action, Alvarez, Kellogg and Volker and I wrote *The Art Therapist As Social Activist.* In 2005, I wrote *The Art Therapist As Social Activist,* which is my life story as a social activist, and in *Mourning, Memory and Life Itself,* with the symbols of the Vietnam Memorial Wall and the AIDS quilt, I explored loss, memory and the healing properties of community. *Our Own Voices: New Paradigms for Art Therapy Research,* (with Debra Linesch) was a treatise on art therapy research that argued for creative methods. Even my published book reviews are idea pieces.

My two books were written to right what I perceived of as a wrong. In 1994, I published the first, and still the only, history of art therapy in America of more than a few pages and in book form, *A History of Art Therapy in the United States* (with Paige Asawa). As an art therapy educator I had become dissatisfied with the histories, often in the beginnings of clinical books, which focused on what I called "the Eastern Block" of art therapists. As a Californian, I knew the story was much broader and that there were many art therapists who remained invisible. My book was published by AATA for its 25th anniversary. An AATA President at the time wanted to give me a "History Award," but because she would not include my collaborator, I turned it down. Shortly after, thanks to Bob Ault and letters from many former students, I was given the Honorary Life Membership award by my art therapy peers, which I accepted with great pleasure. I was very touched.

My other book, *Creative Realities: The Search for Meanings* was published in 1998. It grew out of my lifelong dissatisfaction with attempts to define creativity. Beginning as a dissertation at the Fielding Institute where I earned my Ph.D, (starting at age 45 and ending at 52) it contained my own art work and was a phenomenological study of visual artists and writers. (At Fielding, I trained in social action at the Highlander Center, New Market, Tennessee, and National Training Labs, Bethel, Maine.) My creativity inquiry was unique in the multidiscipline creativity literature and research, in that it employed a four-part alternative realities or world views model as a lens through which to look at creativity. (I do not believe that there is a single reality or "truth.") While not specifically an art therapy book, it was written by an art therapist and with an art therapist's voice and eye.

Occasionally, I took on one of the old AATA arguments which still continue today. Not published is my paper called "The Wars Between Art and Therapy," which looked at the two major theories of our field—art in therapy and art psychotherapy—and called for an integration, not a continuing separation and argument.

Throughout the years from 1973 on, my art remained important to me as I continued it sporadically, but intensely. I had five one-woman shows, some group shows and became a black and white photographer at age 52. Much of my creative work was done in my beloved Mendocino house on the northern California coast.

Poster for Maxine Borowsky Junge's photography exhibit, 2003.

NOW

As Professor Emerita, I retired from Loyola Marymount in 2001. Leaving the cement jungles of Los Angeles behind, I live with two dogs and my collection of folk art in the Pacific Northwest on Whidbey Island, a ferry ride and an hour north of Seattle. Whidbey is a rural land of cows and horses and barns. Leaving LMU, I discovered I wasn't finished with teaching so taught at Goddard College (distance learning) in Vermont for four years and at Antioch Seattle. I still mentor Goddard theses and consult, teaching art therapy and family therapy at Compass Mental Health of Whidbey Island.

My remarkable children are grown and I have a grandchild, Henry. Both my children are multitalented; they are good at art, music, writing, collaboration, teaching and social justice with enough talent so that any one would make them a good career. I am very proud of them both. My daughter lives in Los Angeles, was a founding writer/producer for TV's "Friends." She has written for "Sex and the City," "Now and Again," and "The West Wing," among others. As a young adult, she wrote a musical "Galileo" with her collaborator since college, Jeanine Tesori, and they are working on a commission in development from the Public Theater in New York to write a musical about adolescent girls. What I am most proud of, is that she has helped pay for her brother's doctorate.

My gay son earned his doctorate in Anthropology from Emory University, spring 2006. (He says he hopes to have a job by the time he is 40.) He has been an AIDS activist, a sushi chef, a music counselor, lived in Japan, San Francisco, Rome, Florence, Bolivia, Brazil, and Baltimore where he received a Masters in Public Health from Johns Hopkins. He speaks five languages. He helped found the first needle exchange program in Los Angeles and was researcher for the city of Baltimore's needle exchange. He lived in Brazil for two years where he did field research on gender and politics in a poor area and taught Brazilian transvestites English.

I taught art therapy for more than 30 years and saw about 500 students graduate. I supervised the clinical work of numerous art therapists and postmasters art therapists. I mentored probably 250 masters theses and projects. I am proud of all my students and feel honored to have worked with them. I am proud, too, of the Loyola Marymount art therapy program which has had three HLMs and 12 or more books published by faculty, probably more than any other program in America.

Now I walk in the woods with my dogs, go to the bagel shop afterward, and when I brush my teeth and look in the mirror, I see my mother's face. I work in my studio (the last painting I did was of Andrea Yates, who, in the throes of post-partum depression, drowned her children.) I had two bouts in the hospital this year, so am prone to feel more physically vulnerable than I used to. I do what my Seattle friend calls "backyard 25 cent research" about current culture. I watch "Judge Judy." I am Guest Editor of a series of life stories of art therapy people of color for the American Art Therapy Association journal *Art Therapy* in 2006. And I thought up the idea for this memoirs book and, with Harriet Wadeson as co-editor, will see it published. Harriet and I presented a paper on our research about retired art therapists at AATA's 2005 conference.

I still retain my tremendous enthusiasm for art therapy. The power of the emergent image remains intensely fascinating for me. And how people live their lives never ceases to intrigue and surprise me. The future of art therapy is unseeable. Times have changed since the early days when the mental health business had money and, expansively, looked to creative ideas. Now there is bureaucracy with reams of paperwork; the work is tougher and therapy problems are many and bigger. It is a time when jobs are few and the pioneering spirit is even more important than in the early days of the profession. Art therapy educational programs are often under siege as they scramble to meet the many outside requirements and AATA's increasingly more difficult educational standards. I worry that the increasing standardization will make unbridled creativity very difficult. I hope that educational programs have made a serious curricular effort to address the changing employment climate for art therapists; but I doubt that this is so. I wonder at the American Art Therapy Association's current push to collaborate with counselors and foresee that counselors and others who know art therapy may get employment before art therapists because counselors and other mental health workers are more familiar to the mental health establishment. My questioning includes certificate programs. I have often thought the American Art Therapy Association has "foot-in-mouth" disease. But I have confidence that art therapy will stay alive because it is an important idea and an important practice. And, I remain intentionally an outsider because I have discovered that the view from the outside is more clear.

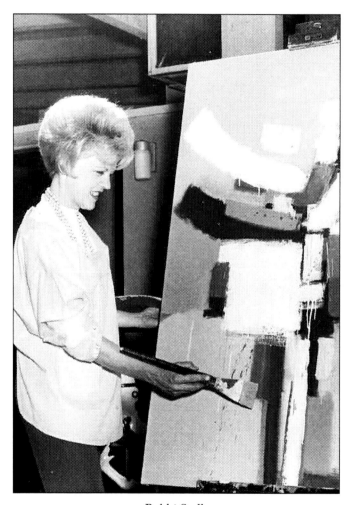

Bobbi Stoll

Chapter 25

BOBBI STOLL

A REWARDING THIRTY-YEAR PARTNERSHIP
OF RIGHT AND LEFT BRAIN

Writing this autobiography as an art therapist of 30-plus years is like birthing a 40-year-old with no past. My yearnings, strivings, aptitude, talent, intuition, bilateral intelligence and experiences coalesced when I was introduced to art therapy, responding positively to art therapy's integrating potential as challenges to both right and left brain.

An only child of parents who divorced when I was five, I spent a vast amount of time drawing and painting. Remaining examples of my masterpieces from ages 4 to 10 portray my mother doing something at home—combing her hair, relaxing on the sofa or reading a book. As a budding artist at 11 or 12 visiting my first female physician, I was intrigued by her vast collection of medical books. She became my medical lending library and for several years I was never without a medical book at home. Unable to understand what I read, I was nonetheless fascinated by the artwork of hands-on bodywork called surgery; diseases held little interest for me. My school reading and book reviews reflected the influence of my family doctor and of the author James Seagrave, whose book *Burma Surgeon* provided me with the pieces missing in the medical books. By age 13, I was set on becoming a doctor—a brain surgeon.

In school, I immersed myself in science classes and each summer took one or two science or history classes to free space in my science-heavy schedule during the school year for art classes. As my interest in artwork increased, my interest in the art in the medical books also increased and I soon modified my career goal to medical illustrator. I was surprised to learn it was offered only at Johns Hopkins University with a prerequisite Bachelors of Fine Arts Degree (BFA).

I applied to Syracuse University art school to major in illustration but, needing freer expression, over four years I changed my major several times to increasingly expressive forms, finally graduating with a BFA in painting. Medical illustration looked increasingly dull! I was also distracted by a budding romance that culminated in my wedding on graduation day in the campus chapel and superseded any remaining interest in graduate school or medical illustration. Coincidentally, technology at the time was rendering medical illustration obsolete so I can say I was saved (from a vanishing career) by the (wedding) bell.

Bobbi Stoll, age 11.

As a newlywed living in Los Angeles with my husband in law school at the University of Southern California (USC), I worked briefly as an advertising artist for a major department store and later as a free-lance advertising artist. Soon I needed more intellectual and creative challenges and human contact which I satisfied as a Social Worker for the County of Los Angeles Department of Public Social Services (DPSS). I relished the direct client contact, the interaction with families, planning for the welfare of multiply disadvantaged children, and locating appropriate community resources for referrals.

The Peter Principle surfaced and I was soon pressured to move into administration where there would be no client contact. I resisted and, when forced to take the test, I *mistakenly* joined 500 males for the wrong test for the newly-emerging computer market! Programmers and systems analysts piqued my interest, and the County Assessor had just ordered a first generation computer from Minneapolis Honeywell. With computer science courses unknown, there were no trained programmers, so job criteria consisted of aptitude testing. I scored high on the test, left DPSS, received training directly from Honeywell engineers, and became a programmer, systems analyst and supervisor.

Being a pioneer in the first generation of computers was a creative challenge for four years, until the lure of the canvas became too seductive and I resigned to dedicate myself to serious painting full time. I was well into the two-step dance between right and left brain that characterized my life. Within a year I'd hung the first of ten gallery shows, in another year I was the adoptive mother of an 18-month-old son and in still another year I had a nine-month old adopted daughter. Studio time was hard to come by, and I worried the children might get into the toxic materials in my home studio.

Miraculously, I was contracted by Permanent Pigment to introduce Liquitex acrylic paints to the art world. They shipped all their products which I was to use for six months in preparation for demonstrating these new products in art supply stores and galleries in Los Angeles. Initially, I was frustrated because they dried too fast or didn't respond like my familiar oil paints. When I allowed them to be what they were, I was free to begin experimenting. I used them in every conceivable way. I tie-dyed t-shirts, filled rotted slats of a broken olive barrel and, to test color-fastness, painted a sunburst to hang on the fence, painted designs on high chairs and children's toys because they were nontoxic, used acrylics as watercolors, for impasto paintings, and sculpted with modeling paste. I found acrylics to be successful in every way except silk-screening (the paint clogged the silk, dried fast and couldn't be removed). I was sold on acrylic paints and free from worry about toxic oils and turpentine around children.

Not an ivory tower type, I needed more social outlets than the four walls of my studio offered. I enjoyed demonstrating Liquitex acrylics and the creative opportunities it provided. During demonstrations, I was frequently asked to teach a class and, when the time-limited demonstrations ended, I eventually taught two acrylic painting classes each week at a city recreation center. I soon tired of repeating the same beginning painting class. I wanted to see artists developing and advancing. The repeating students also outgrew these beginning studio classes and requested private critiques of the work they did at home.

Bobbi Stoll's painting and exhibiting trio.

A small group of former painting students met one Saturday a month for a critique of their work. After a few such meetings, the group began bringing sack lunches and wanting day-long meetings. As these artists related to their work with an apparent focus on composition and aesthetics, deeper personal material was uncovered. I understood this from my own painting but was uncomfortable with their personal disclosures and repeatedly refocused them on aesthetic considerations.

Then in June 1972, a flyer from Immaculate Heart College (IHC) announced Sister Corita's popular serigraphy class and a brief introductory lecture on art therapy by Helen Landgarten. I'd never heard of art therapy but knew this was a lecture I had to attend. What Helen Landgarten described as art therapy also described the process in my group of artists. Since I regarded myself as an artist and not a therapist, I discontinued the Saturday critiques and, to learn what I'd been doing, signed up for the fall class in art therapy. (In hindsight, I can say the art critique groups had been therapeutic, insightful and growthful, not unlike many subsequent art therapy groups.)

Thirty-five to 40 students–half artists, the rest school personnel–attended the fall 1972 class. Artists and school personnel exhibited dramatic differences in perception and degree of interest over the semester. My intense interest in art therapy was complicated by marital problems that resulted in a separation in late November, 1972. I was depressed, trying to soothe two depressed latency-aged children and maintain functioning in a fractured family. I both wanted and needed art therapy. I painted voraciously, read the only art therapy writings available–Margaret Naumburg's books and the *American Journal of Art Therapy* edited by Elinor Ulman–and was supported and soothed by friends and a few classmates. My interest in art therapy was intensified by my emotional vulnerability and loss. As I struggled to settle community property, the art therapy program was the only thing that felt like mine alone and I needed to establish *my* new world. Furthermore, since I was the one wanting out of the marriage I refused spousal support. I needed to make a living as an artist, an art therapist or, if worse came to worse, as a systems analyst, a path I'd already traveled and that held no further interest for me.

In prehistoric times (prior to my introduction to art therapy), my group shows and bi-annual one-woman shows alternately sold out or sold none. Such erratic income was impossible to budget and the scattered few works I managed to complete while a student and later while pioneering my practice were frustratingly inadequate to satisfy the demands of regular exhibits, so I was challenged to make art therapy my career and to earn a living doing it. Being divorced, a single parent, a returning full-time student, head of household, in therapy, and sole wage earner required a revised identity and completely restructured life. With little time for personally satisfying painting, it was sketchbooks to the rescue. I've had one working for me ever since.

Many summers I rented a cabin for a month in Idyllwild, California, where my daughter and I each enrolled in classes at Idyllwild's School of Music and the Arts (ISOMATA). One especially interesting painting class was taught by Francoise Gilot, Picasso's ex-wife, mother of Claude and Paloma, wife of Jonas Salk, artist and author of *Life With Picasso*, published in 1965. I was more star-struck by Francoise Gilot than by any film star in Hollywood! My work was forever influenced by her Picasso-Matisse-Braque approach.

I became one of the most vocal students in the art therapy introductory class petitioning for more art therapy classes. The reward was a one-year certificate program that began in January 1973 with about 16 students, mostly artists from the introductory class. Some students dropped out of the certificate program at Immaculate Heart College (IHC) while others left after receiving their certificate. I was one of seven overzealous artists who clamored for still more and was excited by the announcement of a two year Masters program in Clinical Art Therapy beginning in January 1974 at IHC under Helen Landgarten's direction. All seven of us signed up for the next 18 months (we were given one full semester credit for the one-year certificate).

I attended my first American Art Therapy Association (AATA) Conference at Harding Hospital in Columbus, Ohio, while in the first year of the Masters program. The few students in attendance were barely acknowledged. It was cliquish and difficult to break into AATAs closed system. On returning, I called Membership Chair Robert Wolf to suggest a Student Subcommittee be established to develop student programs at the conferences and stimulate student membership and participation. If students were not welcome in the professional conference program, we could develop a student program to learn from each other. True to the principle of the squeaky wheel, Robert appointed me to chair the first Student Subcommittee.

With no theoretical foundation of its own, our art therapy coursework was psychodynamically-based and our hands-on experience family systems oriented. Classes forming just ahead of us often failed to satisfy my insatiable quest for more. Without knowing what constituted more, Shirley Riley and I searched for seminars, programs, and training in any theoretical or disciplinary mode. It was a time when new concepts and interventions were being developed and promoted for mainstream acceptance: Transactional Analysis, Family Therapy, Group Therapy, Self Psychology, Creative Arts Therapies, Object Relations, Gestalt and Neurolinguistic Programming, to name a few.

California was a popular destination for clinicians on the training circuit and home to many of these new therapies as well as numerous recognized clinicians. I was fortunate to have had opportunities to supplement my university coursework with one-day to five-day trainings with Janie Rhyne, Betty Edwards, Salvador Minuchin, Virginia Satir, Fritz Perls, Irving Yalom, Irving Berkovitz, Carl Whitaker, Cloe Madanes, Bruno Bettelheim, Heinz Kohut, Otto Kernberg, Ira Progoff, Elizabeth Kubler-Ross, Richard Bandler and John Grinder. I applied art therapy to everything I learned in these rich supplemental trainings.

Art therapists came from the east coast to teach intensive weekend courses in our new program: Bernard Levy taught I.Q. Assessment Through Art; Hanna Kwiatkowska taught Family Art Therapy and Evaluation Through Art; Sandra Kagan (later Graves-Alcorn), Christine Sharpes and others presented various topics and theoretical models of art therapy.

Adequate clinical training was not available at Immaculate Heart. Thalians Community Mental Health Clinic at Cedars-Sinai Hospital, familiar with art therapy as Helen Landgarten's employer, included her art therapy students in their training for doctors interning in psychiatry, psychology interns, and social work interns. This excellent training consisted of lectures, case presentations, demonstrations, observations and being observed, videotaped and critiqued in live family art therapy sessions with clients of the clinic.

Five students graduated in June 1975 from the first art therapy Masters program west of the University of Louisville. Over the summer the other two students graduated. Needing a break, I was reenergized by a leisurely and lengthy trip to Japan with a Buddhist group, but no one I asked in Japan had ever heard of art therapy.

On my return, I was ready to get to work and contacted California's Board of Behavioral Science Examiners (BBSE) for a licensing application but was declared unqualified for any existing license. I was shocked to learn that the classes I took at Thalians, for which students in the other disciplines received credit toward their respective licenses, gave me no credit as an art therapist. The same courses were listed on my transcript as "Family Art Therapy," "Art Therapy Practicum," "Introduction to Art Therapy," "Art Therapy Assessment," "Psychopathology in Art," etc. There was no license for art therapists, and California's licensing board had never heard of art therapy.

Nonetheless, eager to practice our new profession, we five June graduates rented an office in Beverly Hills and each had one office day to practice without a license. Having earned a Ph.T. ("Putting Hubby Through") from the University of Southern California, I was not naive about needing a license to open a private practice office. I became a regular in the law library researching options and found the only possibility for licensing was showing that my courses (class by class) for the Masters Degree in Clinical Art Therapy were equivalent in content and substance to those submitted by qualified applicants for Marriage, Family and Child Counselor licenses (MFCC).

My mentor, a purist, and my classmates/officemates considered me a traitor to art therapy for seeking licensure in another discipline. I believed I was qualified as a Marriage, Family and Child Counselor, plus I also had a unique specialty. Lacking their support, I worked directly with the Immaculate Heart Dean and over the next three years submitted lengthy documentation of every class bibliography, test, required paper, practicum experience, lecture, and presentation demonstrating coursework equivalent to that of MFCC graduates. I insisted then and still, that a license grants permission and legitimizes a practice. Once the door to my practice was legally open, I could do what I was trained to do, purchase malpractice insurance and receive third-party reimbursement, none of which was possible for the unlicensed.

No sooner had I graduated than I was asked by Judy Rubin, American Art Therapy Association (AATA) President Elect, to Chair the 9th Annual

Conference in Los Angeles in 1978. It would be the first conference west of the Mississippi; she warned me that only a few of the 680 mostly Eastern members of AATA would attend a conference on the west coast and advised me to plan for a maximum 200 registrations. I saw an opportunity to use the conference to stimulate interest among hospital administrators, clinic directors, special education program directors, school psychologists, teachers, and legislators to develop jobs for art therapists, to educate the public about art therapy and, most importantly, to influence the Board of Behavioral Science Examiners to act favorably on my appeal for licensure. The challenge was explaining to the AATA Board my need for so many printed programs and meeting rooms! With no national office or staff, no Policy and Procedure Manual to follow, the message was clear, "You're on your own!" And it was definitely a three-year task—the same three years during which I was preparing numerous course syllabi for the Dean's approval and signature to establish my eligibility with the BBSE to take the Marriage, Family and Child Counseling licensing exam.

Selecting a conference site, negotiating and signing the hotel contract were frightening and risky. Trying to anticipate every conceivable problem, I was scared enough to negotiate a very tight hotel contract. Special invitations were sent to targeted local individuals and mental health facilities, public service announcements on statewide radio and TV made and a luncheon for AATA Board members and invited California legislators assured good press coverage. The effort was a success. Although by October, 1978 AATA membership had increased to 1,111, the more than 700 conference registrations exceeded everyone's expectation.

Of course, I included a Student Program—the first. Since I lived close to the conference site but would stay at the hotel for the duration of the conference, I turned my house into a student dormitory and assigned two local students to act as "house parents." One of the students staying at my house was presenting a mask-making workshop at the conference. I was informed that plaster of Paris was all over the hotel walls, on the carpet and clogging the sink. I was frantic because I hadn't anticipated such damage when negotiating the contract and now I imagined exorbitant repair costs. In my sternest voice, I insisted the student was responsible for leaving the room in its original condition and any damage found by the hotel would be charged to her. Fearing retribution, I asked the "house parents" to watch that no damage was done to my home. To her credit, that student worked all day and miraculously got the room cleaned and the plumbing unclogged.

The legislative luncheon might have been the magic bullet—I'll never know—but during the conference I received official notice of my eligibility to sit for the MFCC licensing examination early in December, two weeks after the conference! Burned-out after three years of conference planning and with no time to study, I figured if I failed, I'd retake the exam in six months. After taking the exam, it was time for a vacation and I took my teenagers to Guadalajara and Puerto Vallarta for the holidays. I also tried to find any art therapist in either area–it was like trying to find a needle in a haystack since I had no contact. When I returned, I found the notice that I passed the licensing exam and was licensed January 10, 1979. Thus, I was established as a metaphoric "brain surgeon" a.k.a., art therapist.

A year later, I was nominated for Public Information Chair of AATA, a board position at that time, probably as a token westerner. I was elected for 1981–1983 and reelected for 1983–1985, years in which it seemed art therapy was virtually erupting world-wide. I had met art therapists in my European travels and during four summers that I led art therapy growth groups on Skyros, a Greek island. I received letters from isolated art therapists seeking advice, correspondence, information, books, money, letters of support–any echo to assure them they were not alone. I was personally familiar with isolation through my solo licensing efforts, planning a conference with a very small staff for an association whose world view at the time seemed confined to the Eastern seaboard, and successfully arguing for Full Clinical Membership for art therapists in the American Group Psychotherapy Association. It seemed natural to propose in 1982 that the American Art Therapy Association mount an inquiry on the level of world interest in an international art therapy association. AATA agreed and I sent survey questionnaires to four known associations and 49 individual art therapists in 20 countries. Over the next year, 200 surveys were returned–four times more than had been sent. All respondents were eager to see an international association. AATA's continued interest in this project died as a result of the financial crisis in 1983 that forced AATA into survival mode, but the seeds were sown for the eventual establishment of the International Networking Group of Art Therapists (ING/AT) in 1989.

I'd also initiated the first film festival for the 1983 AATA Conference in Chicago. It was very successfully coordinated by Cathy Malchiodi and intended as an annual event, but it became another victim of AATA's financial crisis in its inaugural year. (I was glad to see art therapy films resurrected in 2002 as the Jim Consoli Video/Film Award.)

One by one, my office partners abandoned our shared space in favor of more secure clinical or academic jobs. My intention was to remain in private practice but, now solo, I moved to a smaller and less expensive office until the building was flooded by a major storm in 1982. My little office was the only one to escape water damage and became a popular hourly rental for other mental health professionals, whose offices in the building were seriously damaged and libraries lost. The musty stench left by the flood and the extensive construction taking place on all levels of the building made it unsuitable for therapy sessions, however.

As luck would have it, workmen were already working in my home and I redirected their work to creating a home office with a separate entrance. Within two weeks, I was temporarily seeing clients there while I searched for a permanent office. I saw impressive resiliency in very disturbed clients and heard their comments about the beautiful vistas *en route*, the free parking and especially the greenery outside the wall of glass that was a big improvement over the rooftops visible outside the small window in the other office. I stopped searching, deciding my home office would be permanent. After all, it had a separate entrance and toilet facilities and there was never a need for clients to go through any living areas of the house. Insurance companies insisted that providers have business offices, yet site visit inspectors commented on the tranquil nature, comfort and convenience of my space. Although the site visit was to assess a licensed (MFCC) clinical provider, seeing the art supplies and my framed art therapy registration (ATR) on the wall, brought excited remarks and questions about art therapy from most inspectors. I have never been denied provider status for having a home office and on several occasions was upgraded for having this unique treatment modality.

In addition to legal confirmation, I believed recognition as a legitimate business was equally important. The practice of art therapy is a business with the same challenges and needs as other business enterprises. Many complications followed my move to my home office. Nothing was easy. Initially there was no art therapy business category in the yellow pages and I could not convince Pacific Bell to create one, so I listed my practice as Art Therapy Studio in the white pages. As soon as I was licensed, I would list it under Marriage, Family & Child Counselors in the yellow pages. I had a business license in Beverly Hills; when I moved to my home office, Los Angeles refused to issue a business license to a residential address. I had a business telephone in Beverly Hills, but Pacific Bell balked at a business telephone in a private residence. Without a business phone, I could not have *any* listing in the yellow pages. I fought with Pacific Bell to overcome this ruling. Even the IRS required letterhead stationery, a business card and *a business telephone* in order to file a tax return as an independent business and consulting service. And without these essential business trappings, I would be unable to obtain malpractice or business liability insurance. It seemed like the most convoluted Catch 22, but perseverance paid off and I am still in the same office with a business telephone, liability and malpractice insurance, on Managed Care and insurance provider panels with Art Therapy Studio listings in both white and yellow pages. This listing has been the only way people can locate anything to do with art therapy since educational programs in the vicinity, practicing art therapists and even the Southern California Art Therapy Association cannot be located unless their proper name is known. For 30 years I have answered questions–basic and professional–, made referrals to practicing art therapists, AATA, SCATA (now SoCalATA), IHC (now Loyola Marymount University), and secured a few clients for making art therapy alphabetically accessible in the telephone book.

Following two terms as Public Information Chair, I served a third term on the AATA Board as Membership Chair (1985–1987). During these same years, I visited 16 countries, sometimes as invited speaker or trainer and sometimes as a tourist, but always meeting art therapists and learning of that country's definition, professional acceptance and level of development of art therapy. I continued to receive survey responses from unknown art therapists and from countries where practicing art therapists were previously unknown. Surveys were still coming in five years later. Although no longer sponsored or supported by AATA, I compiled responses and presented the findings at congresses in London (1985), at the 16th AATA conference in New Orleans (1985) and in Brisbane, Australia (1989).

After serving the maximum three terms on the Board, I was forced to retire after the 1987 Miami conference and the next day was involved in an auto accident in West Palm Beach that nearly forced me to retire from life itself! My lengthy recovery interfered with my dream of being free to travel extensively. Instead, I journaled and contacted foreign art therapists to organize an international panel for the 20th AATA conference in San Francisco in 1989. If I couldn't travel to them, I'd get those art therapists here! However, the dangling carrot that I'm convinced hastened my recovery, was my daughter's promised graduation trip to Greece, Egypt, France, Germany and Spain. Still a bit weak in summer 1988, I went on this three-month trip only because she accompanied me. I doubt I could have managed alone.

Seventeen countries sent a panelist or a report to be read *in absentia* on the panel at the 1989 conference in San Francisco. To include all the material, twice as much time was needed as the panel had. Many attended a spontaneous luncheon meeting after the panel. Foreign art therapists reinforced the need for an International Networking Group of Art Therapists and the ING/AT was spontaneously and enthusiastically formed on the spot. The stated mission was to increase the international knowledge base, cross-cultural research, networking and information exchange on art therapy and reduce the isolation of art therapists in third world countries by providing links with other art therapists.

For launching ING/AT as a critical international link, I was awarded the 3rd Annual Bridge Builder Award of the International Arts Medicine Association (IAMA) in 1991 and invited to serve on their Board of Directors. I served on the IAMA Board for 10 years until the organization's demise in 2001. Unfortunately, in these ten years I failed to accomplish what I had hoped–to introduce art therapy *treatment* to physicians who regard artists as patients with unique arts-related maladies. I worked briefly with a doctor who employs the arts in a children's oncology hospital to develop arts therapies training modules for first and second-year medical students. Although I thought this offered hope for the expansion of the arts therapies, the project fizzled prematurely, probably because IAMA, itself, fizzled.

I'd been nominated for AATA President-Elect in the 1989 election and lost by a single vote. There was speculation that I was perceived as still recovering from my accident and not yet up to presidential tasks. However, I was again nominated in 1991 and this time elected to the 1991–1993 term. This was a time I was also actively engaged in planning the ING/AT 1st International Conference in Vilnius, Lithuania, for September 1993. The conference in Vilnius was beautifully hosted by a handful of Lithuanian psychologists and psychiatrists who used art therapy and were eager to learn more. Art therapists from eight countries attended, presented their work and absorbed all that was offered by others.

I conducted an intense 40-hour post conference training for psychiatrists on ways to incorporate art therapy in their psychiatric hospital programs. I have been immensely rewarded by the progress reports from a Chief of Psychiatry who established an art therapy unit on her ward and has presented on art therapy at major psychiatric congresses worldwide for the past six or seven years. She secured a pharmaceutical company sponsorship to produce exquisite yearly calendars featuring the artwork of her patients. I have been honored to receive one each year. She also established and presides over the Lithuanian Art Therapy Association and is developing formal art therapy training programs.

When my travels include countries where art therapists are known, I attempt to meet them and am generally impressed by their accomplishments. Although I have never been to Cuba, I had frequent correspondence and provided support for the development of Cuban art therapy and was honored in 1994 to be named Honorary Member of the Cuban Arterapia Project in Havana.

As various countries reported their professional and organizational problems, a familiar developmental pattern emerged in which gains and obstacles could be predicted with accuracy. The ING/AT Newsletter and personal contacts consistently stressed careful initial planning and networking with neighboring countries to anticipate problems and share solutions. I focused on this phenomenon and the ING/AT as a resource in art therapy in "From Isolation to International Visibility," which appeared in the first issue of IAMA's *International Journal of Arts Medicine* in 1991. An update, "Growing Pains: The International Development of Art Therapy," appeared in the *Arts In Psychotherapy* in 2005. I am convinced that ING/AT is largely responsible for this publication.

On the home front, these were busy years. I was filled with impatience over the American Art Therapy Association's isolationist tendencies and snail-paced responses to rapidly-changing health care, business mergers, intensified legislative activity, and exacting professional standards. I believed, like ING/AT members, AATA also needed links to other professionals, to network more effectively, expand, collaborate, and participate more actively in a broader field.

To compete in this arena, art therapy needed an updated professional definition, outcome studies, a dynamic public image, vastly increased state licensing potential and members knowledgeable and ready to deal with Managed Care. Art therapists know art therapy is a "better mousetrap," but too often we promote our "better mousetrap" to other art therapists who have the same "mousetrap." Promotion of the profession is often confused with promotion of self as a member of the profession. Successful promotion of the profession does not ensure the success of any art therapist's business. Conversely, individual art therapists who successfully use effective clinical and business practices or conduct significant research advance the profession notch by notch and the larger community cannot help but notice. The more we introduce our "better mousetrap" to other professionals as a useful adjunct, the more widespread our sphere of influence and the greater our job potential. In 1994, with all this on our plate, there was no time to waste–AATA was approaching a 25th anniversary.

The Art Therapy Credentials Board (ATCB) was in its first year and relations with AATA were anything but cordial, yet it was important that ATCB succeed as governmental focus shifted from federal to state licensing. Congressional hearings on the Older American Act had concluded; healthcare needed serious revision, and when the Clinton administration abandoned the task, the insurance industry rose to the occasion. The mental health community was challenged to adapt to health care managed by gatekeepers who defined who could be seen, for how long, by whom and at what rate of pay.

My first gesture as 13th President of AATA was to give each Board member a four-inch paint brush to symbolize my intent to avoid micromanagement and focus on the "big picture." The Board accomplished a great deal in two years: revised the Definition of the Profession and Mission Statement; established a Managed Care Committee that kept members informed on trends, panel openings and specialty niches; refocused the Governmental Affairs Committee's attention on state licensing; added color graphics, redesigned AATA's logo and reformatted our printed documents; planned and executed our 25th anniversary celebration with maximum public relations; helped the establishment of a 25th anniversary scholarship with annual contributions by AATA and fund-raising events; and filled a Time Capsule to be opened on our 50th anniversary in 2019. The handle of my "broad brush" was signed by each Board member and placed in the Time Capsule.

With so much of my time, energy and attention devoted to the American Art Therapy Association and professional interests over almost four years, my private practice and income suffered. I envied any Board members who enjoyed perks and support from their institutions or employers—secretarial or office help, postage, copying, and especially, paid time dedicated to AATA. I began to understand the predominance of educators on AATA Boards and committees. Private practitioners can't afford the loss of income and limited attention to their own businesses.

When my term as President ended in 1995 at the San Diego Conference, I thought AATA intentionally planned that conference close to my home to ease my exit since I'd already demonstrated my ungracious way of retiring. This time I arrived home in much better shape, but it was time to consider job retirement. As a Panel Provider for 11 major Managed Care Employee Assistance Programs, I liked the flexibility and limited time commitment of the frequent calls for Critical Incident Debriefings and didn't want to lose these opportunities. I communicated my partial retirement to all 11 panels, continued with two very long-term clients, and chose new clients by their presenting problems and the necessary time commitment. I've perfected this "pick 'n choose" method to free up plenty of travel time.

With a lighter work schedule, I became a Disaster Mental Health volunteer for the American Red Cross and served in 20 national disasters—natural and man-made. Initially a Technician, then a Specialist, I am now a Coordinator. My crisis training and years working with post-traumatic stress have been extremely beneficial in disaster mental health response.

In 1980, Immaculate Heart College closed and the graduate art therapy program moved intact to Loyola Marymount University. The IHC campus was sold to the American Film Institute and has been their residence since. On June 14, 1996, 21 years to the day after my graduation from IHC, my daughter Lisa received her Masters of Fine Arts Degree in cinematography from the American Film Institute. It was strange indeed to walk through the same halls and sit in the same auditorium where I'd once been a student to now witness my daughter's identical looking graduation from a school with a different name.

Since leaving the AATA Board, I've enjoyed much foreign and domestic travel as a tourist, Red Cross Disaster responder, trainer, or speaker, including trips to Brazil, Turkey, Thailand, South Africa, Bosnia, China, Tibet, Taiwan, Mexico, and Hungary.

Since I don't retire gracefully, I've chosen not to retire fully. In March 2005, I had hip replacement surgery and finally felt sufficiently recovered to have planned a trip to Peru in August 2005. I tested the new hip by climbing in Machu Picchu. I also had the opportunity to visit a few art therapists in Lima.

For me art therapy is the only activity that satisfactorily teams both right and left brain. This is why it has seemed more like a welcome integrator than a job and why today I am an art therapist still painting with broad brush strokes on the canvas of life, my metaphoric brain surgery. Still after 30 years, I must admit my right brain is clamoring for more studio time. I'm listening, especially when I'm not traveling. I think I've got a few more one-woman shows waiting to be painted.

Shirley Riley

Chapter 26

SHIRLEY RILEY, 1921–2004

REMEMBRANCES

Bobbi Stoll

In September 1972, Shirley and I were two middle-aged women among 35 or more who enrolled in Helen Landgarten's introductory lectures on art therapy at Immaculate Heart College in Los Angeles. In a class dominated by school personnel, we both were more interested in art in therapy than in education. Enrollment in the introductory class diminished to 17 enrolled in the one- year certificate program that developed from it, and further reduced to seven who matriculated in the Masters Degree program a year later. Shirley and I hung on, enrolled in every additional learning opportunity developed at the college, and persistently sought extracurricular options.

We served our first clinical practicum together at Culver City Child Guidance Clinic, Culver City, California, and were jointly supervised by a psychiatrist for family therapy and by a psychologist for a latency-aged group in which we were co-therapists. We had much to learn about latency, group process, co-therapy and split transference, and it was an exhilarating learning experience. Helen Landgarten, herself, provided art therapy supervision since initially there were no other practicing art therapists. After any supervision, we'd discuss our enlightened understanding and volunteer to read and further research each topic.

By our second year, the Child Guidance Clinic with nine other community clinics was incorporated into a new large mental health center, Didi Hirsh Community Mental Health Center, where Shirley and I again served our *practica*–she in the Family and Child Division and I in the Crisis Day Treatment Unit. (Shirley became a staff member at Didi Hirsh and stayed for more than 20 years. Many of her books were written with case material developed there.) We grew closer as classmates and friends and were viewed by many as inseparable. Our similar interests, ages, and life circumstances had resulted in an immediate attraction and intensified as we commiserated about our rocky marriages to professional husbands, a physician and a lawyer, and discussed expectations, life in the hills of Hollywood and Bel Air, and our social and philosophical similarities.

Throughout our art therapy masters program, Shirley and I were the most diligent seekers of seminars, programs, and training to supplement our art therapy training. We attended weekend training by Salvador Minuchin in Newport Beach and stayed at my San Clemente beach house a few miles south to save money. We independently frequented Esalen in Big Sur, Palo Alto and other northern California areas for trainings in Transactional Analysis, Gestalt and Janie Rhyne's Gestalt Art Therapy Workshop. We attended Virginia Satir's all-day family therapy training together and roomed together at the New York Biltmore for the 1974 American Art Therapy Conference (AATA)–our first.

Shirley's marital problem was temporary and soon resolved; mine resulted in separation two months after beginning the first class and an emotionally devastating divorce over the next two years. Shirley was my comforter, her home my refuge, her husband, Champ, my primary physician and her son Dale, my buddy, the only one of her four sons still at home. Hours and days were spent at Shirley's home on Roscomare Road. I can still hear Dale's melodic greeting, "Hi, Bobbi!" each time I arrived at his house. Dale and I exchanged gold friendship rings. I wore mine as long as it fit any finger on either hand. After a very long absence, Dale remembered our rings with elephant-like memory. I still have and cherish that ring.

One summer Shirley had facial surgery at Stanford University and stayed at a nearby motel for about ten days to recover. Desperate for company, she called me to come to Palo Alto. For a week, we drew pictures, played games, talked, planned, and dreamed about our respective futures as art therapists.

From the beginning, Shirley was drawn to academia; I was headed for private practice. While fighting for a state license, I opened the Art Therapy Studio in Beverly Hills, California, and Shirley and three fellow graduates joined the practice. We five each had one day in the office. Being among the few trained art therapists in Southern California to supervise or instruct students, the next year three of us became faculty in the Immaculate Heart College program. Shirley was in her element and soon abandoned private practice to dedicate herself to teaching. Appealing for a license, chairing the 1978 American Art Therapy Association Conference in Los Angeles, and developing a practice, overwhelmed me and, after two years, I withdrew from academic life.

As consultant to a Family Counseling Agency in San Gabriel Valley, California, I coordinated the student intern program and was in frequent contact with Shirley in her capacity as Coordinator of Practicum Placements at Loyola Marymount University (where the Immaculate Heart program had moved), where she worked for almost 20 years. She was also on the faculty at Loyola Marymount during that time and taught a variety of classes including "Group Dynamics," "Adolescent Art Therapy," and "Advanced Family Art Therapy."

Shirley's dedication to the American Art Therapy Association was central in her life. She was a board member for many years, Chair of the Educational Committee, and a member of the Strategic Planning Committee, among others. She endeavored to raise educational standards and to improve supervision guidelines. Shirley often gave pre-conference courses and presented a workshop or a paper at virtually every conference, usually on family art therapy. Shirley cleared a broad path for understanding family and adolescent art products and effective art interventions and put a premium on good art therapy supervision. She published a number of books: *Group Process Made Visible* in 2000, *Contemporary Art Therapy With Adolescents* in 1999, *Integrative Approaches to Family Art Therapy* in 1996, and *Supervision and Related Issues: A Handbook for Professionals* in 1996 (the latter two written with Cathy Malchiodi). She was particularly interested in integrating art therapy with specific family theoretical ideas.

In her later years, she was most interested in narrative family therapy and the reflecting team innovated by the Milan Group. She called herself a "postmodernist." Shirley was a reader of contemporary ideas and brought those ideas to her art therapy work and to the art therapy field. Although she earned a Marriage and Family Therapy license in California in the 1980s (one of only three licenses in California which enable a person legally to practice psychotherapy), Shirley was always first and foremost an <u>art</u> psychotherapist. In 1990, Shirley received the "Clinician of the Year" award from AATA and in 2000 the Honorary Life Membership award, the highest award given by her art therapy peers in AATA.

After she left Loyola Marymount University and Didi Hirsh Community Mental Health Center, Shirley found the energy to co-start a new art therapy program. At the time of her death she was Associate Director of the art therapy Masters program at Phillips Graduate Institute in Encino, California. In her later years, Shirley focused on writing her books and on her private practice. She continued to adapt art therapy to the treatment of Alzheimer patients and burn victims. She continued to present her work nationally and internationally.

As the years passed, our professional interactions lacked the familiar personal touch and exchanges. We crossed paths in numerous local events and activities but missed our usual mode of being together. Continued focus on our polarized career paths resulted in still fewer social contacts with one another and eventually in fewer professional contacts as well.

It was not until late September 2001, that I chanced to meet Shirley at a day-long training on "Advances in Treating Complex Psychological Trauma & PTSD" by John Briere in Los Angeles. We were immediately back in our student roles sitting together, learning together, eating together, and discussing ways art therapy would maximize treatment of trauma victims and post traumatic stress disorder. It was as if no time had elapsed. When class was over, Shirley's car wouldn't start. She needed a ride to her home nearby which I was happy to provide. We lingered and chatted like old times to catch up on the intervening years and discussed our future goals. Shirley hadn't changed. She was deeply committed to family art therapy, writing on the subject, and to her role as educator in the new graduate program in medical and family art therapy at Phillips. It was the first time in many years that I'd been in her home. It was still familiar, even though her husband was now gone and Dale was living in his own supervised residence.

Now, Shirley, too, is gone. The house is empty but Shirley continues to live through her biological and professional families, through students she touched as mentor or supervisor, her published works, stimulating dialogues, her wry wit, conference presentations, clinical successes, close colleagues, and those she never met. She studied hard, worked diligently, and produced voraciously. She earned a peaceful rest and still she leaves a big vacuum.

Cay Drachnik

Chapter 27

CAY DRACHNIK

CAY'S STORY

When I first meet people and they find out that I am an artist-art therapist, invariably their first question is, "How long have you been painting?" My answer always is, "Since kindergarten," and that is a true statement. I was born and grew up in Kansas City, Missouri. As a child, I was always drawing and painting. We had basements in our houses, and in those days there was no air conditioning. My father built a small desk for me in the basement, and when it got hot in the summer I would retreat to the cool basement and spend hours working on my art. In kindergarten, kids would come around to my desk and ask me to show them how to draw a house or a princess. The satisfaction I got out of being asked must have encouraged me.

When I was about ten years old, there was a Saturday morning program for children at the Nelson Atkins Art Museum in Kansas City. My mother would drop me off on Saturday morning and pick me up around noon. When we first entered the building we went to the auditorium where a slide show and lecture about famous artists and their paintings was presented. Next, we would go to a classroom where we were given drawing lessons, or we would take sketchbooks and be escorted around the museum so that we could draw sculptures that were located in the museum. There were also classes in puppet-making; the puppets were almost always from stories of Greek mythology. Later, we would put on a puppet show for the children in the auditorium. It was a great program, and I've never heard of one as good since.

In high school, although I was shy, my mother encouraged me to become active in theatrical programs, debate teams, and, of course, the art club. The art club members painted murals on the school cafeteria's walls. I became president of the club. I also became involved in drama, appeared in several plays, and I even gave an oration for my literary society.

In my senior year of high school, World War II was on. My father's job as Manager of the Kansas City Electric and Power Association was uncertain.

One of the directors of the association had gone to war and the new director seemed to want younger men in management positions. My mother was not certain that I could finish out my first year of college at Kansas City Junior College, which was where I was slated to go, in case we had to move. She decided to enter some of my art work in a contest for a scholarship to the Kansas City Art Institute. She felt in case of a move, I could drop out of art school more easily than a regular college. I won the scholarship and spent a year and two summer sessions at the Kansas City Art Institute. The class I remembered most was the life drawing class, where the instructor had a female model and a skeleton lined up, side-by-side. When the model moved her arm, the instructor moved the arm bones of the skeleton to show us what was happening both internally as well as externally. It was very enlightening.

My father took a job with the war production board in Washington, D.C. The only university in that area that would accept most of my art credits was the University of Maryland, located about 20 miles from Washington, and the only department that would accept them was the Home Economics Department, which had a minor called "Practical Art."

I was shy and rather lost when I first arrived. I was put into a dorm and shared a room with two other girls, one of whom was even shyer than I was, and the other was a "hot number" who would climb out our window at night to meet boys. Fortunately, the man my father worked for had a daughter who belonged to the Kappa Kappa Gamma sorority at Maryland University, and she saw to it that I went out for sorority rush, and that I pledged Kappa. It was the best thing that could have happened to me at that time. I moved to the Kappa house down the hill from the university and got close to my sorority sisters, some of whom became life-long friends. People often knock sororities, but in my experience, at that time they promoted morals, good grades and activities. The alumni association was a boon to me in later life, as I married a naval officer and we moved frequently. In each new town, I would look up the Kappa Kappa Gamma alumni group, and I had an instant way of making new friends. While at Maryland, I made a life-long friend of my speech instructor, Dr. Ray Ehrensburger. He later became Dean of the University of Maryland Overseas Program, and he either had me look up friends of his in foreign countries or he visited me and my husband wherever we were stationed, including South Vietnam.

I started the art club at the University of Maryland, and became president. I also got heavily into drama and was the star of several productions. I graduated in 1945, with first honors from the College of Home Economics. There weren't many males at the university at that time because of the war, but at Annapolis, just a thirty-minute bus ride down the road, there were! At times, I went there for dates and dances. I thought the men were rather stuffy and swore I'd never marry one.

Upon graduation, my parents sent me to Parsons School of Design in New York for a summer session. I studied "Fashion Illustration" and was offered a scholarship for the next year. Unfortunately, it was discovered that my mother had breast cancer and needed an operation. I felt I was needed at home, so I moved back to Washington, D.C., and took a job as an apprentice fashion illustrator at the Palais Royal department store. Shortly after, the war ended and I moved with my parents to Los Angeles, California, where I got a job in the advertising department of Bullock's department store. I also taught Fashion Illustration one night a week at a local Hollywood art school.

One of my sorority sisters who had married a naval academy graduate whom I had introduced her to moved to San Diego, and they sent Joe Drachnik, a classmate, up to Los Angeles to meet me. I didn't think he was stuffy. We were married four months later. It was then that the moving started: Seattle, San Diego, Hawaii, Monterey, Norfolk, Long Beach, Norfolk, Boston, Vietnam and Washington, D.C. In our first Monterey/Carmel tour, I studied art with Henrietta Shore, a crusty old lady whom Art Museums now try to link with the famous photographer, Edward Weston, just as a they tie Georgia O'Keefe with Alfred Stieglitz. However, there was a real tie between Georgia and Alfred; they were married; whereas Henrietta and Edward were, at most, friends. In addition to my studying art in Carmel, Joe and I built a house, entirely by ourselves, from the ground up. Joe taught at the Naval Post Graduate School, but worked on the house nights and weekends. I did painting there, too, but it was painting the house. I also laid bricks and bought supplies. Orders to move came just as we finished our project. An article about the house was published in *Living for Young Homemakers,* a magazine that was quite popular with young married couples at that time.

From Monterey we moved to Norfolk, Virginia, where Joe had orders to sea duty. He had two tours of duty in the Mediterranean, and I followed the fleet both times. I traveled around while the fleet was out at sea and was able to see some of the great art of Europe at museums in countries such as Spain, Italy, France and Great Britain. The next time he departed, I went back to Los Angeles to live with my parents as my daughter was about to be born and I felt I needed family support. More sea and staff duty for Joe and then we got orders back to Monterey for shore duty. Joe was again on the staff of the Navy Post Graduate School.

The next exciting event was that our son, Kenneth, was born. This time I studied with John Cunningham at the Carmel Art Institute. He had only four or five students. He was a great teacher and a well-known and highly respected Carmel artist. He liked my work and had me enter a painting in the California State Fair. It was accepted, much to my delight. This was my first experience with high-level juried shows.

Cay Drachnik and her daughter Denise in 1952.

In 1960, Joe was on a ship in the far East, so my best friend and college roommate, whose husband was stationed in Japan said, "Bring the kids and come on over." Her husband also was at sea, although he had quarters in Japan. We took turns taking care of the children, her three and my two, while either she or I followed the ship to wherever our husbands were in one or another port in the Orient. While in Japan, I studied with a painter, Tasha Senda. He arranged for one of my paintings to be shown in a juried show in Tokyo. One day on the way to meet Joe in Hong Kong, I sat next to a young man on the plane who said he operated a book store in Saigon. I asked him where Saigon was and he said it was in Vietnam and there was some heavy fighting going on in the country.

I forgot about our conversation until a couple of months later. (This was September of 1961.) Joe got orders to Vietnam. He was to be "frocked" as a Navy Captain. (He was still a Commander; he would have the rank of Captain but only Commander's pay.) His tour would be for one year if he went alone but it would be a two-year tour if he took his family. I started packing the next day: I was not one to be left behind!

Joe was the senior naval officer (Chief of the Navy Section of the Military Assistance Advisory Group) and he had a wonderful counterpart with whom to work, Vietnamese Navy Captain Ho Tan Quyen. The war was in its early stages, but at times it was quite frightening. There were many social events, and on occasion a grenade would be thrown into someone's outdoor party. At other times a grenade would be lying on the sidewalk for someone to pick up and set off. I was concerned about my children as well a my husband, who came back from trips to the Mekong Delta with bullet holes in the airplanes in which he had been flying. Our quarters were a house where one of Bao-Dai's mistresses had lived. It was quite spacious, and required four servants to maintain it. The water was contaminated in Saigon and required an elaborate system to purify it, hence the need for the four servants. When the sewer line was laid it was laid over the water lines and over the years the sewer lines corroded as did the water lines and the sewer dripped into the water. We had a big tank to collect the rain water. Then the water was filtered and boiled and put in sanitized bottles and delivered to the various rooms in the house. In the bath, however, we used water right out of the tanks. One day I was watching my son in the bathtub and he took a sponge and dripped the tank water into his mouth. I guess he had been doing this for so long that he was immune to the contamination in the water. He was the one in the family who never was sick.

My daughter went to the American school for military and diplomatic children and my son went to a French kindergarten. At age four he was able to speak French to his teacher, Vietnamese to the servants and English to me. Unfortunately, he has forgotten all the languages he learned. I took lessons from a Vietnamese artist, Tri Minh, and I gave free lessons to American, Vietnamese, diplomatic, and any other women who were interested. Most of the women had servants and in many cases were bored, as it was difficult for security reasons to leave the city. All had a good time, and I enjoyed the teaching.

The men worked hard during the day, but there was quite a social life at night. We had many visitors, like John Kenneth Galbraith, United States Senators and high-ranking officials who came to see how things were going in Vietnam. We had sit-down formal dinners. All this in the middle of a war. Ambassador Nolting's wife, who was interested in art, became a good friend of mine and ended up buying two of my paintings which showed life as I saw it in Vietnam. Joe was sent back to Hawaii every month to brief Defense Secretary Robert McNamara.

One positive note about this period was that there was no TV in Vietnam. As a result, my daughter became proficient in reading. I started her out with Nancy Drew books and then she progressed to Shakespeare. As one result, she later earned a Master of Business Administration Degree from The University of California at Berkeley. Today, she works for Chevron and recently became Manager for Information Technology for their Eastern

Division of the world. She is now living with her family in Capetown, South Africa. My son, who said he hated all the military traveling, is now Director of Application Integration Products with Sun Microsystems and travels quite frequently, often overseas, as part of the job.

Cay Drachnik in Vietnam, 1963.

There were art exhibits in Saigon. One was an international show with entries from Thailand, Japan, Bali, Argentina and other countries. I won a bronze award.

It seemed all a great adventure until the *coup* on November first of 1963 which overthrew President Diem. I woke up to the sounds of explosives. Some of the generals in Diem's own army decided to get rid of him. There was machine gun fire up and down my street. My children and I got under the stairwell and stayed there for the rest of the day, because by then we knew what was happening, and the presidential palace was only about a mile from our house.

This was very upsetting to us because the first person killed in the *coup* was Joe's counterpart and very good friend, Ho Tan Quyen, the Chief of Naval Operations of the Vietnamese Navy. He had supported the president twice before when *coups* were attempted. In one, he had led one of his marine companies to the Palace and thwarted the *coup*. This time, the supporters of the *coup* took Captain Quyen out and shot him in the head, before they did anything else. He left behind a wife and seven children. Next, they got hold of President Diem and his brother and executed both of them. From then on the war went slowly downhill. More United States soldiers, more defeats, more changes in government. Today, South Vietnam is under communist rule, but is open to tourists. I can't help but feel it was a wasted war on our part. Had we not gone in, I feel Vietnam would be the same today as it was before our troops went in and fought and died. Others feel the Chinese communists would have taken over, but from what I know, both the North and South Vietnamese would have fought the Chinese to the last man.

Joe's tour of duty was up shortly after the *coup* and we moved to Washington, D.C., where Joe had the desk for Thailand, Australia and New Zealand and related treaties. I taught a drawing class for Adult Education. Next came a tour of duty for Joe at the National War College (where he earned an MA in International Affairs), and I taught an art class for the wives of the students. In the class was Margaret Sargent, a well-known portrait painter, who should have been teaching the class. Since her husband retired, she has painted portraits of a president and other highly placed people. The wives were all bright and charming, and it was great fun.

Next we moved to Norfolk, Virginia, and I was again taking art classes, this time at Old Dominion University, where I took enough classes to get a California art teaching credential. We were planning to retire in California. Orders came to go back to Washington, where I tried to get a job teaching high school art, but I had taken so many classes and had so many credits that they would have had to pay me too much. At this point, a friend arranged for me to volunteer as a part-time art teacher at the Arlington Mental Health Clinic in Virginia. This was my first experience working with emotionally-disturbed people. I found out that I really enjoyed it. A couple of months later, they liked what I was doing, and they hired me.

While working at the clinic, I became friends with an occupational therapist. We did some "art" classes together. One day she came in with a newspaper and said, "Cay, do you know anything about something called art therapy? They are offering a class in it at the Washington School of Psychiatry."

I said, "I've never heard of it, but it might be interesting." So she said, "Let's take it." Life is strange. I never would have become an art therapist had my friend not seen that advertisement.

We went to the first class, which was taught by Elinor Ulman. She was a slight, gray-haired woman with a very large nose. She talked about mythology (which I understood from art classes at the museum when I was a child in Kansas City) and other things of which I had no comprehension. When the class was over, I said to my friend, "I think this class is all nutty. I'm not sure I want to waste any more time with it. Do you think we could get our money back?" She said, "I don't know, but how about giving it one more shot?" We did, and after the second class, I knew that I had found what I wanted to do with the rest of my life.

My husband, a Navy Captain with 30 years of service, was about to retire. We had already sent our daughter to the University of California at Santa Barbara, knowing we would live in California. My days in Washington were numbered. Elinor Ulman was wonderful to me. She asked me to write a book review for the *American Journal of Art Therapy*, which gave me confidence that I could write about art therapy, and she gave me names and addresses of subscribers to the Journal who lived in Northern California so I could look them up when I arrived. We knew by then that we wanted to live in Palo Alto. Some of the names she gave me were, Janie Rhyne, Vija Lusebrink, Norman Woodbury and Virginia Goldstein. I called them, and we decided that we should form the Northern California Art Therapy Association. There already was a two-year-old association in Southern California. We advertised and spread the word by word of mouth, and about 150 people showed up to our first meeting. We knew we couldn't deal with that many people to start with, so we scheduled another meeting and this time limited it to those who had worked in or taken a class in art therapy. By the next meeting we had fewer people and got off to a good start.

In the meantime, I applied for a job as an art therapist/teacher at Sequoia Hospital in Redwood City. The head nurse in the psychiatric department, Phoebe Rowles, hired me. We are still best of friends after all these years. I did group work with adults and continued to work there until we moved to Sacramento which was then known as "Cow Town." My husband had done some volunteer work in the national election and as a result got a job as Executive Assistant to the Lieutenant Governor of California. This would prove fortuitous later on for art therapy.

We bought a house, and, while waiting to move in, my husband had the radio on one day and turned to me and said, "Hey, listen Cay, there is someone talking about art therapy." I couldn't believe it; art therapy in "Cow Town?" It turned out to be Dr. Donald Uhlin, who taught in the art department at California State University, Sacramento. He and Dr. Tarmo Pasto, a psychologist who also taught in the art department and had just retired, were interested in the psychology of art. They both belonged to the "Psycho-pathology of Expression" group, which included professionals from all over the world who were interested in that same thing. Since Dr. Pasto had retired, Don really missed having someone to talk to about art therapy. Most others in the art department wanted nothing to do with it. Later, one of them told me that he didn't want anyone analyzing his art. After hearing Dr. Uhlin talk on the radio, I wrote him a letter and told him of my interest. He called a few days later and set up an appointment with me. At the end of our talk, he suggested that I return to school and get a Master's Degree in art with emphasis in art therapy. I said I'd love to, but I was afraid that at 48 I was too old and would not be accepted. He said not to worry, he would fix it, and of course, he did.

Don Uhlin now had someone to talk to about art therapy. I was fascinat-ed by his knowledge. He had studied early-on with Viktor Lowenfeld and had written a book titled, *Art for Exceptional Children.* Several other students joined the art therapy classes, and we spent hours looking at slides of chil-dren's drawings. Don believed that repeated symbols often would give clues about what the problem might be with a child. In the next year, more stu-dents signed up, and an "art with emphasis in art therapy" in the Art Depart-ment was born.

My next problem was that I needed an internship if I were to become a real art therapist and Don needed a hospital to which he could send students for internships. We went to the psych departments of some of the hospitals in Sacramento, and we chose American River Hospital because we both liked what we saw there. I started work in the psych unit, and Dr.Uhlin came out to supervise me. I thoroughly enjoyed my work. Then I learned that the hospital had a mental health outpatient clinic and that the occupational ther-apist who worked there part-time wanted full time work back at the hospital. I wanted to work only half time, so an exchange was made.

My working only half-time and having my husband in an important job at the state capitol turned out really well for art therapy. By working half-time, I could spend the other half-time working for art therapy. By now, I was the Legislative Chair for the Northern California Art Therapy Association. I would drive to the Bay Area once a month to attend art therapy meetings, and I became active in working with other creative arts therapists (music, dance and drama therapists). Since I lived in Sacramento, the state capitol, I was called upon to organize the legislative work. At that time, California laws restricted nonlicensed therapists from private practice and from working in almost all mental health facilities. I organized an art therapy group in Sacramento, and I started visiting legislators at the capitol to gain informa-tion as to how we might get recognition. The Southern California Art Therapy group joined in with us. We wrote letters and testified before the appropriate committees, and finally, after our successful lobbying, we received a state job classification. We were listed, along with occupational, recreational, music and dance therapists, as rehabilitation therapists. The job description called for a Bachelor of Arts Degree. The BA was accepted in as much as no alternative was offered by the State Personnel Board. However, at that time, the few educational programs for art therapists in California were at the master's level, and the American Art Therapy Association (AATA) was also suggesting the Master's as the job entry level for art therapists.

To circumvent the bachelor's degree specified, the California task force worked with the Health Facilities Licensing Board, another state agency that licenses almost all of the state facilities (private as well as state hospitals, nursing homes, and the like). We were able to convince this board to define an art therapist as one with a Master's Degree. Although this resulted in a conflict in law, the task force was informed that state licensing takes precedence over state job classification; therefore the Master of Arts Degree was maintained for state civil service jobs and for all other jobs in state licensed facilities. Behind all this was our thought that one day we could be licensed strictly as art therapists and we wanted to be licensed with a Master's Degree. By this time, the creative arts therapists had united in a coalition to work on other issues of importance within the state–thus, the first California Coalition of Creative Arts Therapists was formed.

Throughout this time, we were getting opposition from the occupational therapists, mainly because in health regulations, it put them in charge of all activity therapists; only they could be the boss, and we wanted equal status. At times, they would go to a legislative meeting and bring with them a patient in a wheelchair for public relations purposes. We learned quickly to make sure that Don Uhlin went with us when we knew the occupational therapists would be at a meeting. Don had been stricken with polio when he was 20 years old but had managed to lead a full and active life in spite of the fact that he was wheelchair bound. At around this same time, because of my husband's connections, I received a gubernatorial appointment to the Health Facilities Advisory Board. I attended monthly meetings and became the watchdog for art therapy and the other creative arts therapies.

In 1975, shortly after I received my Masters' Degree, I became, in addition to my clinical work, a part-time instructor at California State University, Sacramento. I worked with Dr.Donald Uhlin and taught classes in "Art for the Exceptional Child," "Seminar in Art Therapy," and I supervised interns. I also taught art therapy classes in summer school at the College of Notre Dame in Belmont, California, a weekend class at the University of Utah, arranged by my good friend and former student, Cathy Malchiodi. In 1995, I wrote a book, *Interpreting Metaphors in Children's Drawings*, and it was published by my good friend Doris Arrrington's publishing company. It is still in print and still selling well. It is really a manual describing tests used by clinicians over the years to determine through art, children's emotional problems. Today, many of those tests are discredited, but even in my own practice, though I did not use those tests literally, I found that they gave an insight about how to determine symbolically what was going on with the child that was causing the dysfunction.

I had a wonderful place in which to work. It was called Eskaton Mental Health Outpatient Clinic and was a part of American River Hospital. We had several directors over the years when I worked there, one a psychiatrist, one a licensed clinical social worker and another, a minister who was licensed as a Marriage and Family Therapist. As more people found out about the clinic, more staff was hired. Towards the end, we had three half- time psychiatrists, two psychologists, three social workers and four Marriage and Family Therapists, including me. We also had great secretarial staff. We had a play room with a two-way mirror and a large group room. The staff were all highly educated and dedicated people, and we worked together as a team. Some of the best days of my life were spent there.

My greatest interest in teaching and in practice was working with children. I remember well one six-year-old boy who came to me for therapy. He could barely talk. The school counselor felt he was retarded, but in reality he was a victim of severe physical and mental abuse. As we drew pictures together, he slowly began to talk and his drawing progressed from random scribbles to life-like houses and even people. I worked with him for about a year. He had been removed from his parental home and now was sent to live in a foster home in another county. About eight years later, when I was serving as a consultant to a school in this other county, I saw some pictures that the boy had recently drawn. The art work looked normal and his teacher said he was at grade level and was doing well.

In another case, a psychologist at our clinic asked me to look at the drawings of a five-year-old girl. The girl's mother and father were divorced and her mother had remarried. The second husband seemed as concerned about the child as was the mother. The biological father had weekend visitations. I told the psychologist, after looking at a number of drawings, that I felt the child had been sexually abused. The psychologist said she had found no indication of this. She had several more sessions with the child and the child kept drawing pictures. The psychologist showed me more drawings and I kept saying "sexual abuse," because the "tongue" symbol kept appearing in the child's drawings. I had studied this symbol and found that even in ancient times it was regarded as a symbol to ward off evil or had a sexual identity. I was right. It turned out that the child's biological father was sexually abusing her on weekend visitations.

At this time, the Marriage, Family and Child Counselors' (MFCC) licensing law listed five degrees that qualified for licensure; but it also listed sixteen "equivalent degrees." Art therapy was not among those listed. In the fall of 1978, Bobbi Stoll convinced the Board of Behavioral Sciences that art therapy was an equivalent degree. She took the exam in November, 1978 and received her license January 10th, 1979. She was the first person who had a degree in "art therapy" to get the license. In early 1979, Honey Rawlinson, who had an M.A. in psychology, and I, with an art education degree, took the Marriage, Family and Child Counseling exam and we passed. Art therapists could now be licensed as Marriage, Family and Child Counselors. All went well for a few years; then in 1985, the chairman of the Board of Behavioral Science Examiners decided that art therapists, along with several other degree holders would no longer be eligible for licensing as MFCCs. Dance and art therapists, both in Northern and Southern California, developed a plan of action. They got all the groups to write their legislators, and attorneys were consulted. The licensing board was besieged with phone calls. Calls were made to the governor requesting that the Chairman of the Board of Behavioral Science Examiners not be reappointed (he wasn't), and newspapers were notified.

The result was that the Board of Behavioral Science Examiners decided to hold hearings and then made some rapid reversals of policy: If students and graduates "in the pipeline" met core course requirements, they would be allowed to take the examination. Just as we thought we were getting ahead, State Senator Gary Hart introduced a bill that listed only one degree, that of Marriage, Family and Child Counseling (MFCC), as acceptable for licensure as a counselor. This meant that we must be licensed with the MFCCs or not be licensed at all. Meetings were arranged with the MFCC attorney. We wanted to keep our Art Therapy degree title, but we knew that it might not happen at this stage of the game. Their attorney did not want us licensed at all, claiming that we were a modality, not a degree program.

Fortunately, not long after Senator Hart introduced his bill, Assemblyman John Vasconcellos introduced another MFCC licensing bill which fulfilled an art therapist's dream: it contained goals which were to provide solid and professional training while allowing for innovation, individuality and breaking new ground while building on tested values. He also wanted a variety of approaches to the treatment of children. The art therapy task force met with Vasconcellos and offered support for his bill. We continued to write letters and to call upon legislators.

Quite unexpectedly, two people called and offered help. One was David Read Johnson, President of the National Coalition of Arts Therapy Associations, who immediately regrouped the California Coalition of Creative Arts Therapists (which had ceased to function). The other was Paul Minicuicci,

Senior Consultant for the Joint Committee on the Arts (which we had never heard of) that was headed by State Senator Henry Mello. Senator Mello arranged for the arts therapists to testify before the Legislative Joint Committee on the Arts in April of 1986. Finally, a compromise was reached. A degree program approved by the marriage and family therapists' national accrediting body (AAMFT) would be deemed an equivalent degree. We had little choice but to accept this. The Hart and Vasconcellos Bills were joined. State reciprocity was left in and the Governor signed the bill on Sept. 22, 1986.

All went well until the two universities in California offering art therapy degrees were unable to get accredited by AAMFT, the National Marriage and Family Therapy Commission. The pastoral counselors (who had been included in the license) were the first to give in. They made a decision to change their degree title to offer a degree in Marriage and Family Counseling with emphasis in pastoral counseling. Both art therapy programs in the state then followed suit. Art therapists could get a degree in Marriage and Family Counseling with emphasis in art therapy or integrated with art therapy. With the license, they could get jobs in mental health facilities and go into private practice.

I feel that this background information is important, because today art therapists in many states are working to obtain licensure as Mental Health Counselors. Some art therapists are still opposed to being licensed as other than art therapists. I hope that down the road, licensing as art therapists will happen. Because of my work in the legislative process, I know we need to have many more registered art therapists before this will come about. Numbers count heavily in the legislative process.

As an art therapist/MFT (the MFCC was later changed to MFT, marriage and family therapist), I worked in a clinic with both adults and children, singly, and in groups with other therapists. I taught others in the clinic the basics of art therapy. I felt I was helping people both young and old, and I was enjoying every minute of my work. How much difference can a title make if you are well-educated in your field and are working to help those in need? Nonetheless, the sign on my office door read "Art Therapist."

After having succeeded in helping art therapists get licensed in California, in 1987 I became President of the American Art Therapy Association (AATA). As president, I got our finances in order, stressed the need for licensure for art therapists throughout the United States, and I established a scholarship for minority students. My President-Elect Linda Gantt and I called on the National Counseling Association in Arlington, Virginia, to see if they were interested in taking us under their umbrella. They were having financial problems at that time, so we were asked to come back later. That seems to be what is happening today. A number of states now license art therapists as counselors. Even in California, there is a movement to get a counseling license for art therapists because it is very difficult for out-of-state art therapists to meet the Marriage and Family Therapist licensing requirements. In many other states, art therapists are working with legislators. Even in California, art therapists who are currently licensed as MFTs want this counseling licensing bill to go through. It will give more options to California art therapists, will make it much easier for those from out of state to achieve their goals, and it will make it easier for people to get jobs.

Prior to my becoming President of AATA, in addition to being Legislative Chair for the Northern California Art therapy Association in 1986, I was Conference Chair for AATA, on the Search Committee for the Executive Director of AATA and was representative to the National Coalition Committee of Creative Arts Therapists. After my term of presidency ended, I was Chair of the Ethics Committee, served on the Nominating Committee from 1991 to 1994 and worked with the Interface with the Art World Focus Group.

In 1992, the clinic where I worked closed because of state budget cuts. At about that same time my doctor thought I needed an operation. I was offered a job as a school counselor, but decided to wait to make a decision until after the operation was over. After I recovered I decided I would like to try my hand at painting again and then if I didn't like that I would go into private practice. I had friends who wanted me to join them. I took a watercolor class from a talented painter, Jim Estey. I'll never forget my first class. I painted an apple and he asked if it were a tomato. It's a wonder I persisted after that. I then took a class from Gary Pruner, who felt that saying something in a painting was more important than technique. I appreciated that because my work as an art therapist could be expressed in my work as an artist. Early on, I won a "Best of Show" for a painting of three Mexican immigrants by the Sacramento River. Then I painted a hungry child at a women's center, asking for more food. That won the President's Award at the national open California Water Color Association exhibition in San Francisco. Another painting of a pregnant teenager, whose boyfriend is exiting through the doorway and whose goals are crossed out, didn't win an award but I donated it to Planned Parenthood. Next I studied with Gerald Silva, from whom I learned a new way of using watercolor, which I feel made my paintings more interesting. I have received 65 awards in the past twelve years in local and national juried shows and six "Best of Shows." Among those Exhibitions where my paintings have been selected to show are the American Watercolor Society in New York, The Triton Museum in Santa Clara, California, the Haggin Museum in Stockton, the Arizona Watercolor Society, the California State Fair and the Northwest Watercolor Show in Seattle, Washington, among others. I currently show at the Elliott Fouts Gallery in

Sacramento and I also belong to a critique group with eight other award winning artists. We meet every three weeks to critique each others' work and at times show as a group in special galleries. I have done some volunteer work for Victims of Violent Crime and I now also teach Fashion Illustration at Sacramento City College. I enjoy it and it helps pay for the paint. It seems in some ways I'm back to where I started from.

Cay Drachnik's painting, "Along the Sacramento River" (awarded Best of Show in an international exhibit), 1996.

I feel I have contributed to the American Art Therapy Association through both my legislative work and my art work. I feel very proud to have received the Honorary Life Member award. I believe through art and art therapy we, as a group, can make the world a more peaceful and caring place in which to live. At times that seems doubtful but I truly believe if you set a realistic goal and work at it you can be successful.

Cay Drachnik's painting, "Mother Then and Now," 2000.

Virginia M. Minar

Chapter 28

VIRGINIA M. MINAR

MEMOIRS

IN THE BEGINNING

On April 14, 1923, in Kenosha, Wisconsin, a child was born prematurely to Holger and Metha Petersen. Since they already had two-year-old Helen, they were sure the baby would be a boy. They planned to call him William Sofus after the paternal grandfather. Surprise! It was a girl! Metha was reading a love story magazine. The woman in the story was named Virginia, and that's how I got my name. I was a sickly child with severe asthma. The doctors predicted I would not live to my first birthday, but this octogenarian fooled everybody, even myself.

With my two female cousins and my sister, as a child I spent summers on my grandmother's farm near Franksville, Wisconsin, a town famous for its sauerkraut. We took turns writing little skits and performing them on our hay wagon stage. We made our own costumes and props gleaned from grandmother's "trunk of treasures" from Denmark. We entertained our farm neighbors and our parents, who sometimes visited us on weekends. My maiden aunt, my senior by only sixteen years, was an accomplished pianist. She had fun coaching us in singing contemporary songs. On Saturday mornings, she drove us in her roadster to a radio station in Racine where on an amateur hour show, at eight-years-old, I sang a then "sexy" song, in which the final line was "I've got you in the palm of my hand, and I love it!" My father heard the broadcast, and that was the end of my career as a chanteuse.

As teenagers, my sister and I sang in the church choir and were part of a Danish folk dancing troupe that gave performances throughout the Midwest. Because my mother thought that exercise would strengthen my wheezy lungs, she made me take tap and modern dance lessons, and, believe it or not, my partner and I won a teen-age jitterbug contest on the stage of the

Orpheum Theatre in Kenosha, Wisconsin. In junior high and high school I participated in art, music, and drama classes, and had leading roles in both class plays. I had the dual role of the witch and Queen Brangomar in *Snow White and the Seven Dwarfs*, and was the psychotic Julia Price in *Ghost Train*.

Virginia M. Minar, 3, with her sister, 5.

Even though I dreamt of exploring a career in one of the fine arts, my mother, who worked as a practical nurse, wanted me to be a nurse. After high school graduation in February 1941, I traveled to Chicago to complete my application for entering the nursing program at a major hospital. Although my academic qualifications were acceptable, my medical history of severe asthma and chronic eczema on my hands and arms led to a rejection.

Did I feel bad? No! Now I began to plan how to pursue my dream of going to New York where I would become a runway model or stage actress.

Virginia M. Minar, a tap dancer at 14.

December 7, 1941, the "day in infamy" occurred at Pearl Harbor. The marine I was engaged to died on the Arizona, a ship in Pearl Harbor sunk by the Japanese on December 7th. World War II changed my plans and I went to work at the American Brass Company to support the war effort. During the war, I busied myself by joining the Kenosha, Wisconsin, Little Theatre and appeared in several plays. I worked on the stage crew and helped with wardrobes. After the war, I began to date a former high school acquaintance. He had served as a navy pilot. George and I were married on

May 23, 1947, and moved to Milwaukee, Wisconsin, where I worked while he went to college on the G.I. education bill. After the agony of four miscarriages and three premature births, none of whom came home with me, we adopted two beautiful babies, a boy in 1954 and a girl in 1956. Stephan Rolf was named after George's dad and my maternal grandfather; and Karen Marguerite was named after my favorite aunt. Tragically, we lost them both to cancer, our son in 1977 and our daughter in 1981.

Virginia M. Minar, a folk dancer at 16.

ART THERAPY AS PART OF MY LIFE

Some of the following remarks come from the 1995 commencement address I gave for the art therapy graduates of Eastern Virginia Medical School:

The first art therapy book I read was Edith Kramer's *Art Therapy in a Children's Community*. In the introduction she states that the art therapist is at once artist, therapist, and teacher. The theme for the American Art Therapy Association's 1992 Conference was *The Art Therapist: Artist, Teacher, Clinician, Healer.*

My personal journey followed the order of artist, teacher, therapist. As a wife and mother, I engaged in the creative process first by filling notebooks with poetry, selecting those I thought worthy of consideration, sending them off to periodicals, and receiving back those "not-so-pretty" pink slips. A friend of mine encouraged me to resolve my frustration by taking art classes for adults at the local high school. I was filled with a sense of wonder and reverence as my inborn images came to life. One of my art instructors told me that I should take courses for credit at the University of Wisconsin-Milwaukee, and so, at age forty-four and with two elementary school children, I quit my part-time job as a legal secretary and went to school. That led to a Bachelor of Fine Arts degree.

Because I was convinced that very few people make a living as artists, I took art education courses and added "teacher certification" to my Bachelor's Degree. As a student teacher, I was placed at an elementary school that had five classes of children diagnosed as "educable mentally retarded" and at a high school that had two classes of "at-risk" students. As I worked with these children, it became apparent to me that the manipulation of art materials and resulting imagery had a therapeutic effect on student behavior.

For my student practicum in 1971, I went to St. Charles Boys Home, where I observed Brother Arthur working with adolescent boys placed there by the juvenile courts. Brother Arthur was active in the Wisconsin Art Therapy Association (WATA) and was a charter member the American Art Therapy Association (AATA). This was the first time I had seen a real live art therapist in action. He had a wonderful ceramics studio with huge kilns where he fired the pieces created by the boys under his care. He encouraged me to join WATA and throughout his life continued to be a role model for me.

While doing my practicum, the university offered its first art therapy class, with Wayne Ramirez as instructor. My term paper in that class investigated the graphic image development level of the cognitively challenged elementary school children I was working with. Upon graduation in August, 1971, I was hired at the elementary school where I did my student teaching.

In the fall of 1971, Elinor Ulman presented a graduate credit seminar at the university, and the second annual American Art Therapy Association Conference was held in Milwaukee at the Pfister Hotel. I attended that conference and one of the speakers was Robert Wolf, who presented a paper, "Art Therapy in a Public School Setting." Was that prophetic? I considered his paper and said, "This is what I want to do!" My master's thesis explored an hypothesis based on Rhoda Kellogg's belief that retarded children who do well in art have normal mental capacity and the genuinely retarded do not do well in art.

In 1971, I became a member of the Wisconsin Art Therapy Association, AATA in 1975, and received my ATR (Registered Art Therapist) in 1976. Newcomers to the field of art therapy may not know that the Wisconsin Art Therapy Association was incorporated one year before the American Art Therapy Association

Because the State of Wisconsin Department of Public Instruction was offering an Art-Special Education license, I took twelve post-graduate credits in the field of Exceptional Education between 1975 and 1977 to qualify for that certification. Beginning in September 1975, the school district supported a three-year art therapy pilot study under which I serviced both individuals and groups of children with "Exceptional Education Needs," and presented art therapy workshops for art teachers. In 1977, I received a $10,000 federal Arts Education Project Grant which covered workshops for kindergarten and special education personnel. In addition, an annotated bibliography, *Expressive Therapies, The Arts, and The Exceptional Child*, was compiled and published.

Along the way, I taught undergraduate art therapy courses at Alverno College, graduate courses at Mount Mary College, and facilitated art therapy groups for cancer patients at St. Frances Hospital. I also carried on a small private practice, supervising art therapy students doing their practicum and art therapists preparing for registration. Because the hospital limited patient participation to no more than two back-to-back twelve-week sessions, those who wished to continue to work with their original group, or privately, became my personal clients.

INVOLVEMENT WITH CANCER PATIENTS

In the fall of 1989, the Wheaton Franciscan Services of Milwaukee, Wisconsin, contacted the Wisconsin Art Therapy Association (WATA) to see if any of our members would be interested in volunteering their time and expertise to the "Confronting Cancer Through Art" program they were initiating. Its purpose was to recognize that art therapy is effective in alleviating the mental and emotional pain that accompanies the disease. Besides me, seven WATA art therapists participated in this project.

The Cancer Care Center staff at St. Joseph's Hospital recommended patients they felt would benefit from individual art therapy sessions. They were selected because of their interest in art and their willingness to participate. The art therapists were given background information on the patients including diagnosis and prognosis. The purpose of the sessions was to help the patient to express feelings, through the medium of art, that manifest themselves during the various stages of diagnosis, treatment, remission, and even approaching death itself, feelings that can be difficult to convey to someone who has not experienced cancer.

Images from the art therapy sessions were displayed in an exhibit held in the art gallery at Alverno College in June 1990. The patients selected the pieces to be shown, not for their aesthetic appeal, but rather for the nonverbal messages they conveyed. The creative process was more important than the finished artwork itself, for it was through this process that the patients could express the feelings they experienced. The exhibit combined a juried show open to artists, art hobbyists, and crafts persons residing in Wisconsin who had been diagnosed and treated for some form of cancer, and the selected works by the cancer patients working with art therapists under the Cancer Care Center's sponsorship. After this exhibit, an art therapy program at St. Joseph's Hospital was initiated.

At the time of the exhibit, I was an instructor in Alverno's undergraduate art therapy program. I received a call from nearby St. Frances Hospital asking me if I would serve as a guide for a group of their cancer patients as they viewed the contributing artists' artworks, to aid them in their understanding of how art experiences can help cancer patients deal with the traumas caused by the disease. After that tour, I was asked to hold a workshop for patients in the St. Frances cancer therapy groups. As a result of that workshop I began an art therapy program at their women's health care facility.

At the St. Frances workshop, I presented a brief case study on the patient I worked with during the "Confronting Cancer through Art" project. The patient was a fifty-year-old oncology nurse employed at a hospital near my home studio. Her nickname was "Mam." In August of 1989, she was diagnosed with multiple myeloma, a type of cancer of the blood that causes tumors to form in the bone marrow. The prognosis for this disease was survival of from three to ten years.

Our sessions began on November 30, 1989. After the initial background interview, at my suggestion, "Mam" involved herself in the India ink and string procedure described in Evelyn Virshup's *Right Brain People in a Left Brain World*. Multiple images were found within the ink lines on the paper and she refined them with colored pencils. "Mam" identified both Humpty Dumpty and the lady as images of the self; she identified the dog as cancer the hurter. As she worked, healer images appeared: a high-flying balloon, the Madonna, and green shamrocks representing hope, faith, luck, and family.

At our second session, we reviewed the comments "Mam" had expressed while developing the images. She decided she wanted to record her statements, so she wouldn't forget them. I suggested writing a poem. We discussed free-form poetry. She seemed unable to start. I asked if she felt she needed to use a more structured form, since, from our interview, it had been apparent that she liked to keep things organized. I explained haiku poetry, and "Mam" felt she could work with the haiku form, and she created the following poem:

Cancer is a dog!
Need to keep an upper hand;
Its care restricts you.

Can track up your house,
Will take advantage of you,
And leave you on edge.

Need to accept it
This bad dog of mine;
We will survive together.

At just the right time
This lady happened to be
in a certain place.

Caught behind that dog
Will she be soiled, or remain
The proper lady?

What is happening?
Humpty Dumpty on a wall
He's on the way down.

It's hard not to laugh,
Watching him fly through the air.
He's really flying.

We are like Humpty;
As fragile as eggs we live.
We need our balloons.

The green LIFE balloon
Lets us hold onto hope
As we search for peace.

A field of shamrocks
Gives to my mind: peace and hope.
One shamrock, good luck!

Close relationship
Bonding of mother and child
Unqualified love!

During the next few sessions, I let "Mam" experiment with the different media available for her use. "Mam" had once taken a few watercolor classes so she did a few paintings based on her favorite color green and on her unresolved feelings of grief related to the recent death of her beloved brother. She produced a few more watercolor paintings containing images triggered by childhood experiences, birth family relationships, and the stormy anger felt at her diagnosis of multiple myeloma.

At the end of the first session in January 1990, "Mam" talked about the image she really wanted to deal with–a grief spiral. She could visualize it in her mind. The center of the spiral began with a conch shell from which other forms emanated and circled around the shell. Because she wanted to control the images, she chose to work with colored pencils on an 18" x 24" drawing paper. Even though I advised her that drawn images would take much longer to create than a more fluid media, "Mam" assured me that her visualizations needed to be controlled with the pencils, and so began her four-month odyssey wandering through traumatic events that had changed her life.

"Mam's" drawing was finished in May and was professionally framed for entry into the first "Confronting Cancer through Art" exhibit. After the exhibit, "Mam" and I continued to meet once a week, as she was able, until she died in December of 1997, eight years after the original diagnosis. She never used colored pencils again. Instead I introduced her to oil pastels, and she created about twenty-five additional 18" x 24" pictures. Four of these artworks were shown in later art exhibits. "Mam" had preferred to leave her work at my studio, and, after she died, I met with her youngest son and released her portfolio to his care. On the instructions from his mother, he left me her oil pastel "A Candle Burns," inspired by an Edna St. Vincent Millay's poem, *First Fig*, which I had read to her.

VOLUNTEERISM: A MESSAGE TO ART THERAPISTS

At the 1997 Annual Conference during my last year as President of the American Art Therapy Association, I chaired a panel entitled "Commitment to Service: A Professional Responsibility." I opened my introduction with the following statement: "Art therapists toot your horns! This is a call to arms! We need volunteers to fight for the rights of art therapy and art therapists." The need for art therapists' commitment to their profession is as meaningful today and tomorrow, as it was then.

What do I mean by "Commitment to Service?" Commitment is central to the volunteer experience. Paul Ilsley in his book *Enhancing the Volunteer Experience* defines commitment "as a state of being in which one is bound morally, emotionally, and/or intellectually to some entity or idea. Commitment or loyalty determines the object upon which actions are focused. In turn, commitment is shaped by values and beliefs."

If we can agree that the object upon which our actions should be focused is a composite of the art therapy profession and its membership organization, then we can assume that as members of this organization, we are committed to the profession of art therapy: MORALLY because we believe "that the creative process involved in the making of art is healing and life enhancing," EMOTIONALLY because, as I wrote, we have all experienced "that mysterious, magical change in behavior that occurs when individuals can release their images and recognize their meaning," and INTELLECTUALLY because we have studied both the theories of psychology and of art therapy, and have concluded that art therapy is an "effective treatment for individuals with developmental, medical, educational, social or psychological impairments."

The health of any organization depends on the active involvement of all of its members, which leads us to the word "service." There are many definitions of the word. The one applicable to the context of the phrase "commitment to service: a professional responsibility" is work done or duty performed for another or others which is beneficial, helpful, or useful. By making a commitment to serve in your professional organization, you are also serving yourself as you maintain and strengthen the organization, thereby increasing recognition of art therapy as a viable alternative therapy through which we serve the public.

As we look toward the future we recognize that changes will occur. The question is how will we as a community of volunteers deal with those changes? Being a volunteer for your professional organization does not mean that you are subservient to the organization. It does mean that you will offer constructive criticism and solutions to problems you have identified. More importantly, we need to determine how we can initiate changes that are needed to make our organization better, and in so doing advance the profession of art therapy.

In concluding this section, I ask you to recognize your role in volunteering to serve your professional community by reading the following poem, a poem that I wrote some years ago:

> I occupy space, that which exists, and that which I create.
> I may function as an observer, or as a participant.
> If I only observe, then I have no rights as a critic.
> But if I observe and participate, then I may change things
> For my benefit, and for the benefit of others.
> I may accept or arrange things to meet the needs of each day.
> I will not know the possibilities or limitations without trying.

While I will not bore the reader with my volunteerism at the state, local, and national levels of service, I do want to mention my eight years of consecutive service on the American Art Therapy Association Board as treasurer, director, president-elect, and president, beginning in 1990 and ending in 1997. During my time on the Board, the Art Therapy Credentials Board was established and I am proud to have had a part in its adoption. It handles Registration and Certification.The first Certification Exam was given on November 20, 1994, at the Palmer House in Chicago during the AATA 25th Annual Conference. There were 344 test takers. Because I had submitted questions and answers used on the first exam, I was not allowed to sit for the exam until November, 1996. When I took the test, I was so exhausted from multiple meetings throughout the conference, I was afraid I wouldn't be able to concentrate. When I was informed in January 1997 that I had met the certification standards, and could add the initials ATR-BC after my most recent professional degree, I exhaled a huge sigh of relief.

THE HONORARY LIFE MEMBERSHIP

Through the years, as I read the qualifications of others who were nominated to receive the American Art Therapy Association's highest award, I was always impressed when reading their accomplishments. I served as the 1987–1988 Honors Nominating Committee Chair and experienced the difficulties inherent in reading and processing the letters of recommendation and support that the committee receives for the various honorary awards our association presents at our yearly conferences. The task is sometimes difficult, as there are many of our members who qualify for recognition in all the categories under consideration. When Myra Levick, the 2003–2004 Honors Chair, called and told me that the committee was nominating me for the 2004 HLM, I was pleased and humbled by their decision. When the AATA membership voted to approve the nomination, I received copies of the letters of recommendation and support written by colleagues and friends.

When reading these letters, I wondered, "Is this really me they are talking about?" And then, while writing down my thoughts and trying to find something meaningful to say to the members at the awards ceremony, I began to examine some of the terms used in the support letters: role model, mentor, inspiration, and last, but not least, "personal hero." All of these descriptors could be applied to my husband of over fifty-seven years. Because we all have learned from others, I decided to mention those art therapists who strongly influenced me during my journey through this profession.

INFLUENCES AND ROLE MODELS

I have previously mentioned the dynamic Wayne Ramirez's influence on my early work, and how Elinor Ulman was an inspiration, not only when I took her workshop in 1971 and heard her speak at conferences, but through her writings. When I attended my first American Art Therapy Association conference in Milwaukee, Myra Levick was President. What a "class act!!" She showed me how to be in control without alienating the opposition. Oh yes, way back then, there was controversy between those who believed in art AS therapy, and those who believed in art IN therapy. Hopefully, we have now agreed that both approaches are valuable.

In April of 1974, I attended a National Art Education Association Study Institute in Chicago. The topic was "Art, Art Education and Special Education." Judy Rubin was one of the speakers. Who could ask for a better role model? Great authors are not always great speakers. Judy Rubin was, and always has been, both. Through the years, Judy was interested in my work with children and cancer patients and encouraged my involvement in AATA. Inspired by the many excellent presentations at that Institute, I went home and wrote the pilot study discussed in the previous section.

From 1981–1984, I was Wisconsin's liaison to the AATA Governmental Affairs Committee chaired by Nancy Schoebel. Those of you who knew Nancy well know that she was a great role model. It was through my yearly attendance at Govermental Affairs Committee meetings that I learned the importance of being involved at the national level. Nancy was always ready to advise and encourage my efforts in trying to get the State of Wisconsin's

Department of Public Instruction to support my proposal for certification of School Art Therapists. Unfortunately, because I held the Wisconsin Art Special Education license, the licensing board decided that those individuals with that certification could work as art therapists upon the discretion of their school districts.

During 1984–1985, Nancy and I worked with others, including Janet Bush and Audrey DiMaria, on the Governmental Affairs Committee subcommittee "Art Therapy in the Schools." The work of that committee resulted in a position paper on the subject, and the publication of *Art Therapy in the Schools: Resource Packet for Art Therapists in School.* In 1990, her friends and colleagues celebrated Nancy Schoebel's life at a memorial service in Washington, D.C. We miss her always.

My first year as Treasurer on the AATA board was 1990. Linda Gantt was President of the organization. Through the years I have known her I have marveled at Linda's concurrent gentle and dynamic presence. She taught me how to listen, evaluate material presented, and make decisions. Under her administration, everyone had an equal voice. Linda Gantt taught me the value of networking with other health care professionals. When I was President, we attended National Coalition of Arts Therapy Associations (NCATA) meetings, Fair Access Coalition of Testing meetings, and Health Professions Network meetings. We also met with Dr. Tom Clausen of the National Board of Certified Counselors. With other representatives of NCATA, Linda and I met in Washington, D.C., with representatives of the Professional Counselors Association to discuss whether or not Arts Therapies might be considered as a subcategory in their organization, provided our Masters' degrees were comparable to their course-work requirements for certification. However, at that time, it was not possible. In the 2004 fall AATA *Newsletter*, Linda applauded the 2004 Board's commitment to supporting a "Cross-Training Initiative with Counseling," proposed by President Lynn Kapitan. Again, it was evident that Linda is always ready to "listen" to new ideas. I hope we will be able to achieve the goals outlined in Lynn's cross-training initiative without losing our unique identity as art therapists.

In the course of our numerous trips together, Linda introduced me to the many restaurants, art galleries and museums in Washington, D.C., so you see we were not all work and no play. I treasure our relationship.

November, 1995, I was sworn in as President of the American Art Therapy Association. Members of the Wisconsin Art Therapy Association presented me with a Sioux Indian Dream Catcher for good luck. I still have this hanging in my office. In November, 2004, when I received my HLM, they filled my room with a beautiful bouquet and a congratulatory sentiment. So you see, friends and colleagues also influence your life.

I am sure that each one of you had several mentors and role models who have influenced you throughout your professional lives. It is well to remember them, for in remembering, we relive those relationships and reinforce their teachings. Thank you all for remembering me.

RETIREMENT

As the veterans of art therapy know, Wisconsin is my home state. That is where I was born, educated, and worked until I completely retired and moved to Las Vegas, Nevada, in 1998 where I play golf, was the treasurer of the Ladies Executive Golf Club for two years, and count the Sunday offerings for the finance committee at my church. This should not surprise those of you who know that I was treasurer of AATA for three years, and that since the end of my term as President in November 1997, I served on the AATA Finance Committee until September of 2004.

WORDS FOR ART THERAPISTS

Why is it necessary for art therapists to be artists? If we are not engaged in our own art making, we cannot experience the magic of the creative process. That magic, used as an agent of change, is unique to the creative arts therapies in general, and to the art therapy profession in particular. In my own artwork, I am repeatedly awed by the experience of allowing the creative process to work, of finding answers to both recognized feelings and problems. In order to make our images come to life, we must know about the materials of art. If we have not experimented with and used a variety of art materials, we cannot know which are best suited for the particular populations that we serve. We need to be able to answer any and all questions about the media clients choose as their vehicles of expression.

Why do we need to assume the role of teacher? We not only teach others how to use art materials to create their images, but we teach them how to take control of their lives. As teachers, we need to recognize both the limitations and potential of individuals' motoric, cognitive, and socioemotional functioning. Do they process incoming information abstractly or concretely? Can they grasp the whole picture, or is their learning accomplished one step at a time? We need to use our knowledge of the stages of human development to determine their present level of functioning. Little can be accomplished if we present tasks that predispose noncompliance. One of the best ways to teach is by modeling desired behavior. I am sure each one of you remembers one or more teachers who, in your lifetime, have had a profound influence on you. Hopefully those experiences were positive, but conversely, we sometimes learn more from negative ones. We learn what <u>not</u> to do.

What is it we need to know to carry out the role of therapist? Over and over, I have heard art therapists say: "trust the process." What do they mean by that? Do they mean the therapeutic process, or do they mean the creative process? Or, for the art therapist, is it a combination of both? I believe that you need to use therapeutic processes to ready the client to accept being involved in the creative process. It is your task to find ways to unlock the door, open it up, and allow the creative process to enter or reenter the house of their soul. What a privilege to watch someone's images come to life. What a responsibility to help the client read the messages their images send.

What is our responsibility? We are at different times the guide, the helper, the supporter, and sometimes the confronter, but never the intruder. An intruder takes over the client's artwork by overtly applying interpretations to the images. Certainly an image might send you a different personal message than the client receives, but since the picture takes on a life of its own once it is created, you cannot conclude that what you see is what someone else sees in the same image. The therapist can ask informational questions, or discuss possibilities, but first of all you must listen, not only with your ears, but with your eyes, to what the client is saying by voice and body language.

I would urge us to never stop learning. Continue to investigate and, above all, to do research. This is probably the one area of our profession that needs concentrated development. Not enough studies have been published that concretely demonstrate the outcomes of what art therapy services provide our clients. I encourage practitioners and students to find out what kinds of research grants are available through the various divisions of the United States Department of Health and Human Services, the Department of Education, the National Endowment for the Humanities, the National Institutes of Health, and the National Endowment for the Arts.

When federal, state, or local community grants are not available for the type of research art therapists wish to pursue, let us not be discouraged. We can turn to the corporate and private sectors. There are numerous private foundations that offer grants for such interests as cancer support programs, geriatric studies, substance abuse and other mental, medical, and physical disability health issues. In order to find a foundation with interests compatible to your research, consult the Foundation-Center-Regional Collections housed in selected libraries throughout the country. Funding is almost never granted to individuals, but if you have a well thought-out proposal, most institutions will support your efforts and go through the mechanics of making the application.

Concluding, I would like to end where I started with some personal comments. Graduate art therapy students often asked whether I preferred working with individuals or groups. It really depends on what your treatment plan objectives are. When working with emotionally disturbed children, I found that individual art therapy allowed for more direct intervention than working with groups, where their needs were so diverse that it was difficult to find common ground on which to build strengths or remodel behavior.

Virginia M. Minar at her 80th birthday party, 2003.

With cancer patients, the group process seems to have the best results. At the 1992 AATA conference I presented a paper "Living with Cancer: Images of the Hurter and the Healer," which later became the basis for my chapter in Cathy Malchiodi's *Medical Art Therapy with Adults*. I have found that members of cancer groups by the activity of making art, by extending and receiving support throughout the process, and by caring for each other, may find a new sense of purpose for their life.

When working with cancer patients, I have used Betty Levy's successive poetry techniques, sometimes as a warm-up exercise, but often throughout the life of the group. Each contributor writes a line at the top of a piece of paper. This line is the first line of the poem. The paper is passed to the person sitting next to the initiator. The second person adds a line in response, and then folds the first line back and under so that only the second line is visible. The poem is passed in one direction from person to person. The only line any individual sees is the line written by the preceding person. The end of the poem is determined by the end of the page or when it has been returned to the initiator to allow for closure. I would like to share with you a poem written by the women in one of my cancer groups.

The present is all we know of life,
But the future holds glory we can only imagine.
So, live fully in the moment.
Each moment is precious.
And our life is just a moment
In the scope of eternity.

This enables us to face daily challenge
With a new outlook and attitude.
We simply will not have our moments spoiled
With nonsensical problems.
Instead we see them as learning opportunities.

Color me blue with a stroke of pink
And a little sunshine on a green meadow
I am a living collage–shaped and colored
By the people, places and events of my life.
You might call me "A work of art!"

To my new and old colleagues, I want you to recognize that you too, truly are "a work of art." Your life experiences have created the image that is YOU! Project that image with confidence, particularly that part of your picture that is the art therapist. What you have learned in the classroom and experienced in your practicum have helped to shape your image, not only as a caring human being, but also as a qualified art therapist. Remember, there is nobody in the world exactly like you. You are a very special person. Welcome to the profession of art therapy!

ABOUT THE EDITORS

Maxine Borowsky Junge, PhD, LCSW, ATR-BC, HLM, Is Professor Emerita at Loyola Marymount University where she taught for 21 years and for a number of years was Chair of the Department of Marital and Family Therapy (Clinical Art Therapy). She began her art therapy teaching in 1973 at Immaculate Heart College in the program innovated by Helen Landgarten. She has also been a faculty member at Goddard College in Vermont and Antioch University-Seattle and presented papers and workshops nationally and internationally. Dr. Junge has had a clinical art psychotherapy practice since 1973. More recently, she has included organizational consulting. She has contributed chapters to art therapy and psychology texts, the latest being "The Art Therapist as Social Activist." She has published widely including "Feminine Imagery and a Young Woman's Search for Identity," and "Mourning, Memory and Life, Itself: The AIDS Quilt and the Vietnam Veterans' Memorial Wall." Currently, Dr. Junge is Guest Editor of a series of eight life stories of art therapy people of color for *Art Therapy, Journal of the American Art Therapy Association*. Her two books, before this one, are *Creative Realities: The Search for Meanings* and *A History of Art Therapy in the United States*. The *History*, published in 1994, is the only one of its kind and is used in graduate programs across the country. Dr. Junge is the recipient of awards, including an "Award for Excellence" from the South Bay Contemporary Art Museum and Harbor-UCLA Hospital and the Social Justice Award at Fielding Graduate University. She was nominated three times as "Woman of the Year" at Loyola Marymount University. Trained as a painter through graduate studies, she is an exhibiting painter, draftswoman and photographer. She lives on Whidbey Island, in the Pacific Northwest.

Harriet Wadeson, PhD, LCSW, ATR-BC, HLM, Is Professor Emerita at the University of Illinois at Chicago, where she established its Art Therapy Graduate Program, which she directed for 23 years, as well as its Annual Art Therapy Summer Institute at Lake Geneva, Wisconsin, which she directed for 20 years. Her publications include five books, other than this one, beginning with *Art Psychotherapy*, which has been widely used in art therapy training for over 25 years, and *A*

Guide to Art Therapy Research, the first book published by the American Art Therapy Association (AATA). She has contributed chapters to numerous psychology and art therapy texts and has published 68 papers in psychiatric and art therapy journals. Dr. Wadeson is the recipient of many awards, for her art and her professional service, including a first prize in art from the Smithsonian Institution, the Benjamin Rush Bronze Medal Award for scientific exhibits from the American Psychiatric Association, and a Resolution of Commendation from the State of Illinois. She has presented her work worldwide and teaches regularly in Sweden, Finland, and Australia and led professional exchange delegations to China, Indonesia, Bali, and Sweden. Having been active in the American Art Therapy Association since its inception, Dr. Wadeson has held numerous positions in the association, including Associate Editor of its journal, *Newsletter* Editor, Publications Chair, and Research Chair. Currently she is teaching in an art therapy post-graduate program she designed and heads for Northwestern University in Evanston, Illinois, and is working on a novel.

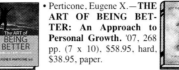

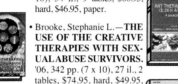
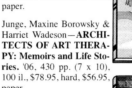
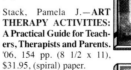

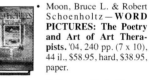